LAW AGAINST

This collection of rich, empirically grounded case studies investigates the conditions and consequences of 'juridification' – the use of law by ordinary individuals as a form of protest against 'the state'. Starting from the actual practices of claimants, these case studies address the translation and interpretation of legal norms into local concepts, actions and practices in a way that highlights the social and cultural dynamism and multivocality of communities in their interaction with the law and legal norms. The contributors to this volume challenge the image of homogeneous and primordially norm-bound cultures that has been (unintentionally) perpetuated by some of the more prevalent treatments of law and culture. This volume highlights the heterogeneous geography of law and the ways boundaries between different legal bodies are transcended in struggles for rights. Contributions include case studies from South Africa, Malawi, Sierra Leone, Turkey, India, Papua New Guinea, Suriname, the Marshall Islands and Russia.

JULIA ECKERT is Professor of Social Anthropology at the University of Bern and head of the research group 'Law against the State' at the Max Planck Institute for Social Anthropology, Halle/Saale, Germany. Her research interests are in legal anthropology, the anthropology of the modern state, social movements, the anthropology of crime and punishment, and changing notions of responsibility and justice.

BRIAN DONAHOE is an independent researcher, writer and editor. From 2004–2010 he was Post-doctoral Research Fellow at the Max Planck Institute for Social Anthropology in Halle, Germany. His thematic interests include the dynamics of constructing, maintaining and asserting ethnic identity and indigeneity, and different approaches to guaranteeing indigenous rights to land.

CHRISTIAN STRÜMPELL is Research Associate in the Department of Anthropology at the South Asia Institute, Heidelberg University. His research interests are in the anthropology of labour, economic anthropology and political anthropology, with a regional focus on South Asia in general and the Indian state of Orissa.

ZERRIN ÖZLEM BINER is Research Associate in the Department of Social Anthropology, University of Cambridge. Her thematic interests include the study of the state, the experience and memory of violence, and the perception of justice and reconciliation in post-conflict settings.

CAMBRIDGE STUDIES IN LAW AND SOCIETY

Cambridge Studies in Law and Society aims to publish the best scholarly work on legal discourse and practice in its social and institutional contexts, combining theoretical insights and empirical research.

The fields that it covers are: studies of law in action; the sociology of law; the anthropology of law; cultural studies of law, including the role of legal discourses in social formations; law and economics; law and politics; and studies of governance. The books consider all forms of legal discourse across societies, rather than being limited to lawyers' discourses alone.

The series editors come from a range of disciplines: academic law; socio-legal studies; sociology; and anthropology. All have been actively involved in teaching and writing about law in context.

Series editors

Chris Arup *Monash University, Victoria*

Martin Chanock *La Trobe University, Melbourne*

Pat O'Malley *University of Sydney*

Sally Engle Merry *New York University*

Susan Silbey *Massachusetts Institute of Technology*

Books in the series

Diseases of the Will
Mariana Valverde

*The Politics of Truth and Reconciliation in South Africa: Legitimizing
the Post-Apartheid State*
Richard A. Wilson

Modernism and the Grounds of Law
Peter Fitzpatrick

Unemployment and Government: Genealogies of the Social
William Walters

Autonomy and Ethnicity: Negotiating Competing Claims in Multi-Ethnic States
Yash Ghai

Constituting Democracy: Law, Globalism and South Africa's Political Reconstruction
Heinz Klug

The Ritual of Rights in Japan: Law, Society, and Health Policy
Eric A. Feldman

The Invention of the Passport: Surveillance, Citizenship and the State
John Torpey

LAW AGAINST THE STATE

Ethnographic Forays into Law's
Transformations

Edited by

Julia Eckert

Brian Donahoe

Christian Strümpell

Zerrin Özlem Biner

CAMBRIDGE
UNIVERSITY PRESS

CAMBRIDGE
UNIVERSITY PRESS

University Printing House, Cambridge CB2 8BS, United Kingdom

Cambridge University Press is part of the University of Cambridge.

It furthers the University's mission by disseminating knowledge in the pursuit of education, learning and research at the highest international levels of excellence.

www.cambridge.org
Information on this title: www.cambridge.org/9781107471078

© Cambridge University Press 2012

First published 2012
First paperback edition 2014

A catalogue record for this publication is available from the British Library

Library of Congress Cataloguing in Publication data
Law against the state : ethnographic forays into law's transformations / [edited by] Julia Eckert, Brian Donahoe, Christian Strümpell, Zerrin Özlem Biner.
pages   cm. – (Cambridge studies in law and society)
Includes bibliographical references and index.
ISBN 978-1-107-01466-4 (hardback)
1. Public interest law–Developing countries.   2. Ethnological jurisprudence–Developing countries.   3. Law and economic development.   4. Government litigation–Developing countries.   5. Law–Political aspects–Developing countries.   6. Indigenous peoples–Legal status, laws, etc.–Developing countries.   I. Eckert, Julia M.   II. Donahoe, Brian.
III. Strümpell, Christian, 1972–
K564.P83L39 2012
344.009172´4–dc23
2012002121

ISBN 978-1-107-01466-4 Hardback
ISBN 978-1-107-47107-8 Paperback

CONTENTS

CONTRIBUTORS

GERHARD ANDERS is Lecturer in African Studies at the University of Edinburgh. His research focuses on the anthropology of emergent regimes of global order in the fields of criminal justice and development, tracking the everyday experiences of civil servants, lawyers and others involved in the production and diffusion of administrative and legal knowledge. He has published on legal anthropology, international criminal justice, good governance and corruption, including the co-edited volume (with M. Nuijten) *Corruption and the Secret of Law* (2007) and the monograph *In the Shadow of Good Governance: An Ethnography of Civil Service Reform in Africa* (2010).

AMITA BAVISKAR is Associate Professor of Sociology at the Institute of Economic Growth, Delhi. Her research focuses on the cultural politics of environment and development. Her first book, *In the Belly of the River: Tribal Conflicts over Development in the Narmada Valley* (2005), discussed the struggle for survival by Adivasis in central India against a large dam. Her subsequent work further explores the themes of resource rights, subaltern resistance and cultural identity. She has edited *Waterlines: The Penguin Book of River Writings* (2003); *Waterscapes: The Cultural Politics of a Natural Resource* (2007); *Contested Grounds: Essays on Nature, Culture and Power* (2008); and *Elite and Everyman: The Cultural Politics of the Indian Middle Classes* (with Raka Ray, 2011). She is currently writing about bourgeois environmentalism and spatial restructuring in the context of economic liberalisation in Delhi. Amita Baviskar has taught at the University of Delhi, and has been a visiting scholar at Stanford, Cornell, Yale and the University of California at Berkeley. She is co-editor of the journal *Contributions to Indian Sociology*. She was awarded the 2005 Malcolm Adiseshiah Award for Distinguished Contributions to Development Studies, the 2008 VKRV Rao Prize for Social Science Research and the 2010 Infosys Prize for Social Sciences.

UPENDRA BAXI is Professor Emeritus at the University of Warwick and the University of Delhi. He was Vice Chancellor of the University of

Delhi and South Gujarat. His most recent works include *Human Rights in a Posthuman World* (2007) and *The Future of Human Rights* (2008). His work *A Tale of Three Cities: Aspects of Justice* is scheduled for publication in 2012.

ZERRIN ÖZLEM BINER is Research Associate in the Department of Social Anthropology at the University of Cambridge. Her research includes the study of the state and the experience of minority citizens in post-conflict settings in contemporary Turkey. Furthering her interests in the areas of political and legal anthropology, she conducted research on diasporic Assyrian-Syriac communities in Sweden, with a special focus on transnational movements and their effects on claims for citizenship rights. Among her publications on this research are *The Politics of Victimhood*, a co-edited special issue of the journal *History and Anthropology* (2007); 'Retrieving the dignity of a cosmopolitan city: contested perspectives on culture, rights and ethnicity in Mardin', in *New Perspectives on Turkey* (2007); 'Acts of defacement, memory of loss: ghostly effects of Armenian crisis in Mardin, Southeast Turkey', in *History and Memory*, (2010); and 'Multiple imaginations of the state: understanding a mobile conflict of justice and accountability from the perspective of Assyrian-Syriac Christians', in *Citizenship Studies* (2011). She is currently working on a special journal issue on the themes of reconciliation and transitional justice.

BRIAN DONAHOE is an independent researcher, writer and editor living in Kyzyl, Republic of Tyva. From 2004–2010 he was Post-doctoral Research Fellow at the Max Planck Institute for Social Anthropology in Halle/Saale, Germany. His research compares four closely related indigenous communities inhabiting the Eastern Saian mountain range that separates Siberia from Mongolia. His thematic interests include the dynamics of constructing, maintaining and asserting ethnic identity and indigeneity, and different approaches to guaranteeing indigenous rights to land. Recent publications include 'Size and place in the construction of indigeneity in the Russian Federation' in *Current Anthropology* (2008), and 'The law as a source of environmental injustice in the Russian Federation', in the edited volume *Environmental Justice and Sustainability in the Former Soviet Union* (2009). He is also co-editor of the volume *Reconstructing the House of Culture: Community, Self and the Makings of Culture in Russia and Beyond* (2011).

JULIA ECKERT is Professor of Social Anthropology at the University of Bern and head of the research group 'Law against the State' at the

Max Planck Institute for Social Anthropology, Halle/Saale, Germany. Her research interests are in legal anthropology, the anthropology of the modern state, social movements, the anthropology of crime and punishment, and changing notions of responsibility and justice. She is currently writing a book on the police in Bombay, focusing on everyday conflicts over norms of justice, citizenship and authority. Among her publications on this research are 'The Trimurti of the state', in *Sociologus* (2005), and 'From subject to citizens: legalism from below and the homogenisation of the legal sphere', in *The Journal of Legal Pluralism* (2006). She has worked extensively on the rise and practice of Hindu-nationalist movements in India (e.g. *The Charisma of Direct Action*, 2003). In addition to her work in India, she has conducted research in Uzbekistan and Afghanistan. She was a researcher at the German Institute for international pedagogical research, Frankfurt am Main, and Lecturer at the Humboldt University, Berlin and the Free University of Berlin, from where she holds a Ph.D. She was a member of the Young Academy of the Berlin-Brandenburg Academy of Sciences. Among other awards, she has received a Jean Monet Fellowship to the Robert Schumann Centre of the European University Institute in Fiesole Italy, and the Akademie Stipendium of the Berlin-Brandenburg Academy of Sciences.

HARRI ENGLUND is Reader in Social Anthropology at the University of Cambridge. He is also Research Associate in Social Anthropology at the University of Cape Town and Docent of African Studies at the University of Helsinki. He has carried out research among Chichewa/Nyanja speakers in south-central Africa for over two decades. He has written and edited several books on rights discourses, Christianity, war and displacement, mass media and democratisation. His most recent books are *Human Rights and African Airwaves: Mediating Equality on the Chichewa Radio* (2011) and the edited volume *Christianity and Public Culture in Africa* (2011).

ERDEM EVREN is a doctoral candidate at the Institute for Middle Eastern and North African Politics, Free University, Berlin, and has recently taken up a position as Post-doctoral Fellow at the Zentrum Moderner Orient in Berlin. His Ph.D. thesis, tentatively titled *Convulsions of Reason: State, Mandatory Military Service and Political Subjectivity in Turkey*, focuses on political activism against mandatory military service in Turkey. During his fieldwork in Istanbul and Ankara (2008–2009), he worked with conscientious objectors and gay men who seek to be medically exempted from the service on the grounds of their sexual orientation. His broader research interests include the study of social, political and ecological movements, political subjectivity, law, violence and non-violence, and the anthropology of the state and capitalism. His next research project will be on environmental activism against the construction of small-scale hydro-electric facilities (HES) in the eastern Black Sea region of Turkey.

STUART KIRSCH is Associate Professor of Anthropology at the University of Michigan. He earned his Ph.D. at the University of Pennsylvania in 1991. He has worked for many years as an ethnographer and an advocate for the people affected by pollution from the Ok Tedi copper and gold mine in Papua New Guinea. This work was published as *Reverse Anthropology: Indigenous Analysis of Social and Environmental Relations in New Guinea* (2006). He recently co-edited a special issue of the journal *Dialectical Anthropology* (2010) on corporate oxymorons and edited a collection of post-graduate essays on engaged anthropology in the journal *Collaborative Anthropologies* (2010). He is currently completing a book on corporations and their critics, which he hopes to publish as *Mining Capitalism: The Rise and Corporate Response to Indigenous and NGO Critique*. He has consulted widely on indigenous rights and environmental issues, including work for the World Bank, the United Nations, the US Nuclear Claims Tribunal and numerous NGOs and law firms.

CHRISTIAN STRÜMPELL is Research Associate in the Department of Anthropology at the South Asia Institute, Heidelberg University, and Research Fellow for the project *Stress and Stress Relief in a Transcultural Perspective*, part of the cluster of excellence *Asia and Europe in a Global Context: Shifting Asymmetries in Cultural Flows*. He received his doctorate from the Department of Social Anthropology, Free University of Berlin, in 2004. His research interests include the anthropology of labour, economic anthropology and political anthropology, with a regional focus on South Asia. He has conducted long-term fieldwork on two separate occasions in Orissa, India, the first among migrant workers in a public-sector power plant, the second among migrant and local workers of the public-sector Rourkela Steel Plant. He has recently initiated field work on private-sector labour in Dhaka, Bangladesh. Among his publications are 'We work together, we eat together: conviviality and modernity in a company settlement in south Orissa', in *Contributions to Indian Sociology* (2008), and 'On the desecration of Nehru's temples:

Bhilai and Rourkela compared' (co-authored with Jonathan P. Parry), in *Economic and Political Weekly* (2008). He is currently working on a co-edited volume on processes of neo-liberalisation in India.

OLAF ZENKER is Ambizione Research Fellow of the Swiss National Science Foundation (SNSF) at the Institute of Social Anthropology, University of Bern, where he previously worked as Assistant Professor. He received his M.Sc. in social anthropology from the London School of Economics and his M.A. in linguistics and literature from the University of Hamburg. As a doctoral student at the Max Planck Institute for Social Anthropology in Halle/Saale, Germany, he conducted research on Irish language and identity issues in Northern Ireland. He received his Ph.D. from the Martin Luther University Halle-Wittenberg in 2008. He then became a postdoctoral research fellow in the project group *Law, Organization, Science and Technology (LOST)*, also at the MPI. He currently investigates South African land restitution as an exemplary site where the moral modernity of the new South African state is contested, renegotiated and made. His research interests include statehood, the rule of law, modernity, conflict and identity formations (especially ethnicity, nationalism and autochthony), and linguistic anthropology. Among his publications are the co-edited volume *Beyond Writing Culture: Current Intersections of Epistemologies and Representational Practices* (2010), as well as articles in the journals *Paideuma* (2006), *Nations and Nationalism* (2009), *Social Science & Medicine* (2010), *Critique of Anthropology* (2011) and *Zeitschrift für Ethnologie* (2012).

ACKNOWLEDGEMENTS

This volume is the culmination of the work of the research group Law against the State, or: The Juridification of Protest (2005–2010), jointly funded by the Max Planck Society and the Max Planck Institute for Social Anthropology in Halle/Saale Germany. The research group was headed up by Julia Eckert, and included Zerrin Özlem Biner, Brian Donahoe and Christian Strümpell. Franz and Keebet von Benda-Beckmann, the heads of the Project Group Legal Pluralism at the MPI for Social Anthropology, generously agreed to host the research group. For this we are deeply indebted to them. We also wish to express our gratitude to Gesine Koch, who provided invaluable logistical support for the duration of the project. With one exception, all the chapters collected in this volume developed out of presentations given at a workshop held at the Max Planck Institute for Social Anthropology, 14–16 April, 2010. The exception is the epilogue, which Upendra Baxi graciously offered to contribute ex-post facto. In addition to those represented here, there were three more participants at the workshop – Lori Allen, Ronald Niezen and Arzoo Osanloo – who greatly enlivened the workshop with their stimulating presentations and insightful comments. We also wish to acknowledge the workshop discussants – Franz von Benda-Beckmann, Tobias Kelly, Daniel Münster and Klaus Schlichte – who found the common threads among the papers and cogently wove them into a coherent set of talking points for discussion and debate. Their creative input, challenging questions and valuable insights are evident throughout the volume, and especially in the editors' introduction. Needless to say, responsibility for any shortcomings in this volume is borne solely by the editors.

INTRODUCTION: LAW'S TRAVELS AND TRANSFORMATIONS

Julia Eckert, Zerrin Özlem Biner, Brian Donahoe and Christian
Strümpell

INTRODUCTION

The contributors to this volume start from the premise that in the use of
law, law transforms those who use it, their understanding of the world,
of their conflicts and their normative orientations – in other words, their
political subjectivities. At the same time, the essays trace the ways that
law itself is transformed in iterative processes. These transformations are
historically contingent on the dialectic between the transformations of
social relations and subjectivities that law can effect, on the one hand,
and the transformations in the meaning of laws produced by the interpretations of those who mobilise law for their particular social, political
or economic struggles, on the other hand. This dialectic reflects the two
sides of the sociality of law: first, law's formative impact on social perceptions; and secondly, its very constitution in the social. Attention to
these dynamics opens our eyes to the creation of new legal understandings – *jurisgenesis*, to use Robert Cover's (1992) term – that result from
the active use of existing law.

THE GLOBALISATION OF LAW

Law travels, and there are different ways in which it does so. It matters to normative processes whether law is imposed by colonial rule or
imported by a national elite as a component of the modernisation and
development project; whether it is propagated by activists to claim rights
or by nation-states to legitimise their power; whether it is transmitted via

rumours among laypersons who hope it might help them attain justice or via networks of experts trying to achieve international standardisation and global 'harmonisation' (Benda-Beckmann *et al.* 2005). These different forms of law's travels rarely come alone. As David Westbrook has elaborated, 'the imperial, the fashionable, the systemic and the tribal' forms of law's travels 'are interrelated' (Westbrook 2006: 504). Law's travels are almost always at one and the same time a matter of export and import, of imposition and adoption, of expert knowledge and lay rumour. These modes of the spread of law and the dynamics between them are central to the phenomenon of 'juridification', a term that refers to a variety of social processes entailed in the proliferation of law.

In recent years, we have been observing an increasing juridification of social and political protest worldwide. The global 'rights discourse' has projected law, particularly human rights law, as the internationally intelligible and acceptable language of voicing demands, providing categories of global scale and linking local concerns with international forums. Analyses of these processes of juridification have often examined governmental and commercial actors who propagate the activation and implementation of legal norms, such as international organisations (e.g. Li 2009), NGOs (e.g. Keck and Sikkink 1998; Merry 2006; Levitt and Merry 2009), law firms (e.g. Garth and Dezalay 1996) and judicial institutions such as the International Criminal Court (e.g. Anders, this volume; Clarke 2010). Considering the economic and political impact that these actors have, analyses of the ways they promote law and the networks within which they operate are indispensable for an understanding of law in current global relations.

Boaventura de Sousa Santos and César Rodríguez-Garavito, however, assert that such 'realist' analyses of law's travels only take into consideration the top-down processes of the globalisation of law, that which Upendra Baxi in this volume and elsewhere has called the politics *of* human rights. Santos and Rodríguez-Garavito hold that such a focus on the top-down processes of the globalisation of law reproduces the silencing of those subjected to the processes in question: 'Missing from this top-down picture are the myriad local, non-English-speaking actors ... [T]hese subaltern actors are a critical part of processes whereby global legal rules are defined' (Santos and Rodríguez-Garavito 2005: 11). We argue that such analyses of the top-down processes of globalisation of law, important as they are, do more than just dismiss the voices of those marginalised. They also assume a unidirectional change and thereby render impossible any analysis of the dialectic between the implementation of legal norms and the diverse ways that local actors adopt them; they do not take into account the constitutive effects of what Baxi calls the politics *for* rights. In this way, they foreclose a differentiated understanding of normative change.

Santos and Rodríguez-Garavito modestly hold that their notion of 'subaltern cosmopolitan legality' does not quite amount to a theory (2005: 13). Nevertheless, we believe that such an approach is indispensable for a theory of normative change in two ways: firstly, it directs us toward a practice-oriented approach that overcomes assumptions of cultural determinism in the normative realm; secondly, such a perspective opens up the possibility for a radically *social* theory of legal change such as we are espousing here.

Our approach is thus inspired by the observation that people demonstrate a startlingly persistent faith in 'the law', as evidenced by their ever-increasing recourse to legal means to settle conflicts, alleviate suffering and further their causes. The contributions to this volume explore the effects of people's legal choices, trials and errors in eclectic situated processes of juridification. While other notable anthropologists have also dealt with such processes of 'juridification', they have generally focused solely on one body of law, such as Dembour and Kelly (2007) and Clarke (2010) on international criminal law, and Merry (2006), Goodale (2009, 2010) and Wilson and Mitchell (2003) on human rights law. They critically examine the effects of such legal processes on the construction and regulation of particular types of crimes and identities. While we agree with these approaches, our starting point is different: we explore how such legal mobilisations articulate with other practices of negotiating conflicts, sometimes replacing non-legal means of protest, sometimes forming mutually reinforcing interdependent strategies with them. This implies following the hopes and practices of people into whatever arenas happen to become relevant. In our view, juridification entails not only the application of state law against the state, but also the mobilisation of different legal orders, such as international human rights law, customary law and 'travelling' models of conflict resolution. People tend not to be trained in the finer distinctions of bodies of law and their jurisdictions, and many make their claims with reference to a certain body of law (e.g. human rights) even though their specific cases would not fall under the purview of that particular body of law as traditionally understood. By not focusing on a single body of law we attempt to highlight the heterogeneous geography of law and the ways boundaries between different legal bodies are blurred in the struggles for rights.

DEPOLITICISATION

From its very origins in debates on labour law in the German Weimar Republic, the term 'juridification' has critically described processes of depoliticisation that are concurrent with the relocation of issues into legal arenas. Kirchheimer (1972 [1933]; cf. Anders, Chapter 4 in this volume) deployed the term as a polemic against the legal formalisation of labour relations, which he saw as severely restricting the possibilities for workers and unions to engage in more militant actions. In this way juridification drastically depoliticised labour relations (cf. Teubner 1987: 9).[1] The concept gained prominence in academic debates after Habermas observed that the development of modern law closely corresponds to wider social developments, and showed how they shape each other. Habermas distinguished four thrusts of juridification (*Verrechtlichung*) in his theory of legal evolution. The first thrust reflects and moulds the development of the bourgeois state, separating the economy from politics and constituting the legal person as a subject free to enter into contracts, acquire and dispose of property (Habermas 1985). Habermas's second thrust entails the development of a legal constitutionalisation establishing the notion of 'the rule of law'. The third thrust refers to the democratisation of the constitutional powers of the state by the introduction of universal franchise and the freedom of organisation for political associations. Finally, the fourth thrust marks the constitutionalisation of the economic system or the establishment of labour laws guaranteeing collective bargaining and the welfare state.[2]

Blichner and Molander (2008) further refine the concept of juridification according to five dimensions of socio-legal processes. The first dimension they call 'constitutive juridification', which simply describes the establishment of a legal order such as a formal constitution. The second dimension of juridification they define as law's expansion and differentiation, i.e. its expansion into 'life-worlds' it had hitherto not regulated. The third dimension is marked by the tendency to solve conflict increasingly by reference to law, both in the sense that citizens take recourse to courts and in the sense that citizens outside the judiciary also

---

[1] This concept of juridification has been criticised for the voluntarism inherent in its preoccupation with strategic choices of conflict or cooperation of labour unions, and for the fact that its use has been limited to the politics of organised labour, and thus to only one segment of society (Teubner 1987: 10).

[2] The latter three thrusts thus all aimed at protecting the 'life-worlds' that the first thrust endangered by placing them 'at the disposal of the market and absolutist rule' (Habermas 1985: 206).

refer to laws in their attempts to settle disputes.[3] Blichner and Molander's fourth dimension of juridification refers to a process by which judicial power increases, owing to the indeterminacy and non-transparency of law and its applications. The fifth dimension distinguishes processes where juridification occurs as legal framing, i.e. the 'increased tendency to understand self and others, and the relationship between self and others, in light of a common legal order' (Blichner and Molander 2008: 47). This dimension describes the development and the internalisation of legal cultures without which – as Blichner and Molander argue – complex legal orders can barely gain stability. It gets at law's power to shape subjectivities, as is illustrated in a number of the chapters in this volume (e.g. Biner, Chapter 9; Eckert, Chapter 6; Englund, Chapter 3; and Evren, Chapter 10). All of Blichner and Molander's dimensions are represented to one degree or another in the case studies collected here; however, our focus corresponds most closely to Blichner and Molander's third dimension of juridification, referring to the process whereby law is employed to further hopes and express aspirations or protest.[4]

Juridification has since the coining of the term thus pointed to a process of depoliticisation; with juridification, a vast array of social conflicts that were once sorted out by political means – in bodies of elected representatives or through strikes, boycotts, protests and demonstrations – are ever more often mediated through the judicial system (cf. Blichner and Molander 2008: 45). In this perspective political decision making is reduced to the application of existing law, thereby increasing the power of definition and decision making of the judiciary and legally trained experts (Bourdieu 1987).[5]

---

[3] Blichner and Molander (2008: 44) emphasise that this lay legal reasoning does not necessarily correspond to law 'by the book', and may even refer to laws that do not actually exist, an insight that is supported by Julia Eckert's analysis of rumours of rights (Chapter 6, this volume).

[4] As Blichner and Molander point out, these dimensions are not exclusive. They are all closely bound up with one another, and all of them are relevant to a greater or lesser degree to our case studies.

[5] Juridification is also often accompanied by a proliferation of institutionalised legal arenas. With their overlapping jurisdictions and competencies these new arenas likewise remain largely unintelligible to the citizenry, thereby increasing legal uncertainty rather than strengthening citizens' rights and enforcing the accountability of governmental institutions. For a good example, see Shalini Randeria's (2011) ethnographic study of the dynamics of juridification around the forced displacement of residents of a Mumbai slum for a World Bank-funded development project. It addresses the disorienting proliferation of 'quasi-judicial arenas of mediation, arbitration and inspection at various scales' (Randeria: 188) that comes along with contemporary development projects.

In this manner, '[p]olitics itself is migrating to the courts', where 'ordinary political processes [are] held hostage to the dialectic of law and disorder' (Comaroff and Comaroff 2006: 26). Therefore, the widespread 'culture of legality' is often nothing more than 'lawfare', defined by Jean and John Comaroff (2006: 30) as 'the resort to legal instruments, to the violence inherent in the law, to commit acts of political coercion'. These legal instruments often serve powerful political elites and corporate cap-ital to further their predatory interests in 'plundering' natural resources (Mattei and Nader 2008).

Nevertheless, the 'culture of legality' has also come to underpin claims of marginalised people everywhere in the world. It is 'not uncommon nowadays to hear the language of jurisprudence in the Amazon or Aboriginal Australia, in the Kalahari or the New Guinea highlands, or among the poor in Mumbai, Mexico City, Cape Town, and Trench Town' (Comaroff and Comaroff 2006: 26).

Whether law can actually serve as a 'weapon of the weak' (Scott 1985) is, however, an empirical question. While law has the inherent char-acteristic of legitimating and reproducing the status quo, it can also serve to bind those who impose it (Thompson 1975: 266–68; Lazarus-Black 1994: 257). Donahoe's case studies (Chapter 2) show how legal instruments are often selectively implemented to allow national and international oil and gas companies in Russia to gain access to lands his-torically inhabited by indigenous peoples. This, however, does not stop Russia's indigenous peoples from trying to use the courts to protect their interests. Stuart Kirsch's examination of the juridification of indigen-ous politics (Chapter 1) exemplifies how recourse to the courts can serve the interests of indigenous peoples. Kirsch notes that the gap between indigenous people's claims and the expression of those claims in legal language can in fact create new political opportunities by yielding 'legal precedents which generate change' and facilitating 'the critique of power by providing glimpses of alternative ways of being human'. Julia Eckert (Chapter 6), too, demonstrates how law 'gave an [institutionalised] name to hopes; it made specific vague ideas of entitlements and the grounds on which they were based', and thus made possible their communication and enforcement.

It is thus not a question simply of the effectiveness of law for those de-privileged by it, but also one of the particular structuring qualities of different arenas in which issues are negotiated. As Olaf Zenker and Zerrin Özlem Biner discuss in their contributions (Chapters 5 and 9), the question of how law relates to more overtly political means of social transformation is an empirical matter that requires ethnographic scrutiny. Zenker (Chapter 5), referring to Luhmann (1995), argues that

> representing [an issue] either in 'political' terms that overstate the agency
> and power of the involved actors to define collectively binding rules
> largely at their discretion *or* in 'legal' terms that understate such agency
> and power (as well as the indeterminacy of law) ... seems to be more a
> matter of switching between two different and ultimately incommensur-
> able codes than an issue of differential ontology ... Switching from one
> code to another opens up a limited range of new potential consequences,
> while simultaneously precluding an equally limited set of others. Against
> this backdrop, it becomes an empirical question whether a certain phe-
> nomenon is being processed by actors in terms of the political or legal (or
> any other) code.

DISTANCES

We started by asking what effect law's travels have on law itself and on
the understanding of the world, of the conflicts and the normative orientations of those who use it. This is because attention to the dialectic
between the two is necessary to understand normative change that occurs
as law travels and produces situations of legal pluralism (see, e.g., Benda-
Beckmann *et al.* 2005). Several dimensions of this have been addressed
in the debates of legal anthropology. First, legal scholars have shown how
so-called universal norms as expressed in the legal language and procedures of Western law often fail to adequately capture the understandings of situations, relationships and conflicts of those they are meant to
protect (Felstiner *et al.* 1980/1981; Merry 1990). Anthropologists in particular have pointed to the increasing hegemony of a Western notion of
the person, with its ideological baggage of autonomy, free will and the
primacy of the individual and individualistic 'interests', which is prom-
ulgated by the spread of (Western) law (Collier *et al.* 1995). Scholarly
works increasingly focus on the legal classifications that are used to categorise people on the basis of their experiences of subjugation, exclusion, deprivation and other forms of suffering (Ross 2002; Hastrup 2003;
Wilson 2003). Notions of community (e.g. James 2006), indigeneity (e.g.
Donahoe *et al.* 2008), gender (e.g. Merry 2003) and 'victimhood' (e.g.
Mamdani 1996; Borneman 1997; Wilson 2001, 2003; Ross 2002; Hastrup
2003; Biner 2007) become embedded in law and are transmitted by various discourses of rights and justice. This can lead to the transformation
of the self-understanding of persons and groups who are recognised as

belonging to certain legal categories. For example, Wilson argues that human rights discourse 'draws upon Manichean dualisms (violated/violator; powerless/powerful) to construct its subjects as innocent victims', and how it presents images of its subjects 'as in "need" and inhabiting a social and global position of marginality' (2009: 215). This has the effect of homogenising the category of victim by removing subjects from their social, family and class backgrounds, and thereby decontextualises and depoliticises human rights violations (Wilson 2009: 224).

This process is clearly illustrated in Zerrin Özlem Biner's analysis (Chapter 9) of a law designed to compensate people for losses incurred as a result of the military conflict between Turkish armed forces and militants of the Kurdistan Workers' Party (PKK). The manner in which the law was implemented reduced the traumatic experiences of applicants to a cost-benefit calculation. In their well-intentioned efforts to help people take advantage of the compensation law, human rights activists and lawyers instructed them to frame their highly personal experiences in terms of a standardised narrative of violence, which had the unintended effect of homogenising applicants and lumping them into a single undifferentiated category of 'victims'.

Secondly, and in a more general way, Biner's case throws into high relief the fundamental gap between people's aspirations for justice, on the one hand, and the legal interpretation of 'justice', on the other hand; between the 'experience-near' formulation of personal, localised understanding and awareness of a situation, and the 'experience-distant language of jurisprudence', as Stuart Kirsch (Chapter 1) describes it. In many ways, this gap is asymptotic; it can never be completely closed. Many of the contributions in this volume show that it is impossible ever to seamlessly translate the innumerable diverse experiences of people's everyday lives into a legal language of any kind. This is particularly evident in Gerhard Anders's case (Chapter 4 in this volume), in which the Special Court for Sierra Leone, established to prosecute war criminals, not only imposed specific narratives of violence and conflict, but raised and ultimately disappointed ordinary citizens' expectations for a more encompassing vision of justice that they located in development and distributive justice.

As Derrida (1992) argues in his essay 'Force of Law', while law is an authorising, legitimising form, justice as it is *imagined* carries the 'messianic promise' of setting wrongs right, a promise that can only be imperfectly, if ever, captured, contained or actualised. This points us to the hope that is invested in law – and at the same time towards the unbridgeable hiatus between this messianic promise and law's mundane translations of hope into procedures. To what degree and under what circumstances this gap is actually experienced as problematic is an empirical question; it depends on law's promises in different legal fields and the expectations that it raises. There are many situations in which nobody expects legal representations of a situation, a relation or an issue to fully express their hopes and aspirations (see e.g. Zenker, Chapter 5). In other cases, particularly those dealing with social processes that fall under the rubrics of 'reconciliation' and 'transitional justice' (e.g. Anders, Chapter 4; Biner, Chapter 9), law is overburdened with expectations and is therefore necessarily experienced as deficient and inadequate.

TRANSLATIONS

Notwithstanding the fundamental hiatus between law's representations and people's experiences, a third question – that of the degree to which it is possible to 'translate' legal concepts and terminologies from one socio-politico-cultural milieu into another (Watson 1974; Legrand 1997) – has remained contentious. Several authors have proposed theories of what actually happens when law travels and is, for better or for worse, transported, transplanted, transmitted or translated from one context to another. One example of such a vision is the notion of 'vernacularisation'. Vernacularisation suggests that a specific norm is transformed to fit into a specific cultural order – and is thus changed. Levitt and Merry (2009) distinguish situations in which only the name of an imported norm or institution is changed in order to create the semblance of conformity with existing norms, while the content remains for the most part unaltered. This is a 'replication'. At the other end of the spectrum is 'hybridisation', a merging of imported transnational norms or institutions with local ones. An extreme form of hybridisation is subversion, in which the recognised 'global name' is adopted, but it is applied to a practice that is fundamentally in keeping with existing cultural practices. In such cases, while the name is retained the transnational institution or norm is fundamentally transformed (Merry 2006: 44).

Merry (2006) uses the notion of translation, originally adopted from Actor Network Theory, to analyse the networks of translators, namely the members of NGOs who 'translate' legal norms between the vernacular notions of their clients and the legal language of the wider arenas. The focus on such translators points our attention to the structured interaction between different arenas: local concerns and international forums in which these local concerns are connected to particular norms and thereby attributed relevance. The view on translators thus provides an insight into the power relations in which these networks relate to each other. What is translated by the translator is determined also by fashions and agendas set in arenas different from those whose concerns are negotiated.

While attention to translators can elucidate the power relations in which legal norms are negotiated, this use of the notion of translation suffers from the problem that the process of translation is cut short. Translation does not stop at professional translators: users, clients, subjects of law themselves make meaning of legal norms, and thus extend the chain of translations. One way to extend this chain, according to Harri Englund (Chapter 3), would be to actively engage in a process of reverse translation, in which the claims that are expressed through local interpretations of law would be translated back in such a way that they have the possibility of influencing the global rights discourse. Referring to Anna Tsing (2005), Englund concludes: 'If "globalization" is to have any other meaning than the diffusion of ideas and institutions from centres into peripheries, it must include the possibility that those ideas and institutions may encounter friction that propels fresh travels.'

Moreover, vernacularisation, in as much as it assumes the convergence (in whatever way) of two distinct normative systems as the relevant process of legal pluralism, assumes a great deal of overlap between a social group and a delineated normative order, with the group being defined by shared norms and values. It must perceive people (particularly those 'with culture' and 'without history' – cf. Wolf 1982) as primordially norm-bound, and their societies as normatively integrated and homogeneous. Such a perspective abstracts from the heterogeneity of normative orientations within social groups; it excludes from its analysis the struggles over the meaning of norms *within* normative orders that are a defining feature of all social interaction.

The concept of culture that lies at the base of such notions has in many ways long been problematised. The ontological concept of coherence and in this sense of normative integration disappeared with functionalism – and with this a fundamental change of the concept of culture was developed. With a 'pragmatic notion of culture' (Schiffauer 2004: 252) we can analyse culture as a continuing process of synthesis, distinction, differentiation and articulation within structured figurations. Such a perspective could inform our thinking about normative processes and legal pluralism; it can further the understanding of the intertwining of norms by overcoming dichotomous notions of authenticity and alienness.

Specific interpretations of norms and their validity are thus the result of negotiations within social relations. Contestations over the meaning of norms and categories, classifications such as nature, citizenship, gender, community and others are not processes of vernacularisation, but relate to historical social struggles. These struggles are what Peter Fitzpatrick once pointed to with his notion of 'combined law' (1983: 168). But the term 'combined law' also implies the meeting of two (or more) normative orders (if only in the terminology). Fitzpatrick himself describes a process more defined by the interactions and historical struggles than by the mixing of distinct normative orders. Focusing on the meeting of the norms often diverts attention from the social processes in which they are negotiated.

These contentions over meaning are what we consider the central site from which to understand normative change. We hold that when people turn towards legal norms to express their hopes and strive for their future, they interpret norms in the light of these aspirations rather than simply in terms of existing normative orders. Of course, these aspirations are shaped by the normative orders that prevail in the historical situation within which they live; their perception of the world, of what it should be and what is wrong with it, are structured by their moral parameters that relate to what Bourdieu has called 'doxa' (Bourdieu 1977), that which is not questioned and cannot be named because it is taken as the given natural order beyond reflection. However, people's habitual normative orientations always entail a measure of openness: situations demand interpretation; they entail alternatives even within habitually restricted realms of normative orientation (Bourdieu 1977: 225).

THE DIALECTIC OF LAW'S TRANSFORMATIONS

In order to move away from the more culturalist assumptions that inform analyses focusing on the meeting or mixing of distinct normative orders, we suggest looking at changes in law through the notion of iteration. Iteration suggests that any use, any engagement with an institution, implies an interpretation, a variation and a selection, and is, thereby, a constitutive act (Derrida 1991: 90). Or, as Seyla Benhabib (2004: 179) has put it, 'every iteration transforms meaning, adds to it, enriches it in ever so subtle ways'. Iteration focuses our attention on interactions, and thus on situations and constellations of actors. It can occur at the level of single interactions, or, as Benhabib (2004: 171–212) has suggested (in a somewhat strange detour via Derrida towards Habermas's discourse theory of law), at the level of the emergence of collective opinion, a process well exemplified by the emphasis on 'publics' (Niezen 2010) in the debates over justice, as described by Gerhard Anders (Chapter 4). Both levels are important for our understanding of normative change: individual interactions reveal the scope for action that opens up before people, despite their habitual normative orientations; examination of collective opinion helps us begin to get at what Robert Cover has called *jurisgenesis*.

Cover theorises law as a social construct that takes place through interaction and that develops within a normative universe. This normative world 'is held together by the force of interpretive commitments – some small and private, others immense and public. These commitments – of officials and of others – do determine what law means and what law shall be' (1992: 99). In Cover's words (1992: 103), the production of 'legal meaning, jurisgenesis, takes place always through an essentially cultural medium … [T]he creative process is collective or social.'

We use the concept of iteration to highlight the situational interpretative processes that are not in their entirety shaped by particular pre-given normative orders, and as such are not captured by the term vernacularisation. We see such interpretative processes particularly clearly in the contributions of Stuart Kirsch, Harri Englund, Olaf Zenker and Julia Eckert in this volume. They show processes in which law is transformed to incorporate values that otherwise would not have been considered. Kirsch's Papua New Guinea case (Chapter 1) shows how 'subsistence values' became incorporated into legal decisions and then took on a life of their own, being propagated through precedence in other cases. His Suriname case shows how 'freedom' is a multivalent cultural value that is 'neither exclusively indigenous nor modern', and is 'simultaneously a shared concern of members of the state and the basis of a claim to difference … The multivocality of freedom means that any gaps or differences in the interpretation of the concept may be concealed by the shared meanings it also invokes.' Kirsch's case studies clearly demonstrate the law-changing potential of iterations, which he, citing Hacking (1994), discusses as the '"looping effect" through which indigenous ideas and practices are refashioned through their engagement with the courts'.

Harri Englund (Chapter 3) also invokes a culturally specific form of freedom that Malawian villagers want to have recognised in law. One of the rights the villagers are fighting for is the right to be dependent on the headman of their own choosing. This is clearly not the kind of right envisioned by the framers of the Universal Declaration of Human Rights, with its underlying assumption of personal autonomy, and Englund himself makes a clear distinction between 'human rights' and what he has dubbed 'relationship rights'. But the Malawian villagers insist on expressing their demands in terms of human rights (or rather 'birth freedom', the Chichewa concept that most closely approximates human rights), and Englund suggests that this local appropriation of human rights has the potential to transform the concept at the international level.

Julia Eckert's cases from the slums of Bombay (Chapter 6) show how law and legal knowledge are spread and transformed through rumours. Rumours constitute an unauthenticated, uncertain and unsystematic body of knowledge; as such, they make possible the exploration of the interpretative processes that affect legal norms and ultimately propel normative change. This is because, Eckert asserts, 'in the spread of rumours selection happens at every stage: what is transmitted and what is heard depends on what is deemed important either for hopes or for fears'. She concludes that the study of the rumoured ways of horizontal knowledge transmission can shed light on the ways in which fears and hopes affect the interpretation and adoption of specific notions of right and law.

Finally, in his analysis of land restitution in South Africa, Olaf Zenker (Chapter 5) shows how, through persistent 'timid and modest appeals to existing sets of overarching rules' and declaring themselves 'to be concerned with following, not changing rules', the communities of Kalkfontein, a farm north of Pretoria, managed to establish new rules over time, a feat they were not able to accomplish through more overtly political means. Through repeated and reiterated attempts to work within the existing legal framework, the people of Kalkfontein 'both profoundly altered the standing of the co-purchasers vis-à-vis the local tribal authority and substantially changed the overall order at various levels'.

Thus, rather than using notions of vernacularisation that imply the convergence of two different normative orders, we suggest looking at the processes through which norms – whichever norms are deemed relevant by those concerned – are interpreted in a given situation. People subsume their concerns under specific laws, thereby interpreting these laws and 'making' them (cf. Benda-Beckmann 1991). This is the notion of translation that Stuart Kirsch and Harri Englund employ in their articles in this volume, a notion of translation that does not focus on privileged translators, but takes into view the simultaneous, sometimes diverging, but mutually related processes of translation of actors engaged in a situation.

Whenever such interpretative or translating processes occur in legally plural situations, they can blur the differences between different normative systems, ignore them, form hybrids (Kirsch, this volume) or inadvertently synthesise them (Eckert, this volume). They can bring forth new meanings of legal terms that relate to the specific experiences of different people, as is evident in Harri Englund's contribution. They can, of course, also produce further differentiation between two or more normative systems; just as assimilation is always a possibility in legally plural situations, so is differentiation.

TRANSFORMING SUBJECTIVITIES

Such an approach demands a re-evaluation of the position that subjectivities are determined by legal categories. Our insistence on the structured agentic possibilities of people can more precisely be put in terms of the dual characteristics of subjection as employed by Judith Butler. In her project to understand the disciplinary notion of power (with reference to Foucault), Butler acknowledges the subordinating and at the same time productive effects of power, and argues that power that appears to pressure the subject into subordination actually constitutes the subject's identity (1997: 2). In her view, subjection is not a linear and straight process. Where submission to power is constantly maintained and re-iterated, the subject is constantly in the process of becoming (Butler 1997: 13–16). In this process, Butler argues, 'agency exceeds the power by which it is enabled' (Butler 1997: 15).

Erdem Evren's case of conscientious objectors in Turkey helps to illuminate the process of subjection, where political subjectivity is produced through the transformative re-iteration of norms. Evren addresses the ambivalent position Turkey's conscientious objectors find themselves in as outspoken anarchists and dissenters who at the same time appeal to an international legal body such as the European Court of Human Rights (ECHR). He shows that by challenging the Turkish state in a legal forum, conscientious objectors' subjectivities are transformed and take on characteristics that call to mind Agamben's *homo sacer* (1998). According to Evren, Agamben's *sacer* is an 'emblem of a new subjectivity that is constituted at the intersections of the juridical and biopolitical models of power in liberal democracies'. Like Agamben's *homo sacer*,

Turkey's conscientious objectors are thrown into the bare life; however, unlike *sacer*, for which there can be no sacrifice or law, Evren demonstrates that 'law ... mediates intricately with sacrifice', and it is in this 'convoluted mediation' that conscientious objectors' political subjectivities come into being. They sacrifice their own freedom for the sake of other conscientious objectors and to generate public awareness of conscientious objection.

Julia Eckert's cases also show the dual nature of law's transformative force: those who employ law to express their needs and their experiences of justice come to see themselves in a new light as 'rights-bearing persons', or as women who are subject to women's rights. This emergent self-understanding creates specific and thus limited and structured possibilities of self-realisation that replace former (equally limited and structured) self-understandings and at the same time articulate with other such possibilities, thereby creating new meanings of what it is to be a woman and from what grounds rights arise.

THE STRUCTURATION OF ITERATION

This conceptualisation of the dialectic of law's transformations in and of itself does not tell us anything about the extent of the transformations effected in iterations, or the different characteristics of such shifts. We therefore complement the use of the concept with an analysis of the particular fixity of law, the limits of iteration that are given in specific norms and procedures. More importantly, the notion of iterative transformation needs to be complemented with a method for analysing the structuration of such iterations. Attention to iterations alone cannot reveal the conditions of specific iterations, the factors that determine which course they take and whether through them a status quo is actively reproduced or actually transformed. The processes by which specific norms gain dominance can be analysed, and the processes by which they remain dominant can likewise be analysed. Change and continuity of normative orders can both be seen as social process and are as such in need of explanation.

We want to stress therefore that iterations of law occur within figurations, historically contingent 'networks of interdependencies' (Elias 1978), i.e. the relations between actors that are defined by their roles and historical positioning, and that restrict to a greater or lesser degree the transformative potential of iterations. Franz von Benda-Beckmann has examined in detail the conditions and limits of iterative interpretations of law by differently positioned actors. In the final analysis, *which* interpretation comes to predominate in a given situation depends on social and political power relations (Benda-Beckmann 1991: 225). The historical transformation of political relations and their effect on the interpretation of law is particularly evident in Amita Baviskar's contribution to this volume (Chapter 7). She demonstrates how the legal instrument of public interest litigation, once successfully employed to address the violation of constitutional rights of the poor in India (Baxi 1987), has increasingly been utilised by the newly-empowered middle classes in Indian cities. They have pitted environmental rights against the socio-economic rights of the urban poor, and in an uncanny alliance with the judiciary founded on a mutual distancing from 'politics', have managed to quash alternative interpretations of constitutional rights. Thus, the attempt of the judiciary to preserve and emphasise its autonomy vis-à-vis the executive, which earlier had led to the judiciary's pro-poor social activism, has, under conditions of changed political relations that govern the new India, produced an alignment with middle-class interests. This generates interpretations of (largely the same) law that radically differ from earlier interpretations: political relations have been transformed by the new weight and power of the middle class.

Christian Strümpell's analysis (Chapter 8) of the struggles of people displaced by the construction of a public-sector steel plant in Rourkela, India to assert their right to public-sector employment is also evidence of this same historical trajectory within India. He shows how Nehru's early post-colonial policies of industrial modernisation, based on a 'vanguard working class' leading to a 'socialistic pattern of society', were re-interpreted by regional elites in the province of Orissa to serve their political interests. This in turn seriously threatened the local displaced tribal villagers' participation in the nation-building project. Their position worsened in the 1990s with the advent of neo-liberal structural adjustment policies. Their attempts to bring the issue of their rehabilitation into the courts, where they hoped they might take the issues out of the political and into the judicial realm and perhaps stand a better chance of effecting real, long-lasting change to their advantage, have been thwarted by the fact that the courts here too interpret law and constitutional rights according to a vision of justice that emerged in line with the neo-liberal restructuring of the public sector. Within these shifting figurations the juridification of their protest has led the local displaced tribal people to perceive the current regime in western Orissa as an illegal regime of plunder.

Zerrin Özlem Biner's discussion of Turkey's Compensation Law (Chapter 9) likewise illustrates the complexity of figurations and their transformations. Turkey's persistent failure to address human rights issues related to the treatment of its Kurdish minority has been perhaps the main obstacle to Turkey's acceptance into the European Union. The Compensation Law was one of the most effective legal policies that the Turkish state has enacted to counter its diminishing credibility on the international stage. Subsequently, the ECHR ruled that the applicants must exhaust the procedures of the Compensation Law before filing action in Strasbourg. This decision, itself resulting from the negotiations between Turkey and the EU, and from the conflicts over EU membership within Turkish society itself, has transformed the relations between the Turkish state and Kurdish citizens, on the one hand, and the ECHR and displaced Kurds on the other; it has transformed issues of accountability and justice into an entirely internal affair between lawyers, displaced Kurdish citizens and local bureaucrats who implement the law and act as representatives of the state.

As these cases show, such historically transforming figurations shape the interdependencies within which different social forces operate and articulate their interests and norms. The studies collected in this volume demonstrate how and where the struggles over the meaning of norms and categories occur and continue to produce new legal meanings. The emplacement of these negotiations in their historically contingent matrices of politics, institutions and identities reveals that they are always relational (Emirbayer 1997) and, in the final analysis, radically social. The particular trajectory of more global normative developments in the current era is demonstrated by Upendra Baxi in his epilogue to this volume: he sees what he calls the 'politics for rights' overtaken by a 'trade-related, market friendly human rights paradigm' that emerges from a specific historical figuration, overriding earlier understandings of rights.

BETWEEN *DOXA* AND THE FUTURE

Upendra Baxi has insisted that it is precisely 'the struggles of the multitudes of mass illegalities which enact forms of citizen understandings and interpretations of the rule of law notion' (Baxi 2004: 326). He distinguishes in his contribution in this volume and elsewhere between the politics *of* human rights and the politics *for* human rights, arguing passionately that 'law is always and everywhere a terrain of people's struggle to make power accountable, governance just, and state ethical' (Baxi 2004: 327). His intention is to overcome the Eurocentric understanding of the shaping of legal norms and construct 'multicultural ... narratives of the rule of law' (2004: 340) by pointing to the ways in which these norms were reformulated and creatively constituted in the interpretations of different historical struggles.

We thus propose a radically social theory of law's transformations. The interpretative processes that cumulatively generate *jurisgenesis* come out of normative orientations that draw on an all-encompassing experience of life, what Rapport has called 'human' (2010: 88). He relates this to Victor Turner's 'emphasis on the voluntary, active and intentioned nature of change, [and] the renunciation of communitarian classification in favour of human communitas' (Rapport 2010: 89). We can relate it also to the conceptualisation of 'life' that Veena Das (2011) proposes, life that is contextually specific in its needs but in its fundamental neediness is in principle universal. Hopes towards what ought to be and ideas of justice are not determined by 'custom' or legal norms, but by a more encompassing experience of life that underlies moral or legal norms. These hopes rise above immediate needs and project 'anyone's' human existence towards a future that goes beyond customary or communitarian circumscription and transcends the repetition of doxic certainties. Such creative visions of the future inspire the struggles against what is perceived as wrong, and for what ought to be.

References
Agamben, Giorgio 1998. *Homo Sacer: Sovereign Power and Bare Life*, trans. Daniel Heller-Roazen. Stanford University Press.
Baxi, Upendra 1987. 'Taking suffering seriously: social action litigation in the Supreme Court of India', in Neelan Tiruchelvam and Radhika Coomaraswami (eds.) *The Role of the Judiciary in Plural Societies*. London: Pinter, pp. 32–60.
    2004. 'Rule of law in India, theory and practice', in Randall Peerenboom (ed.) *Asian Discourses of Rule of Law: Theories and Implementation of Rule of Law in Twelve Asian Countries, France and the U.S.* London: RoutledgeCurzon, pp. 324–45.
Benda-Beckmann, Franz von 1991. 'Pak Dusa's law. Thoughts on legal knowledge and power', in Eberhard Berg, Jutta Lauth and Andreas Wimmer (eds.) *Ethnologie im Widerstreit*. München: Trickster, pp. 215–27.
Benda-Beckmann, Franz von, Benda-Beckmann, Keebet von and Griffiths, Anne (eds.) 2005. *Mobile People, Mobile Law, Expanding Legal Relations in a Contracting World*. Aldershot: Ashgate.

Benhabib, Seyla 2004. *The Rights of Others, Aliens, Residents and Citizens.* Cambridge University Press.

Biner, Z. Özlem 2007. 'From terrorist to repentant: who is the victim?', *History and Anthropology* 17 (4): 339–53.

Blichner, Lars C. and Molander, Anders 2008. 'Mapping juridification', *European Law Journal* 14 (1): 36–54.

Borneman, John 1997. *Settling Accounts: Violence, Justice, and Accountability in Postsocialist States.* Princeton University Press.

Bourdieu, Pierre 1977. *Outline of a Theory of Practice.* Cambridge University Press.

1987. 'The force of law: toward a sociology of the juridical field', *Hastings Law Journal* 38: 814–53.

Butler, Judith 1997. *The Psychic Life of Power.* Stanford University Press.

Clarke, Kamari 2010. 'Rethinking Africa through its exclusions: the politics of naming criminal responsibility', *Anthropological Quarterly* 38 (3): 625–51.

Collier, Jane, Maurer, Bill and Suarez-Navaz, Liliana 1995. 'Sanctioned identities: legal constructions of modern personhood', *Identities* 2 (1–2): 1–27.

Comaroff, Jean and Comaroff, John L. 2006. 'Law and disorder in the postcolony: an introduction', in Jean Comaroff and John L. Comaroff (eds.) *Law and Disorder in the Postcolony.* University of Chicago Press, pp. 1–56.

Cover, Robert 1992. '*Nomos* and narrative', in Martha Minow, Michael Ryan and Austin Sarat (eds.) *Narrative, Violence, and the Law: The Essays of Robert Cover.* Ann Arbor: University of Michigan Press, pp. 95–172.

Das, Veena 2011. 'State, citizenship and the urban poor', *Citizenship Studies* 15 (3–4): 319–33.

Dembour, Marie-Benedicte and Kelly, Tobias 2007. *Paths to International Justice: Social and Legal Perspectives.* Cambridge University Press.

Derrida, Jacques 1991. 'Signature, event, context', in Peggy Kamuff (ed.) *A Derrida Reader: Between the Blinds.* New York: Columbia University Press, pp. 80–111.

1992. 'Force of law: the mystical foundation of authority. Deconstruction and the possibility of justice', in Drucilla Cornell, Michel Rosenfeld and David G. Carlson (eds.) *Deconstruction and the Possibility of Justice.* New York: Routledge, pp. 3–67.

Donahoe, Brian, Habeck, Joachim Otto, Halemba, Agnieszka and Sántha, István 2008. 'Size and place in the construction of indigeneity in the Russian Federation', *Current Anthropology* 48 (6): 993–1020.

Elias, Norbert 1978. *What is Sociology?* London: Hutchinson.

Emirbayer, Mustafa 1997. 'Manifesto for a relational sociology', *The American Journal of Sociology* 103 (2): 281–317.

Felstiner, William, Abel, Richard L. and Sarat, Austin 1980/1981. 'The emergence and transformation of disputes: naming, blaming, claiming …', *Law & Society Review* 15: 631–54.

Fitzpatrick, Peter 1983. 'Law, plurality, and underdevelopment', in David Sugarman (ed.) *Legality, Ideology and the State*. London: Academic Press, pp. 159–82.

Garth, Bryant and Dezalay, Yves 1996. *Dealing in Virtue: International Commercial Arbitration and the Construction of a Transnational Legal Order.* University of Chicago Press.

Goodale, Mark 2009. *Surrendering to Utopia: An Anthropology of Human Rights.* Stanford University Press.

    2010. 'Response', *PoLAR: Political and Legal Anthropology Review* 33 (S1): 155–60.

Habermas, Jürgen 1985. 'Law as medium and law as institution', in Gunther Teubner (ed.) *Dilemmas of Law in the Welfare State*. Berlin, New York: De Gruyter, pp. 203–20.

Hacking, Ian 1994. 'The looping effects of human kinds', in Dan Sperber, David Premack and Ann James Premack (eds.) *Causal Cognition: A Multidisciplinary Approach*. Oxford: Clarendon, pp. 351–94.

Hastrup, Kirsten 2003. 'Violence, suffering and human rights', *Anthropological Reflections* 3 (3): 309–23.

James, Deborah 2006. 'The tragedy of the private: owners, communities and the state in South Africa's land reform programme', in Franz von Benda-Beckmann, Keebet von Benda-Beckmann and Melanie G. Wiber (eds.) *Changing Properties of Property*. Oxford: Berghahn Books, pp. 243–68.

Keck, Margaret and Sikkink, Kathryn 1998. *Activists beyond Borders: Advocacy Networks in International Politics*. Ithaca: Cornell University Press.

Kirchheimer, Otto 1972 [1933]. 'Verfassungsreform und Sozialdemokratie', in Otto Kirchheimer (ed.) *Funktionen des Staates und der Verfassung*. Frankfurt am Main: Suhrkamp, pp. 79–99.

Lazarus-Black, Mindie 1994. *Legitimate Acts and Illegal Encounters: Law and Society in Antigua and Barbuda*. Washington, DC: Smithsonian Institute Press.

Legrand, Pierre 1997. 'The impossibility of legal transplants', *Maastricht Journal of European and Comparative Law* 4: 111–24.

Levitt, Peggy and Merry, Sally 2009. 'Vernacularization on the ground: local use of global women's rights in Peru, China, India and the United States', *Global Networks* 9 (4): 441–61.

Li, Tania 2009. 'The law of the project: government and "good governance" at the World Bank in Indonesia', in Franz von Benda-Beckmann, Keebet von Benda-Beckmann and Julia Eckert (eds.) *Rules of Law and Laws of Ruling*. Aldershot: Ashgate, pp. 237–56.

Luhmann, Niklas 1995. *Social Systems*. Stanford University Press.

Mamdani, Mahmood 1996. *Citizen and Subject: Contemporary Africa and the Legacy of Late Colonialism*. Princeton University Press.

Mattei, Ugo and Nader, Laura 2008. *Plunder: When the Rule of Law Is Illegal.* Malden, Oxford: Blackwell Publishing.

Merry, Sally 1990. *Getting Justice and Getting Even: Legal Consciousness among Working-Class Americans.* University of Chicago Press.

2003. 'Rights talk and the experience of law: implementing women's human rights to protection from violence', *Human Rights Quarterly* 25 (2): 343–81.

2006. 'Transnational human rights and local activists: mapping the middle', *American Anthropologist* 108: 38–51.

Niezen, Ronald 2010. *Public Justice and the Anthropology of Law.* Cambridge University Press.

Randeria, Shalini 2011. 'The (un)making of policy in the shadow of the World Bank: infrastructure development, urban resettlement and the cunning state in India', in Cris Shore, Susan Wright and Davide Però (eds.) *Policy Worlds: Anthropology and the Analysis of Contemporary Power.* London: Berghahn Books, pp. 187–204.

Rapport, Nigel 2010. 'Apprehending anyone: the non-indexical, post-cultural, and cosmopolitan human actor', *Journal of the Royal Anthropological Institute* 16: 84–101.

Ross, Fiona 2002. *Bearing Witness: Women and the South African Truth and Reconciliation Commission.* London: Pluto Press.

Santos, Boaventura de Sousa and Rodríguez-Garavito, César A. (eds.) 2005. *Law and Globalisation from Below: Towards a Cosmopolitan Legality.* Cambridge University Press.

Schiffauer, Werner 2004. 'Anthropologie als Kulturwissenschaft', in Friedrich Jaeger, Burkhard Libsch and Jürgen Straub *Handbuch Kulturwissenschaften, Bd. II.* Stuttgart: Kultur in der Wissenschaft, pp. 235–56.

Scott, James 1985. *Weapons of the Weak: Everyday Forms of Peasant Resistance.* New Haven, CT: Yale University Press.

Teubner, Gunther 1987. 'Juridification: concepts, aspects, limits, solutions', in Gunther Teubner (ed.) *Juridification of Social Spheres: A Comparative Analysis in the Areas of Labor, Corporate, Antitrust and Social Welfare Law.* Berlin, New York: De Gruyter, pp. 3–48.

Thompson, Edward P. 1975. *Whigs and Hunters: The Origin of the Black Act.* London: Allen Lane.

Tsing, Anna L. 2005. *Friction: An Ethnography of Global Connection.* Princeton University Press.

Watson, Alan 1974. *Legal Transplants: An Approach to Comparative Law.* Edinburgh: Scottish Academic Press.

Westbrook, David A. 2006. 'Theorising the diffusion of law: conceptual difficulties, unstable imaginations and the effort to think gracefully nonetheless', *Harvard International Law Journal* 47 (2): 489–505.

Wilson, Richard A. 2001. *The Politics of Reconciliation in South Africa: Legitimizing the Post-Apartheid State*. Cambridge University Press.

    2003. 'Anthropological studies of national reconciliation processes', *Anthropological Theory* 3(3): 367–87.

    2009. 'Representing human rights violations: social contexts and subjectivties', in Mark Goodale (ed.) *Human Rights: An Anthropological Reader*. Blackwell: London, pp. 209–28.

Wilson, Richard A. and Mitchell, J. P. (eds.) 2003. *Human Rights in Global Perspective: Anthropological Perspectives on Rights, Claims and Entitlements*. Routledge: London.

Wolf, Eric 1982. *Europe and the People without History*. Berkeley: University of California Press.

CHAPTER 1

JURIDIFICATION OF INDIGENOUS POLITICS

Stuart Kirsch

The emergence of the 'indigenous' as an international legal category has opened up new avenues for claims to recognition and redistribution (Barsh 1994; Anaya 1996; Rosen 1997; Niezen 2003, 2010; Gilbert 2006). However, the juridification of indigenous politics requires translation across cultural and political boundaries (Clifford 1988; Bunte and Franklin 1992; Kirsch 2001; Miller 2001; Graham 2002; Povinelli 2002; Richland 2008). This process produces gaps between the *experience-near* formulation of indigenous knowledge and practices and the *experience-distant* language of jurisprudence. Clifford Geertz (1983: 57–8) invokes these terms with reference to ethnographic representation, distinguishing between the language through which people naturally and effortlessly refer to what they think, feel and believe in contrast to how these thoughts, emotions and beliefs are described by anthropologists and other social scientists. This distinction may also be applied to the process of juridification through which indigenous peoples and their interlocutors, including lawyers, judges and anthropologists, represent their claims in legal terminology that has the capacity to alienate the participants from their own speech (Das 1989: 316).

Post-colonial scholars express strong reservations about the juridification of indigenous politics. Veena Das (1989: 316) refers to the

Earlier versions of this chapter benefitted from discussion at York University, the University of Iowa, the University of Manchester, and the workshop on 'Law against the State' at the Max Planck Institute for Social Anthropology, although I bear sole responsibility for the result. I am especially grateful to Julia Eckert for suggesting the rubric that helped frame the text.

imposition of 'legal domination ... in all spheres of life' as part of the contract 'such groups have been compelled to establish with the forms of domination belonging to the structures of modernity'. Arif Dirlik (2001: 181) argues that the reduction of political opposition to the 'language of jurisprudence ... signals a consolidation of hegemony'. Elizabeth Povinelli (2002: 159) questions whether legal systems can adequately address past injustices 'without performing an ideological critique of the institutions themselves'. Dipesh Chakrabarty (2000: 85) describes how cross-cultural translation involves the mediation of homogenising middle terms that cloak implicit claims to universality. However, he also recognises that social and political movements require access to information encoded by these universalising terms, which are the categories employed by 'bureaucracies and other instruments of governmentality', and consequently serve as reservoirs of power (Chakrabarty 2000: 86).[1] He defines the task of analysis as attending to the gaps or traces of difference produced by these acts of translation (Chakrabarty 2000: 93–94).

In this chapter, I compare three international legal cases concerned with indigenous rights, paying particular attention to the gaps between indigenous discourse and the language of jurisprudence. In contrast to post-colonial arguments about hegemony, these cases suggest a range of potential outcomes. The claims articulated in these legal proceedings may have a kind of 'looping effect' (Hacking 1994) in which indigenous ideas and practices are refashioned through their engagement with the courts. Here, the gaps produced by juridification undergo partial closure as indigenous peoples appropriate and deploy the language of the courts. What may initially have been experience-distant terminology can become internalised as indigenised concepts (Sahlins 1999) offering new political resources. Another possibility for closing the gap is the transformation of legal discourse as a result of interaction with unfamiliar concepts and practices, resulting in the formation of hybrid legal precedents. Alternatively, the courts may fail to recognise or incorporate indigenous concerns into their decisions, reifying difference. A final possibility is that the discourse used in legal proceedings may elide certain forms of difference. The

---

[1] These disjunctions might be compared to what Kim Fortun (2001: 8) refers to as the double-binds faced by political activists, which may 'foreclose certain lines of inquiry, disable certain forms of knowledge, and legitimate discriminatory social categories'. She describes how political and legal struggles create new subject positions and require new vocabularies: 'Subjects are drawn into new realities and fields of reference [in which] traditional constructs of society and culture no longer seem adequate' (Fortun 2001: 13).

examples considered here illustrate some of the potential consequences of juridification, including the internalisation of new concepts, the creation of new hybrids and the reification or elision of difference.

This chapter examines these transformations by drawing on examples from my experience as an engaged anthropologist working with and on behalf of indigenous communities in three legal venues. The first case considers subsistence rights in a lawsuit against the Australian-owned Ok Tedi mine in Papua New Guinea. The second example addresses claims for compensation regarding the loss of culture (or a 'way of life') and the right to a healthy environment in the wake of US nuclear weapons testing in the Marshall Islands. The third case involves ongoing legal claims regarding the recognition of indigenous land rights in Suriname. By examining the gaps that emerge through the juridification of indigenous politics, this essay addresses the following questions: what are the different pathways through which indigenous rights claims are formulated? How do they draw on local understandings, national histories and international discourses? What role do lawyers, anthropologists and NGOs play in this process? How do the constraints of the legal regimes in which these claims are articulated affect their content or presentation? Finally, how does the juridification of indigenous politics create new resources, reify or elide difference, or lead to new hybrids?

SUBSISTENCE RIGHTS IN PAPUA NEW GUINEA

The pivotal issue in the Ok Tedi case was subsistence rights. The Ok Tedi copper and gold mine in Papua New Guinea has discharged 80,000 metric tons of tailings and waste rock into the Ok Tedi and Fly rivers daily since production began in 1984, and more than 1 billion metric tons of sediment in total, polluting these waterways beyond recognition and causing widespread deforestation (Kirsch 2006; Bolton 2009). Since the mid 1980s, the people living downstream from the mine have objected to its environmental impacts and demanded compensation commensurate with its consequences for their subsistence practices (Kirsch 2007). They circulated petitions, staged protests and lobbied the company for change and the state for enforcement of existing laws. They travelled from Papua New Guinea to Australia, to Rio de Janeiro for the 1992 Earth Summit, and to North America and Europe to enlist support from environmental NGOs, church groups and governments. Their participation in the 1993 International Water Tribunal in Amsterdam (International Water Tribunal 1994) inspired their lawsuit against Broken Hill Proprietary

Ltd. (BHP), the majority shareholder and managing partner of the Ok Tedi mine, in the Supreme Court of Victoria in Melbourne, where BHP is incorporated (Banks and Ballard 1997).

The legal case against BHP and the Ok Tedi mine initially addressed the environmental impact of the project on the property of the downstream landowners. However, BHP challenged the lawsuit on the basis of legal doctrines which prevent the Australian courts from determining claims related to 'land or immoveable property situated in another jurisdiction' (Gordon 1997: 153). The lawyers needed to restate their claims without making reference to property rights.

Ethnographic information proved to be the key. The rights of the Yonggom people who own land along the west bank of the Ok Tedi River, where most of their contemporary villages were established in the 1970s, differ from the rights of the people who relocated to these villages from smaller Yonggom settlements scattered throughout the rainforest. The Yonggom refer to landowners as *ambip kin yariman*, the persons responsible for lineage land. The other people living in these villages are known as *animan od yi karup*, persons who derive their livelihood (food and wealth, *animan* and *od*) from the land. Yonggom settlers in the new villages were granted use rights to the land and the river for subsistence purposes: extracting the starch that is the mainstay of their diet from the sago palms that grow along the river and in the swamps that crisscross the region; growing bananas and other crops in their gardens; and hunting, fishing and harvesting timber and other forest products. Both groups of people experienced losses as a result of the mine's impact on the riverine environment and the surrounding forests. Consequently, access to resources for subsistence use became the central issue in the case rather than property rights (see Ribot and Peluso 2003).

The lawyers subsequently reformulated the case to focus on the impact of the Ok Tedi mine on the subsistence economies of the people living downstream, arguing that:

> what distinguishes these claims from the usual claims that come before courts is that these plaintiffs are people who live a subsistence lifestyle. They live substantially, if not entirely, outside the economic system which uses money as the medium of exchange. But to say that does not alter the fact that if they are deprived of the very things which support their existence, they suffer loss. Of course it is a loss which appears in an uncommon guise because typically the courts have dealt with claims that are rooted in society's adherence to the monetary medium of exchange … What Mr Myers [the lawyer for BHP] says really proceeds from the

unstated assumption that a thing is only economic if it is passed through the system of monetary exchange, and there is simply no reason in theory or in law for that to be so.

(Julian Burnside, cited in Gordon 1997: 154–55)

The judge in the case endorsed this line of reasoning, determining that:

to restrict the duty of care to cases of pure economic loss would be to deny a remedy to those whose life is substantially, if not entirely, outside an economic system which uses money as a medium of exchange. It was put that, in the case of subsistence dwellers, loss of the things necessary for subsistence may be seen as akin to economic loss. If the plaintiffs are unable or less able to have or enjoy those things which are necessary for their subsistence as a result of the defendant's negligent conduct of the mine, they must look elsewhere for them, perhaps to obtain them by purchase or barter or perhaps to obtain some substitute.

(Byrne 1995: 15)

With this judgement, the court confirmed the commensurability of subsistence rights and the economic rights associated with property ownership, establishing important legal precedents for both the subsistence rights of indigenous peoples and corporate liability for abrogating those rights. While not legally binding beyond its original jurisdiction, such legal determinations circulate widely and may influence lawyers and judges in related cases (Gordon 1997: 154).

Despite its deployment in the courts, there is no Yonggom equivalent to the concept of subsistence rights. The relationship between the *yariman* and his land may be translated as ownership but has other meanings as well. The central actor in divinations held to seek the cause of a persistent illness, or *anigat*, is the *anigat yariman*. This role is filled by the senior kinsman or guardian responsible for the patient's well-being. Similarly, the sponsor of an *arat* feast, who coordinates the labour and exchange relations of the participants, is known as the *arat yariman*. The *yariman* relationship is based on the responsibilities of kinship, guardianship and sponsorship. Given that *ambip kin* refers to both a specific parcel of land and the lineage that holds the rights to that land, *ambip kin yariman* refers to the person or persons responsible for the land belonging to the lineage. With these responsibilities comes the political authority to limit the access of others as well (Schoorl 1970). Although the Yonggom are able to acquire use rights to land from others through assertion or appeal (Schieffelin 1976), they do not recognise subsistence rights in the abstract.

27

Despite the gap between Yonggom concepts and the legal argument made on their behalf, the notion of subsistence rights adequately represented the interests of the plaintiffs. It is well established that indigenous commitment to hunting, fishing and other subsistence practices often persists even in the context of a predominantly cash economy (Sahlins 1999). At its most fundamental level, the Ok Tedi case addressed the capacity of the affected communities to preserve their relationships to the land, both in terms of the ability to carry out traditional subsistence practices and the larger significance of these practices (Kirsch 2006). The concept of subsistence rights provided a valuable shorthand for the stakes in the Ok Tedi case: the ability to sustain meaningful and productive relationships to the land in the face of devastating environmental change.

The concept of subsistence rights also proved useful to the Yonggom in their negotiations over the case. They affirmed the distinction made by the courts between a subsistence economy and 'an economic system which uses money as a medium of exchange', as indicated by the following complaint about the inadequacy of compensation payments in 1998, two years after the lawsuit was settled out of court: 'The company doesn't face this problem [of inadequate resources]. They eat in the mess, while we live on hunting and gardening. We cannot afford to buy fresh meat in the stores. Once our [compensation] is spent, it is difficult to make ends meet. The environment has already been destroyed; the only option is to provide us with additional funds' (Kirsch 2006: 212). During a village meeting the same year, one of the leaders of the campaign against the mine raised the following question: 'What are we going to do without money? When we say fortnightly [compensation] payments, it means survival' (Kirsch 2006: 208). In arguing that compensation must be paid every two weeks, he compares the wages people earn in a monetary economy to subsistence practices. Although he does not use the term subsistence, he argues that environmental degradation threatens their survival. The concept of subsistence rights, whether directly or indirectly invoked, becomes a key trope for indigenous politics when their ability to obtain one's livelihood from the land is threatened or abrogated rather than taken for granted (see Ivy 1995). In other contexts, subsistence practices have become metonymic of indigenous ways of life and consequently key symbols of indigenous identity (Sahlins 1999; Nadasdy 2003), and therefore central to the questions about culture and loss that are the subject of the next section of this chapter.

In the Ok Tedi case, lawyers for the plaintiffs introduced the novel concept of subsistence rights, which established an important legal precedent and provided the people living downstream from the mine with the means to express their concerns about the economic consequences of pollution. The juridification of indigenous politics resulted in changes to both legal concepts and local political claims.

LOSS OF A WAY OF LIFE AND THE RIGHT TO A HEALTHY ENVIRONMENT IN THE MARSHALL ISLANDS

The second case addresses damages resulting from US nuclear weapons testing in the Marshall Islands during the 1940s and 1950s.[2] In 1999, I was one of three anthropologists invited to conduct preliminary research in support of a claim by the people of Rongelap Atoll to the US Nuclear Claims Tribunal, which was established to adjudicate claims for property damage, loss and suffering (Kirsch 2001; Johnston and Barker 2008). The people we interviewed expressed concerns about their 'loss of a way of life' and the violation of their 'right to a healthy environment'.[3] During an advisory committee meeting, we were told that: 'Land gives you the meaning of life and the role of each individual in society' (Johnston and Barker 2008: 63). Another participant at the meeting told us: 'You cannot put enough value on land ... How do you put a value on something that people consider as a living thing that is part of your soul?' (Johnston and Barker 2008: 63). A third person at the meeting framed his concerns in terms of culture and society: 'When the bomb exploded, the culture was also gone, too. It is impossible for people to act in their proper roles' (Johnston and Barker 2008: 186). During one of our interviews, we were told that: 'We have lost our knowledge, our ability, our moral standing and self-esteem in the community. What we were taught is no longer practical. To be a good fisherman, you have to know where to fish on an island. A lot has been lost, not just our land' (Johnston and Barker 2008: 189).

---

[2] It is the Rongelap case to which Dirlik (2001) refers in the comment cited above.

[3] The 'right to a healthy environment' was initially recognised in Principle 1 of the 1972 Stockholm Declaration on the Human Environment, and subsequently elaborated by the 1992 UN Conference on Environment and Development in Rio de Janeiro, which argued that 'human beings ... are entitled to a healthy and productive life in harmony with nature'. While not legally binding, these declarations form the basis for discussion about the right to a healthy environment.

My colleagues Barbara Rose Johnston and Holly Barker (2008) document these claims in greater detail in their submission to the Nuclear Claims Tribunal. They point out that earlier awards for compensation by the tribunal were based on land values derived from a record of lease payments in the Marshall Islands. They argue that real estate values fail to take the social and cultural values of land into account. Conventional real estate values also ignore the marine resources that sustained the Marshallese way of life. Johnston and Barker's (2008: 57) focus on 'the loss of access to use a healthy ecosystem … [and the] problems resulting from the inability to interact in a healthy landscape and seascape in ways that allow the transmission of knowledge and the ability to sustain a healthy way of life' suggests a more holistic way to assess the consequences of nuclear weapons testing for the people of Rongelap.

During previous testimony before the Nuclear Claims Tribunal, the anthropologist Laurence Carucci discussed the hardships experienced by the people from Enewetak after they were relocated to Ujelong, a remote, uninhabited and largely desolate atoll. Carucci described how the women from Enewetak were unable to weave mats because there were no pandanus trees on Ujelong. The lack of mature breadfruit trees also meant that a generation of young men grew up without the opportunity to make and sail canoes, skills and experiences that were both essential and highly valued by their predecessors (Carucci, cited in Kirsch 2001: 173). Such material losses can have significant cultural consequences. However, contemporary anthropologists have generally avoided the issue of culture loss, which is associated with a disciplinary past in which it was commonly assumed that people would assimilate and cultures would disappear (Kirsch 2001). Yet these examples from the Marshall Islands, and similar claims by other indigenous peoples (Kambel 2002; Wood 2004; Demian 2006), indicate the need for additional attention to the question of culture loss.[4]

On 17 April 2007, the Nuclear Claims Tribunal issued its decision in the Rongelap case, 'calling for payment of just over $1 billion in compensation to the claimants, a figure reflecting the costs for remediation and restoration of Rongelap (and associated islands/atolls), future lost property value and compensation for damages from nuclear testing'

---

[4] The proliferation of claims about cultural property (Brown 2003; Hirsch and Strathern 2004) index these concerns.

(Nuti 2007: 42). The amount of compensation awarded was substantially greater than in prior judgements by the Nuclear Claims Tribunal for Enewetak ($323 million in 2000), Bikini ($563 million in 2001), and Utrik ($307 million in 2005). Each successive award incorporated and expanded upon prior judgements in terms of the calculation of their losses (Johnston, cited in Nuti 2007: 43).

However, specific claims by people from Rongelap about the loss of a way of life and the right to live in a healthy environment were explicitly downplayed by the three judges of the Nuclear Claims Tribunal. The tribunal weighed two methodologies for assessing the value of land. The 'residential/agricultural use approach' calculated the 'damages to natural resources, real or personal property, subsistence use, revenues, and profits and earning capacities' (Plasman and Danz 2007: 14, n.32). The second methodology relied on real estate values in which property had been rented or sold, and yielded the higher value. However, the tribunal previously established that compensation rates should be set with reference to the 'highest and best use' of the land, which they identified as agricultural and residential use rather than government purchase or rental. Consequently, the award to the people on Rongelap was based on lost use values rather than real estate values (Plasman and Danz 2007: 11–12).

In making its determination, the tribunal disputes Johnston and Barker's assertion that 'lost use values assessed by the appraisers are incomplete in that they fail to address ... natural resource damage and loss of lagoon, reef heads, clam beds, reef fisheries, turtle and bird nesting grounds'. Instead, the tribunal argues that the assessment of agricultural and residential use 'explicitly includes these uses' because in many cases the rights to marine resources were directly linked to the ownership of land (Plasman and Danz 2007: 14, n.32). Similar reasoning applied to the symbolic or cultural value of resources, including 'cultural resource damage and loss of access to family cemeteries, burial sites of *iroij* [chiefs], sacred sites and sanctuaries, and *morjinkot* land [given by the chiefs to commoners for bravery in battle]' (Plasman and Danz 2007: 14, n.32). The tribunal even argued that land which was culturally significant but had no discernable economic value – providing the example of an uninhabited and unused outer island in an atoll – was implicitly included in their analysis (Plasman and Danz 2007: 19, n.41). According to the tribunal, all of these specific cultural values were taken into account by the generic procedures of economic accounting and therefore did not require independent assessment. The tribunal also determined that 'the loss of access to a healthy ecosystem' was adequately addressed by the award for the loss of use (Plasman and Danz 2007: 19, n.41). Additional compensation was provided for the pain and suffering caused by inadequate and unhealthy living conditions, and by subjecting people from Rongelap to unnecessary medical procedures.

Specific claims made by the people of Rongelap about the loss of a way of life and the right to a healthy environment were not explicitly recognised by the Nuclear Claims Tribunal. But based on the larger value of the award for Rongelap in comparison to previous judgements by the tribunal, these claims were implicitly folded into their assessment of land values. The judgement significantly expanded prior valuations of land in the Marshall Islands even though it did not assign specific economic values for the loss of culture or the right to a healthy environment.

The hearings of the tribunal also failed to contest the fundamental power of the state to reduce its subjects to the conditions of *bare life* (Agamben 1998). Even though the tribunal cannot question the sovereign power of the state, it can unmask that power by showing how it operates, thereby revealing false claims made by the state concerning its responsibilities towards its subjects. Thus the hearings provided the people from Rongelap with the opportunity to challenge the state's claim to moral authority through testimony about their experiences. Johnston and Barker (2008: 225) conclude that the 'expert witness report and the tribunal hearings served as a truth and reconciliation committee, with Marshallese experts providing the testimony and the declassified narratives of scientists and scientific findings providing the damning substantiation'. Chakrabarty's (2000: 93) observation that 'the point is to ask how this seemingly imperious, all-pervasive code [of history or the law] might be deployed or thought about so that we have at least a glimpse of its own finitude, a glimpse of what might constitute an outside to it' is applicable to the proceedings of the Nuclear Claims Tribunal. The testimony of the people from Rongelap, and in particular their claims about the loss of a way of life and the right to live in a healthy environment, remains independent from the language of the court; there is no fusion or merger of the two. Yet this alternative accounting of events acts as a mirror in which the state is forced to view its own image.

FREEDOM IN SURINAME

The final example addresses indigenous land rights in Suriname. In 2009, the Lokono (Arawak) and Kaliña (Carib) peoples filed a complaint with the Inter-American Commission on Human Rights against the Republic of Suriname. Their complaint challenges the state's refusal to recognise indigenous land rights despite their obligation to do so under the UN Declaration of the Rights of Indigenous Peoples, to which Suriname is a signatory. It builds on the landmark 2007 judgement in the case of *Saramaka People v. Suriname* (2007, 2008), in which the Inter-American Court on Human Rights 'expanded the scope of protection for groups seeking to protect ancestral lands and resources, moving for the first time beyond indigenous peoples to extend protection to other tribal groups', namely the Maroon peoples who escaped from slavery during the seventeenth and eighteenth centuries to establish largely autonomous communities in the rainforest (Shelton 2008: 168; Price 2011). The Lokono and Kaliña territories in the lower Marowijne region of east Suriname have been progressively reduced and degraded by mining, logging and the expansion of the town of Albina onto indigenous lands. Three nature reserves have been established on indigenous land without permission, one of which has become a major industrial zone. BHP Billiton, the mining company responsible for the Ok Tedi mine in Papua New Guinea, mines bauxite in the Wane Creek Nature Reserve.[5] The Wane Hills mine has ravaged the landscape, transforming rainforest into barren red earth. A decade of restoration efforts amount to scattered plots of stunted trees. Mining company roads through the nature reserve have attracted legal and illegal logging, and the removal of the bauxite layer has spurred extraction of the underlying kaolin deposits. Until recently, Wane Creek was the most important hunting and fishing ground of the indigenous communities living in the lower Marowijne region. In January 2009, I was invited by the Association of Village Leaders in Suriname (VIDS) and the Forest People's Programme in the UK to conduct research on these issues and the question of indigenous land rights for submission to the Inter-American Court on Human Rights (Kirsch 2010).

Like the Yonggom people living downstream from the Ok Tedi mine, the Lokono and Kaliña attest to the impacts of development and environmental degradation on their subsistence practices, which require them to become more deeply involved in the monetary economy. As

---

[5] BHP merged with Billiton to form BHP Billiton in 2001.

one person told me: 'Before it was okay if you didn't have money, but now we need money [to survive].' They are no longer able to feed their families by hunting, fishing and agriculture. Members of these communities told me that participation in the monetary economy is fine for those persons who possess the skills required to earn a living wage, but that others are unsuccessful. Even though they share food among themselves when they hunt and fish, they do not redistribute the wages earned through employment. This leads to new structural forms of inequality.

Like the people from Rongelap affected by nuclear weapons testing, the Lokono and Kaliña also describe how these economic and environmental changes have affected their ability to reproduce their own culture. Many of the practical skills associated with subsistence production are no longer regularly taught by fathers to their sons and mothers to their daughters: 'In some families, there are no elders to teach them these things. And even to get the materials needed ... you can no longer find them locally because of logging, but have to travel long distances.' However, new markets for Amerindian products including cassava bread and beer (*kasiri*), agricultural produce and wild fruits have recently emerged in the town of St Laurent du Maroni, across the river from Albina in French Guiana. Participation in these markets provides them with the opportunity to improve their standard of living by using local knowledge and skills. But the viability of these practices remains at risk owing to environmental degradation from mining and logging.

The Surinamese legal scholar Ellen-Rose Kambel (2002: 148–53) identifies three discourses used by the Kaliña and Lokono to challenge the state's refusal to recognise indigenous land rights: (1) the argument that the land cannot be owned, which appears to be an older discourse now on the wane given its incompatibility with contemporary political objectives, (2) the reference to historical precedent, that they were the original inhabitants of the land and therefore have the right to exclude others, and (3) the importance of land rights for preserving their freedom. Kambel (2002: 154) notes that only the first two rationales for indigenous land rights have been taken up in national debates. However, it is the link between land rights and freedom that emerged most emphatically in my discussions with the Lokono and Kaliña in east Suriname. This corresponds with anthropologist Joanna Overing's (1986: 151) observation that 'Amerindians of the South American rain forest, and particularly of the Guianas, place a strong value upon the freedom of the person, have an aversion to political tyranny, and demonstrate concern over the ambiguous relations between personal freedom and both socio-political right and constraint' (1986: 151, references omitted).

I first became acquainted with Amerindian concerns about freedom in Suriname while examining BHP Billiton's plans for a new bauxite mine in the Bakhuis Mountains in west Suriname (Goodland 2009). Initially, the Lokono communities living closest to the proposed mine site were enchanted by the prospect of economic development. Although the Lokono I spoke with recognised that modern mines provide relatively few jobs, they hoped the project would have a multiplier effect on the local economy. Their desire for greater economic opportunity evokes economist Amartya Sen's (1999) definition of the goal of development as enhancing human freedom, including a people's ability to shape their own destiny.[6] However, their views differed from Georg Simmel's (1978) observations about the relationship between money and modernity. Simmel describes how the universal form of value created by money is a vehicle for realising new forms of the self that are freed from prior attachment to particular people, places and things. Thus the attraction of money has generally been taken to signify the negation of tradition, which is replaced by the modern project of self-realisation (Maclean 1994). But when I interviewed young men about their desires for the future, their answers always included living in their villages: they did not dream of the bright lights of the city, but wanted economic opportunities that would allow them to stay home. They did not think of money as the path to individualisation and modernity, but as the means to remain traditional (see Sahlins 1999).

The women I spoke with in west Suriname also invoked the discourse of freedom in relation to money, albeit differently from the men. Women had their own reasons for supporting the mining project. What concerned them the most were recent economic changes that gave men privileged access to money through wage labour. They told me that traditional gender roles were complementary: in their gardens, men cleared the forest and wove the *matapi* for squeezing cassava while the women planted, weeded, harvested and prepared the root crop for consumption. Each gender needed the other's labour. In contrast, today women find themselves dependent on their husbands for money and object to their loss of autonomy. For them, regaining their freedom requires access to

---

[6] However, Chakrabarty (2000: 44–45) argues against the identification of the modern state with freedom, as the state achieves its goals through projects of reform, progress and development that may be coercive or violent.

their own source of income. They see potential development opportunities associated with the mine as a means to earn the money required to overcome their current dependence on their husbands. In contrast to Simmel (1978), Lokono women seek financial independence in order to reclaim their autonomy and ensure they can provide for their families. Access to money becomes the means to achieve traditional values, to reassert the interdependence of women and men and to fulfill their responsibilities to their children.[7]

In focus groups and interviews with the Lokono and Kaliña people in east Suriname, the most striking element of discussions about land rights was also their invocation of freedom. People told me that they only feel free on their own land, where they are able to do as they please. Without land rights, they emphasised, one is not truly free, because 'anyone can show up with a piece of paper and say they own our land'. Many people described freedom in terms of their ability to hunt and fish in the rainforest. When I asked the young men about their future, they told me they wanted to stay on their land because: 'We love this place. We want our own place where we can live. We like to be free.' Today, however, they are 'not free enough [because] other people are coming into our territory'. When describing the nature reserve established on their land, they expressed their criticism in terms of the resulting constraints on their freedom: 'Before we were free to go there, but now someone is imposing rules on us'. Many people also brought up stories about 'no trespassing' signs on indigenous lands that have been alienated from their rightful owners.

When the Lokono and Kaliña spoke to me about freedom, they also mentioned the freedom to be indigenous, to possess their own culture and follow their own way of life. Kambel (2002) notes that the Lokono and Kaliña are familiar with the provisions of the UN Declaration on the Rights of Indigenous Peoples, including the 'collective right to live in freedom, peace and security as distinct peoples' and the ability to express 'indigenous cultural diversity' without prejudice. In this sense, the freedom to be indigenous implies the right to determine and reproduce important cultural values, which resonates with claims made in the Rongelap case about the 'loss of a way of life'.

---

[7] When BHP Billiton withdrew from the project after the economic downturn in 2009, and the results of an independent review of the mining project (Goodland 2009) were presented to the community and in the capital of Paramaribo, the Lokono began to express doubts about the Bakhuis project. People also questioned their earlier enthusiasm that money would solve their problems, recognising that it will create new problems as well.

The concept of freedom also has broad historical resonance in Suriname, a Dutch colony from 1667 until 1975. Most of the inhabitants of Suriname are descendants of slaves or indentured labourers. Creoles make up 32 per cent of the population and are the strongest political faction; the Maroons, descendants of escaped slaves who settled in the rainforest, constitute another 10 per cent of the population. The largest group of people in the country is composed of the descendants of Hindi-speaking Indians who moved to Suriname as indentured labourers after the abolition of slavery, and comprise 37 per cent of the population. Another 10 per cent of the population is made up of the descendants of indentured labourers from Java. Given the historical significance of forced and coerced labour in Suriname, freedom is a powerful unifying discourse among its citizens, including the Amerindian communities, which comprise between 1.5 and 2.0 per cent of the country's population.[8]

In these examples from Suriname, freedom is a multivalent concept that simultaneously references traditional ideas about persons, gender and social relations; the freedom to hunt and fish in the rainforest; the UN Declaration on the Rights of Indigenous Peoples, which supports the freedom to be indigenous; and freedom in a recently independent country comprised largely of the descendants of slaves and indentured labourers. Concerns about freedom are neither exclusively indigenous nor modern, and are simultaneously a shared concern of members of the state and the basis of a claim to difference. The importance of freedom resonates across social divides in Suriname even as it is invoked in support of indigenous land rights. Its multivocality means that any gaps or differences in how freedom is invoked may be partially concealed by these shared meanings.

CONCLUSION

This chapter examines the gaps created through the juridification of indigenous politics. Are indigenous claimants alienated from their own speech by being forced to formulate their claims in the language of legal jurisprudence? In the Ok Tedi case, claims based on indigenous practices challenged a fundamental principle of the common law, which

---

[8] As Nikolas Rose (1999) argues, freedom is also a pervasive discourse of modernity that goes hand in hand with the modern state's capacity to organise and regulate the behaviour of its population.

previously restricted claims for damage to property owners. Local sub-sistence practices provided a new model for redressing industrial forms of pollution and the consequences of environmental degradation for the people living downstream from the Ok Tedi mine, establishing import-ant legal precedents. The concept of subsistence rights was equally novel for the indigenous plaintiffs, although it provided them with a powerful means of expressing their grievances. In the Marshall Islands, the claim-ants from Rongelap articulated their concerns in terms of previously cir-culating discourses about the loss of a way of life, or culture, and the right to a healthy environment. Although the Nuclear Claims Tribunal avoided ruling directly on these claims, its final assessment of the dam-ages caused by nuclear testing was clearly influenced by the presentation of indigenous views at the hearings. The gap between local conceptions and judicial verdict remains, but the people from Rongelap welcomed the opportunity to present their testimony to the tribunal. Finally, the Amerindian communities in Suriname invoke the multivocal discourse of freedom in presenting their claims, which simultaneously incorporates their relationship to the rainforest, social relations, new claims about indigenous rights and national history. Their claim unifies what might otherwise be disjunctive social positions.

There are other consequences of these claims as well. Some travel as legal precedents for other indigenous communities to adopt, such as the notion of subsistence rights in the Ok Tedi case. In the Marshall Islands, however, claims about the right to a way of life and the right to a healthy environment were not endorsed by the court but may still circulate as contemporary political discourses rather than legal precedents. The Nuclear Claims Tribunal was unable to challenge the sovereign power of the state, but the people of Rongelap were able to call attention to the moral failings of the state. We do not know how the Inter-American Court on Human Rights will respond to claims about freedom and land rights in the Suriname rainforest. There are concerns about privacy and governmentality in all three cases, as participating in legal processes always invites the scrutiny of the court, but this also reflects the larger paradox of indigenous politics, in which those who are different must bear the responsibility for commensuration (see Povinelli 2002).

Another important question concerns efficacy. It may take so long for a case to reach the courts that problems are compounded, as in the Ok Tedi case, in which legal remediation has provided more than one bil-lion dollars in compensation to the state and the affected communities, but came too late to save the river (Kirsch 2007). In the Marshall Islands case, the Nuclear Claims Tribunal made a record award to the people of Rongelap for the harms they experienced, although full monetary payment is contingent on the US Congress substantially increasing its funding to the programme. At present the tribunal is only able to make payments for the medical consequences of nuclear testing. Finally, even if the Amerindian land rights case is successful in the Inter-American Court on Human Rights, this does not guarantee that the Republic of Suriname will change its laws accordingly. Despite being a signatory to the Inter-American Commission, and therefore bound by its decisions, Suriname has thus far failed to implement its findings in the Saramaka case (Price 2011), although pressure on the state through various multi-lateral development agencies and banks may eventually compel it to do so. Turning to the courts for justice does not guarantee a positive outcome, and may only partially deliver on the claims being made.

Success in court and the objectives of social movements are not identical, however, although the cases analysed here indicate that questions of meaning, claims for recognition and redistribution, the opportunity to put state power on trial and the possibility of defining the terms of contestation that drive social movements may be addressed in legal proceedings. These cases also provide opportunities for indigenous claimants to influence both legal jurisprudence and political contests, either through the universal language of legal precedent, or through the horizontal exchange of ideas among indigenous peoples (Appadurai 2002). This development represents an important political accomplishment, as the opportunities of indigenous peoples to influence legal knowledge as well as larger debates about state power, the environment and freedom have historically been limited. However, their success is contingent on their willingness to enter into intercultural conversations that have the potential to transform all of the participants.

Finally, these cases require consideration of the role played by engaged anthropologists in mediating between legal language and indigenous knowledge and practices. Although the gap between legal concepts and indigenous ideas may initially seem too great to bridge, interventions by anthropologists can help frame problems in ways that prove valuable to the indigenous participants. This may be true even for rapid ethnographic assessment, despite its shortcomings in comparison to long-term ethnographic research (Macdonald 2002). Although there is no template or formula for making such interventions, these practices may not be as remote from conventional ethnographic work as they appear, as all ethnography is contingent on acts of translation and representation, and must align empirical findings with the aesthetic requirements of particular languages of expert knowledge and genres of writing.

There will inevitably be gaps between some indigenous claims and their legal presentation. They may be reduced through looping effects in which new claims are internalised. They may yield legal precedents which generate change or contribute to related political projects. They may also facilitate the critique of power by providing testimony about the moral failings of the state. Alternatively, they may conceal their own presence through the use of multivocal terms which elide difference and consequently mobilise recognition and support. However, they may also end up reifying difference. The juridification of indigenous politics cannot escape the universalising power of legal language, but can create new political opportunities.

References

Agamben, Giorgio 1998. *Homo Sacer: Sovereign Power and Bare Life.* Stanford University Press.

Anaya, S. James 1996. *Indigenous Peoples in International Law.* Oxford University Press.

Appadurai, Arjun 2002. 'Deep democracy: urban governmentality and the horizon of politics', *Public Culture* 14 (1): 21–47.

Banks, Glenn and Ballard, Chris (eds.) 1997. *The Ok Tedi Settlement: Issues, Outcomes, and Implications.* Canberra: Australian National University.

Barsh, Russell Lawrence 1994. 'Indigenous peoples in the 1990s. From object to subject of international law', *Harvard Human Rights Journal* 7: 33–86.

Bolton, Barrie R. 2009. *The Fly River, Papua New Guinea: Environmental Studies in an Impacted Tropical River System.* Amsterdam: Elsevier.

Brown, Michael 2003. *Who Owns Native Culture?* Cambridge, MA: Harvard University Press.

Bunte, Pamela and Franklin, Robert 1992. 'You can't get there from here: Southern Paiute testimony as intercultural communication', *Anthropological Linguistics* 34 (1): 19–44.

Byrne, J. 1995. *Rex Dagi et al. v. the Broken Hill Proprietary Company Limited.* No. 5782 of 1994 and others, Victorian Supreme Court of Melbourne, 10 November.

Chakrabarty, Dipesh 2000. *Provincializing Europe.* Princeton University Press.

Clifford, James 1988. 'Identity in Mashpee', in James Clifford (ed.) *The Predicament of Culture: Twentieth-century Ethnography, Literature and Art.* Cambridge, MA and London: Harvard University Press, pp. 277–346.

Das, Veena 1989. 'Discussion: subaltern as perspective', in Ranajit Guha (ed.) *Subaltern Studies VI: Writings on South Asian History and Society*. New Delhi: Oxford University Press India, pp. 310–24.

Demian, Melissa 2006. 'Reflecting on loss in Papua New Guinea', *Ethnos* 71: 507–32.

Dirlik, Arif 2001. 'Comment on Stuart Kirsch, lost worlds', *Current Anthropology* 42 (2): 181–82.

Fortun, Kim 2001. *Advocacy after Bhopal: Environmentalism, Disaster, New Global Orders*. University of Chicago Press.

Geertz, Clifford 1983. '"From the native's point of view": on the nature of anthropological understanding', in Clifford Geertz (ed.) *Local Knowledge: Further Essays in Interpretive Anthropology*. New York: Basic Books, pp. 55–70.

Gilbert, Jérémie 2006. *Indigenous Peoples' Land Rights under International Law: From Victims to Actors*. Ardsley, NY: Transnational Publishers.

Goodland, Robert (ed.) 2009. *Suriname's Bakhuis Bauxite Mine: An Independent Review of SRK's Impact Assessment*. Paramaribo, Suriname: Bureau VIDS.

Gordon, John 1997. 'The Ok Tedi lawsuit in retrospect', in Glenn Banks and Chris Ballard (eds.) *The Ok Tedi Settlement: Issues, Outcomes and Implications*. Canberra: Australian National University, pp. 141–66.

Graham, Laura 2002. 'How should an Indian speak? Amazonian Indians and the symbolic politics of language in the global public sphere', in Kay B. Warren and Jean E. Jackson (eds.) *Indigenous Movements, Self-representation, and the State in Latin America*. Austin: University of Texas Press, pp. 181–228.

Hacking, Ian 1994. 'The looping effects of human kinds', in Dan Sperber, David Premack and Ann James Premack (eds.) *Causal Cognition: A Multidisciplinary Approach*. Oxford: Clarendon, pp. 351–94.

Hirsch, Eric and Strathern, Marilyn (eds.) 2004. *Transactions and Creations: Property Debates and the Stimulus of Melanesia*. Oxford: Berghahn Books.

International Water Tribunal 1994. 'Ecological damage caused by the discharges from the Ok Tedi copper and gold mine', in L. Bijvoet, E. de Lange and A. van Norden (eds.) *Mining. The Second International Water Tribunal Case Books*. Utrecht: International, pp. 49–85.

Ivy, Marilyn 1995. *Discourses of the Vanishing: Modernity, Phantasm, Japan*. University of Chicago Press.

Johnston, Barbara Rose and Barker, Holly M. 2008. *Consequential Damages of Nuclear War: The Rongelap Report*. Walnut Creek, CA: Left Coast Press.

Kambel, Ellen-Rose 2002. *Resource Conflicts, Gender, and Indigenous Rights in Suriname: Local, National and Global Perspectives*. Ph.D. dissertation, University of Leiden.

Kirsch, Stuart 2001. 'Lost worlds: environmental disaster, "culture loss" and the law', *Current Anthropology* 42 (2): 167–98.

2006. *Reverse Anthropology: Indigenous Analysis of Social and Environmental Relations in New Guinea*. Stanford University Press.

2007. 'Indigenous movements and the risks of counterglobalization: tracking the campaign against Papua New Guinea's Ok Tedi mine', *American Ethnologist* 34 (2): 303–21.

2010. *Inter-American Commission on Human Rights case 12.639 Kaliña and Lokono indigenous peoples (Suriname)*. Expert report.

Macdonald, Gaynor 2002. 'Ethnography, advocacy and feminism: a volatile mix. A view from a reading of Diane Bell's *Ngarrindjeri wurruwarrin*', *Australian Journal of Anthropology* 13 (1): 88–110.

Maclean, Neil 1994. 'Freedom or autonomy: a modern Melanesian dilemma', *Man* 29: 667–88.

Miller, Bruce G. 2001. *The Problem of Justice: Tradition and Law in the Coast Salish World*. Lincoln, NB: University of Nebraska Press.

Nadasdy, Paul 2003. *Hunters and Bureaucrats: Power, Knowledge, and Aboriginal-state Relations in the Southwest Yukon*. Vancouver: University of British Columbia Press.

Niezen, Ronald 2003. *The Origins of Indigenism: Human Rights and the Politics of Identity*. Berkeley: University of California Press.

2010. *Public Justice and the Anthropology of the Law*. Cambridge University Press.

Nuti, Paul J. 2007. 'Reordering nuclear testing history in the Marshall Islands', *Anthropology News* 48 (6): 42–43.

Overing, Joanna 1986. 'Men control women? The catch 22 in the analysis of gender', *International Journal of Moral and Social Studies* 1 (2): 135–56.

Plasman, James H. and Danz, Gregory J. 2007. Memorandum of decision and order. Nuclear Claims Tribunal, 17 April.

Povinelli, Elizabeth 2002. *The Cunning of Recognition: Indigenous Alterities and the Making of Australian Multiculturalism*. Durham, NC: Duke University Press.

Price, Richard 2011. *Rainforest Warriors: Human Rights on Trial*. Philadelphia: University of Pennsylvania Press.

Ribot, Jesse C. and Peluso, Nancy Lee 2003. 'A theory of access', *Rural Sociology* 68 (2): 153–81.

Richland, Justin 2008. *Arguing with Tradition: The Language of Law in Hopi Tribal Court*. University of Chicago Press.

Rose, Nikolas 1999. *The Powers of Freedom: Reframing Political Thought*. Cambridge University Press.

Rosen, Lawrence 1997. 'The right to be different: indigenous peoples and the quest for a unified theory', *Yale Law Journal* 107 (1): 227–60.

Sahlins, Marshall 1999. 'What is anthropological enlightenment? Some lessons of the twentieth century', *Annual Review of Anthropology* 28: i–xxiii.

Saramaka People v. *Suriname* 2007. Preliminary objections, merits, reparations and costs. Judgement of 28 November 2007. Series C No. 172, at para. 194–96. Electronic document: www.corteidh.or.cr/dos/casos/articulos/seriec_172_ing.pdf.

    2008. Interpretation of the judgement on preliminary objections, merits, reparations and costs. Judgement of 12 August 2008. Series C No. 185. Electronic document: www.corteidh.or.cr/docs/casos/articulos/seriec_185_ing.pdf.

Schieffelin, Edward L. 1976. *The Sorrow of the Lonely and the Burning of the Dancers.* New York: St Martin's Press.

Schoorl, J. W. 1970. 'Muyu land tenure', *New Guinea Research Bulletin* 38: 34–41.

Sen, Amartya 1999. *Development as Freedom.* New York: Random House.

Shelton, Diana L. 2008. 'Saramaka judgment', in Ole Kristian Fauchald and David Hunter (eds.) *Yearbook of International Environmental Law 2007.* Volume 18. Oxford University Press, pp. 168–72.

Simmel, Georg 1978. *The Philosophy of Money*, trans. Tom Bottomore and David Frisby. London: Routledge and Kegan Paul.

Wood, Michael 2004. 'Places, logging and loss among the Kamula', *Asia Pacific Journal of Anthropology* 5 (3): 245–56.

CHAPTER 2

NAMING, CLAIMING, PROVING? THE BURDEN OF PROOF ISSUE FOR RUSSIA'S INDIGENOUS PEOPLES

Brian Donahoe

Much has been written about the importance of land rights for the eco-nomic and cultural maintenance and continuity of indigenous peoples the world over.[1] Land and the resources located within it not only provide a material base for subsistence, but also the foundation for cultural con-tinuity (and in some cases for cultural revitalisation).[2] Throughout much of Siberia, sacred sites such as mountain peaks and passes, unusual rock formations, lakes and rivers are believed to be inhabited by spirit masters with whom local people establish personal relationships. The social per-son comes into being through his/her relations to others, including other non-human persons (spirits, animals, etc.). The recognition that such social relations are constitutive of individuals (Strathern 2004; Cowan 2009 [2006]: 322) should be the starting point from which indigenous claims to land as a fundamental human right are evaluated. In this way, 'culture' can be 'analytic to rights', in Cowan, Dembour, and Wilson's terms (2001: 13–15).

Fieldwork for this chapter was supported by the Max Planck Institute for Social Anthropology and the project *Dynamics of Circumpolar Land Use and Ethnicity* (CLUE), funded by the US-based National Science Foundation through the International Polar Year (IPY) initiative (award # ARC-0755832). Thanks go to my colleagues in the *Law against the State* research team – Zerrin Özlem Biner, Julia Eckert and Christian Strümpell – as well as to the leaders of the CLUE project: Hugh Beach, Dmitrii Funk and Thomas Thornton.

[1] There are countless examples, among them Wilmsen 1989; Anderson 1998, 2000, 2002; Fondahl 1998; Novikova 1999; Anaya 2000; Ivison *et al.* 2000; Nadasdy 2002; Osherenko 1995.
[2] See, for example, Myerhoff 1976; Myers 1986, 1989; Chatwin 1987; Basso 1996; Berkes 1999; Jordan 2003; Halemba 2006; Syrtypova 2007; Thornton 2008.

The discussion of indigenous land rights in much of the literature on Canada, the United States and Australia is about native title to land, and the burden falls generally to indigenous peoples themselves to prove that they deserve title to land on the basis of prior occupation and/or treaties signed with the colonising powers that demonstrate a pre-existing 'native title' (Greaney and Bohill n.d.). This is the case in countries with common law. In Russia, whose legal system is based on civil law, the approach is quite different. There were never any treaties signed, and native title to land is not even on the table. Russia's indigenous people's claims are much more modest than those of indigenous peoples in the 'West', focusing on the right to lead a 'traditional' lifestyle, which of necessity implies some sort of priority rights of access to land and resources. Nevertheless, the burden falls to indigenous peoples to demonstrate that they deserve these limited rights by proving that they are 'indigenous' enough, that their land use activities are 'traditional' enough, and that their lands deserve to be designated as 'places of traditional inhabitance and traditional economic activities of indigenous peoples'.[3]

In this paper I want to start by trying to locate Russia's official position in the 'culture and rights' debate, with a particular focus on land rights, because that goes a long way toward illuminating Russia's indigenous policies and the way Russia's indigenous peoples engage with those policies. Following that I will develop two case studies of legal actions taken by representatives of indigenous peoples in Russia, which demonstrate that, while Russia's indigenous peoples have been involved in creating the categories ('naming') that provide them with the necessary terms of reference for making various claims to land and resources, they generally find themselves on the losing end of legal battles, often because they are not able to prove in a court of law that they deserve the rights they are claiming.

RUSSIA AND 'CULTURE AND RIGHTS'

The task of placing Russia's approach to its indigenous peoples within the context of the 'culture and rights' debate deserves more attention than

---

[3] In Russian law, the working definition of the term *indigenous small-numbered peoples* (*korennye malochislennye narody*) is 'peoples living in the territories of traditional settlement of their ancestors, preserving a traditional way of life, traditional economic system and economic activities, numbering fewer than 50,000 persons within the Russian Federation, and recognising themselves as independent ethnic communities' (Federal Law no. 82 of 30 April 1999, 'On Guarantees of the Rights of the Indigenous Small-Numbered Peoples of the Russian Federation'). It was first articulated in the law 'On the Fundamentals of State Regulation of Socioeconomic Development of the North of the Russian Federation' (19 June 1996).

I can give it here, but for the purposes of my argument a brief outline is in order. The most thorough treatment of this I have come across in the Russian-language literature is a book called *Regulation and protection of the rights of national [ethnic] minorities and indigenous small-numbered peoples in the Russian Federation* (2005), by Liudmila Andrichenko, who is the head of the Department of Legal Problems of Federative and National Relations at the Institute of Law and Comparative Jurisprudence of the Government of Russia. I will dwell here at some length on Andrichenko's treatment not only because she is a recognised authority and her book is thorough, well-argued and engages with some of the Western literature, but also because her position reflects the official government position (she is, after all, a professor at an institute directly under the government) and also the popular opinion I hear voiced throughout Russia by non-indigenous people.

Andrichenko spends a great deal of time dismissing various definitions of 'indigenous' as inapplicable to the Russian case because most of these international definitions (Martínez Cobo 1987: 379; the definitions provided in ILO 169 and World Bank Operational Directive 4.20) a) presuppose a previously existing colonial relationship between the indigenous peoples and the ancestors of the present-day dominant majorities; b) emphasise autochthony and/or prior occupation; and c) assert fundamental differences between the cultures of indigenous peoples and the culture of the dominant majority, and some degree of continuity of indigenous institutions.

Andrichenko asserts that 'Russia can hardly be considered a colonial power in its relations with the peoples living on her territory in the way that it applies to, for example, the states of North America' (2005: 50).[4] She cites both the 'blue water doctrine' (2005: 57) and the 'salt-water test' (2005: 69) in support of her argument that Russia cannot be considered a colonial power because it never colonised lands that lie across an ocean from Russia. For this reason, Russia is not obligated to address indigenous peoples' claims to self-determination in the same way that they should be addressed in former colonial lands. Andrichenko reviews the distinction between 'internal' and 'external' aspects of the right to self-determination, citing the 1975 international court decision on Western Sahara. 'External' self-determination is when peoples, independent of external interference, define their own political status within the system of international

---

[4] All quoted material from Andrichenko's book has been translated from the Russian by the author of this chapter.

relations, either through creating a completely new state of their own, or through joining another state in a federated or confederated relationship (2005: 72). According to the 'majority of specialists,' the right to 'external' self-determination 'belongs only to peoples living in a colonial relationship or other type of dependence on a foreign power, or in situations of occupation by a foreign power' (2005: 73). 'Internal' self-determination includes full rights to participate in the social and political life of the country within which indigenous peoples find themselves, and the right to develop their own culture as they see fit (2005: 73). Andrichenko ultimately concludes that those governments that do not have a history of colonial relationships with indigenous peoples (including Russia) and have 'restricted the right of self-determination of indigenous peoples to their right to "internal" self-determination is, from our point of view, completely just' (2005: 90). 'A state must act on the interests of the entire population of the country, and not on the interests of separate groups' (2005: 97).

With regard to arguments of autochthony and prior occupation, she asserts that 'the majority of ethnic societies living in Russia, including Russians, can be considered indigenous peoples' (2005: 54). Again:

> Indigenous origin (i.e., autochthony or the fact that representatives of a given people were the first to be settled on a certain territory) is, undoubtedly, a distinctive peculiarity of indigenous peoples. This factor, however, as practice has shown, does not help clarify many situations arising in many countries, including ours [Russia], where both the dominant as well as the non-dominant population groups within a single state can lay claim to indigenous origins.
>
> (2005: 59)

Needless to say, this approach to Russia as non-colonial simply because the lands into which the Russian Empire expanded were contiguous to its own and not separated by an ocean conveniently ignores the fact of the Russian Empire's west-to-east expansion and colonisation of Siberia by taking the present-day borders of the country as the baseline. Thus Siberia is within the borders of present-day Russia, so by definition all ethnic Russians living in Siberia are indigenous.[5] This is a very commonly voiced argument to refute the accusation that Russia colonised Siberia and to deny special rights to indigenous peoples in Russia.

---

[5] Interestingly, this approach is reinforced in the teaching of geography throughout the former Soviet Union, in which Eurasia is recognised as a single landmass (as it indeed is) and a single continent, and not as two separate continents divided by the Ural mountains, as is taught in the West.

The final issue of fundamental differences between indigenous peoples and the dominant majority is less unequivocal in Andrichenko's analysis. First, as part of her rejection of the ILO 169 (Indigenous and Tribal Peoples Convention) definition, she denies that any peoples in Russia still lead a 'tribal' way of life: 'in Russia at the present time practically all peoples have progressed beyond the period of a tribal way of life' (2005: 50).[6] Then she notes that 'indigenous peoples as well as ethnic minorities the world over assert that they have a unique culture that distinguishes them from all from other peoples and cultures. Because of this both minorities and indigenous peoples not infrequently claim that it is precisely their unique culture that is the reason they are striving for recognition of collective legal status and rights to self-determination' (2005 58), but goes on to call that into question, noting that cultures are changing rapidly, some peoples are losing touch with their unique cultures, and even within ethnic groups, some peoples are closer to their traditions than others. While she does not deny the fact that some groups are striving to 'preserve their cultural uniqueness', she concludes that this in and of itself 'must not be a defining criterion for establishing the legal claims of a given group' (2005: 59).

Throughout the book, Andrichenko is careful to distinguish 'ethnic minorities' from 'indigenous peoples'. However, she also takes pains to point out the similarities, noting that both strive to assert their distinctiveness from the majority population, that both are in non-dominant positions, and that both claim a special relationship to their lands (2005: 58–62). With regard to their relations to land, for example, Andrichenko notes that 'indigenous peoples assert that there is a special bond between them and their lands' (2005: 61), and that this is the basis for many of their land claims. However, it is 'necessary to remember that the character of many indigenous peoples' relationship to the environment has essentially changed in industrially developed countries, and the majority of them no longer live within the territories where their ancestors lived. Nevertheless, the lands of their ancestors often still hold great symbolic and political significance, even in conditions of industrialisation and economic integration' (2005: 61). But, she notes, this also describes the situation for many ethnic minorities who

---

[6] This assertion reflects the social evolutionism that characterised the Soviet approach to ethnic politics, in which it was believed that the social organisation of ethnic communities progressed from tribes (*plemia*) to peoples (*narodnost'*) to nations (*natsiia*), and that all peoples, by virtue of their inclusion in the Soviet Union, had already progressed beyond the tribal stage of social organisation.

have migrated from their countries of origin for a variety of reasons. In fact, 'ethnic minorities' could be considered 'indigenous' in those places from which they have migrated, so does that mean they should be able to make claims to land in those countries from which they have come? Ultimately, she concludes that the difference between indigenous peoples and ethnic minorities with regard to their cultural uniqueness, efforts to maintain their culture and their connection to land is 'a difference of degree and not of kind' (2005: 61), and therefore their claims (to land) should be treated the same – either all indigenous peoples and all ethnic minorities have the same claims to land, or none of them does. Noting that it would be impossible to satisfy all such claims to land, she opts for the latter understanding and denies that any of them have justifiable claims to land. The emphasis on autochthony is misplaced also because it suggests preferential treatment for those who have managed to stay in their places of origins, in other words, those who have been fortunate enough not to have been displaced, while those who have been forcibly removed lose their right to count themselves among the numbers of the 'indigenous'.

As for the right to self-determination, Andrichenko sees it as 'belonging to the ranks of exclusively collective rights' (2005: 74). She then goes on to build an elaborate argument that culminates in the rejection of collective rights, echoing many of the well-known arguments against collective rights.[7] Andrichenko then refers to Kymlicka's distinction between two different kinds of claims to self-determination that an ethnic or national group might make: 'internal restrictions' are claims made by the group to limit the liberty of its own members; and 'external protections' are claims of the group to limit the negative impacts of economic and political power exercised from without. Kymlicka asserts that 'history has shown that the most effective way to protect indigenous communities from this external power is to establish reserves where the land is held in common and/or in trust, and cannot be alienated without the consent of the community as a whole' (Kymlicka 1995: 43).

---

[7] Andrichenko's main objections to the idea of collective rights can be condensed into two major points: (1) as indigenous groups and minorities can only be recognised as 'objects' of legal regulation and not as 'subjects', anything that might be termed 'collective rights' would be best realised through the provision of rights to individuals because individuals are 'subjects' of legal regulation; and (2) that the lack of clear criteria defining collective rights renders the concept legally inchoate and, because of that, lumping collective rights in with human rights unnecessarily complicates the notion of human rights and therefore weakens its effectiveness and impact (Andrichenko 2005: 95–100).

Andrichenko notes that the main task of legislation regarding indigenous peoples is the provision of special laws in the sphere of land use (2005: 105). She notes that

> in the traditions of indigenous peoples there never was private property in land and natural resources. Reindeer pastures, hunting grounds, water resources for fishing, and especially sacred places and burial grounds were always objects of general access for indigenous peoples ... This raises a completely different aspect of the interrelationship between indigenous peoples and land ... Because of this we can talk about the collective rights of indigenous peoples to land (parcels of land).
>
> (2005: 105)

This and other issues related to the rights of indigenous peoples should be decided on the basis of a combination of four principles. The first two and most prominent of these principles are (1) 'respect for the territorial integrity of the state'; and (2) 'the guarantee of equality and non-discrimination in the sphere of social interests'. With this she is clearly referring to equality for the general population vis-à-vis indigenous peoples and minorities, thereby rejecting the idea of special rights for indigenous peoples and minorities. The third and fourth principles are much more understated and come across more as concessions to the political correctness of multiculturalism than as convictions; (3) 'the state has the obligation to protect the cultural uniqueness of minorities and enable cultural pluralism on the basis of tolerance for other cultures'; and (4) 'where necessary and possible, the provision of territorial autonomy on the principles of self-administration [note here: not self-determination], but only on a democratic basis' (2005: 105). Again, the emphasis on a 'democratic basis' is an oblique way of insisting that indigenous peoples and minorities do *not* get preferential treatment at the expense of the general populace.

Andrichenko devotes all of her Chapter 2 (approximately 120 pages) to a detailed comparison of the protection of the rights of ethnic minorities and indigenous peoples in international law and legislation of foreign countries. Her far-ranging comparison includes not only the US, Canada and Australia, but also Bangladesh, Brazil, Bolivia, India, the Philippines, Madagascar, Panama and others. She is particularly critical of the United States, and uses US policies toward Native Americans as her poster child for bad treatment of indigenous peoples (2005: 166ff). However, in all her detailed and thorough treatment, she never once mentions any of the famous land claims settlements such as the Alaska

Native Claims Settlement Act (1971),[8] the Acoma Pueblo Mineral Rights legislation (2002), or the US Code Title 25, all US legislation that has granted not only title to Native Americans, but also their rights to some of the subsurface resources on the lands to which they have been granted title. Nor does she mention the fact that numerous Native American groups have been recognised as sovereign nations within their territories, with full rights of self-determination. She also does not mention any of the famous Canadian cases, such as the 1984 recognition of the MacKenzie Delta Inuvialuits' title to land (Osherenko 1995: 228) or the 1993 Nunavut Land Claims Act. Andrichenko's only mention of a precedent-setting land claims case settled in favour of indigenous peoples is the Mabo case in Australia (2005: 168), but she notes only that it overturned the *terra nullius* doctrine, and fails to mention that it led to the Australian Native Title Act of 1993.

This failure to mention any of the major land claims settlements that have granted land and self-determination to indigenous peoples is a glaring omission in such an otherwise thorough treatment of the rights of indigenous peoples and, I believe, reflects Russia's current official position to avoid granting land rights and the sort of broad collective rights of self-determination, which James Anaya aptly calls 'the mother of all group rights' (Anaya 1999: 257), that have come along with precedent-setting agreements and legal cases in other countries such as those mentioned above. There was a brief moment, however, when it looked as if Russia would grant something approaching 'the mother of all group rights'. Back in the 1990s and early 2000s – the highpoint of progressive and positive legal activity for Russia's indigenous peoples – Russian legislators passed a series of quite progressive laws granting broad rights to Russia's indigenous peoples. With regard to protecting Russia's indigenous peoples' rights to land, the most highly touted of these new laws was the law 'On Territories of Traditional Land Use' (Federal Law no. 49 of 7 May 2001 – hereafter 'TTLUs'). TTLUs are defined as 'specially protected nature territories [*osobo okhraniaemye prirodnye territorii*], formed for the realisation of traditional nature use and traditional lifeways of the indigenous small-numbered peoples'. According to the law, such TTLUs can be established at the federal, regional or local levels, depending on which administrative

---

[8] The ANCSA has not been without its problems and controversies (see, for example, Garber 1985), and is a good example of how indigenous peoples have been forced to negotiate their land claims within an imposed European discourse of property and rights that is often not compatible with indigenous conceptions (see Nadasdy 2002 and Niezen 2003 for cogent discussions of this).

level is responsible for the land in question. And in fact quite a number of TTLUs have been established at the local and regional levels throughout Russia. These are, however, for the most part, symbolic and without legal standing, because, according to the Land Codex, almost all territories that might be candidates for TTLU status are either partly or wholly on federal land (70 per cent of Russian territory is categorised as 'forest fund' (*lesnoi fond*), which is federal property); therefore, local and regional organs of power do not have the authority to transfer control over such lands to indigenous peoples (Murashko 2002: 54). Only the federal government has the authority to do so. For a number of reasons (discussed in Donahoe 2009), including the lack of an implementation procedure and contradictions with other laws, not a single TTLU has been established at the federal level since passage of the law (Murashko 2006). Legal expert Vladimir Kriazhkov suggests that the various omissions and contradictions in the law are the result of 'the unwillingness of organs of power to create TTLUs as long as the alienation of property for the exploitation of natural resources is occurring, giving rise to situations in which rights of control over the use of such resources would have to be shared with indigenous peoples' (Kriazhkov 2008: 48).

In general, the overwhelming public opinion in Russia is NOT to recognise indigenous peoples' rights to land. There was never a history of treaties between the Russian Empire (or the USSR) and indigenous peoples, so there is not the same sort of legally binding, contractual evidence supporting indigenous peoples' rights to territory in Siberia that there is in the Canadian and US contexts. Also, since no one owned land in Soviet times, and all land was considered state property, the approach to land is significantly different. Even still it is impossible to own land in most of Russia, on lands categorised as forest fund, agricultural lands, etc. The best anyone can hope for is a long-term lease. Given this background, it is no wonder, then, that very few citizens of Russia (outside of the indigenous population) support indigenous peoples' claims to land and self-determination. For these reasons Russia's indigenous peoples do not name their claims in terms of native title, but rather try a variety of different strategies to claim a limited degree of control and access to resources, as the following case studies illustrate.

NAMING, CLAIMING, PROVING

In earlier articles I have written about the construction of the category 'indigenous small-numbered peoples' in Russia, and how, once it became enshrined in the 1993 Russian Constitution there was a push from many groups to be 'named' as such, in part so that they could lay claim to certain rights and forms of state support that come along with the status (Donahoe 2009b, 2011; Donahoe et al. 2008). This entailed a complicated process of having to prove that they deserve the status, often requiring the expert testimony of state ethnographers.

But getting named in this way is just the first hurdle in the race to turn this status into a political and economic reality. The next step is to get certain territories 'named' – as *sacred sites, territories of traditional land use, places of traditional inhabitance and traditional economic activities of indigenous small-numbered peoples*, or *specially protected nature territories* – in order to lay claim to control over them and limited access to the natural resources on them, a process that places a heavy burden of proof on indigenous peoples and other residents of such territories. In this paper I intend the terms 'naming' and 'claiming' to refer not only to the transformation of disputes that comes about through the social processes of naming a perceived experience as injurious and the voicing of a grievance in order to claim remediation, to use Felstiner *et al.*'s terms (1980/1981), but more principally to refer to the act of trying to 'name' certain territories in order to 'claim' the rights to control of access to the land and the resources on the land. These processes transform not only the dispute, but also the land, the people and the relationships between them, as the case studies below illustrate (see also Donahoe 2011).

However, despite great effort going into these processes, Russia's indigenous peoples have been highly unsuccessful in their endeavours, because naming and claiming of both kinds butt up against a heavy burden of proof. The burden of proving that a particular territory deserves a particular status falls squarely on the shoulders of indigenous peoples. Such proof includes intensive professional surveying of land so that it can be 'passportised' as a *territory of traditional land use*, and documentary proof of 'traditional' inhabitance and of the sacredness of sites. These procedures are extremely difficult, time-consuming and expensive, and therefore virtually impossible for indigenous peoples to conduct. Furthermore, the burden of proof that extractive activities will be (or have been) injurious also falls on the shoulders of local residents, rather than the burden of proof falling on extractive companies to show that the activities will be safe.

Irkutsk Oblast' and territories of traditional land use

In the offices of the environmental NGO Baikal Ecological Wave in the Siberian city of Irkutsk, I met Viktor Alekseevich Kuznetsov. Kuznetsov cuts an imposing figure, a burly man with a long full grey beard and intense blue eyes. He worked for three decades as an *okhotoved*, a state-employed specialist trained in assessing wild animal resources. His disillusionment with the state's treatment of the indigenous Evenki (sing.: Evenk) of Irkutsk Oblast' gradually led him into activism for the rights of the indigenous peoples of Irkutsk Oblast'.[9] He now puts his considerable experience and skills to work for Baikal Ecological Wave, and is Acting President of the Association of Indigenous Small-Numbered Peoples of Irkutsk Oblast' (despite the fact that he is not indigenous himself).

In his work as an *okhotoved* Kuznetsov had already witnessed how the construction of the Baikal-Amur railway (BAM), and following that the establishment of the organisation KI-450, an amalgamation of twelve correctional 'colonies' (i.e. prison camps) created to cut timber over an enormous swath of taiga lands, had encroached on lands historically inhabited by Evenki and negatively impacted their ability to conduct their subsistence hunting and reindeer herding activities. In 2002 a new threat emerged: RUSIA Petroleum announced plans to begin extracting gas condensate from the Kobyktinskii natural gas fields, which lay under lands of a recognised Evenki *obshchina* (a non-commercial family- and/or territory-based collective structure for administering economic activities, limited to Russia's recognised indigenous peoples). With this development it became imperative to establish a baseline from which to monitor changes in the natural environment and to measure the losses incurred by the Evenki.

Kuznetsov wrote up a project to establish this baseline, in which he developed a new methodology using the most up-to-date equipment. His project was reviewed and overwhelmingly approved by the Faculty of Hunting Resources (*okhotovedenie*) at the local university. While all this was in process, Kuznetsov participated as an expert in the state *ekologicheskaia ekspertiza* (environmental impact assessment) that was being conducted as a normal part of the procedure for granting a licence to develop the Kobyktinskii natural gas fields. Part of this procedure includes reviewing the *otsenka vozdeistviia na okruzhaiushchuiu sredu* (OVOS – the evaluation of the impact on the environment, an earlier step in the environmental impact assessment, which is conducted by the company that is requesting permission to do the work) of borehole drilling for the planned natural gas extraction project. He was shocked to

---

[9] An *oblast'* is a semi-autonomous administrative unit within the Russian Federation, somewhat analogous to a state in the United States.

see that the OVOS came back saying that the compensable damages for loss of potential income to the Evenki over the course of twenty-six years for the one existing exploratory borehole was calculated at 234 rubles and 32 kopeks (approximately $9 US), a figure that, according to the report, included a factor for inflation! This is because the damages were calculated using only the area of direct impact, i.e. the few square meters contained within the fencing surrounding the borehole. It also came to light that a second borehole had already been drilled and another was in the process of being drilled, despite the fact that the *ekspertiza* had not been completed prior to commencement of drilling, which was completely illegal. Despite the absurd compensation figure and the violation of laws, the OVOS received a positive assessment and the project was given the green light.

As Kuznetsov says: 'There was nothing left to do but take them to court.' First, the court refused to recognise Kusnetsov as a 'victim'. He then took it to the arbitration court (he got power of attorney from the *obshchina*), but they said he needed to do a qualified, professional assessment of the wild animal resources in the area. As he had already developed the necessary methodology to do precisely this, he set out with Dmitrii Leont'ev, the docent of the Department of Economics and Organisation of Hunting Economies at Irkutsk State Agricultural Academy, and for one and a half years they analysed the degree of anthropogenic impact caused by the single existing borehole and the 37-km road that led to it. They conducted a wild game population count twice, and compared the current wild animal populations to the population figures from before the road and borehole were built. Looking only at the three most economically important wild animal resources – sable, squirrel and moose – Kuznetsov and Leont'ev came up with a figure for damages that was 2,000 times higher than the figure arrived at by RUSIA Petroleum. 'However', recounts Kuznetsov, 'it must be emphasised that we were only counting the loss of income for a single year, but the company's figure was for twenty-six years' (Kuznetsov 2006: 3).

The judge said the essence of the disagreement was clear and that the proof was convincing, but said a decision would have to wait for the next session. 'At the following session, the lawyers and I went to court fully expecting a positive, precedent-setting case for the use of legal means to protect the interests of a local population confronted with the threat of large-scale exploitation of natural resources by a transnational company' (Kuznetsov 2006: 3). Just before the case was to begin, the judge was handed a statement signed by the chairperson of the Council of the Khandinskii Evenki Obshchina saying: 'We request that the Arbitration Court of Irkutsk Oblast' not hear this case.' Later the chairperson told Kuznetsov that she had been pressured into withdrawing the case by the district administration. 'They forced me to go against my own people', she told Kuznetsov (Kuznetsov 2005: 17; Kuznetsov 2006: 3).

Despite this very disappointing experience, Kuznetsov continues to work to protect the lands of the Evenki and other hunting and herding communities in Irkutsk Oblast'. He had already established one TTLU of about 660,000 ha (on the regional level) for local Evenki, and was working on the second (300,000 ha).[10] He explained to me what needs to be done to establish the scientific foundation for a TTLU, as well as what needs to be done to challenge compensation offered by a company. The work requires a great deal of very detailed surveying and mapping. This second territory was first divided into three sections: one designated for each of two *obshchinas*, and the middle strip still 'unoccupied'. These sections were divided into areas for different types of land use, such as hunting grounds, reindeer pasturage, non-timber forest product gathering and settlements. Each of these segments was further subdivided into much smaller cells representing specific types of habitat, more than 300 in all. He had to conduct animal population counts on 10 per cent of the cells of each type of habitat, on the basis of which he was able to extrapolate population estimates (high and low) for each species for each type of micro-environment, and also the projected growth of each species, from which he derives the amount of a species that can be sustainably harvested. Then he had to make a 'passport' for each of these little cells, which is a little map of it with a unique identifying number and a description of the cell (size, location, types of ecosystems, types and numbers of animals, etc.). He pulled out a ring-bound folder containing several hundred of these laminated 'passports' for the area he was working on. All this is needed to show how a place can be used as a TTLU, and what needs to be done to make it economically viable. Even after all this work, there is no guarantee that a territory will be granted TTLU status, and even if it is, as mentioned above, it will only be recognised at the local or regional level and therefore the status is easily overruled in a dispute because the land in question is under federal jurisdiction.

[10] These territories may sound enormous in other contexts, but given the low biological productivity of Siberia, such expanses are necessary for reindeer herding and hunting activities.

Sakhalin Island and the case of the 'wild' domestic reindeer
My second case study comes from Sakhalin Island in the Russian Far East. Sakhalin is home to approximately 3,500 members of four recognised small-numbered indigenous groups: Nivkh, Uil'ta (Orok; Orochon), Nanai and Evenki. The Nivkh and Nanai historically subsisted on fishing, while the the Uil'ta and Evenki were hunters and reindeer herders. In all cases their access to reindeer pasturage and hunting and fishing grounds is being severely curtailed by massive development of oil and natural gas resources and the infrastructure required for the oil and natural gas industry (pipelines, off-shore drilling rigs, refineries, storage facilities, etc.). These mega-projects include Sakhalin 2, the world's largest integrated oil and gas development project, owned and operated by Gazprom and Sakhalin Energy, a consortium made up of Shell, Mitsubishi and Mitsui. Indeed, it was on Sakhalin where in 2005 the island's indigenous peoples staged a rare public protest against these developments, attracting international attention (Graybill 2009; cf. Wilson 2002).

In the small office of the Legal Information Centre of the Indigenous Small-Numbered Peoples of the North and the Far East on the fourth floor of the same high-rise office complex that houses Sakhalin Energy in Yuzhno-Sakhalinsk, the capital of Sakhalin, we met Vladimir Machekhin, at the time a 37-year-old Evenk (b. 1972) who has been very active in the indigenous movement on Sakhalin. In addition to running the Legal Information Center, Machekhin is the director of 'Oron', an *obshchina* devoted to hunting and based in the village of Viakhtu on the western part of the island. He is also the vice-president of the Council of Evenki People of Russia. In 1999 he was chosen to take over operation of the *sovkhoz Olenevod* (state farm 'Reindeer Herder'), which, like many state farms since the collapse of the USSR, had been severely neglected throughout the 1990s and was on the verge of bankruptcy. He restructured the state farm into a private limited share-holding enterprise, also called *Olenevod*, with eighteen families and approximately 2,800 reindeer, which he ran until 2007. His hope was to bring reindeer herding back from the brink of extinction (according to Machekhin, there had been some 14,000 reindeer in the 1980s) and give the reindeer herding Evenki a viable economic base upon which to rebuild their lives and maintain their culture.

The Legal Information Center employs five lawyers, and was one of the first private law firms in Yuzhno-Sakhalinsk. It got in on the ground floor as privatisation was just getting started in the 1990s, and the centre is now a recognised expert specialising in the legal issues surrounding privatisation. Because of its independent status, the lawyers working at the centre feel that they have greater latitude and are relatively immune to local political pressures. In their spare time, the lawyers also support, on a pro-bono basis, Machekhin's legal efforts to establish some degree of control over land and resources for the Evenki reindeer herders and hunters living on the western side of the island. Machekhin has filed numerous law suits against the regional administration and against the oil and gas companies. A brief examination of some of these cases will illustrate the interaction between naming, claiming and proving.

Briefly, in 1986 the state farm *Olenevod* was granted a twenty-five-year lease on 1,191,001 ha of land that was carved out of state forestry lands from each of three districts in central Sakhalin. Most of this land was declared reindeer pasturage for the state farm's reindeer herding activities.[11] In the course of the 1990s, the state farm went into decline and in 1999 Machekhin was elected director of the state farm, which he proceeded to reorganise into a limited joint-stock enterprise (*zakrytoe aktsionernoe obshchestvo* – ZAO). According to the enterprise's registration documents, it was the legal successor to the state farm and took over all of the state farm's assets, including the lease on the land (which at that point was still valid for some eleven more years) and the remaining reindeer. In 1999, at the time Machekhin was elected director of the state farm *Olenevod*, a land-use map for the state farm was created in collaboration with the directors of the state forestry divisions from the three districts involved (Okhinskii, Noglikskii, and Aleksandrovsk-Sakhalinskii), authorities from the Committee for Land Resources and Land Use from the three districts involved, and a representative of the Oil and Gas Extraction Directorate *Okhaneftegaz*. The map marked out some 1,141,656 ha for the state farm, the great majority of which was categorised as 'reindeer pasturage' for the 2,588 reindeer the state farm declared as its property.

The series of court cases started in 2002 when, in response to preliminary reconnaissance and preparatory work prior to constructing a pipeline through the reindeer pastures of *Olenevod*, Machekhin took Exxon and its subcontractors to court (three separate cases), saying that the work frightened the reindeer, damaged the land and rendered it unsuitable for use as reindeer pasturage, and was a violation of the rights of the members of the enterprise as indigenous persons. He requested that the

---

[11] Machekhin showed as proof of this Order of the Council of Ministers of the RSFSR No. 1551-r from 14.11.1986, in which this transaction is detailed.

court require the companies to stop such work, remove the work they had already done, pay a small amount of compensation for damage done to the land, and prohibit further work on the lands of the enterprise without prior written consent from the enterprise. As proof of exclusive proprietorship (*vladenie*), Machekhin presented an order of the Council of Ministers of the USSR from 1986 that detailed the transference of 1,191,001 ha of state forest land to the control of the state farm for twenty-five years, and the registration documents of the ZAO *Olenevod* showing that it is the legal successor in all rights and duties to the state farm and that it is a registered 'national' (i.e. ethnic) enterprise of the indigenous Evenki people of Sakhalin, and as such 'has the right to pro-tect the original environment, including reindeer pasturage, to conduct their traditional activities'. The defendants countered, claiming that *Olenevod's* proprietorship was not valid because it had not been properly re-registered; that the relevant legislation does not require prior written consent; and that the plaintiffs had not proven the existence of property, i.e. reindeer, because they only showed written records claiming that the reindeer exist. The court sided with the defendants, saying that the case is one of negatory action and as such the plaintiff must prove rights of proprietorship. The order of the Council of Ministers presented by the enterprise as proof of ownership was no longer valid because of various changes in the Land Codex of 1991 and the Law on Land Reform that had taken place in the post-Soviet period, and neither the state farm nor the enterprise had completed the necessary registration documenta-tion in accordance with the newer laws, therefore the enterprise 'had not proven the presence of rights of proprietorship or usufruct of the lands'.[12] The enterprise appealed this decision on a number of occasions, present-ing supporting documentation, but in each case the appeals were denied on the same grounds of lack of proof of proprietorship.

The second set of law suits brought by the ZAO *Olenevod* was against the Hunting Directorate of Sakhalin Oblast' for selling licences to hunt wild reindeer on *Olenevod's* reindeer pastures. Partly in response to Machekhin's repeated attempts to stop the work on the oil pipeline, the Hunting Directorate unilaterally declared all reindeer existing on *Olenevod's* territory to be 'wild' reindeer, therefore under the jurisdiction of the Hunting Directorate, and started selling licences to hunt them.

---

[12] Law on Land Reform: Law No. 374–1 of 23.11.1990 'On Land Reform' (coming into force on 24 December 1993). From the decision of the Arbitration Court of Sakhalin Oblast' #A 59–2405/2002-C23, dated 31 October 2002.

According to Machekhin, this was all done without any investigation into the question of whether the deer were indeed wild or domestic, an issue easily determined as the external appearance of wild reindeer differs from domesticated ones. In turn, the administration declared that since there were no domestic reindeer anymore, the lands formerly designated as reindeer pasturage could no longer be considered reindeer pasturage and therefore could no longer be protected as such. According to Machekhin, this decision was in direct contradiction to the Committee for Land Resources and Land Use, which had approved the map designating all that territory as reindeer pasturage.

In order not to be arrested for poaching, *Olenevod* had to purchase a licence to 'hunt' fifty 'wild' reindeer in the 2001–2002 hunting season so there would be meat for the herders and their families. 'Under these circumstances we were forced to buy hunting licences just so we could have access to our own deer', Machekhin complained.[13] As representative of the ZAO *Olenevod*, Machekhin asked the court to forbid the Hunting Directorate from issuing any more hunting licences for wild reindeer or any other wild animals on the pasture lands of the ZAO *Olenevod*, from conducting any sorts of activities at all on these pasture lands without prior written consent from *Olenevod*, and from interfering with the reindeer herding activities of *Olenevod*. He also asked the court to make the Hunting Directorate pay damages to the amount of 7,500 rubles (approximately $300 US at the time), the cost of the fifty licences *Olenevod* had to purchase. In its defence, the Hunting Directorate responded by asserting that 'the reindeer existing on the pasture territories of the plaintiff are wild and do not belong to the plaintiff, but rather belong to the state's fund of wild animal resources'. The defendant supported this statement by claiming that *Olenevod* had not been carrying out the necessary tasks of marking, protecting and maintaining official counts of reindeer. Machekhin responded by saying that he and his herders had been threatened at gunpoint by employees of the Hunting Directorate and prevented from carrying out these functions.

The court ruled in favour of the Hunting Directorate, saying:

> The plaintiff has not proven the existence of domestic reindeer in his own possession. The plaintiff has not produced an account of these reindeer. The reindeer existing on the pasture territory of the plaintiff are not marked, they are not protected, they are not pastured, and even

---

[13] Interview with V. V. Machekhin in Yuzhno-Sakhalinsk, 25 August 2009.

the plaintiff does not refute these facts … As the representative of the defendant has explained, the reindeer indicated by Machekhin – 2,198 in number – as belonging to the ZAO *Olenevod*, belong to the wild population. As the reindeer grazing on pasturage granted to the plaintiff cannot be identified as domestic, the defendant has correctly considered them wild animals and therefore as belonging to the state's fund of hunting resources.[14]

Machekhin appealed the decision twice, once in the appeals court of Sakhalin Oblast', and once in the federal arbitration court in Khabarovsk. The appeals were turned down once again for lack of proof that the Hunting Directorate had in fact threatened the herders and interfered with their ability to carry out herding activities, and for lack of proof of the existence of domesticated reindeer in their possession.

More recently Machekhin has been working with other indigenous peoples to try to stop operation of an existing pipeline that runs from Exxon's oil fields on the north-eastern part of Sakhalin Island across the north-central part of the island and to the De-Kastri export terminal in Khabarovskii Krai on the eastern coast of the Russian mainland. Believing there would be power in numbers, in 2008 they filed a collective lawsuit representing 204 indigenous persons from whom Machekhin had power of attorney. 'Look at all these applications', he says, pulling a stack of papers out of the cabinet. 'Two hundred and four of them. All these people trusted me to defend their rights in court.' He said he had to make 204 copies of all the various documents and send them to all the plaintiffs. 'Can you imagine? We went through dozens of printer cartridges. I asked all my friends and acquaintances to help print all this. We were working like a publishing house!'

In the case, the plaintiffs referred to the 1999 law 'On guarantees of the rights of the indigenous small-numbered peoples of Russia' to claim that the construction and operation of the pipeline and its associated installations occupied land necessary for conducting traditional indigenous activities and therefore violated the rights of the plaintiffs, and requested that the court order Exxon to halt operation of the pipeline. In response to this, Machekhin explains, Exxon's lawyers

> demanded proof that these petitioners in fact, for example, gather berries, that they are involved in reindeer herding, that they lead a traditional

[14] From the decision of the Arbitration Court of Sakhalin Oblast' in case # A59–2100/2002-C8, dated 11 November 2002.

way of life – they were supposed to prove this, but they live right in the forest, in these villages … I think that there are some things that do not need to be proven. People live there, they have their proof of residence there (*propiska*), they all live in a territory recognised as a region of inhabitance of indigenous peoples. In this case, it's *a priori*, their rights are already defined. They were born there, they live there, and by virtue of that they should have these rights. And sometimes when there's a different dispute before the public prosecutor, for example if they want to invalidate the results of a competitive tender, they simply throw it out on the basis that there are a few indigenous enterprises on that territory, or if they just want to fine a private company for something. And when something like that happens they don't appeal to these processes – it's not necessary to *prove* anything, only to show that indigenous people live there. It's selective application (*izbiratel'noe primeneniye*) of the demand for proof.

Furthermore, the plaintiffs argued that the environmental impact assessment of the project was carried out without their participation or involvement, and that the pipeline is being operated on land necessary for their traditional activities but without any monitoring by the indigenous peoples, both of which are violations of their rights according to the law 'On guarantees'. Finally, Article 1065 of the Civil Codex of the Russian Federation states that a danger that could potentially lead to harm in the future may be considered justification for a law suit to prohibit the activity that is creating the potential danger. The courts in at least three instances (the original suit and at least two appeals) dismissed the claims of the plaintiffs, noting that (1) the pipeline had been built in accordance with all legal requirements; (2) the plaintiffs hadn't provided proof of danger to their lands and livelihoods; and (3) since the plaintiffs petitioned as *individual members of indigenous peoples*, and not as an *indigenous people or its associations*, Article 8 paragraph 1 of the law 'On guarantees' upon which the plaintiffs based their claim, is inapplicable and they have no rights *as individuals* to participate in the environmental impact assessment or in the monitoring of the operations. 'So you see what kind of *yerunda* (nonsense) is going on here', vented Vladimir Denisov, one of the lawyers working with Machekhin. 'That means that an association of an indigenous people has rights, and a people has rights, but you as a representative or an individual member of that people, you don't have rights.' This catch-22 is particularly interesting in light of Andrichenko's rejection of collective rights as outlined above.

From Machekhin's point of view, the problem with the pipeline is not so much one of environmental damage (although he's quick to point out that the damage is very real, as is the ever-present threat of oil spills). Rather, the issue is that Sakhalin's indigenous peoples are being deprived of their rights:

> What harms indigenous peoples most is their situation without rights. Because as long as indigenous peoples don't have any rights to this land, where their ancestors were born and carried out their traditional activities, then they don't even have the right to say anything about the fact that here there is ecological damage – they don't have even that right, you understand? They have the general civil right to say, 'I was born, so I have the right to live'. But what is that? The right to sit in the village, where we're only allowed to drink, and dance, and die, and that's all.[15]

In addition to his legal activities, Machekhin also orchestrated a hunger strike in front of the regional administration building in Yuzhno-Sakhalinsk. The strike involved twelve Evenki people under the slogan, 'Stop the genocide of the Evenki people of Sakhalin'. Machekhin believes it is fair to call the actions of the administration in favour of the oil and gas companies a 'genocide' because it deprives the Evenki people of their land, which is the foundation of their culture and livelihoods. In support of this claim, Machekhin says that sixteen of the eighteen herders with whom he started the enterprise *Olenevod* have committed suicide as a result of the actions of the administration and the decisions of the courts in favour of the administration's actions.[16] 'They had nothing left to live for', he explains. 'There were families where several people committed suicide. People said, "Of course! Look at them – they're all drunks!" But they were good families when they had something to live for.'

For his efforts Machekhin has been rewarded with six criminal cases against him and his family for poaching. In other words, he is being prosecuted for killing his own domestic animals, which the state has unilaterally declared wild, and therefore subject to regulation as wild animals by the regional hunting directorate. As long as these cases are pending, Machekhin is forbidden from leaving Sakhalin. 'The administration said to me, "Stop your actions, and we'll drop these cases against you"', Machekhin explains.

---

[15] From a meeting with Machekhin in his office on 25 August 2009.
[16] This sounds highly implausible, and I had no way of confirming or disconfirming this statement.

RUMOURS AND PROOF

These different processes of naming and claiming interact in a variety of ways. There is a productive dialectic between the naming of a territory and the naming of a perceived injurious experience: once a territory has been named, it can provide the legal vocabulary through which the injurious experience can be voiced. In Soviet times, when there was no legal framework protecting the rights of indigenous peoples, no such thing as 'territories of traditional land use', and the state's unlimited rights to all land and resources went unquestioned, raising such issues and making such claims were simply unthinkable. Nowadays, in some cases, the designation of a territory as a TTLU or as a sacred site can create the perception of injury where none had existed before. Similarly, the claiming of rights to territory can be a process to prevent an anticipated perceived injurious experience, or it can be part of the claim for remediation.

Russia's indigenous peoples are not simply working within existing legal categories, however. They are also trying to use the legal system to create new categories by which to name and claim land. For example, when efforts to use the law to protect sacred sites as sacred sites failed in the Khanty-Mansi Autonomous Okrug (because 'sacred sites' as such are not recognised in the law), indigenous leaders were forced to frame their legal claims as their right to protect 'sites necessary for the perpetuation of living folklore' (Wiget and Balalaeva 2004). Other examples include efforts to have sacred sites protected as 'sites of cultural heritage' (Syrtypova 2007; Kuleshova n.d.);[17] and as nature parks (Donahoe 2009a).

Getting a certain category of land recognised under the law can be seen as a successful act of naming. Rumours of these new legal categories travel swiftly (cf. Eckert, Chapter 6), inspiring hope and encouraging people to use the law to try to make certain claims to land. But the naming and the claiming are just the beginning of the process. Indigenous leaders must 'prove' that the territory deserves the name,

---

[17] Until passage of Federal Law 73, 'On objects of cultural heritage (monuments of history and culture) of the peoples of the Russian Federation' (25 June 2002), such important cultural places had no protection under the law. Article 3 of the law specifically mentions 'places where religious rituals are conducted', and also 'monumental places and cultural and natural landscapes connected with the historical formation of peoples and their ethnic societies in the territory of the Russian Federation' as being among the types of objects of cultural heritage that may qualify for protection if designated as such.

and it is this burden of proof that most often stymies indigenous peoples' efforts to lay claim to land, especially when their interests run counter to the interests of more economically and politically powerful players, as is usually the case. This process of rumour inspiring hope that is ultimately defeated is best exemplified by the frenzied efforts to have parcels of land recognised as 'territories of traditional land use' (see Donahoe 2009b). Strangely enough, rumours of the complete and total failure of all efforts to use that particular federal law do not seem to have travelled as far or lasted as long as the news of the law itself. Perhaps, paradoxically, this is because failures are so much more common and expected that they become unworthy of notice, whereas successes, being rarer, still excite the imagination. Failures, moreover, can be written off to the procedural specifics of the case at hand, including the burden of providing documentary proof, while substantive law in its abstraction can still inspire the hope that 'springs eternal in the human breast'.

Moreover, each attempt to fit the landscape into a legally protected category entails a shift in the terms of reference and forces indigenous leaders to enact a different 'public transcript' with regard to their relationship to the land in question. While these various public transcripts may be more or less based in the peoples' actual sense of their relationship to the land, forcing them to shift the terms of reference and at the least to foreground a different aspect of their relationship to land has the potential to subtly shift their actual relationships to land, to one another and to themselves as indigenous peoples (i.e. their 'subjectivities'). This recalls the 'transformation perspective' championed by Felstiner, Abel and Sarat, which 'directs our attention to individuals as the creators of opportunities for law and legal activity: people make their own law, but they do not make it just as they please' (1980/1981: 633).

As the legal terms of reference change, so too do the images and rhetoric indigenous peoples use to represent themselves. This is an example of what Cowan et al. have termed the 'essentializing proclivities of law', defined as 'the proclivity of legal systems to demand clearly defined, context neutral categories (including categories of identity and membership) in order to classify persons', which contributes to the 'strategic essentializing of culturally defined groups' (Cowan et al. 2001: 10–11). The cases detailed here demonstrate how the legal rights granted and, all too frequently, rescinded can be 'productive of subjectivities, of social relations, and even of the very identities and cultures they claim merely to recognize' (Cowan 2009 [2006]: 307).

References

Anaya, James 1999. 'Superpower attitudes toward indigenous peoples and group rights', *American Society of International Law Proceedings* 1999: 251–60.
2000. *Indigenous Peoples in International Law.* Oxford University Press.
Anderson, David G. 1998. 'Property as a way of knowing on Evenki lands in Arctic Siberia', in Chris M. Hann (ed.) *Property Relations: Renewing the Anthropological Tradition.* Cambridge University Press, pp. 64–84.
2000. *Identity and Ecology in Arctic Siberia.* Oxford University Press.
2002. 'Entitlements, identity and time: addressing aboriginal rights and nature protection in Siberia's new resource colonies', in Erich Kasten (ed.) *People and the Land: Pathways to Reform in Post-Soviet Siberia.* Berlin: Dietrich Reimer, pp. 99–123.
Andrichenko, Liudmila 2005. *Regulirovanie i zashchita prav natsional'nykh men'shinstv i korennykh malochislennykh narodov v Rossiiskoi Federatsii* (Regulation and Protection of Rights of National Minorities and Indigenous Small-numbered Peoples in the Russian Federation). Moscow: Gorodets.
Basso, Keith 1996. *Wisdom Sits in Places.* Albuquerque: University of New Mexico Press.
Berkes, Fikret 1999. *Sacred Ecology: Traditional Ecological Knowledge and Resource Management.* Philadelphia, PA: Taylor & Francis.
Chatwin, Bruce 1987. *The Songlines.* New York: Viking.
Cowan, Jane 2009 [2006]. 'Culture and rights after culture and rights', in Mark Goodale (ed.) *Human Rights: an Anthropological Reader.* Oxford: Wiley-Blackwell, pp. 305–33.
Cowan, Jane, Dembour, Marie-Benedicte and Wilson, Richard 2001. 'Introduction', in Jane Cowan, Marie-Benedicte Dembour and Richard Wilson (eds.) *Culture and Rights: Anthropological Perspectives.* Cambridge University Press, pp. 1–26.
Donahoe, Brian 2009a. 'The law and environmental injustice for Russia's indigenous peoples'. Unpublished paper presented at the Society for Applied Anthropology Annual Meetings, Santa Fe, NM, 18 March.
2009b. 'The law as a source of environmental injustice in the Russian Federation', in Julian Agyeman and Yelena Ogneva-Himmelberger (eds.) *Environmental Justice and Sustainability in the Former Soviet Union.* Cambridge, MA: MIT Press, pp. 21–45.

2011. 'On the creation of indigenous subjects in the Russian Federation', *Citizenship Studies* 15 (3–4): 397–417.

Donahoe, Brian, Habeck, Joachim Otto, Halemba, Agnieszka and Santha, István 2008. 'Size and place in the construction of indigeneity in the Russian Federation', *Current Anthropology* 48 (6): 993–1020.

Felstiner, William, Abel, Richard and Sarat, Austin 1980/1981. 'The emergence and transformation of disputes: naming, blaming, claiming', *Law & Society Review* 15 (3–4): 631–54.

Fondahl, Gail 1998. *Gaining Ground? Evenkis, Land, and Reform in Southeastern Siberia*. Boston: Allyn and Bacon.

Garber, Bart 1985. '1991: Balancing individual and group rights after ANCSA', *Alaska Native News* vol. 2 (January 1985), p. 21.

Graybill, Jessica 2009. 'Places and identities on Sakhalin Island: situating the emerging movements for "sustainable Sakhalin"', in Julian Agyeman and Yelena Ogneva-Himmelberger (eds.) *Environmental Justice and Sustainability in the Former Soviet Union*. Cambridge, MA: MIT Press, pp. 71–96.

Greaney, Jennifer and Bohill, Ruth n.d. 'Proof of native title: Australia, Canada, and the United States'. Unpublished manuscript provided by the authors.

Halemba, Agnieszka 2006. *The Telengits of Southern Siberia: Landscape, Religion, and Knowledge in Motion*. London: Routledge.

Ivison, Duncan, Patton, Paul and Sanders, Will 2000. *Political Theory and the Rights of Indigenous Peoples*. Cambridge University Press.

Jordan, Peter 2003. *Material Culture and Sacred Landscape: The Anthropology of the Siberian Khanty*. Lanham, MD: Rowman & Littlefield.

Kriazhkov, Vladimir 2008. 'Territorii traditsionnogo prirodopol'zovaniia kak realizatsii prava korennykh malochislennykh narodov na zemli' ('Territories of traditional land use as the realisation of the rights of the indigenous small-numbered peoples to land'), *Gosudarstvo i Pravo* 1 (January): 44–51.

Kuleshova, M. E. n.d. 'Nasledie i krizis prava' ('Heritage and the crisis of rights'). (Unpublished manuscript provided by the author).

Kuznetsov, Viktor 2005. *Materialy vtorogo s'ezda Assotsiatsii korennykh malochislennykh narodov Irkutskoi oblasti* (Proceedings of the second congress of the Association of Indigenous Small-Numbered Peoples of Irkutsk Oblast').

2006. 'Obshchestvennoi inspektsii po okhrane prirody, obshchestvennykh ekologicheskikh ekspertiz, obshchestvennogo monitoringa' ('Public inspection for the protection of nature, public environmental impact assessment, public monitoring'). *Orlinga* (Bulletin of NGO Baikal Wave) 6 (November).

Kymlicka, Will 1995. *Multicultural Citizenship: A Liberal Theory of Minority Rights*. Oxford: Clarendon Press.

Martínez Cobo, José. 1987. *Study on the Problem of Discrimination against Indigenous Populations*. United Nations publication No. E.86.XIV.3, vol. 5.

Murashko, Ol'ga 2002. 'Pochemy ne rabotaet federal'nyi zakon o territoriiakh traditsionnogo prirodopol'zovaniia?' ('Why is the federal law on territories of traditional nature use not working?'), *Zhivaia Arktika* 11–12: 54–57.

——— 2006. 'Zemel'nyi vopros, ili gde teper' zhit' narodam Severa' ('The land question, or where are the peoples of the north to live now?'), *Russkaia Tsivilizatsiia* 27 (11), www.rustrana.ru. Last accessed 12 August 2011.

Myerhoff, Barbara 1976. *Peyote Hunt: The Sacred Journey of the Huichol Indians*. Cornell University Press.

Myers, Fred 1986. *Pintupi Country, Pintupi Self: Sentiment, Place, and Politics among Desert Aborigines*. Washington, DC: Smithsonian.

——— 1989. 'Burning the truck and holding the country: Pintupi forms of property and identity', in Edwin Wilmsen (ed.) *We Are Here: Politics of Aboriginal Land Tenure*. Berkeley: University of California Press, pp. 14–42.

Nadasdy, Paul 2002. 'Property and aboriginal land claims in the Canadian subarctic: some theoretical considerations', *American Anthropologist* 104 (1): 247–61.

Niezen, Ronald 2003. *The Origins of Indigenism: Human Rights and the Politics of Identity*. Berkeley: University of California Press.

Novikova, Natalia I. 1999. 'Prava cheloveka i prava korennykh narodov Severa Rossii: Garmoniia ili antagonizm?' (Human rights and the rights of the indigenous peoples of the North of Russia: harmony or antagonism?), in Natalia I. Novikova and V. A. Tishkov (eds.) *Chelovek i Pravo* [*Man and Law*]. Moscow: ID Strategiia, pp. 54–63.

Osherenko, Gail 1995. 'Indigenous political and property rights and economic/ environmental reform in northwest Siberia', *Post-Soviet Geography* 36 (4): 225–37.

Strathern, Marilyn 2004. 'Losing (out on) intellectual resources', in Alain Pottage and Martha Mundy (eds.) *Law, Anthropology, and the Constitution of the Social: Making Persons and Things*. Cambridge University Press, pp. 201–33.

Syrtypova, Surun-Khanda 2007. *Sviatyni Kochevnikov Transbaikal'ia: Traditsionnye Kul'tovye Ob'ekty kak Pamiatniki Istorii i Kul'tury* (Sacred Sites of the Nomads of Transbaikaliia: Traditional Cult Objects as Monuments of History and Culture). Ulan-Ude: Buriat State University.

Thornton, Thomas 2008. *Being and Place among the Tlingit*. Seattle: University of Washington Press.

Wiget, Andrew and Balalaeva, Olga 2004. 'Culture, commodity, and community: Developing the Khanty-Mansi Okrug law on protecting native folklore', in Erich Kasten (ed.) *Properties of Culture, Culture as Property: Pathways to Reform in Post-Soviet Siberia*. Berlin: Dietrich Reimer, pp. 129–58.

Wilmsen, Edwin (ed.) 1989. *We Are Here: Politics of Aboriginal Land Tenure.* Berkeley: University of California Press.

Wilson, Emma 2002. 'Est' zakon, est' i svoi zakony: Legal and moral entitlements to the fish resources of Nyski Bay, North-Eastern Sakhalin', in Erich Kasten (ed.) *People and the Land: Pathways to Reform in Post-Soviet Siberia.* Berlin: Dietrich Reimer, pp. 149–68.

CHAPTER 3

HUMAN RIGHTS AND VILLAGE HEADMEN IN MALAWI: TRANSLATION BEYOND VERNACULARISATION

Harri Englund

Tinyade lero pamene tatuluka muukapolo, 'Let us be proud today, for we have left slavery behind.' These were the Chichewa words sung by a group of women in Azunga village in Malawi's Dedza District in 2006. The occasion was a public event during which their new headman was formally recognised by the chief responsible for the villages in their area. The selection of a new village headman was a form of claims-making against other villagers whom they saw as the cause of discontent that had mounted over a period of several years. In this moment of triumph, villagers likened other leaders' oppressive rule and bias towards their own kin to 'slavery', which was the condition these villagers were leaving behind. But other villagers were not the only adversaries. As they highlighted the oppression they were leaving behind, these villagers also deployed the concept of freedom (*ufulu*) to counter the reluctance of the state to recognise their new headman. They pointed out that since the early 1990s, Malawians had been granted their 'birth freedom' (*ufulu wachibadwidwe*) to live as they please. The principle that it is 'not the government but the people who choose village headmen' (*boma sisankha mfumu koma anthu*) constitutes one important element of this freedom.

Ufulu wachibadwidwe had become the Chichewa concept for human rights, enshrined in law by the new constitution in 1995 and by countless pamphlets and educational documents prepared by the government and NGOs (Englund 2006). However, villagers' use of constitutionally defined principles to counter the reluctance of the state to recognise their new village headman did not simply embrace those principles. As a basis for claiming dependence on a particular headman, the constitutional freedom they invoked was radically different from the content politicians and human rights activists had given it.

No vernacularisation of human rights was at play here, as the followers of Sally Engle Merry's (2006) subtle argument might suggest. Fully aware of the difficulties of translating the principles and provisions of international law into non-European languages, the proponents of vernacularisation approach the problem of translation in a metaphorical sense to explore how the meanings attached to concepts and principles such as human rights shift as they travel from one historical and cultural setting to another. However, fundamental to the idea of vernacularisation is the assumption that a set of core meanings can be discerned within the dizzying array of actual uses. The choice between relativism and universalism no longer needs to arise, because the scholarly momentum has veered towards the exploration of situated, contingent universals (compare Tsing 2005). What often goes unnoticed in this welcome move beyond relativism is the origin of vernacularised concepts and principles in apparently translocal artefacts such as international law. The scale of applicability remains highly uneven – vernacularised concepts and principles are, by definition, applicable in their own particular contexts, whereas international law and the idea of human rights are the ones that travel, however vernacularised they become in the process. Malawian villagers' use of the translated concept of human rights would, depending on the perspective, appear as a result of either vernacularisation or ignorance, but never as a possible origin for fresh travels.

Rather than assessing how villagers and the framers of Malawi's constitution have understood the concept of human rights, the aim of this chapter is to examine the emergence of new village headmen in order to *translate back* what villagers might have intended with their use of the concept of birth freedom. In effect, their use was doubly subversive. On the one hand, it turned the constitutional provision against the very state that was supposed to be its guardian. On the other hand, by conflating freedom and dependence, they went far beyond vernacularisation to transform the very meaning of *ufulu wachibadwidwe*. When translating back their use, the anthropologist has to be equally inventive in finding concepts to convey villagers' intents. It does not seem advisable to continue describing their claims as though they subscribed to the idea of human rights. Instead, it is worth exploring whether a notion of *relationship rights* captures the sense in which freedom presupposes dependence. At once specific to the predicament in which villagers struggled to make their claims heard *and* capable of travelling widely, the notion of relationship rights draws our attention to the variable meanings of possibility and constraint in claims expressed through legal provisions and principles. Those variable meanings inevitably expand the scope of subjectivity associated with law, with the double meaning of subjection particularly evident in the notion of relationship rights. The subjects of relationship rights are acting subjects in so far as they are subject to their relationships.

POVERTY AND FREEDOM

Both ethnography and the philosophical debate I address here relate to an influential practice in poverty alleviation in the Global South, namely the effort to provide aid that targets the poorest of the poor, or as they are often called, the most vulnerable members of society. After Bingu wa Mutharika became president of Malawi in 2004, the immediate reason for the appearance of new headmen and the accompanying splitting up of existing villages was the government's policy of enlisting headmen and chiefs as major local partners in its farm input subsidy programme.[1] Although not strictly targeting the poorest of the poor, the subsidy programme certainly sought to address vulnerability as it is often understood in contemporary development theory and practice (Ellis 2007). The philosophical justification is the notion that severe poverty violates human rights by undermining people's personal autonomy (Kreide 2007), as well as their capacity to act as moral agents. While such policies are driven by the need to distribute limited aid in the most efficient way and are often enacted with the best of intentions, there are still two fundamental problems: first, these policies assume a categorical distinction between individual and society; and second, the notion that the 'most vulnerable' can be separated from the ordinary poor for analytical and policy-making purposes is based on neo-liberal notions that personal autonomy and capability are the pathways out of poverty. Ethnographic evidence from Malawi calls for an appreciation of an alternative sense of freedom that requires no such distinction between individual and society and that recognises human relationships and dependence, rather than autonomy, as the keys to poverty alleviation.

---

[1] The headman of a particular village discharges his duties, as is described below, within a hierarchy of gradually more encompassing authorities, from group village headmen to chiefs. Although the majority of authorities in this hierarchy are men, women can also occupy positions in it in many parts of Malawi.

The subsidy programme earned Malawi some international renown as a country where, at the macro level, chronic food insecurity was transformed into a surplus of maize, the main food crop. The subsidy took the form of coupons for inputs such as chemical fertiliser and seeds. The coupons were distributed among what the government called the most vulnerable farming families. Headmen and chiefs were instrumental in the programme as the ones who, together with local representatives of the Ministry of Agriculture, identified those who were entitled to this aid. A somewhat cynical explanation for the emergence of new village headmen became popular among both government officials and the so-called civil society based in urban centres. Villagers, so the explanation went, were simply manipulating the programme to get as much material benefit as possible. The multiplication of village headmen would, in this view, also multiply the amount of input subsidies.

The cynical explanation did little justice to the locally compelling circumstances within which these transformations were taking place. Although the positions in the state-recognised hierarchy of so-called traditional authority are considered hereditary, they are in practice subject to negotiation and contestation. Candidates with tenuous genealogical credentials can emerge as village headmen after consultations that place an emphasis on the person's character (*khalidwe*). The predicament among chiefs and headmen described in foundational ethnographies from the region still rings true despite the contemporary difficulties, caused by the scarcity of land and high population densities, to physically relocate villages. 'A chief is a chief by grace of his tribe' (Schapera 1937: 184) went the saying among the Tswana. In colonial Zambia, Audrey Richards (1956: 38) observed among the Bemba that 'the headman's prime difficulty was in fact to persuade relatives to join him or if they had already done so to persuade these kinsmen not to leave him'. However, already by the time these observations were made, the selection of chiefs and headmen was not simply a local affair. As is described below for Malawi, British officials in the protectorate could appoint chiefs of their own choice and imposed rules that they were expected to enforce. Traditional authority continued to enjoy legal status in the independent state, but both the autocratic regime, in power from independence in 1964 until 1994, and the more democratic regimes thereafter kept chiefs and headmen under state surveillance, albeit through somewhat different rhetorics and with different objectives. After 2004, the farm input subsidy programme was not the only immediate context for the emergence of new headmen. Another context was the 'podium elevations of chiefs' that President Mutharika was criticised for in Malawi's media and among many villagers.[2] Using his presidential prerogative to promote and remove chiefs, Mutharika on several occasions announced changes in chiefs' statuses during his political rallies, from the podium so to speak.

The villagers celebrating their new headman were therefore assert-ing more than their attachment to custom. The reference to birth free-dom invoked the republican constitution, which had been rewritten after the democratic transition. Its Bill of Rights protects a handful of human rights and enshrines the rest as the principles of state policy (see Chirwa 2005; Mbazira 2007). A noteworthy aspect of the consti-tution, and the human rights regime it served to establish in Malawi, is the emphasis on individual freedom as the essence of human rights, with the very concept of human rights translated into Chichewa as *ufulu wachibadwidwe*, literally 'birth freedom', the freedom one is born with (Englund 2006: 47–69). Thus the Chichewa concept of birth freedom became the most widespread translation for human rights in Malawi and the Chichewa- (or Nyanja-) speaking areas in Zambia and Mozambique. I rarely encountered the notion otherwise while working with the rural and urban poor, and it was apparent that human rights as birth freedoms was a concept that appealed first and foremost to the urban-based NGOs and independent journalists who had appeared after the democratic transition in the early 1990s. They tended to define human rights primarily as political and civil liberties, a preference that was per-fectly understandable after three decades of dictatorship but that was also unlikely to engage Malawi's impoverished majority, whose mater-ial conditions had improved little (or had indeed deteriorated) since the democratic transition (Chirwa 2005). Moreover, while ruling politicians would invoke liberties as the achievement of their struggle for democ-racy, many Malawian human rights activists used the same idea of lib-erties to criticise the government's betrayal of democratic principles by manipulating elections, curtailing press freedoms and appointing public officials more on the basis of political allegiance than merit, to name but a few such practices. Despite the funds that foreign agencies provided for NGOs to conduct civic education on human rights, villagers rarely used the concept of *ufulu wachibadwidwe* in any other than a cynical sense. According to elders, 'too much freedom' had resulted in disobedience and insecurity, whereas young people, unless they were NGO volunteers

---

[2] See, for example, 'Commentators against podium elevations of chiefs', *The Nation* (Blantyre), 22 February 2009.

or employees themselves, commented on the limited relevance of such liberties for their pursuit of income and opportunities. I had produced a critique of this human rights regime before I encountered the notion of birth freedom in the context of the emerging new headmen and farm input subsidies (see Englund 2006). I was, therefore, somewhat startled when the concept of *ufulu wachibadwidwe* began to appear in villagers' reflections on the emergence of new headmen.

Was the reference to the constitutional freedoms merely a belated appreciation of the new democratic conditions in which villagers found themselves? To assume that this was the case would make it difficult to grasp what villagers were actually saying. With their invocations of slavery and freedom, the villagers cited in the beginning were at once voicing their grievances in terms of human rights and asserting a break between their concept of human rights and the one advocated not only by Malawi's civil-society activists but by a wide range of development aid donors and even moral and political theorists. What the villagers were claiming was the freedom to be the subjects of the authority they had chosen themselves. The subject-citizen dichotomy outlined in Mahmood Mamdani's (1996) influential thesis would not be able to depict such a claim in any other way than as an instance of false consciousness. For Mamdani, the colonial-era bifurcation of the African state laid the groundwork for post-colonial African 'society'. A tiny minority of Europeans and Westernised Africans enjoyed citizenship rights, while the majority of Africans were the subjects of tribally defined 'native authorities'. The post-colonial legacy of this policy of indirect rule is, in Mamdani's view, the tendency to turn every democratic struggle into a tribal conflict, with the mode of rule providing a model for the mode of resistance. However, when the claims and practices informing subjection are not investigated in any detail, it becomes all too easy to dismiss popular appeals to traditional authority as uncritical responses to the very way that the state has sought to govern rural people. Subjection serves, in this perspective, the functionalist imperative of maintaining a mode of rule that systematically excludes or marginalises those who do not have full citizenship rights.

What escapes Mamdani's purview is the possibility that dependence might be a mode of action. However, another perspective that does recognise subjects' capacity for action is no less committed to a certain functionalist idea of governance. Authors inspired by Michel Foucault, such as Nikolas Rose (1999) and Barbara Cruikshank (1999), have argued that the liberal art of governance has always involved the exercise of political and economic power through making people free. This principle of governance achieved new depths of regulation with a neo-liberal emphasis on 'rolling back the state' in favour of self-management and participation. Attempts to promote the free market are, in other words, compatible with new forms of governance that emphasise personal freedom and liberties. It is only in recent years that scholars, largely as a result of developments in feminist theory, have been able to question this association of subjection with a freedom that serves the interests of those in power (see e.g. Hirschmann 2003; Mahmood 2005). Reaching beyond debates on neo-liberalism, a fundamental distinction here is between freedom and autonomy, rather than between subjects and citizens. Fresh analytical space is created for debating those instances in which persons are able to act as free subjects only in and through their relationships with others. These observations advise caution with the interpretation that Malawian villagers were either misguided or uncritical in their adoption of a new vocabulary for making claims.

THE TRAVAILS OF TRADITIONAL AUTHORITY

In their appeals to law, villagers could have referred to the Chiefs' Act rather than the constitution. Passed in 1967 and amended in 1999, the Act builds on a history of legislating the nature and limits of traditional authority in Malawi. Introduced soon after independence, it reaffirmed the state's interest in supporting traditional authority. This policy was contrary to the trend in Malawi's neighbouring countries, which moved away from traditional authority as they pursued different forms of socialist modernisation after independence. Tanzania, Mozambique and Zambia all abolished or curtailed the institution of chieftaincy.[3] Malawi followed a path signposted by both neo-traditionalism and capitalist development, embodied in its 'Life President' Kamuzu Banda's apparently contradictory tendencies to act as an arbiter of Chewa culture while at the same time displaying Anglophilia in many aspects of his lifestyle (Vail and White 1989). Unsurprisingly in this context, chiefs and headmen were given the role of custodians of culture, with particular responsibility for customary law, while remaining assistants to district commissioners, the most senior civil servants at the district level. Coming in the wake of

---

[3] In these countries, as in many other African countries since the wave of democratisation in the early 1990s, a state-recognised revival of chieftaincies has taken place (see e.g. Buur and Kyed 2007).

colonial impositions, and continued by democratic presidents' powers to appoint and remove chiefs, this piece of legislation has had an ambiguous status among rural Malawians, on the one hand granting recognition to custom (*mwambo*), and on the other hand operating as an instrument of state power. By the time the farm input subsidy programme was introduced, villagers had come to regard the constitution as a more potent legal weapon to defend their claims.

The imperfect fit between the state legislation on traditional authority and actual practices in rural Malawi has to be understood historically before villagers' particular appropriation of constitutional provisions is investigated further.[4] A part of that history tells the familiar tale of indirect rule in colonial Africa. The British began to govern Malawi (then Nyasaland) as their protectorate in 1891, and in 1912 the District Administration (Native) Ordinance imposed a hierarchy of principal headmen and village headmen across the territory. With little regard for the historical patterns and regional variations of authority, it made principal headmen 'responsible for the maintenance of discipline, the encouragement of taxpaying, the reporting of crime, the apprehension of criminals, the provision of sanitation, control of cattle movement, and the general welfare of their administrative areas' (Rotberg 1965: 49). Appointed by the governor on the basis of their previous service to the colonial government, principal headmen supervised a number of village headmen, who all met in a council of headmen presided over by British representatives in various districts. The policy of indirect rule proper reached the protectorate in 1933, when the headmen's councils were transformed into local governments. They lacked, however, financial responsibility and control. The ordinances by which this transformation took place turned African rulers into officially recognised 'native authorities', but in one historian's estimation, '"indirect rule" was never real' (Rotberg 1965: 50). District commissioners resisted any devolution of power suggested by the Colonial Office in London, arguing that native authorities were not fit to exercise certain responsibilities.

Between 1953 and independence in 1964, local government was consolidated through statutory district councils where native authorities were *ex officio* members (Chiweza 2007). The fear of anti-colonial agitation made the colonial government give the minister of local government

---

[4] Chiefs and headmen are also recognised in many urban areas, some of them elected by local residents, others claiming hereditary authority in townships that have emerged in the territory of their villages (see Cammack *et al.* 2008).

the powers to establish and abolish councils and decide on membership. The closer to independence Malawi came, however, the more resources these councils had at their disposal through self-financing services, direct government grants and local taxes. As a consequence, the enhanced service provision that native authorities could be associated with gave them unprecedented popular legitimacy. Because of the ambiguity of their position – promptly identified by anthropologists working at the Rhodes–Livingstone Institute in present-day Zambia (see Gluckman *et al.* 1949) – native authorities were both the representatives of their subjects and answerable to the colonial government.

This ambiguity by no means vanished with the achievement of independence. Many chiefs had instigated and encouraged disobedience against the colonial government, and when Banda, upon his return to Malawi in 1958 after a forty-year absence, was presented with the skin of a civet cat customarily worn by Ngoni chiefs, the association between the nationalist movement and traditional authority looked seamless (Rotberg 1965: 287). The 1967 Chiefs' Act replaced the title 'native authority' with that of 'traditional authority' and reaffirmed their role as assistants to district commissioners and as custodians of customary law (Cammack *et al.* 2008: 4–5). The one-party state entailed a centralisation of power that gradually stripped local councils of human resources and financial means. Malawi Congress Party officials, supported by the paramilitary Malawi Young Pioneers and the women's league in the party, emerged as formidable agents of local government, ensuring the enforcement of state-imposed rules in villages and mobilising villagers for public works and political meetings. Chiefs were, nevertheless, indispensable to Banda's regime, which sought legitimacy by appealing to tradition and deployed traditional courts to persecute and punish dissidents.

After increasing pressure for reform from both within and outside of Malawi, the democratic transition commenced in earnest in 1993 with a referendum on the system of governance. Once Banda had accepted multipartyism as a result, competitive elections were held in 1994. Bakili Muluzi and the United Democratic Front were to rule the country for the next decade, and among the liberal principles enshrined in the new constitution was the promotion of local democratic institutions and democratic participation (Cammack *et al.* 2008: 5–7). The new government abolished all local councils and, after considerable delay, allowed local council elections to take place in 2000. The Local Government Act of 1998 had established district and town/city assemblies as the principal instruments of local government, with elected councillors expected to share membership with members of parliament for the areas and *ex officio* persons such as chiefs. The story of local assemblies in democratic Malawi has, however, been dismal, and after the tenure of the first assemblies came to an end in 2005, the central government lacked the political will to hold new local elections for several years. The poor resources of the assemblies and their fragmented implementation of projects undermined decentralisation even when the assemblies were in place. Thus although chiefs had in elected councillors potential rivals in mediating contacts with the district commissioner's office, the short duration and weakness of assemblies posed little challenge to chiefs' position in practice. They have actually gained in importance since the democratic transition, if only because of their assumed capacity to mobilise votes in the multiparty era (Chiweza 2007). President Muluzi increased the allowances paid to leaders at different levels in the hierarchy of traditional authority and initiated the pattern, continued by his successor Mutharika, by which the state president appoints and promotes chiefs during high-profile events.

During the period of Muluzi's and Mutharika's regimes, the state-recognised hierarchy of traditional authority comprised, in order of increasing authority: village headmen, group village headmen, sub-traditional authorities, traditional authorities, senior chiefs and paramount chiefs. A notable feature of the 'podium elevations' was the creation of paramount chiefs where none had existed before, such as among the Lomwe, an ethnic group in whose revival President Mutharika had taken personal interest.[5] The higher a chief is in this hierarchy, the more likely he or she is to become the subject of politicians' and state officials' interest. High-ranking chiefs were summoned to facilitate political manoeuvring during both Muluzi's and Mutharika's regimes. Chiefs were paraded in the public media to demand an unconstitutional (and ultimately unimplemented) third term for Muluzi and to pledge support for Mutharika's younger brother to succeed him as state president. The

---

[5] The chairperson of the Lomwe association Mutharika helped to create has been cited as saying that the Lomwe make up 'about half of the country's population'. See 'Bingu shoots at two faced chiefs', *The Nation* (Blantyre), 26 October 2008. The chairperson played on the notion of the silent majority that is the title of an academic book about the Lomwe published decades before Mutharika's ascension to power (Boeder 1984). Chichewa is spoken as the first language by over 70 per cent of the population, but as a national and regional lingua franca, it has long ceased to belong exclusively to the Chewa. Malawians with Lomwe identity are among those who have increasingly lost their ethnic language to Chichewa.

2007–2008 national budget also increased the allowances paid across the hierarchy by 1,000 per cent.

While rarely of consequence to national political leaders, village headmen are by no means immune to politicians' attentions. Multipartyism has introduced a potentially competitive context in which aspirants to parliament seek access to votes through village headmen. The extent to which village headmen can withstand the multiple pressures posed by their subjects, politicians and high-ranking traditional authorities varies greatly. The Anti-Corruption Bureau's survey in 2009 discovered that headmen and chiefs were the second most corrupt authorities after the traffic police.[6] This finding was based on the corruption complaints received by the Bureau, of which 12 per cent involved traditional authorities. Rather than indicating their lack of legitimacy, however, the finding revealed the broad range of situations in which traditional authorities were expected to be involved and, accordingly, the contested boundary that exists between corrupt practices and customary gestures of respect.

These ambiguities of traditional authority cannot be captured by the polarised framework suggested by Mamdani's (1996) thesis. Scholarship on contemporary chieftaincy in Africa has moved beyond it to explore the possibilities and constraints of this form of power in the context of political pluralism (see e.g. Nyamnjoh 2003; Oomen 2005). Apart from being subject to manipulation by politicians, traditional authority presents a challenge to democratisation also when governmental and non-governmental agents regard chiefs as the only important local rulers, work through them to undermine, inadvertently or not, elected local government and give little thought to the ways in which traditional authority might marginalise the interests of women and youth. At the same time, however, it is particularly at the level of village headmen that diverse interests can be articulated and local and national policies contested. As the scholarship on traditional authority in Africa develops, it is important that empirical investigation replace normative proclamations. The recognition of ambiguities by anthropologists working in the colonial era (Gluckman *et al.* 1949) may well serve as a model for detailed investigations of the contemporary moment.

One source of ambiguity in the present case is villagers' simultaneous appeal to tradition and the new constitution. Despite its increasing sophistication, the paradigm of legal pluralism provides few clues to understand how constitutional principles rather than the Chiefs' Act

---

[6] 'ACB rates village heads most corrupt', *Daily Times* (Blantyre), 11 October 2010.

came to support the villagers' demand for a new leader. The notion of the 'semi-autonomous social field' (Moore 1978) qualified the earlier emphasis in legal pluralism on distinct normative and moral orders by acknowledging that those orders existed within other social fields without being entirely governed by them. A more decisive break with the paradigm of legal pluralism asserted that customary law originated in the colonial period, with both colonial and customary law regarded as instruments of dispossession (Chanock 1985, 1991). Certainly in Malawi, where the so-called traditional courts could become arenas for political persecution, the interest among the officials of the newly independent state in customary law was rarely innocuous.[7] It is, therefore, vital to realise what sort of rupture villagers were claiming by their allegiance to the village headman they had selected themselves. The rupture was less between different normative orders than between the uses of traditional authority by successive governments and villagers' own sense of legitimate leadership. In this regard, villagers' appeal to constitutional principles was a rare instance of constitutionalism in a country where the commitment of national leaders to the constitution has by no means been guaranteed (see Kanyongolo 1998).

Villagers' appeal to the constitution in the dispute about the new village headman is all the more striking because the constitution has little to say about traditional authority. In contrast to the elaboration of cultural rights and traditional authority in, for example, South Africa's 1996 constitution and other recent legislation (see Oomen 2005: 50–9), Malawi's 1995 constitution has only this to say about cultural rights: 'Every person shall have the right to use the language and to participate in the cultural life of his or her choice' (section 26). Chiefs appeared in sections 68–72, which sought to establish a two-chamber structure by stipulating the composition and objectives of a senate. These sections, however, were repealed in 2001. Although some high-ranking chiefs have continued to call for the establishment of the senate or a house of chiefs to comment on national affairs, the official policy has kept traditional authority as an instrument of local government. It is here that the contradiction between the official policy and local aspirations has been most acutely felt by villagers. Far from being left to local concerns, local government through traditional authority has been a thoroughly national project, as illustrated by the podium elevations mentioned above. Villagers did not take issue with this contradiction as ethnically or culturally defined

---

[7] For an account of customary law in Malawi until the 1970s, see Benda-Beckmann 2007.

subjects. They had in mind those constitutional provisions that had given rise to the ubiquitous rhetoric about personal freedom, a rhetoric familiar to them through NGOs' civic-education campaigns and politicians' speeches. Few villagers were able to cite a particular section in the Bill of Rights, and their invocation of birth freedom had connotations radically different from those promoted by NGOs and politicians. Rather than confronting the state as individuals seeking personal autonomy and individual civil and political liberties, villagers were asserting their freedom to be the subjects of a leader they themselves had chosen.

This contrasts sharply with human rights theorists' consensus about freedom as personal autonomy. These scholars often assert that severe poverty violates human rights by depriving poor people of their capacity for self-rule and for making the right choices in their lives. For example, persons are said to lose their capacity to act as moral agents when severe poverty undermines their freedom as personal autonomy (Kreide 2007). This idea is of course something very different from a libertarian position. These authors do not celebrate personal autonomy in purely individualistic terms, as if any influence from others represented an infringement on individual rights. However, while most of the scholars writing about poverty as a human rights violation emphasise the diversity of the ideas of the good life, they still make a categorical distinction between individual and society. Ethnography from Malawi calls for an appreciation of an alternative sense of freedom that requires no such distinction. Inspired by ethnography, I propose a notion of *relationship rights* to pave the way beyond individual rights and collective rights as the conventional templates for describing human rights.

CONTESTED AUTHORITY

State officials could in practice do little else than issue missives to condemn the emergence of new villages. The district commissioner of Dedza, the highest-ranking civil servant in the district, sent out a circular to chiefs and displayed copies of it outside his office. In the circular, he stated that chiefs had no mandate to appoint new headmen without the consent of his office. The only tangible sanction the district commissioner could impose was the refusal to include the new headmen on the government's payroll for allowances. He also let it be known that these new headmen were not entitled to receive and distribute the coupons provided by the farm input subsidy programme. However, the district commissioner had little direct control over how low-ranking civil servants such as agricultural extension workers living close to villages actually implemented his directives. Locally workable arrangements did involve the new headmen in the area where I do fieldwork, because extension workers often felt more pressure to comply with the demands of their neighbours than those of the district commissioner, who virtually never visited them where they were stationed. In practice, therefore, the new headmen became intermediaries in facilitating their subjects' access to resources from the state.[8]

Beyond the refusal to grant them recognition through material means, the district commissioner was also incensed by the way in which the new villages disturbed his sense of what villages should properly look like. He despaired that the new villages no longer adhered to spatial boundaries. In an interview with me he explained that in the past one would know where one village ended and another village started, because they were spatially separate from each other. Because of land scarcity and high population densities, however, new villages were not created by splitting up existing villages and physically dispersing their members. People stayed where they were but could still come within a new headman's territory and be members of the same village even while living miles apart from one another, surrounded by people belonging to other villages. This pattern was a remnant of widespread mobility in earlier times, when disputes drove people out of existing villages or they married or looked for arable land other than in the place of their immediate relatives.[9] 'We know each other' (timadziwana), villagers would respond when I reported to them the district commissioner's complaint. But in any case it became apparent that the establishment of new villages whose members remained spatially dispersed did involve much extra effort on the part of new headmen and their supporters.

Even once a new village had come into existence through common agreement and the recognition granted by the chief, some households that were more marginal than others needed to be persuaded to recognise

---

[8] The extent to which chiefs and headmen have been allowed to participate in the distribution of coupons has varied over the years since the programme has been implemented. Persistent reports of corruption have made the government experiment with different systems of delivery, but it should be apparent that the emergence of new headmen was partly a local response to the illegitimate use of power at higher levels.

[9] Ethnographies on this region from the late colonial period frequently reported the relatively short life-spans of particular villages. In some parts of the region, the so-called slash-and-burn method of agriculture required periodic relocation over vast areas of land, but even in the more densely populated parts of the region the genealogical depth of villages was often found to be shallow (see e.g. Mitchell 1956; Turner 1957; Marwick 1965).

the new headman's authority. New leaders had to produce compelling historical narratives to justify the new villages not only to their own subjects but also to those who continued to live as neighbours while belonging to different villages. One case involved some dozen houses located three miles from the largest cluster of houses in Azunga, the new village mentioned at the beginning of this chapter. These separated houses were situated by the main road and were, in spatial terms, indistinguishable from the village that surrounded them. Azunga's first headman paid them several visits, sometimes accompanied by elders from his and other villages, to convince them that they were his subjects. The complicating issue was as much social as it was spatial. These houses belonged to the descendants of a man who had married a woman in what was now called Azunga village. She moved to live with him in Blantyre, then Malawi's only major town, but returned before him to the village. She wanted to use some of their capital to start a business and settled to brew beer by the main road, which was at the time sparsely populated. Her husband eventually joined her there, but he brought with him a new wife whom he had married in Blantyre. The woman was from a district adjacent to Dedza, and she invited a number of her sisters to establish their own houses at the new site. Four decades later and with the original protagonists long dead, Azunga's new headman faced the difficult task of explaining to their children and grandchildren that they belonged to his village. He argued that the land on which these houses were built, and the fields they cultivated, had been given to the first wife by her elders, who were members of the Azunga clan that had now given rise to the new village. The argument appeared to meet with uncertain success, and the issue remained unresolved several months after the new headman had started to pursue it.

While the village (*mudzi*) was the central idiom to express claims to resources such as input subsidies, it could not guarantee a stable set of relationships. As the above case indicates, not only were the spatial limits of villages subject to constant negotiation, the question of who properly belonged to a village was also prompted by a range of considerations beyond spatial dispersal. New villages were established on the basis of kinship (*pachibale*), but cross-cutting ties beyond family units, along with the possibility of identifying ever smaller units within the encompassing clan, ensured that new headmen had to deal with complicated matters of loyalty and affiliation. As clan-based units, the new villages had established hierarchies of elders (*akuluakulu*) and guardians (*ankhoswe*), who had presided over marital and other family disputes when they were the subjects of old villages. It was not, however, these elders and guardians who selected the candidates for the headmanship, but rather groups of adult and often elderly women. The involvement of women in selecting headmen arose from their insight into candidates' characters, because they were said to have had intimate knowledge of the candidates since their infancy. Women's deliberations were not made public, and they usually came up with only one name. It was the elders' and guardians' burden to persuade the named candidate to accept the position. Many candidates were reluctant because of the conflicts, rivalry and occult threats the position was seen to involve.

Madalitso Mpofu's ascendancy to the headmanship in the above-mentioned Azunga village and his subsequent tribulations illustrate many of these complexities. Mpofu's genealogical position and his residence in a different village made his selection to the headmanship unlikely. The unschooled second son of an unmarried third-born daughter in Azunga's founding cluster, Mpofu emerged as the preferred candidate against a field of several more senior and better educated men. He was in his early thirties when the selection took place, and lived a few miles away in his wife's village. The women in the founding cluster convened to discuss and compare the eligible candidates and agreed that Mpofu had shown throughout his life exemplary conduct by avoiding conflict, maintaining sobriety and assisting his impoverished mother. The mother herself was the only woman in the group to protest, tearfully describing to me after the meeting what I already knew about the headman's ambivalent position: his vulnerability to other people's envy and hatred, all too often resulting in occult attacks on his person or family. Sure enough, Mpofu found himself embroiled in controversy as soon as the coupons for input subsidies were next distributed.

Some of 'those who had married elsewhere' (*okwatira kwina*), as women in Azunga referred to their sons and grandsons scattered in different villages and towns, paid visits to their village of origin when they heard that it had been recognised as a separate entity. The distribution of coupons brought to a head the resentment some of these men felt over Mpofu's selection as headman. They convened a meeting with other villagers without Mpofu's knowledge and argued that he had not distributed the coupons in a fair manner. Mpofu became concerned about rebellion (*kuukira*) when he was told about the meeting, and called his own immediately afterwards. 'I do not know war' (*nkhondo sindidziwa*), he told his subjects, and explained that when he was asked to take on the headmanship, 'I neither refused nor agreed' (*sindinakane ndipo sindinavomere*).

All he wanted to know then was how he could lead (*kutsogolera*) others, and if anyone wished to try out the position, he was prepared to relinquish it. Moreover, in another instance of how constitutional matters had penetrated villagers' understandings of justice, he announced that he would call a referendum (*riferendamu*) to settle his disputed headmanship. He alluded to a controversy surrounding President Mutharika's departure from the political party that had sponsored his campaign, and Mutharika's suggestion that he could organise a referendum to settle the issue. Elders in Azunga village ultimately dissuaded Mpofu from calling a referendum, arguing that he was the only headman acceptable to the women who had selected him. They also highlighted his personal integrity, noting that because Mpofu was himself living in a different village, he did not demand a share of the coupons for his own household as some of the other *okwatira kwina* had done.

Chiefs, and not the district commissioner, were crucial to the public recognition of new headmen's authority in villages. Despite the fact that the district commissioner attempted, as was seen above, to prevent established chiefs from exercising their prerogative to recognise new headmen, the chiefs themselves were in practice just as entangled in complex personal loyalties and animosities as the local-level civil servants were. The recognition of new headmen went against the directives of the state, and some chiefs refused to participate in such subversive practices, but this was not necessarily proof of their endorsement of state policy. When Kabudula village, one of the largest in the area, split up after the district commissioner's disapproval had become common knowledge, it exposed a cleavage between the two most senior chiefs in the area, Kachindamoto and Kamenyagwaza. The former was, as senior chief, formally above the latter in the hierarchy, but Kamenyagwaza was the chief whose approval was sought by the subjects of new village headmen in the first instance. The immediate reason for Kachindamoto's intervention was the decision by Kabudula's splinter faction, known as Kabudula 2, to invite the masked dancers of the *gule wamkulu* (great dance) to celebrate the recognition granted by Kamenyagwaza. The decision was controversial because *gule wamkulu* was seen as the key custom of the Chewa people, whereas all of Kachindamoto's subjects were thought to be Ngoni, a people whose origins lay in the northbound migrations sparked by Shaka Zulu's expansive state in nineteenth-century South Africa (Barnes 1954; Hamilton 1995). Kachindamoto summoned the headman and elders of Kabudula 2 to explain their decision, pressing them to answer the question of 'who had dressed their headman' (*anaveka mfumu ndi ndani?*). The question was whether their new village had been recognised by Kasumbu, the nearest Chewa chief in Dedza District, or Kamenyagwaza. Because it had been Kamenyagwaza, Kachindamoto made them pay a fee as compensation for bringing a wrong group of dancers to their celebration. The penalty was seen as a rebuff of Kamenyagwaza, who had endorsed the celebration, and not as a penalty for having recognised the new village against the wishes of the district commissioner.

What this example illustrates is that although they were in theory – and often in practice too – closer to the state, high-ranking traditional authorities had a more complex field of relationships to negotiate than their service to the government would seem to suggest. By the same token, as the examples in this section indicate, the installation of new village headmen was not a cynical reaction to the opportunity to access input subsidies through traditional authority. The emphasis their subjects placed on character was consistent with the broad range of responsibilities new headmen were expected to assume, from distributing coupons for fertiliser to hearing disputes to mobilising villagers for public events in the village and beyond. Moreover, just as past loyalties and migrations could become critical issues in the present, so too was the emergence of new villages often the outcome of a process that had begun well before the current programme of input subsidies. The fragmentation of Kabudula village into Azunga, Kabudula 2 and three other new villages, for instance, has to be understood in light of the conflicts and grievances that were associated with the decreasing popularity of its long-serving headman. His tendency to impose unreasonable penalties for minor offences had coincided with his fraternisation with chiefs and politicians whose moral credentials were by no means obvious to Kabudula villagers. It was to such locally compelling experiences of conflict that the song quoted at the beginning of this chapter alluded when it celebrated release from slavery. The reasons for the emergence of new villages were not, in other words, as transparent as the district commissioner and NGO executives thought, nor did their cynical explanation leave much room for appreciating the specific sense of freedom that informed these processes.

TRAVELLING CONCEPTS

The events and claims described in this chapter should not be taken merely as instances of villagers discovering, however belatedly, resources in the constitutional Bill of Rights to resist injunctions handed down by state officials. The appeal to freedom, as human rights were translated in the Chichewa constitution, certainly opposed villagers' interests to those of the state, but it also transformed the meaning that politicians and non-governmental activists had given to that concept. Villagers were not simply parroting what they had heard on the radio and during civic-education campaigns. The new village headmen embodied the freedom of their subjects in so far as they were selected by those subjects, mediated their access to resources and were goodnatured in their conduct of village affairs. Freedom, in other words, did not inhere in the villagers' individual personal autonomy, nor was its invocation a reflection of individualistic aspirations. Freedom, in the sense that villagers invoked it, revealed the empowering potential of subjection. Far from being beleaguered by the 'clenched fist' (Mamdani 1996: 23) of traditional authority, villagers were active subjects in so far as they subjected themselves to a higher authority. It would be wrong to interpret this orientation as another instance of the communalism that has, depending on a given author's outlook, inspired either despair or pride over Africans' alleged commitment to the community rather than the individual.[10] What has been described above are conflicts as well as communal solidarities, leadership determined more by personal character than genealogical position, multiple and cross-cutting loyalties rather than adherence to one particular community. The challenge posed by freedom-through-subjection is to understand rights and obligations in terms of relationships rather than in terms of individual or group autonomy.

It is a challenge of translation, albeit not in the sense of the vernacularisation that has become an influential paradigm in the anthropology of human rights (Merry 2006). This paradigm has approached the challenge of translation in a metaphorical sense, drawing a parallel to the way in which national languages came to replace Latin in nineteenth-century Europe. Merry's (2006) distinction between replication and hybridity recognises different modalities in vernacularisation, but whether human rights norms are imposed without modification (replication) or merge with locally salient institutions and meanings (hybridity), the traffic in translation appears to go in one direction only. Hybridity in this sense assumes the priority of pure forms, such as international law, against which the practice of human rights appears in its

---

[10] Compare, among many other examples, Howard 1990 and Mutua 2002.

multiple, culturally inflected instances.[11] Such an approach obscures the need to *translate back* what claims expressed through local translations of human rights actually say (Goodale and Clarke 2010: 7–8). If 'globalisation' is to have any other meaning than the diffusion of ideas and institutions from centres into peripheries, it must include the possibility that those ideas and institutions may encounter friction that propels fresh travels (see Tsing 2005). In other words, it is incumbent on anthropologists and others engaged in field research to consider carefully whether the claims they investigate are best regarded as culturally specific hybrids or whether they entail insights that have more general consequences for theorising human rights. The first task is to appreciate the challenge of translation in more than a metaphorical sense.

The reason why the claims expressed by villagers in Dedza District have not entered global circulation is plain to see. Made in a language that, although spoken by millions, is not one of the world languages, and emanating from the predicament of severe poverty, they stand little chance of influencing metropolitan theorising. Yet if translated back into a world language, they may start doing so. The fundamental issue they throw into sharp relief is whether the claims described here should be translated back in terms of human rights at all, despite the use of a vernacularised human rights concept. The question is, in effect, whether the anthropologist should allow himself to be so influenced by the burgeoning human rights talk across the globe that even these claims would be translated as its particular instances. As Richard Ashby Wilson remarks, 'human rights have gone from a general list of what governments should not do to their citizens in the 1940s to a full blown moral-theological-political vision of the good life' (2007: 349). With some despair, he notes how 'new rights are added all the time, thus expanding the rights framework into areas for which it was not originally designed or intended' (2007: 350). Such an approach may end up diluting the very idea of human rights and the legal architecture that can take violators to task. Conversely, it may also make academics and activists deaf to the specific features of claims they hear in widely different contexts (for more discussion, see Englund in press).

---

[11] The paradox is that social theorists offered 'hybridity' in the 1980s and 1990s as a critique of pure forms while making, in Marilyn Strathern's words, 'frequent appeals to categories such as race and gender which [were] presented, uninflected, prior to the work that the concept of the hybrid [was] supposed to do in undermining them' (1996: 520).

The argument here is not that Malawian villagers are, for whatever cultural or political reasons, oblivious to the idea of human rights as it is understood in mainstream legal practice. This idea does figure in their reflections and disputes about, for example, electoral politics and gender relations, but what makes the claims they occasion different from the claims described in this chapter is their evocation of individuals and groups as rights-bearers. Individuals or groups claim to be disenfranchised by fraudulent elections; women assert their rights to reproductive health and independent income as individuals or a group separate from men. Alongside such claims voiced in terms of human rights exist other kinds of rights claims that pursue justice by describing claimants' relationships to others. They belong to the domain of relationship rights within which subjects have rights in so far as they have relationships. As the case of new village headmen indicates, relationships do not presuppose harmonious communities, but are both specific and hierarchical in their effects. They are specific to the claim subjects wish to make, and hierarchy is the very means by which those claims can achieve their objectives. Where human rights presume generic individuals and groups that are as abstract as they are thought to be equal, relationship rights *produce* particular rights-bearing subjects instead of being predicated on them.

This kind of translation may allow the anthropologist to revise his/her initial, unexamined conflation of villagers' claims with human rights talk. Equally importantly, it can delimit the scope of human rights in order to expand the purview of academics and activists to accommodate other kinds of rights claims. Translation is, therefore, a generative process that influences the original concept as much as it gives birth to a new one. Walter Benjamin captured this generative potential when he observed that translation is 'charged with the special mission of watching over the maturing process of the original language and the birth pangs of its own' (1970: 73). The concept of relationship rights, as it travels from the ethnography of rural Malawi to other contexts of claims making, will qualify the current academic and activist preoccupation with human rights by introducing an alternative way in which rights might be related to freedom and subjectivity. Severe poverty may well be a paradigmatic condition for relationship rights. Yet various forms of vulnerability can belong to the scope of relationship rights, revealing the ways in which those who are deemed vulnerable by public policy or private charity, such as the disabled and the very poor, ameliorate their situation by claiming relationships with others. Critical to this fresh approach to rights is the capacity of concepts to travel from, rather than merely into, out-of-the-way places such as rural Malawi.

References

Barnes, John A. 1954. *Politics in a Changing Society: A Political History of the Fort Jameson Ngoni*. Oxford University Press.

Benda-Beckmann, Franz von 2007. *Legal Pluralism in Malawi: Historical Development 1858–1970 and Emerging Issues*. Zomba: Kachere Series.

Benjamin, Walter 1970. *Illuminations*, trans. Harry Zohn. London: Jonathan Cape.

Boeder, Robert B. 1984. *The Silent Majority: A History of the Lomwe in Malawi*. Pretoria: African Institute of South Africa.

Buur, Lars and Kyed, Helene M. (eds.) 2007. *State Recognition and Democratization in Sub-Saharan Africa: A New Dawn for Traditional Authorities*. Basingstoke: Palgrave-Macmillan.

Cammack, Diana, Kanyongolo, Edge and O'Neil, Tam 2008. '*Town Chiefs*' *in Malawi*. London: Overseas Development Institute.

Chanock, Martin 1985. *Law, Custom and Social Order: The Colonial Experience in Malawi and Zambia*. Cambridge University Press.

1991. 'Paradigms, policies and property: a review of the customary law of land tenure', in Kristin Mann and Richard Roberts (eds.) *Law in Colonial Africa*. London: James Currey, pp. 61–84.

Chirwa, Danwood M. 2005. 'A full loaf is better than half: the constitutional protection of economic, social and cultural rights in Malawi', *Journal of African Law* 49 (2): 207–41.

Chiweza, Asiyati L. 2007. 'The ambivalent role of chiefs: rural decentralization initiatives in Malawi', in Lars Buur and Helene M. Kyed (eds.) *State Recognition and Democratization in Sub-Saharan Africa: A New Dawn for Traditional Authorities*. Basingstoke: Palgrave-Macmillan.

Cruikshank, Barbara 1999. *The Will to Empower: Democratic Citizens and Other Subjects*. Ithaca, NY: Cornell University Press.

Ellis, Frank 2007. 'Vulnerability and coping', in David A. Clark (ed.) *The Elgar Companion to Development Studies*. Northampton, MA: Edward Elgar, pp. 671–75.

Englund, Harri 2006. *Prisoners of Freedom: Human Rights and the African Poor*. Berkeley: University of California Press.

in press. 'Cutting human rights down to size', in Mark Goodale (ed.) *Human Rights at the Crossroads*. Oxford University Press.

Gluckman, Max, Mitchell, J. Clyde and Barnes, John A. 1949. 'The village headman in British Central Africa', *Africa* 19 (2): 89–106.

Goodale, Mark and Clarke, Kamari M. 2010. 'Introduction: understanding the multiplicity of justice', in Kamari M. Clarke and Mark Goodale (eds.)

Mirrors of Justice: Law and Power in the Post-Cold War Era. Cambridge University Press, pp. 1–27.

Hamilton, Carolyn A. (ed.) 1995. *The Mfecane Aftermath: Reconstructive Debates in Southern African History*. Johannesburg: Witwatersrand University Press.

Hirschmann, Nancy 2003. *The Subject of Liberty: Toward a Feminist Theory of Freedom*. Princeton University Press.

Howard, Rhoda 1990. 'Group versus individual identity in the African debate on human rights', in Abdullahi A. An-Na'im and Francis M. Deng (eds.) *Human Rights in Africa: Cross-cultural Perspectives*. Washington, DC: Brookings Institution, pp. 159–83.

Kanyongolo, Fidelis Edge 1998. 'The limits of liberal democratic constitutionalism in Malawi', in Kings M. Phiri and Kenneth R. Ross (eds.) *Democratization in Malawi: A Stocktaking*. Blantyre: Christian Literature Association in Malawi (CLAIM), pp. 353–75.

Kreide, Regina 2007. 'Neglected injustice: poverty as a violation of social autonomy', in Thomas Pogge (ed.) *Freedom from Poverty as a Human Right: Who Owes What to the Very Poor?* Oxford University Press, pp. 155–81.

Mahmood, Saba 2005. *Politics of Piety: The Islamic Revival and the Feminist Subject*. Princeton University Press.

Mamdani, Mahmood 1996. *Citizen and Subject: Contemporary Africa and the Legacy of Late Colonialism*. Princeton University Press.

Marwick, Max G. 1965. *Sorcery in Its Social Setting: A Study of the Northern Rhodesian Ceŵa*. Manchester University Press.

Mbazira, Christopher 2007. 'Bolstering the protection of economic, social and cultural rights in Malawi under the Malawian constitution', *Malawi Law Journal* 1 (2): 220–31.

Merry, Sally E. 2006. *Human Rights and Gender Violence: Translating International Law into Local Justice*. University of Chicago Press.

Mitchell, J. Clyde 1956. *The Yao Village: A Study in the Social Structure of a Nyasaland Tribe*. Manchester University Press.

Moore, Sally F. 1978. *Law as Process: An Anthropological Approach*. New York: Routledge.

Mutua, Makau 2002. 'The Banjul Charter: the case for an African cultural fingerprint', in Abdullahi A. An-Na'im (ed.) *Cultural Transformation and Human Rights in Africa*. London: Zed Books, pp. 68–107.

Nyamnjoh, Francis B. 2003. 'Chieftaincy and the negotiation of might and right in Botswana democracy', *Journal of Contemporary African Studies* 21 (2): 233–50.

Oomen, Barbara 2005. *Chiefs in South Africa: Law, Power and Culture in the Post-Apartheid Era*. Oxford: James Currey.

Richards, Audrey I. 1956. *Chisungu: A Girl's Initiation Ceremony among the Bemba of Zambia*. London: Faber and Faber.

Rose, Nikolas 1999. *Powers of Freedom: Reframing Political Thought.* Cambridge University Press.

Rotberg, Robert I. 1965. *The Rise of Nationalism in Central Africa: The Making of Malawi and Zambia, 1873–1964.* Cambridge, MA: Harvard University Press.

Schapera, Isaac (ed.) 1937. *The Bantu-Speaking Tribes of South Africa.* London: Routledge & Sons.

Strathern, Marilyn 1996. 'Cutting the network', *Journal of the Royal Anthropological Institute* 2 (3): 517–35.

Tsing, Anna L. 2005. *Friction: An Ethnography of Global Connection.* Princeton University Press.

Turner, Victor W. 1957. *Schism and Continuity in an African Society: A Study of Ndembu Village Life.* Manchester University Press.

Vail, Leroy and White, Landeg 1989. 'Tribalism in the political history of Malawi', in Leroy Vail (ed.) *The Creation of Tribalism in Southern Africa.* Berkeley: University of California Press, pp. 151–92.

Wilson, Richard A. 2007. 'Tyrannosaurus lex: the anthropology of human rights and transnational law', in Mark Goodale and Sally E. Merry (eds.) *The Practice of Human Rights: Tracking the Law between the Global and the Local.* Cambridge University Press, pp. 342–69.

CHAPTER 4

JURIDIFICATION, TRANSITIONAL JUSTICE AND REACHING OUT TO THE PUBLIC IN SIERRA LEONE

Gerhard Anders

> All domains were characterised by juridification, decisions with real impact, affecting actual power relations were avoided. Whether it concerns the authority of the president or the resolution of labour conflicts, everything is neutralised by framing it in the juridical form. This is the rule of law in its pure form. The state's legitimacy has come to rest exclusively on the law. As a consequence, legal decisions appear bland and barely authoritative. This results in the belief that decisions are purely legal, pronounced by a universally recognised authority … The state depends on the law, but it is a legal machinery rather than real law.
>
> Otto Kirchheimer (1928: 597, author's translation)

INTRODUCTION

'We bring the court to the people', Raymond Kamara told me while we were mounting his motorcycle. On that day in March 2009, I was accompanying him to Mukump Gbana, a village on the road connecting Makeni and Magburaka, the two main towns in northern Sierra Leone. Raymond was one of the dozen 'outreach officers' employed by the Special Court for Sierra Leone. Outreach officers were posted in all district capitals of Sierra Leone with the task of informing the population about the court, the trials being heard there and the principles of international humanitarian law. They visited villages, town halls, schools, police stations and army barracks to conduct 'outreach events', usually comprising the screening of footage of the trials, a brief presentation and an opportunity for the audience to ask questions and make comments.

Raymond and the other outreach officers who toured the towns and villages acted as foot soldiers in the global movement against impunity that had emerged after the end of the Cold War. The Special Court for Sierra Leone and the other international criminal tribunals set up during the 1990s and at the beginning of the twenty-first century are manifestations of a transnational process of juridification in a sphere that used to be the domain of diplomatic relations between states, the traditional subjects of international law. The Special Court was established in 2002 by agreement between the government of Sierra Leone and the United Nations to hold accountable those 'bearing greatest responsibility' for crimes against humanity and war crimes committed in Sierra Leone during the civil war. During the late 1990s the civil war in Sierra Leone had become synonymous with senseless violence against civilians, horrific atrocities and the ruthless plunder of natural resources.

Following discussions about the nature of the planned court, the United Nations and the government of Sierra Leone signed an international agreement to establish the Special Court for Sierra Leone in January 2002. Shortly afterwards the court commenced its operations and already in March 2003 the chief prosecutor issued the first eight indictments against leaders of the various armed factions who were accused of bearing the 'greatest responsibility' for the crimes committed during Sierra Leone's civil war. In 2004 the first trial chamber, consisting of three judges appointed by the UN Secretary General and two appointed by the government of Sierra Leone, was established. It commenced hearing two trials, one against three senior commanders of the Revolutionary United Front (RUF), the notorious rebel group that had waged war against successive governments for a decade, and the other against three leaders of the Civil Defence Force (CDF), a government militia that fought against the RUF. In 2005 the second trial chamber began hearing the trial against three leaders of the Armed Forces Revolutionary Council (AFRC), a group that had ousted the government in May 1997 and formed an alliance with the RUF.

Between June 2007 and March 2009 the trial chambers handed down judgements in these three trials. All accused were found guilty and sentenced to long prison terms. Both defence and prosecution appealed the trial chambers' judgements. In all three trials the appeals chamber confirmed the guilty verdicts, in one case even increasing the sentences. A fourth trial against the former Liberian president Charles Taylor was heard between 2008 and 2011 in The Hague. The prosecution accused him of being responsible for the crimes committed by combatants of the RUF and the AFRC because he supported and directed both organisations.

Juridification, or the expansion of legal norms, is highly ambivalent. On the one hand, it may have an empowering effect. Especially since the end of the Cold War, the idea of the rule of law and the idiom of individual and collective rights have been appropriated by social movements and indigenous peoples to claim the recognition of political and social demands. Since the 1970s, for instance, indigenous groups have learned to use the law and the institutions charged with its enforcement to their advantage, beating the system with its own tools and using the legal categories once employed to deprive them of their ancestral lands to claim restitution or compensation. The other chapters in this volume describe how marginalised or oppressed groups attempt to use the law against the state. The language of human rights provides a globally cir- culating vocabulary for these groups, who adapt it to voice their com- plaints and demands, as recent socio-legal and anthropological studies show (Dezaley and Garth 2002a; Santos and Rodríguez-Garavito 2005; Eckert 2006; Merry 2006; Goodale and Merry 2007). Of course, they face powerful interests and many a legal battle is lost while their struggle for recognition continues.

On the other hand, juridification was originally coined to describe the gradual depoliticisation of political and social conflict due to the expan- sion of legal regulation into all social domains (Kirchheimer 1928). Later Habermas and others used the term to describe the 'colonization of the life world' (Habermas 1981: 522) by the welfare state. In this latter sense juridification denotes the encroachment on the rights of the individual and democratic decision-making processes by the flood of regulation produced by the bureaucracy of the modern welfare state (Voigt 1980; Teubner 1985, 1987).

This chapter examines one of the facets of the expansion of inter- national criminal law. Rather than addressing the centres of this devel- opment – the courtrooms and conferences where international criminal law is made – it focuses on the margins, the villages and towns in Sierra Leone's hinterland, where ordinary Sierra Leoneans were exposed to the retributive vision of justice driving the project of international criminal justice. During my fieldwork among the Special Court's outreach offi- cers I learned that the audiences they encountered on their daily tours were highly critical of the court and insisted on raising fundamental concerns about justice that were not addressed by the court's representa- tives. People used the outreach events to express a fundamental critique of the Special Court and international criminal justice in general. This critique hinged on two pillars. On the one hand, audiences across Sierra Leone suspected that the court was politically biased and was being instrumentalised in the national political arena. On the other hand, a widely shared feeling across Sierra Leone was that the court's vision of retributive justice did not address people's fundamental concerns. They demanded development in the form of schools, roads and hospitals rather than the symbolic punishment of a few individuals.

The encounters of the outreach officers with audiences across Sierra Leone constitute a specific type of ethnographic data. In a recent book Ronald Niezen (2010) draws attention to the importance of publics for the anthropology of law. According to Niezen, 'publics, however intangible, have also become part of the social worlds of those whom it is possible to know intimately' (Niezen 2010: 1). The audiences the outreach officers encountered on their daily tours constituted an important part of their social world. Niezen underlines the importance of publics in current debates about law and justice, and indeed the work of the outreach officers was deemed crucial for the Special Court's success. Public opinion mattered to court officials, who were keen to show to their supporters and donors in the West that the court met the demand for justice in Sierra Leone.

The first part of this chapter situates the ethnographic evidence in relation to the scholarly debate about juridification. The second part describes how the Special Court has influenced the domestic political landscape in Sierra Leone. The third part presents ethnographic evidence from two outreach events to show how the fundamental critique of the Special Court was voiced by audiences in Sierra Leone.

THE FIFTH WAVE OF JURIDIFICATION

The global movement for human rights has fanned out in many directions and spawned the global legal order and the transnational movement against impunity (Dezaley and Garth 2002b; Robertson 2006). In a way, international criminal justice is the flip side of human rights because it also attributes to individuals the status of legal subjects under international law. International criminal law ascribes criminal responsibility to individuals in positions of authority who violate international humanitarian law and human rights law.

According to Simpson (2007), the global expansion of international criminal law is characterised by juridification. The term juridification was used by Habermas to describe the 'colonization of the lifeworld' (Habermas 1981: 522). According to Habermas, 'the term "juridification" refers to the tendency of formal law to increase, which can be observed in all modern societies. In this regard, the expansion of law, the legal regulation of new, hitherto informally regulated social domains, can be distinguished from the densification of law, the transformation of general rules into specific, highly detailed rules' (1981: 524). He identifies four waves of juridification in European history. The first wave occurred during the formation of the early absolutist state. The second wave accompanied the rise of individual rights during the nineteenth century, which was followed by the third wave, when democratic rights became more widespread. Finally, the fourth wave came about in the second half of the twentieth century with the advent of the modern welfare state (Habermas 1981: 522–47). Following Habermas's periodisation, the current expansion of international criminal justice would reflect a fifth wave of juridification, transcending the boundaries of the nation-state.

According to Habermas, juridification is decidedly ambivalent, empowering the individual and guaranteeing individual rights on the one hand, and curtailing individual liberties by prescribing the form in which demands can be expressed and regulating all domains of social life on the other hand. This ambivalence is also well exemplified by this fifth wave of juridification, the expansion of the human rights discourse and its twin, international criminal justice, beyond the borders of the nation-state. On the one hand, human rights discourse empowers people by providing them with an idiom for making claims, but, on the other hand, it also limits possible demands by defining the scope of rights and obligations, and by individualising them.

This observation resonates well with Otto Kirchheimer's (1928) early writings on liberal democracy and juridification. Kirchheimer, a student of Carl Schmitt, was at the time highly critical of the Weimar Republic, an attitude he shared with his teacher. But while his teacher was a prominent representative of the conservative and Catholic right who had sympathies for the Nazi movement, Kirchheimer formulated a fundamental critique of the Weimar Republic from the left. According to Kirchheimer, liberal democracy had once been driven by the moral values and political ambitions of the bourgeoisie, but later turned into a mere shell for the class conflict between bourgeoisie and working class. Far from operating as sovereign above the conflicting interests, the state had, according to Kirchheimer (1928: 597), become 'the borderline between two opposing forces, both of which deny the state's claim to act as impartial arbiter'. Liberal democracy is characterised by juridification, the increase of legal regulation extending into all social domains. As the epigraph at the beginning of this chapter shows, Kirchheimer believed that juridification 'neutralises' the political struggle by formalising and regulating it. He lamented this 'transportation of issues from the realm of the factual into the legal mechanics' of the constitutional liberal state

(Kirchheimer 1928: 598). For Kirchheimer, labour law exemplified the negative consequences of juridification. He argued that the codification and regulation of labour law eventually weakened the working class because it lost the most devastating weapon in class struggle, the general strike. Later his critique was taken up by a number of German socio-legal scholars (Voigt 1980; Teubner 1985, 1987) and Habermas (1981). Habermas explicitly refers to Kirchheimer in his analysis of juridification and appears to share Kirchheimer's view, although in general his liberal perspective is at odds with the radicalism of Kirchheimer in the 1920s. Generally, these authors framed juridification in rather negative terms, although not all went as far as Teubner, who described it as an 'ugly affair' (Teubner 1985: 290).

This critique of juridification is echoed in recent studies of the post-colonial state in Africa. Comaroff and Comaroff (2006: 26) observe a similar trend in Africa, where 'conflicts once joined in parliaments, by means of street protests, mass demonstrations, and media campaigns, through labour strikes, boycotts, blockades and other instruments of assertion, tend more and more – if not only, or in just the same way everywhere – to find their way to the judiciary'. In Sierra Leone, the advent of international criminal justice has influenced discussions about the country's difficult past and future, redirecting attention from issues of social justice to retributive justice. The Special Court for Sierra Leone is therefore one aspect of a wider trend towards juridification of political and social issues that has not gone unnoticed by people in Sierra Leone, as the following sections will show.

TRANSITIONAL JUSTICE AND POPULAR OPINION IN SIERRA LEONE

While conducting fieldwork in 2009 I accompanied Raymond and several of his colleagues in five districts of Sierra Leone (Bombali and Tonkolili in the north, Kailahun, Kenema and Bo in the east) as they conducted their outreach activities. The audiences they encountered were usually polite but also highly critical of the court. The villagers who assembled in the court barry on that day in March 2009 when I accompanied Raymond to the village of Mukump Gbana were no exception.[1] Their criticisms broadly fell into two categories: first, several people

---

[1] A court barry is a roofed structure situated in the middle of a village or town housing the local court.

criticised the court for trying Issa Sesay, the former interim leader of the RUF, which had its headquarters in Makeni during the last two years of the war. They considered Sesay 'a good man'. To them, Sesay played a key role in bringing the decade-long civil war to an end by agreeing to disarm the combatants under his command. Secondly, several audience members criticised the court for spending money that could be used for the benefit of the general population, which had endured great suffering during the war but had not received any compensation. They echoed general complaints heard all across the country about poverty and the lack of development in terms of infrastructure, healthcare and education.

The audience in Mukump Gbana, as in the other villages I visited with the court's outreach officers, provided a perfect example of Stuart Hall's (2005) reception theory. The people who voiced their criticisms rejected the court's preferred reading of contributing to national reconciliation by bringing to justice 'those bearing greatest responsibility' for the crimes committed during the civil war. Instead, they proposed their own reading of a court they perceived as being deeply implicated in national power struggles and mainly serving foreign interests. Indeed, my informants outside the court referred to the court as a 'white man's show'. People also suspected the court of political partisanship and a regional bias in selecting specific individuals for prosecution. When confronted with the court's legalistic narrative they insisted on raising fundamental concerns about the politics of transitional justice in Sierra Leone and the problems of the retributive vision of justice espoused by the court's representatives. They demanded recognition and compensation and rejected the perpetrator-centred approach of the Special Court.

Audience reactions to the court's preferred reading put two positions in the academic debate into perspective. On the one hand, they challenge often taken for granted assumptions about a general demand for retributive justice in the regions affected by widespread violence and civil war. As Allen (2006) shows for Uganda, there are usually intense debates about how to deal with the violent past and whether punishment is the best option for what is known in German as *Vergangenheitsbewältigung* – coping with the past. On the other hand, my fieldwork in Sierra Leone relativises anthropological accounts that overgeneralise in their focus on cultural differences between African conceptions of justice and the Western model of criminal justice to explain the challenges faced by international criminal justice in Africa (Clarke 2009; Kelsall 2009).

Since the 1990s, ideas about transitional justice, humanitarianism and global legal order have gained widespread currency, informing the establishment of the *ad hoc* international criminal tribunals and a variety of other legal and quasi-legal mechanisms such as truth commissions and the *gacaca* courts in Rwanda. Generally, mainstream Western observers, academics, policymakers and journalists have tended to present these transitional justice mechanisms in a favourable light, deeming them instrumental in promoting the rule of law (Minow 1998; Bass 2000; Rotberg and Thompson 2000; Chuter 2003; Ambos *et al.* 2009). Recently, a more critical strand has emerged in academic (Hagan *et al.* 2006; Dembour and Kelly 2007; Simpson 2007) and popular writing (Moghalu 2006; Laughland 2008) questioning some of the fundamental assumptions driving the global movement for transitional justice and international criminal justice. In spite of this critique, most Western commentators and policymakers do not question the desirability of international criminal tribunals and other transitional justice mechanisms as principal agents in realising the vision of a global legal order that can be traced back to Kant's concept of Perpetual Peace (1795), although there is considerable debate about the question of what constitutes the best avenue to justice. Especially relevant for this chapter is the demand for reparations for victims, which is increasingly seen as key to the legitimacy of transitional justice institutions (Ferstman *et al.* 2009; Zenker, this volume).

Popular acceptance or legitimacy is deemed crucial for the success of these institutions. The proponents of transitional justice tend to present the level of popular support in a positive light, but closer examination reveals a much more ambiguous picture. Allen's study (2006), for example, highlights a heated political debate about the long-running conflict in northern Uganda. People's opinions ranged from the demand for an intervention by the International Criminal Court (ICC) to calls for so-called African reconciliation mechanisms such as the *gacaca* courts or neo-traditional reconciliation ceremonies. Haslam (2007) draws attention to the discontent and demands for justice voiced by civil society associations in Rwanda representing victims' interests. These organisations demanded compensation and support for victims, while the court's representatives argued that the court's mandate did not include compensation payments. Both studies show that popular support for international criminal tribunals in the regions affected by widespread violence cannot be taken for granted, and a serious analysis must unpack abstract categories such as the public, the population and the victim.

Officials at the Special Court for Sierra Leone, the only *ad hoc* international tribunal established in the same country where the crimes under adjudication were committed, have been keenly aware of the importance of public opinion for the court right from the beginning. Public opinion has played an important role in legitimising the court. Unlike the other international tribunals, the Special Court relies on voluntary contributions of UN member states, primarily the United States, Britain, Canada and the Netherlands. As a consequence, the court has been forced to acquire funding – often with great difficulty. In March 2007, Lovemore Munlo, the court's second registrar (2005–2007), described the court's financial situation as 'living from hand to mouth'. Frequently, the continuation of the trials was threatened by a lack of sufficient funding. Over the years, registrars, chief prosecutors and presidents of the Special Court frequently travelled to Western capitals and the United Nations to present the court's achievements and drum up financial support. High public approval rates in Sierra Leone were key to convincing governments to contribute to the court's budget. For instance, at a lecture at the influential British think-tank Chatham House, the court's third registrar, the Dutchman Herman von Hebel, cited the results of a survey of 10,000 people, in which '91 per cent of the respondents said that the court is contributing to peace and reconciliation in Sierra Leone' (Chatham House 2007). Statements such as these echo the rationale behind setting up the court. In 2000, the UN Secretary General stated in his report to the UN Security Council: 'As the Security Council itself has recognized, in the past circumstances of Sierra Leone, a credible system of justice and accountability for the very serious crimes committed there would contribute to the process of national reconciliation and to the restoration and maintenance of peace in that country' (UN 2000: 13).

It was well understood that the court could only realise these goals if it communicated effectively with the general public in Sierra Leone. Shortly after arriving in Sierra Leone in August 2002, the court's first chief prosecutor, the US military lawyer David Crane, and the first registrar, Robin Vincent, toured the country 'to establish rapport with the people of Sierra Leone' (Special Court for Sierra Leone (SCSL) 2006: 11). David Crane in particular went to great lengths to engage the public and 'held town hall meetings around the country', where he addressed audiences to explain the court's mandate and 'listen to the Sierra Leonean people, and to the extent possible, answer their questions' (SCSL 2004: 16). Crane and Vincent also quickly formed a Special Court Working Group with several civil society organisations that had been campaigning for an international criminal tribunal. The Special Court Working Group comprised representatives of Sierra Leonean and international NGOs, and held regular meetings with the registrar. This proved to be an effective means to keep in touch with the mainly Freetown-based Sierra Leonean NGO community and the international NGOs with a presence in the country. The support of these organisations was crucial. The Sierra Leonean NGOs acted as representatives of the general population and powerful conduits for public relations activities. The international NGOs, in turn, exercised considerable influence on public opinion in the countries providing financial support for the court.

In 2003, the registrar institutionalised the court's outreach activities and established the Outreach Section 'with the aim not only of ensuring that the purpose of the Special Court is understood across Sierra Leone, but also to grant to all sections of civil society in the country the opportunity to have their voices heard and their expectations of the court identified' (SCSL 2004: 6). According to its mission statement, the outreach section's task 'is to promote understanding of the Special Court and respect for human rights and the rule of law in Sierra Leone' (SCSL 2004: 1). According to representatives of the Special Court, the work of this department has been extremely successful in raising awareness about the court. It is presented as a model for other international tribunals such as the ICC. In each district the Outreach Section employed outreach officers who regularly visited villages, schools, police stations, army barracks and other locations. Following a set schedule and a work plan, they showed video recordings of the trials and conducted outreach events on the mandate and jurisdiction of the Special Court and on the general principles of international humanitarian law. Occasionally, more extensive events with expatriate senior staff of the court were held in the larger towns. Apart from these rare instances the court's expatriate staff were hardly ever confronted with these challenges to the legitimacy of the court, as they lived and worked in heavily fortified compounds and rarely interacted with ordinary Sierra Leoneans.

The outreach officers were locally recruited junior employees of the court who had not received any training in international law beyond a cursory introduction at the court's headquarters in Freetown. One or two of them were posted in each of the country's twelve district capitals, while events on the Freetown peninsula were conducted by the outreach section's headquarters in Freetown. All outreach officers were Sierra Leonean nationals, male (except for one woman, the outreach officer in Magburaka), and between the ages of 35 and 55. Most had an NGO background and experience in carrying out extension work. For example, three were former teachers and one was a self-appointed reverend and NGO activist. They were all highly educated (university or college) and had a fairly elite social background. All of them hailed from the respective district where they were based. This was a conscious decision by the management of the outreach section because the outreach officers were supposed to have an intimate knowledge of the district. They earned about US $600 per month excluding allowances, a handsome salary in Sierra Leone. All of them had been working for the court since 2004. By 2009, when I conducted fieldwork, their job had become less exciting than in the beginning when the Special Court captured the popular attention. The audiences they encountered on their tours through the districts had heard their presentations many times before, but refused to accept the court's official narrative of bringing justice to Sierra Leone, as the following section illustrates.

DIFFICULT ENCOUNTERS

In this section I present ethnographic evidence from two outreach events I observed during my fieldwork in 2009. The first one was the above-mentioned event in Mukump Gbana near Makeni, where I accompanied Raymond Kamara. The second was an outreach event in a village near Kenema, in the eastern part of the country. Both events were typical of the ordinary outreach events conducted by the outreach officers on their regular tours through their districts. They featured a brief introduction providing an update on the trials heard before the Special Court, followed by a question and answer session. Then the outreach officers showed a video with footage from the court hearings produced by the audio-visual department of the outreach section. This part of the outreach events constituted the main attraction, according to the outreach officers. These events usually lasted between one and two hours, and the outreach officers had to provide the TV set, the video recorder, a loudspeaker and a generator. Occasionally they also distributed leaflets and brochures about the work of the court and international humanitarian law. Both events were held in the village court barry in the afternoon when people were returning from their daily work.

Upon arriving in Mukump Gbana, we met the town chief, and Raymond rented a TV set and video recorder from the local trader who usually screened the popular mix of Nigerian soaps and war films. This was unusual as only a few villages had this kind of equipment available. The outreach officers had been equipped with a TV set, a video recorder, a loudspeaker and a generator, but it was cheaper for Raymond to travel to the village on his motorcycle and to rent the equipment there than to bring his equipment in a rented car. While the equipment was being set up, some children who had been watching a war film when we arrived quickly converged on the court barry, excited about the spectacle. Then the older men settled in on their chairs in the front row, and other men and women populated the rough wooden benches. Latecomers sat on the waist-high wall forming the enclosure of the barry. Conspicuous was the absence of young men, although soon after the event started a group of them gathered at some distance from the court building.

After an opening statement by the town chief and the customary prayer, Raymond took the floor and gave a brief update on the trials heard before the Special Court. Not counting children, there were about thirty adults gathered in and around the court barry, including those peeping in from the outside. Raymond gave his presentation in Krio, the creole language widely spoken in Sierra Leone, and the town chief translated into Temne, the local language. Like many of the younger generation belonging to the educated elite, Raymond's first language was Krio and his command of Temne was rather tenuous. His presentation followed the standardised script of introducing the court as an international criminal tribunal established to hold accountable those 'bearing greatest responsibility' (interestingly both Raymond and the town chief used the English phrase to add weight and authority to the court) for 'war crimes and crimes against humanity' (again in English, followed by the Krio phrase 'big crime').

Then he gave a cursory update on the trials, two of which had been concluded at the time. Three leaders of the Armed Forces Revolutionary Council (AFRC), a group of renegade soldiers who had toppled the government in 1997 and formed an alliance with the Revolutionary United Front (RUF), had been convicted in 2007 and were serving their prison sentences of fifty, fifty and forty-five years. Two leaders of the Civil Defence Forces (CDF) had been found guilty in 2007 and sentenced to six and eight years. In February 2008, however, the court's appeals chamber partly overturned the trial chamber's judgement and increased the sentences to fifteen and twenty years. Then he talked about the more recent trial against the leaders of the RUF. Just one week before our visit the trial chamber had found them guilty but had not passed sentences yet. He moved on to the trial against Charles Taylor, telling the assembled villagers that the prosecution had closed its case after calling ninety-one witnesses. When Raymond had finished it was time for the Q&A session. It should be noted that the Q&A session, like the entire outreach event, was highly regulated, and questions were asked in order of status. First those at the top of village society, the town chiefs, sub-chiefs and councillors, would ask questions. Then it was the educated people's turn, those who 'know book', to use the Krio phrase. Women would virtually never pose questions in public, with the notable exception of women holding political office. During the outreach event in Mukump Gbana only the chiefs and elders who sat in the front row asked questions.

The town chief and the sub-chiefs were surprisingly frank. The town chief criticised the court for putting Issa Sesay, the RUF's interim leader between 2000 and 2002, on trial. In the town chief's opinion, Sesay was a responsible commander and peacemaker who had ordered the RUF to disarm. The headman went on to say that the court should take Sesay's good conduct as RUF leader into account and let him go free. Many in the audience murmured assent and a few applauded. In response, Raymond stuck to the official narrative and pointed out that no one was above the law. Sesay might have done some good, he conceded, but as the top RUF commander he was responsible for numerous war crimes and crimes against humanity for which he had to be held accountable.

The chief's opinion was shared by the group of young men who had gathered at some distance from the court barry. I joined them after the Q&A to share a smoke. They were cautious at first, but they soon became more outspoken. They have fond memories of 'General Issa'. In Krio they explained to me that he enforced discipline among his troops and treated the civilians well: 'We General Issakam, no more looting, no more killing, no more raping. He do good things dem. I do good.' When I asked them what the court should do with Sesay, some of them said: 'Let him go free.' Another one said: 'Just give him five years of prison.' Raymond told me later that some of these young men had belonged to the RUF, which might explain their positive opinion of Issa Sesay. In fact, the RUF had a detachment posted in a hamlet just a mile down the road, and many villagers engaged in trade with them, provided accommodation, entered into personal relationships, did chores for them or otherwise interacted with them in various ways. This finding highlights the fact that experiences of the war may vary considerably and that extreme forms of violence were less common than is often assumed.

It has to be noted that these questions and comments are by no means 'representative' in a quantitative way, although they did reflect widely held views. The empirical material presented here is not an opinion poll, but constitutes 'the anthropology of publics', to use Niezen's term (2010). The strict village hierarchy structured the outreach events. Only those with high social status asked questions or made comments, while women, uneducated younger men and children virtually never spoke up. The important point for the purposes of this chapter is the fact that these questions were raised at all, that they were raised consistently at all outreach events I observed, and that they continued to be raised even after several years of villagers' exposure to such outreach activities. They were not questions to be answered in the sense of demanding information. The villagers were already relatively well-informed. The questions constituted a critique, a constant reminder of disappointment and an assertion of different needs.

It is noteworthy that the villagers were so positive about a rebel group that was notorious for its trademark atrocity, the amputation of limbs. At this point it is necessary to put the villagers' comments into context. As mentioned in the introduction, Makeni was the RUF headquarters between 1999 and 2002. During those years the RUF was preparing the transition to a post-conflict order. RUF personnel treated civilians much better than during the war, and, as I learned during my fieldwork there, many people had positive memories of that time. I was also surprised at the degree to which people identified with the RUF. This could hardly be explained only by the fact that the RUF had its headquarters in Makeni during the final years of the civil war. In fact, the identification with the RUF in many parts of northern Sierra Leone was more a comment on Sierra Leone's current political landscape than a reflection of historical facts. The 2002 elections were won by the Sierra Leone Peoples Party (SLPP), which traditionally has its main powerbase in the east and among the Mende ethnic group. Many northerners feared the SLPP and the Mende, accusing them of expanding their powerbase by marginalising other regions and ethnic groups, in particular the north and the Temne, the main ethnic group in the north. The victory of the SLPP coincided with the disarmament of the RUF in 2002 and the unsuccessful attempt of the RUF to transform itself into a political party. In fact, the RUF had been neutralised as a political force in 2000, when President Kabbah and Vice-President Berewa (both SLPP) dissolved the power-sharing agreement during the violent clashes of May 2000 (discussed in more detail below). The identification of the north with the RUF was further fuelled by the fact that the two principal leaders of the RUF at the end of the war, Issa Sesay and Foday Sankoh, came from the north and belonged to the Temne ethnic group, despite the fact that most RUF cadres actually hailed from the eastern part of Sierra Leone. The marginalisation of the RUF and the perceived marginalisation of the north after the 2002 elections fused with long-running complaints about the neglect of the north and its marginal position relative to the south-east and the capital, Freetown. As a consequence, the court's indictment against Sesay and two other RUF leaders was seen by many in the north as a political move and an attempt by the SLPP government to consolidate its grip on power.

Several chiefs and elders raised the issue of the enormous sums of money spent on the court and the prosecution of a mere dozen individuals. By Sierra Leonean standards the court was spending an exorbitant amount of money. It had an annual budget of roughly US $25 million. At the time of fieldwork a total sum of about US $150 million had been spent on the court, mainly contributed by Britain, the United States and Canada. The villagers were not informed of these exact numbers, but they knew that it was a lot of money. They argued that this money could have been better spent on development projects, the improvement of infrastructure, new schools or hospitals, rather than on punishing a few individuals. Their demands for compensation for the victims of the violence, as opposed to the punishment of the perpetrators, reflected the abject poverty of the overwhelming majority of the population. Sierra Leone is one of the poorest countries in the world. Healthcare is only poorly developed and has suffered from the civil war. Malaria is widespread and there have been frequent outbreaks of cholera, yellow fever and meningitis. Life expectancy is only forty-one years, and the country has one of the highest levels of child mortality and maternal mortality in the world. One of the younger chiefs demanded to know why the inmates of the Special Court's detention facility in Freetown were 'growing fat' on three meals a day and had electricity and satellite television while the villagers in Mukump Gbana were hungry. Instead, the money should be spent on them, the 'victimised' villagers, he said, using the English word.

Just how hard life in Mukump Gbana really was and how much it was focused on daily survival dawned on me when our discussions turned to the events of May 2000, when a violent incident at the nearby UN Disarmament, Demobilization and Reintegration (DDR) camp led to the abduction of hundreds of UN peacekeepers, the near collapse of the UN peacekeeping mission, violent clashes in Freetown and elsewhere, and a national political crisis. The villagers had fond memories of the Kenyan peacekeepers that were stationed there. The Kenyans provided employment for the villagers and bought various goods the villagers had to offer. The villagers had even nicknamed the DDR camp 'Poverty Done Go', which in Krio means 'the end of poverty'. In fact, they were still using this name for the camp even though it had been abandoned years ago. When the Kenyan UN peacekeepers were deployed to this area, locals developed personal ties with the peacekeepers, and when the DDR camp came under attack from RUF forces, the villagers helped the peacekeepers escape. It was striking that they associated the DDR camp with the improvement of the local economy and never referred to the disarmament process *per se* or the mission of the peacekeepers. Neither did they experience conflicting loyalties in their relations to the RUF and the Kenyans, as they framed them mainly in personal and economic terms. The villagers' memories of the DDR camp highlight the paramount importance of survival in an environment characterised by abject poverty and scarcity of resources. They criticised the Special Court for not responding to their demands for social or distributive justice and rejected the court's claim of political neutrality. To them the conviction of Issa Sesay and the other RUF commanders had to be seen in the context of the North's political and economic marginalisation since independence.

The other outreach event I would like to present in this chapter took place in a village about ten miles from Kenema, in the eastern part of Sierra Leone. The outreach officer in Kenema, Francis Nuni, was in his late fifties. He used to be a French teacher in one of the country's most prestigious secondary schools, the Bo School, originally set up in 1906 by the British colonial masters to educate the sons of the indigenous elite. In fact, he himself came from a ruling house in Bonthe district and was educated at Bo School. He was a member of the coalition of civil society groups that formed the Special Court Working Group in 2002, and had been working as an outreach officer since 2004.

In this village, Tissor, people's statements revealed the considerable regional differences in opinion about the trials heard before the Special Court. Right from the beginning opinions about the court were divided along regional and ethnic lines. The town chief in Tissor demanded to know why the court had indicted Sam Hinga Norman, who had defended their community against the rebels. Norman was an influential Mende traditional ruler who played a central role in forming the CDF and had emerged as its national coordinator. He had also served as deputy minister of defence (1996–2002) during the war and minister of internal affairs (2002–2003) in President Kabbah's cabinet. His arrest at the behest of the Special Court in March 2003 came as a surprise, and many Sierra Leoneans criticised the court for arresting a national hero who had defended the democratically elected government of President Kabbah against the rebels of the RUF and AFRC. The CDF was mainly associated with the *kamajors* of the Mende ethnic group in the south-east of the country and the SLPP, which ruled Sierra Leone from 1996 until 2007 (Hoffman 2007). According to a conspiracy theory with wide currency, it was suspected that the indictment against CDF leader Sam Hinga Norman was actually the result of a conspiracy within the SLPP to get rid of a political rival who enjoyed widespread popular support, especially in the SLPP's heartland. Francis explained that the area around Kenema had been a stronghold of the CDF, and the town chief and many men in Tissor had been members of the CDF. When Norman died in March 2007 while undergoing medical treatment in Senegal, the people in Kenema even accused Francis 'of having Sam Hinga Norman murdered'. When Sam Hinga Norman was buried in a village near Bo, he and the other outreach officers were called to the outreach head office in Freetown for their own safety. People in Kenema District were very disappointed about the convictions of the remaining two accused.

During outreach events in Bo and Kenema people in the audience would invariably ask why Sam Hinga Norman had been put on trial. Francis, who had heard the same criticism countless times over the years, responded with the official statement, 'in war there are laws', and reminded the villagers of the Nuremberg trials against German war criminals. He explained that all factions in the Sierra Leonan civil war had committed crimes and that no one, not even those defending the country, was above the law. The issue, Francis stated, was 'how you fight the war', and one of the basic rules of international humanitarian law stated that civilians should not be attacked. The town chief clearly was not satisfied with this answer, although he must have heard it before.

With regard to one issue the villagers in Tissor and Mukump Gbana were in absolute agreement: the money spent on the court should have been used for development projects and the compensation of victims. One of the sub-chiefs said the court should pay compensation to the victims. The white man – and here he looked at me – should bring education, healthcare and good roads. 'Yes, them guilty,' he said, 'but let them go'. To my mind, this comment put the issue of justice in a wider perspective. From the perspective of this man and many others the international community should not spend money on realising a vision of retributive justice. What they demanded was recognition of their suffering. Indeed, the advocates of transitional justice asserted that recognition of the victims' suffering was one of the aims of the Special Court, but for the local villagers suffering did not begin or end with the war. For them suffering meant abject poverty and endemic illness. As a consequence, they called for development in very concrete terms such as building schools, hospitals and a tarmac road, and improving the water supply.

Francis explained that justice does not have a price tag and that the court contributed to national reconciliation by punishing those 'bearing greatest responsibility' for the crimes committed during the civil war. He defended the court (and himself), noting that Sierra Leonans should be grateful to the international community for the Special Court. Obviously fed up with this line of questioning, he somewhat lamely concluded that it was the decision of the international community to spend the money on a court rather than other things.

These and other questions were a source of anxiety for Francis. In private he admitted that 'often I don't know how to answer their questions', and that 'they make you sweat'. In general, villagers were the most difficult audience for him because they were 'illiterate' and it was 'difficult to explain those things to them'. He preferred outreach events with more educated audiences such as police officers and soldiers. Francis's statements reflected a certain ambivalence. On the one hand, he felt far superior to them because he was educated while they were 'illiterate'. 'Here', he told me, 'I personify the court'. On the other hand, he felt exposed and vulnerable: 'I have no office. Here everybody can approach me.' Although he was never physically threatened and was well-known in the area, he experienced constant anxiety because the general attitude toward the court was hostile.

After the Q&A, which had lasted about fifteen minutes, Francis's assistant started the video, the show's highlight. Here we were in the village court, a basic structure with a zinc roof, a few rough wooden benches and chairs, villagers loitering around and half-naked children huddling in front while the generator supplying the electricity was rattling outside and we peered through a telescope in which the sterile high-tech courtroom in Freetown materialised. We could see Moses Blah, former Liberian vice-president, under direct examination by the prosecutor, who had called him as a witness. Blah's questioning was conducted in English. This was no exception. The outreach office was supposed to dub all tapes into Krio but managed to do so only with a few. In any case, the sound quality was poor and the voices were difficult to understand because of the noise and the bad quality of the speaker. Francis stopped the tape several times and briefly explained what Blah had said, but he did not contextualise the statement in relation to the trial against Charles Taylor, nor did he explain whether Blah was a prosecution witness or a defence witness and how his testimony fitted into the case against Taylor. Taylor, former warlord and Liberian president between 1997 and 2002, was accused of supporting the RUF in neighbouring Sierra Leone. He was arrested in March 2006 and stood trial before the Special Court between 2008 and 2011. Unfortunately I was not able to check what the villagers made of it, but perhaps it was not really important to know exactly when Blah had testified and why.

Observing this event and others, it occurred to me that outreach events were not primarily about conveying information. Echoing Marshall McLuhan's 'the medium is the message', the act of 'reaching out' to the population itself was the message conveyed by the court. Of course, the outreach officers did provide information about the court and the trials to the audiences they encountered. The information was usually limited to the basic facts, such as how many witnesses had testified, when the defence case would begin or the number of counts the accused had been charged with. Sometimes a particular count was emphasised, such as forced marriage in Mukump Gbana, but the explanation provided by Raymond was so summary that it would have been impossible for anyone to understand what constituted forced marriage under international criminal law. Instead of explaining what forced marriage was and why it was a crime under international humanitarian law, he merely stated that this was the first time ever an international criminal tribunal had convicted someone for this specific crime. It appeared to me that it was often difficult to actually grasp what the outreach officers were saying. They themselves were often at a loss and some, like Francis, experienced considerable anxiety because of this. They all had an elite background and their Krio, Mende or Temne was rife with English expressions and legal terms. Often the outreach officers focused on legal findings and the court's mandate. Rarely if ever did they mention the court's factual findings or contextualise the screenings of witnesses' testimonies.

These observations should by no means imply that the villagers were ignorant or refused to be 'educated', as several of the outreach officers complained. Quite the contrary; generally the officers met well-informed audiences who were keen to discuss fundamental questions about justice or the court's relation to the national political landscape, but invariably they were provided with the standard script of a court that does justice, that no one was above the law and that the court only focused on a small number of individuals. These explanations failed to address their concerns and needs.

CONCLUSIONS

Based on my reading of Habermas's and Kirchheimer's critiques of juridification I argue that people in Sierra Leone were in fact challenging the official discourse on transitional justice and its focus on retribution by demanding social or distributive justice instead. The outreach events were one of the few opportunities where people could directly engage with the discrepancies between their ideas about justice and the court's vision of retributive justice. Usually, development agencies, international organisations and government officials succeeded in separating these issues, drawing a clear dividing line between development and criminal justice. Drawing on Kirchheimer's critique of juridification, I argue that this separation was the result of the removal of debates about Sierra Leone's violent past from the political sphere into the ambit of international criminal law. Issues such as power relations, the accountability of political leaders and inequality were depoliticised by framing them in terms of individual criminal responsibility.

The outreach officers struggled to answer the audiences' critical questions and comments, but did not succeed in convincing them. When challenged, outreach officers would stick to the official script, invoking the court's limited jurisdiction and the scope of international criminal justice, which did not include development or social justice. Of course, these answers were absolutely legitimate – a court of law is not a development agency and a trial is primarily an instrument to establish the guilt or innocence of the accused – but it was striking that people who had been exposed to these outreach events for several years continued to insist on raising issues of distributive justice and reminding the court of its failure to address their elementary concerns. They responded to the court's claim to bring justice and the rule of law to Sierra Leone by taking this claim seriously and reminding the court's representatives of the original promises to bring justice and contribute to reconciliation. Confronted with this stubbornness, the outreach officers were exasperated and complained about 'impolite' or 'uncivilised' villagers who simply didn't understand these complex issues and refused to be 'educated' or 'sensitised'.

While it is true that the outreach officers were not trained in law and did not have the necessary cultural skills to translate highly complex legal issues into the vernacular languages, I do not think that the real problem lay there. The questions were simply not answerable for them because they transcended legal formalities such as the scope of the court's jurisdiction and its rules of procedure. It seems to me that people in Sierra Leone had a keen eye for the contradictions of the humanitarian project of international criminal justice in practice. They stubbornly insisted on questioning the politics of the court, situating it within the national political landscape and relating it to the influence of the white man, the donor agencies and foreign governments. This demonstrates that for them transitional justice was not about fuzzy concepts such as national reconciliation or the symbolic punishment of a few individuals, but about concrete development in their communities, including roads, schools, hospitals, clean water, electricity and, above all, employment.

It should be noted that the Special Court's outreach events constituted just one facet of the plethora of sensitisation workshops and activities aimed at inducing behavioural change conducted every day in Sierra Leone and elsewhere in the global South. They appear strangely devoid of any substance but serve to bring peace to the humanitarians' troubled conscience. The trials heard before the Special Court operated as spectacles of justice, dramas or 'secular rituals' in Moore's and Myerhoff's terms (1977), aimed at projecting an image of justice being done and effecting a sense of closure in the audience, the citizens of Sierra Leone and other places where such courts operated. In other words, they were manifestations of juridification in the field of international criminal law. Kirchheimer's critique of juridification allows one to interrogate the darker sides of projects such as international criminal justice, taking seriously the fundamental critique formulated by ordinary Sierra Leoneans and their demands for distributive justice and development, which tend to be eclipsed by official representations of transitional justice and the spectacles of justice being done.

References

Allen, Tim 2006. *Trial Justice: The International Criminal Court and the Lord's Resistance Army.* London: Zed Books.

Ambos, Kai, Large, Judith and Wierda, Marieke (eds.) 2009. *Building a Future on Peace and Justice Studies on Transitional Justice, Conflict Resolution and Development. The Nuremberg Declaration on Peace and Justice.* Berlin: Springer Verlag.

Bass, Gary J. 2000. *Stay the Hand of Vengeance: The Politics of War Crimes Tribunals*. Princeton University Press.

Chatham House 2007. *The Special Court and How It Will End*. Summary of the Chatham House International Law Discussion Group Meeting, 9 July.

Chuter, David 2003. *War Crimes: Confronting Atrocity in the Modern World*. Boulder, CO: Lynne Rienner.

Clarke, Kamari M. 2009. *Fictions of Justice: The International Criminal Court and the Challenge of Legal Pluralism in Sub-Saharan Africa*. Cambridge University Press.

Comaroff, John L. and Comaroff, Jean 2006. 'Law and disorder in the post-colony: an introduction', in Jean Comaroff and John L. Colmaroff (eds.) *Law and Disorder in the Postcolony*. Chicago University Press, pp. 1–56.

Dembour, Marie-Bénédicte and Kelly, Tobias (eds.) 2007. *Paths to International Justice: Social and Legal Perspectives*. Cambridge University Press.

Dezaley, Yves and Garth, Bryant G. (eds.) 2002a. *Global Prescriptions: The Production, Exportation, and Importation of a New Legal Orthodoxy*. Ann Arbor: University of Michigan Press.

2002b. 'From the Cold War to Kosovo: the rise and renewal of international human rights', *Annual Review of Law and Social Science* 2: 231–55.

Eckert, Julia 2006. 'From subject to citizens: legalism from below and the homogenisation of the legal sphere', *Journal of Legal Pluralism* 53/54: 45–75.

Ferstman, Carla, Goetz, Mariana and Stephens, Alan (eds.) 2009. *Reparations for Victims of Genocide, War Crimes and Crimes against Humanity: Systems in Place and Systems in the Making*. Leiden: Martinus Nijhoff Publishers.

Goodale, Mark and Merry, Sally E. (eds.) 2007. *The Practice of Human Rights: Tracking Law between the Global and the Local*. Cambridge University Press.

Habermas, Jürgen 1981. *Theorie des kommunikativen Handelns, Band 2: Zur Kritik der funktionalistischen Vernunft*. Frankfurt am Main: Suhrkamp. Translated as Jürgen Habermas 1987. *The Theory of Communicative Action*, vol. 2: *Lifeworld and System: A Critique of Functionalist Reason*. Boston: Beacon Press.

Hagan, John, Levi, Ron and Ferrales, Gabrielle 2006. 'Swaying the hand of justice: the internal and external dynamics of regime change at the international criminal tribunal for the former Yugoslavia', *Law and Social Inquiry* 31: 585–616.

Hall, Stuart 2005. 'Encoding/decoding', in Stuart Hall, Dorothy Hobson, Andrew Lowe and Paul Willis (eds.) *Culture, Media, Language: Working Papers in Cultural Studies, 1972–1979*. London: Routledge, pp. 117–27.

Haslam, Emily 2007. 'Law, civil society and contested justice at the international criminal tribunal for Rwanda', in Marie-Bénédicte Dembour and Tobias

Kelly (eds.) *Paths to International Justice: Social and Legal Perspectives.* Cambridge University Press, pp. 57–82.

Hoffman, Danny 2007. 'The meaning of a militia: understanding the civil defence forces of Sierra Leone', *African Affairs* 106: 639–62.

Kant, Immanuel 1795. *Perpetual Peace: A Philosophical Sketch.* Königsburg: Nicolovius.

Kelsall, Tim 2009. *Culture under Cross-Examination: International Justice and the Special Court for Sierra Leone.* Cambridge University Press.

Kirchheimer, Otto 1928. 'Zur Staatslehre des Sozialismus und Bolschewismus', *Zeitschrift für Politik* 17: 592–611.

Laughland, John 2008. *A History of Political Trials from Charles I to Saddam Hussein.* Oxfordshire: Peter Lang.

Merry, Sally E. 2006. *Human Rights and Gender Violence: Translating International Law into Local Justice.* Chicago University Press.

Minow, Martha 1998. *Between Vengeance and Forgiveness: Facing History after Genocide and Mass Atrocities.* Boston: Beacon Press.

Moghalu, Kingsley C. 2006. *Global Justice: The Politics of War Crimes Trials.* Westport, CT: Praeger.

Moore, Sally F. and Myerhoff, Barbara G. 1977. 'Introduction. Secular ritual: forms and meaning', in Sally F. Moore and Barbara G. Myerhoff (eds.) *Secular Ritual.* Assen: Van Gorcum, pp. 3–24.

Niezen, Ronald 2010. *Public Justice and the Anthropology of Law.* Cambridge University Press.

Robertson, Geoffrey 2006. *Crimes against Humanity: The Struggle for Global Justice*, 3rd edn. London: Penguin Books.

Rotberg, Robert I. and Thompson, Dennis (eds.) 2000. *Truth v. Justice: The Morality of Truth Commissions.* Princeton University Press.

Santos, Boaventura de Sousa and César A. Rodríguez-Garavito (eds.) 2005. *Law and Globalisation from Below: Towards a Cosmopolitan Legality.* Cambridge University Press.

Simpson, Gerry J. 2007. *Law, War and Crime: War Crimes Trials and the Reinvention of International Law.* Cambridge: Polity Press.

Special Court for Sierra Leone 2004. *First Annual Report of the President of the Special Court for Sierra Leone for the Period 2 December 2002–2001 December 2003.* Freetown: Special Court for Sierra Leone.

2006. *Special Court Outreach Report 2003–2005.* Freetown: Special Court for Sierra Leone.

Teubner, Gunther (ed.) 1985. 'Verrechtlichung – Begriffe, Merkmale, Grenzen, Auswege', in Friedrich Kübler (ed.) *Verrechtlichung von Wirtschaft, Arbeit und sozialer Solidarität.* Frankfurt am Main: Suhrkamp, pp. 289–344.

1987. *Juridification of Social Spheres: A Comparative Analysis in the Areas of Labor, Corporate, Antitrust and Social Welfare Law.* Berlin: Walter de Gruyter.

United Nations 2000. *Report of the Secretary-General on the Establishment of a Special Court for Sierra Leone*. 4 October, S/2000/915.

Voigt, Rüdiger (ed.) 1980. *Verrechtlichung. Analysen zu Funktion und Wirkung von Parlamentarisierung, Bürokratisierung und Justizialisierung sozialer, politischer und ökonomischer Prozesse*. Königsstein: AthenäumVerlag.

CHAPTER 5

THE JURIDIFICATION OF POLITICAL PROTEST AND THE POLITICISATION OF LEGALISM IN SOUTH AFRICAN LAND RESTITUTION

Olaf Zenker

INTRODUCTION

The development of apartheid in South Africa was closely related to state laws regulating access to land. Since the Natives Land Act (1913), successive legislations not only engendered massive land dispossessions, but also provided the basis for 'racial' segregation, on which the ideology of 'separate development' could build. It is, therefore, not surprising that with the end of apartheid, the legal process of restituting land rights, in the course of which the new South African state compensates former victims of 'racial' land dispossession, has been crucial in terms of both alleviating poverty and restoring justice. The transition towards a legitimate new form of governance has thereby been marked by a pronounced shift towards a substantively understood rule of law, on the one hand, and the juridification of former protest against apartheid's landed policies that is embedded in it, on the other. In this

I am grateful to the Berne University Research Foundation for financially supporting the ethnographic fieldwork on which this text is based. During my stays in South Africa, the Departments of Anthropology at the University of the Witwatersrand, Johannesburg, and the University of South Africa (UNISA), Pretoria, provided me with welcoming and inspiring research environments. Earlier versions of this text were presented in 2010 at the workshop 'Law against the State' at the Max Planck Institute for Social Anthropology, Halle/Germany, and the research seminar of the Institute of Social Anthropology at the University of Bern, Switzerland. Apart from helpful comments by various participants on these occasions, the text further benefitted from critical interventions by Zerrin Özlem Biner, John Comaroff, Brian Donahoe, Julia Eckert, Henk Smith, Christian Strümpell and Julia Zenker. Needless to say, all factual mistakes and argumentative weaknesses that remain are mine.

sense, the post-apartheid government has used new laws – especially the Restitution of Land Rights Act (1994) – to undo the political injustices committed by the old state.

With regard to the transition towards a legitimate new form of governance, three interlinked arenas can be distinguished: first, the interface between international politics, where 'the rule of law' is demanded as the acceptable mode for 'behaving' like a state, and national ways of doing politics; second, the national terrain of land restitution, which is framed by new constitutional and other legal arrangements; and third, the micro-level of concrete land struggles, where local actors make variable usage of 'rules of law' to further their interests in land. In this chapter, I will follow these interconnected settings by first showing how apartheid's 'rule *by* law' came to be transformed into a 'substantive rule of "good" law' – in other words, how political values of the anti-apartheid protest became enshrined in the legal foundations of the successor state. In a second step, I will describe the parallel emergence of the specific legal framework affecting land restitution, in which law amendments, policy shifts and additional legislations have provided changing orientations for both administrators and claimants in the struggle over land. This is exemplified in a third step, in which the case of the Kalkfontein communities is presented, who over the past decades have used various political and legal means against the South African state to restore their land ownership. Most recently, this has also entailed their successful constitutional challenge to the Communal Land Rights Act (2004) that, had it been enacted, would yet again have threatened the security of their tenure. Having traced this exemplary struggle for land within a shifting terrain of international relations, national land policies and profoundly transformed legal arrangements, the chapter concludes with a reflection on some theoretical implications of South African land restitution for the juridification of political protest and the politicisation of legalism.

THE TRANSNATIONAL REGIME OF RULES OF LAW AND THE SOUTH AFRICAN TRANSITION

In his overview of the history, politics and theory of the rule of law, Brian Tamanaha (2004: 1–3) starts with the observation that 'the rule of law' constitutes the most important political ideal today: it represents an orthodoxy in the liberal West, while being exported by the World Bank and IMF as a condition for financial assistance to 'the Rest', where the apparent unanimity of its support by leaders from a broad spectrum of systems is unparalleled in history. By now, it seems, 'adherence to the rule of law is an accepted measure worldwide of government legitimacy' (Tamanaha 2004: 3); it provides a discourse of self-legitimation in a world that is increasingly preoccupied with what Jean and John Comaroff call the 'fetishism of the law' (Comaroff and Comaroff 2006: 22, 2009: 32–40).

Rather than reconstructing an intellectual history of this notion from its origins in Western antiquity, I will here merely engage with a brief analytic elaboration of different types of 'rules of law', functioning as a backdrop for the subsequent discussion of shifts in the South African transition from apartheid to its current state of legality. There is no shortage of alternative definitions of 'rule of law'. Nevertheless, many theorists distinguish between 'formal' and 'substantive' conceptions (e.g. Summers 1993; Craig 1997), which are regularly equated, respectively, with 'thinner' and 'thicker' definitions of the rule of law (Tamanaha 2009: 4). Another approach is taken by Brian Tamanaha, who cross-tabulates formal and substantive approaches with three variants in terms of increasing comprehensiveness, leaving him with six distinct forms (Tamanaha 2004: 91). For the purposes of this paper, however, a tripartite distinction will be sufficient, which, according to degree of thickness, differentiates between 'the rule by law', 'the formal rule of law' and 'the substantive rule of "good" law'.

The 'rule by law' constitutes the thinnest version of the rule of law. It is based on nothing more than the notion 'that whatever a government does, it should do it through laws' (Reynolds 1989: 3). As Tamanaha (2004: 92–93) observes, when ruling by law the state thus simply uses the law as the means to conduct its affairs without, however, being itself limited by the law. As Joseph Raz (1979: 213) cynically notes, such a definition of the rule of law ultimately amounts to 'an empty tautology, not a political ideal'. By contrast, the somewhat thicker 'formal rule of law' is crucially defined on the one hand by the fact that the government itself is limited by law. Such legal limitations on government consist in two norms: first, that state officials must themselves abide by the currently valid positive law; and second, that governments' law-making power is itself legally restrained – whether by natural, divine or customary law, constitutional bills of rights or human rights declarations. This is typically ensured by a sufficiently independent judiciary (Tamanaha 2004: 93–99, 114–19; Palombella 2009). On the other hand, this variant of the rule of law also entails the related concept of 'formal legality', i.e. the minimal requirements that 'law must be set forth in advance (be pro-spective), be made public, be general, be clear, be stable and certain, and be applied to everyone according to its terms' (Tamanaha 2009: 3).

While adherence to the formal rule of law prevents completely arbi-trary discretion by the state, this variant ultimately remains silent about the actual content of the law. In the absence of any separate criteria of what constitutes good or just law, the formal rule of law is thus quite compatible with ruthless, authoritarian regimes as long as they fulfil its formal requirements. It is with regard to this problem that the third and thickest version of the rule of law can be defined: 'the substantive rule of "good" law' incorporates the elements of the formal variant (comprising, in turn, the rule *by* law) but adds vari-ous content specifications. These usually include fundamental rights (typically individual ones), democracy and/or other criteria of justice such as substantive equality. The obvious problem with such substan-tive approaches consists in the fact that there is no uncontroversial way to determine the content of 'good' laws; they necessarily remain deeply contestable in meaning and reach (Tamanaha 2004: 102–13; Tamanaha 2009: 4).

With regard to the former South African state, it has been widely noted that 'the infrastructure of apartheid – an administrative night-mare more complex and bureaucratic than the combined tax code, crim-inal law, regulatory apparatus, and welfare system of most countries – was constructed out of law' (Abel 1995: 13), requiring 'a quite extraordinary degree of state planning' (Crush and Jeeves 1993: 359) and legislation. State officials frequently boasted about the government's respect for the rule of law and the great reputation of its impartial judiciary (Abel 1995: 2–3, 12–13). However, seen in the light of the above distinction between various types of the rule of law, apartheid South Africa arguably exhib-ited merely the thinnest form, i.e. the rule *by* law. To begin with, the South African parliament was expressly supreme, unconstrained by a bill of rights, an unwritten constitution or natural law, and to a great extent exempted from independent judicial review (Abel 1995: 3, 489, 540). As the government could thus change the law at will, this arrange-ment violated the first criterion of the formal rule of law, namely that governments' law-making power be itself legally restrained. Furthermore, apartheid legislation repeatedly violated the criterion of formal legality. Abel (1995) provides countless examples in which the legislature vali-dated laws that had been successfully challenged in the Supreme Court and/or the Appellate Division either by retroactively changing these laws or – even more bizarrely – by retroactively ruling that the violated law had to be treated as if it had been followed. Yet, as Tamanaha (2004: 97) dryly observes, 'a retroactive rule is an oxymoron' and incompatible with the formal rule of law. Given the frequent changes to and additions of new laws with far-reaching consequences for the population (a considerable part of which had been denaturalised), the requirements of the formal rule of law (i.e. that laws have to be sufficiently clear, stable and certain) were arguably violated as well.

The negotiated revolution (Waldmeir 1997) in South Africa in the early 1990s thus began with the apartheid state under the rule *by* law. This was to be profoundly transformed through the adoption of the current Constitution of the Republic of South Africa (1996) into a new state under the substantive rule of 'good' laws as entrenched in an extensive bill of rights and with an independent judiciary (including a strong constitutional court) under the auspices of a new constitutional, rather than parliamentary, supremacy. Heinz Klug (2000) describes in detail how this shift towards strong constitutionalism ultimately came about. A commitment to constitutionalism and a bill of rights had been a tradition within the anti-apartheid movement before, as is most notably demonstrated by the adoption of the Freedom Charter in 1955 by the Congress of the People. In 1988 the African National Congress (ANC) also published its *Constitutional Guidelines for a Democratic South Africa*, expressing openness to a negotiated solution and assuring the world of its dedication to constitutionalism. This document subsequently formed the basis of the Harare Declaration by the Organisation of African Unity in 1989, which was later adopted by the UN General Assembly and specified the minimal conditions for a negotiated constitution acceptable to the international community (Klug 1996: 2–11). During the late 1980s the apartheid government likewise started to publicly explore the possibilities of a bill of rights and constitutionalism, eventually producing an Interim Report on Group and Human Rights (1991) by the South African Law Commission (Klug 1996: 2–12).

However, Klug (2000) suggests that the ultimate form of strong constitutionalism was also heavily conditioned by international pressures on all local stakeholders to accept such a constitutional solution, as well as by practical necessities emerging from stalemates during the negotiation process. By acknowledging and thereby postponing disputes to be resolved by future legislation and, if necessary, by an impartial judiciary, constitutionalism offered a viable strategy for containing differences concerning, for instance, the degree of state centralism vs. federalism (even political self-determination for minorities), individual vs. group rights (including the role of traditional authorities and customary law), and the protection of property vs. the demand to address past 'racial' dispossession through restitution. It is against the backdrop of this new constitutional supremacy that the ongoing South African land restitution process, with its persistent reference to 'the rule of law', needs to be seen. As the former Minister for Agriculture and Land Affairs, Ms Lulama Xingwana, aptly put it (Commission on Restitution of Land Rights 2007: 4), it is a process essentially concerned with 'putting land rights into the right hands under the rule of law'.

THE NATIONAL ARENA OF LAND RESTITUTION: THE JURIDIFICATION OF ANTI-APARTHEID PROTEST

It is hardly surprising today that the adherence to the rule of law should be routinely invoked in the context of South African land restitution in order to reassure both current and future landholders within the country, as well as the international community at large, especially given the next-door example of Zimbabwean land redistribution since 2000. There a decisive policy shift at the turn of the new millennium has reconceptualised the repossession of land as a purely political and expressly non-legal issue, entailing a liberation from restrictions imposed by 'the rule of law' (Hellum and Derman 2004: 1789–94). In other words, the policy shift in Zimbabwe has led to the political control of land redistribution merely *by* law rather than, as before, within a regime of substantive rule *of* law. That the situation with regard to land restitution in South Africa would ultimately be considerably different from this scenario in Zimbabwe, drawing instead on a strictly juridified market-based approach under the rule of law (see below) as a means of returning dispossessed land to its former owner(s), was not at all clear at the outset of the transitional negotiations.

As Cherryl Walker (2008: 50–51) observes, the history of race-based land dispossession had always occupied a prominent position in the ANC's understanding of the liberation struggle. For decades, land activists in and around the ANC had politically protested, legally fought and meticulously documented the race-based dispossessions of land and forced removals, involving an estimated 3.5 million blacks between 1960 and 1983 (Platzky and Walker 1985: 10; Abel 1995: 385–522; James

2007: 7.[1] However, Klug – who was involved in the ANC's internal Land Commission at that time – recalls the low priority rural issues actually had on the mainly urban-based ANC political agenda during the late 1980s, despite the latter's general rhetoric highlighting the land question (Klug 2000: 125). While many within the ANC cadre at that time still assumed that a future land reform would prominently entail a politically endorsed nationalisation of existing land holdings, senior ANC policy makers were apparently already starting to look critically at such socialist approaches. According to Walker (2008: 51–52), an emergent scepticism towards state farms in other socialist countries, growing fears about the potential destruction of the commercial agricultural sector and mounting pressures by the international and South African business lobby favouring market-led reforms, as well as worries about an ensuing massive capital flight from the country, all combined to tip the balance towards an approach that increasingly favoured enshrining land rights and the right to redress in the constitutional bill of rights. In addition, the actual process of negotiating the transition to democracy

> led to further moderation of its [the ANC's] land reform proposals. This was consistent with the organisation's general shift to the political centre as it turned its attention from fighting a liberation struggle towards fashioning substantive economic policies that could 'win consensual endorsement'. Once back in South Africa, furthermore, key members of the ANC's land desk concluded that a radical programme of land nationalisation was unlikely to find much support among rural communities, who yearned for tenure security and harboured deep suspicions of 'government' as an unaccountable, untrustworthy force.
>
> (Walker 2008: 53)

Against the backdrop of the ANC's general preoccupation with urban-industrial issues and the strong emphasis on property rights by the still ruling National Party (NP), especially concerning agricultural land, land reform developed into a matter of strategic compromise (Walker 2008: 54). Although prolonged and intense debates around these issues were still to complicate the negotiations leading, first, to the Interim Constitution of 1993 (Chaskalson 1994: 131–32; 1995), and then to the

---

[1] I use the conventions of African, Indian, coloured, black (as inclusive of the previous three categories) and white to describe the different social groups that were identified as 'distinct' under the apartheid system, while acknowledging, of course, the dilemma that the inevitable usage of these socially constructed terms might reinforce their alleged 'reality' as biologically predetermined categories.

current Constitution of the Republic of South Africa of 1996, a balanced constitutional protection of both property rights and the right to redress for racially based violations of past property rights thus emerged as the likely, and ultimately the actual, outcome (Klug 2000: 124–36; Spitz and Chaskalson 2000: 313–29; Walker 2008: 50–69).

Let me now turn to the content of those legislative acts that eventually came to regulate the juridified restitution of land rights under the new rule of law. Section 25(7) of the current constitution stipulates that a person or community dispossessed of property after 1913 as a result of past 'racially' discriminatory laws or practices is entitled, to the extent provided by an act of parliament, either to restitution of that property or to equitable redress. The act of parliament in question – the Restitution of Land Rights Act (1994) – defined the legal framework for the actual restitution process and established the 'Commission on Restitution of Land Rights', including the 'Chief Land Claims Commissioner' and the 'Regional Land Claims Commissioners', and the 'Land Claims Court' as its key players. The end of December 1998 was established as the cut-off date for lodging claims. The subsequent examination of claims by the commission ultimately validated about 80,000 claims as legitimate and in need of resolution. Since then, commission bureaucrats have mediated between claimants and (usually) white landowners in order to settle on a largely market-oriented agreement whereby the state buys the land and, based on certain conditions, hands it over to the claimants.

Originally, the Land Claims Court was established to grant restitution orders for all cases and to determine the conditions that must be met before land rights can be restored. However, owing to the slow process of handling claims, amendments to the restitution act have been made, shifting the approach from a judicial to an administrative one in 1999. Now the minister, and by delegation the land claims commissioners, have the power to facilitate and conclude settlements by agreement, and only claims that cannot be resolved this way take the judicial route through the Land Claims Court. This also entails the possibility of expropriation – an option that is also constitutionally enshrined (Hellum and Derman 2009: 128–31).

Based on figures from 2011, there are still about 5 per cent of restitution claims (i.e. 3,673 cases) that remain outstanding (Department of Rural Development and Land Reform 2011: 40). These cases are typically quite complex and present numerous challenges. Yet it is not only the outstanding restitution claims that continue to be haunted by many problems, but also the officially 'resolved' cases. To begin with, restitution is only one subcategory within the overarching tripartite land reform policy, which aims for the transfer of 30 per cent of agricultural land into the hands of black agriculturalists. While this goal was originally projected to be reached by 2014, the Department of Rural Development and Land Reform (formerly the Department of Land Affairs) has recently acknowledged that 2025 might be a more realistic target date (Walker 2008: 200; Zigomo 2010). Besides the *restitution* of land to former rights holders, the second policy subdivision of *redistribution* is aimed at people who have never previously had secure claims to landed property, and is designed to enable them to pool settlement grants provided by the state and buy their own farms. Finally, *tenure reform* is 'aimed to safeguard the rights of residents of white farms and state land in the former homelands. It was designed to protect poor people from summary eviction by securing their existing rights, or buy alternative land on which they could live' (James 2006: 247; see also James 2007: 8). Given that the land reform is strongly centred on the protection of *private property*, even when concerned with communal land, these three approaches sometimes come into conflict. This is especially the case with regard to current farm workers on white farms, who are meant to be protected by tenure reform, while their tenure on subsequently restituted farms often continues to be highly insecure (James 2006, 2007; Hellum and Derman 2009).

Within restituted farms difficulties have also persisted, and are addressed by the administration by continuously changing and adapting the conditions that must be met by claimants before land rights can be restored. Based on the Communal Property Associations Act (1996), claimants often have to form a legal entity, with a constitution regulating issues pertaining to fair and equal membership and decision making, which then becomes the owner of the land. These 'Communal Property Associations' (CPAs) elect their own committees that actually run the farms. In the context of extensive agricultural 'de-skilling' throughout the apartheid era of the very people who now own the land, and without substantial state funding, these CPAs have often proven to be quite dysfunctional. This has also been the case because committee members have often come from the ranks of the local elite, who do not necessarily reside on the land, but rather live and work in remote urban areas. Their negligence often results in inefficient management and can lead to the deterioration of the farms and cause new conflicts within claimant communities. Ambiguities of proclaimed gender and status equality in the context of persistent local hierarchies, often based on chieftaincies, have further made problematic the CPA approach (James 2006, 2007; Hellum and Derman 2009).

Another approach of the commission has consisted of propagating the establishment of a trust-style legal entity that facilitates decisive action. Within this model, the communal property is often conceptualised as an asset, owned by the trust, which members must lease by paying a monthly rent. While this approach has implemented some safeguards against 'tragedy of the commons'-type scenarios, it has continued to be problematic as it is based on the inappropriate assumption that every local can afford to pay rent on a regular basis. Furthermore, there continues to be a shortage of managerial and organisational skills, leading to problems with the day-to-day running of the farms (James 2006, 2007; Hellum and Derman 2009).

In recent years, the state has also increasingly embraced a new 'strategic partnership' model, especially with regard to huge and highly productive commercial farms, in order to ensure that the restituted farms continue to bear fruit:

> Under the strategic partnership model, the claimant community, organized in a communal property association or a trust, takes outright ownership of the land, which is directly transferred to it on the following conditions: that the community cannot sell or mortgage the land, and that the community (a) forms an operating company with the strategic partner to run the farm, and (b) agrees to lease the farm to the new operating company for an extended period, typically 10 or 15 years. In cases where there are permanent farm workers on the land who are not themselves members of the claimant community, farm workers may also be included as shareholders in the operating company as members of a workers' trust, yet to be formed.
>
> (Hellum and Derman 2009: 137)

This model envisions that the benefits to the claimant communities will include rent paid by the company for use of the land, a share of its profits, and employment and training opportunities for community members. While it is still too early to evaluate the overall effects of this new model, it seems clear that the strategic partnership diminishes the control of the land by the claimant community, entails a tension between the economic interests of the strategic partner and those of the claimants and does not provide for the actual transition in farm management at the end of the strategic partnership. This model further entrenches the overall shift in emphasis within South African land reform from a more state-driven economic development and procurement of social justice, which somewhat prevailed during the first five years of the ANC government, to a more market-oriented business venture in the new millennium, measured mainly in terms of economic growth (James 2007: 27–51; Hellum and Derman 2009).

This whole picture of a juridified land restitution process under the rule of law was made considerably more complicated by two additional laws enacted in 2003 and 2004, namely the Traditional Leadership and Governance Framework Act (2003) and the Communal Land Rights Act (2004). The first of these statutes more or less recognises anew the legitimacy of tribal authorities, which were defined in the controversial Bantu Authorities Act (1951), and reforms them into newly established 'traditional councils' (Love 2008: xiii). The second act, meant to improve tenure security as demanded by section 25(6) of the South African constitution, is concerned with the profound reorganisation of property rights in 'communal land', which encompasses the former homelands, state trust land and also private communal land registered in the name of chiefs, community trusts or CPAs – i.e. restituted land – and thereby affects an estimated 21 million people in South Africa (Love 2008: xii; Smith 2008: 40). Among the many controversial aspects of this second statute, three deserve special mention here: first, that in areas where the newly established 'traditional councils' exist, these councils would be likely to completely take over the land allocation process under this act, even if prior CPAs or trusts exist; second, that – ironically – this act controls such traditional councils even less in their land allocation practices than did colonial and apartheid jurisdictions; and third, that the Minister of Land Affairs acquires quasi-judicial functions through this act in determining the existence and boundaries of communal lands, while the affected people have only very limited rights to object to such discretion (Smith 2008; see also Ntsebeza 2005: 295–99). Recently, the constitutionality of both of these laws has been challenged – a process launched in April 2005 on behalf of communities in Kalkfontein, Dixie, Mayaeyane and Makuleke by the Legal Resources Centre, a public interest law firm, and Webber Wentzel Bowens, a private law firm (Claassens and Cousins 2008b: x). It is the case of the two Kalkfontein communities, which have been using various political and legal means against the South African state for decades and for whom the recent constitutional challenge is but the latest effort in their seemingly endless struggle to secure their land rights, to which I turn now.

USING THE RULES, SETTING THE RULES: THE KALKFONTEIN COMMUNITIES AND THEIR LAND STRUGGLE

The two communities on whose case I will focus here reside near the town of Settlers north of Pretoria, on the farm Kalkfontein (deed number: 143 JR), which is situated right on the border with Limpopo Province, while itself falling into Mpumalanga Province. Like several other South African farms with the same name, Kalkfontein derives its name from the local occurrence of water in limy soil. I became aware of the communities in Kalkfontein through the high-profile media coverage of their constitutional challenge of the Communal Land Rights Act that – as just mentioned – was recently litigated on behalf of one of these two communities in Kalkfontein (residing on portions B and C), as well as of three other communities, by the Legal Resources Centre (LRC) and Webber Wentzel Bowens. While this litigation was still pending before the Pretoria High Court, Aninka Claassens and Ben Cousins published the edited volume *Land, Power and Custom: Controversies Generated by South Africa's Communal Land Rights Act* (2008a) in collaboration with the LRC. This volume brings together critical analyses related to the act by many of the experts that have acted on behalf of applicants in the actual litigation. The book comes with a CD-Rom appendix, containing extensive litigation documents provided by both applicants and respondents, and thus constitutes an invaluable source of information. With regard to the situation in Kalkfontein, the overview chapter by the LRC lawyers Aninka Claassens and Durkje Gilfillan (2008) is also particularly helpful. During nine months of multi-sited fieldwork on South African land restitution in 2010 and 2011, I followed a set of exemplary cases (including Kalkfontein) from their localities to their legal representatives, the Commission on Restitution of Land Rights, the Land Claims Court and beyond. In this context, I also interviewed LRC lawyers and applicant experts in the constitutional challenge, obtained additional Kalkfontein files from the LRC and, most importantly, talked extensively to various members of the communities in Kalkfontein itself. These data provide the basis for the following reconstruction of the land struggle in Kalkfontein.

The current members of the two Kalkfontein communities are descendants of ethnically mixed groupings who clubbed together in the 1920s to buy farm land. However, the Natives Land Act (1913) had prohibited the acquisition of land by blacks outside the 7 per cent of South

Africa scheduled in this act for black occupation. But the same act also envisioned the enlargement of these scheduled areas by subsequent legislation, even though it would be another twenty-three years before this was accomplished by the Native Trust and Land Act (1936), which expanded the scheduled areas to about 13 per cent of South Africa. In the meantime, as section 1 of the Natives Land Act allowed the governor general to approve exemptions, purchasers could apply for permission to buy non-scheduled land. The farm Kalkfontein was non-scheduled land, yet fell within those areas that had been recommended by the Beaumont Commission in 1916 to be subsequently released (and indeed became part of the released areas through the Native Trust and Land Act in 1936), so exemption was applied for and granted. As always in such cases, however, title was not transferred directly to the co-purchasers. Instead it was registered in the name of the Minister of Native Affairs, who held it in trust on behalf of the co-purchasers and their executive bodies. This happened for one community of 127 individuals, who bought portion A of the farm in 1923; and again in 1924–1925 for another community of twenty-six individuals, who purchased the remaining portions B and C of the Kalkfontein farm. This is the origin of 'the two communities' in Kalkfontein, consisting of the original co-purchasers and their descendants (in the following: 'the co-purchasers'). Over time, these groupings of 'rightful owners' of the land, as they see themselves, also incorporated external members through marriage.[2] However, due to later excesses by a superimposed chief (see below), since the late 1970s many more people were brought in to live, especially on Kalkfontein A, who neither had nor established immediate family ties to the co-purchasers. It is thus important to distinguish between the original buyers and their heirs, whose fate constitutes the primary subject of this chapter, and those other residents that only moved in much later.[3]

While both communities of co-purchasers originally consisted of ethnically mixed groupings with Ndebele, Pedi and Tswana origins, the situation was somewhat different in Kalkfontein A than in Kalkfontein B and C. While the twenty-six co-purchasers of portions B and C apparently just came together from different backgrounds in order to acquire

---

[2] Group interview with committee members of the 'Kalkfontein Community Trust' (managing portions B and C), 31 August 2010.

[3] See the founding affidavit by Stephen Tongoane, the representative of Kalkfontein B and C, in *Tongoane and Others v. The Minister of Agriculture and Land Affairs and Others* (TPD 11678/06), vol. I: 21–26, 30–31; Claassens and Gilfillan 2008: 295–99), and data generated during an interview with Stephen Tongoane on 31 August 2010.

the land as private communal landowners, a sizeable majority of the original buyers of portion A seemingly did have some tribal intentions right away. As I learned from Johannes Mahlangu, an elected representative of the co-purchasers in Kalkfontein A and long-term opponent of local chiefly rule, the bulk of the 127 co-purchasers of Kalkfontein A belonged to a Ndzundza Ndebele tribal section under Chief Januarie Mahlangu, who wanted to buy land in the area.[4] However, the former white landowner of portion A, Mr Jacobs, did not want to sell the land to 'a tribe', as he sought to prevent his farm workers (who were not Ndebele) from being driven off the land. The landowner thus only agreed to sell his portion if his workers were included in the group of co-owners and the land subsequently held as communal land under a committee rather than as tribal land under a chief. So it was agreed and an executive committee was correspondingly formed (including Januarie Mahlangu).[5] By contrast, Chris van Vuuren (1992: 141–43) states in his account of the history of the Ndzundza Ndebele in Kalkfontein that it had been clear from the start that the ethnically mixed group of 127 co-purchasers of Kalkfontein A would accept the leadership of chief Januarie Mahlangu. These deviating accounts nicely illustrate that there have existed considerable tensions right from the start between those co-purchasers who wanted the farm to be run by a committee (as written into the title deed) and those who rather wished to install a local Ndebele chief.

Over the next decades the communities on portions A and B and C were administered by their respective committees under customary-law type arrangements, regulating access to residential, farming and grazing land for each family of co-purchasers. From time to time, conflicts arose between the communities over access to water and the trespassing of boundaries. In the late 1950s, other tensions that cross-cut the farm boundaries and related to ethno-linguistic affiliations emerged with regard to local schooling, leading the Ndebele-dominated Katjebane Primary School to split off from the newly-founded Tswana-medium Thabong Primary School. In addition, attempts by Ndebele tribalists

---

[4] 'Mahlangu' is the praise name for a very large section of the Ndzundza Ndebele, extending far beyond Kalkfontein. Given that numerous Ndzundza Ndebele are thus referred to as 'Mahlangu', sharing this name implies neither close kinship ties nor the involvement in any common cause.

[5] Interview with Johannes Mahlangu, 25 October 2010; cf. the answering affidavit by Christopher Mahlangu, the chairperson of the Ndzundza (Pungutsha) Traditional Council, in *Tongoane and Others v. The Minister of Agriculture and Land Affairs and Others* (TPD 11678/06), vol. 2D: 1599–1602.

to establish an expressly chiefly rule on Kalkfontein A and beyond continued to cause problems.[6]

It was in this respect that another dispute arose in the early 1960s when, after the death of Januarie's son Cecil, yet another Ndebele from the local royal family made explicit claims to chieftainship in Kalkfontein. Many Pedi, Tswana and even Ndebele co-purchasers strongly objected to this and insisted that they did not want to be ruled by a chief. Officials from the Department of Bantu Affairs extensively investigated the local situation.[7] The senior state ethnologist, N. J. van Warmelo, pointed out in a comment to one of the department's reports that

> the problem [in Kalkfontein] is caused by the Department's efforts to force the owners of private land to constitute themselves as tribes and to be governed as such when they are neither tribes, nor do they wish to be tribes. Given that tribal government is built on voluntary support, the absence of voluntary affiliation shows that the tribal system is not wanted here.[8]

Within this atmosphere of pronounced opposition to tribal government, the committees continued into the 1970s to run the everyday administration of the land in Kalkfontein A and B and C, despite recurrent attempts by Ndebele tribalists to install their chief as the only legitimate authority.

This situation was profoundly altered in the late 1970s when, without proper involvement or democratic consent of the co-purchasers in Kalkfontein, the South African government created an Ndebele homeland in that very area. Aninka Claassens and Durkje Gilfillan summarise this process:

> [I]n 1978, the apartheid government constituted the Kalkfontein communities into a tribe. The Native Administration Act 38 of 1927 was used to 'establish' the Ndzundza (Pungutsha) tribe and to appoint as chief Daniel Mahlangu, a descendant of a Kalkfontein A co-purchaser [namely Januarie Mahlangu and his chiefly heir]. Then in 1979, the Bantu Authorities Act [of 1951] was used to create the Ndzundza (Pungutsha)

---

[6] Interviews with Stephen Tongoane on 31 August 2010 and with Johannes Mahlangu on 25 October 2010.

[7] Interview with Johannes Mahlangu on 25 October 2010; see Claassens and Gilfillan 2008: 298–99, as well as the file on this matter in the National Archives Repository, Pretoria, TAB. KHK2/2/116. File Reference N2/10/3/45.

[8] Quoted in Claassens and Gilfillan (2008: 299) in their English translation. The original Afrikaans report can be found in the National Archives Repository, Pretoria, TAB.KHK2/2/116. File Reference N2/10/3/45.

Bantu Authority, and its area of jurisdiction was defined as the three portions of the Kalkfontein farm. The KwaNdebele Legislative Assembly was established in October 1979 with the Ndzundza (Pungutsha) Bantu Authority included as part of the 'homeland' of KwaNdebele. Six members of the Bantu authority were made members of the legislative authority. In 1981, KwaNdebele was made a self-governing state in terms of the National States Constitution Act 21 of 1971.

(Claassens and Gilfillan 2008: 299–300)

This process in effect forcibly displaced the residents of Kalkfontein from South Africa by unilaterally moving homeland borders.

What followed in the 1980s was a reign of excesses by chief Daniel Mahlangu, who treated Kalkfontein as if it was his private property: he 'sold' residential slots to over 1,000 outsider families, often allocating residential sites on agricultural land of the original owners (mostly in Kalkfontein A). He also established a police station, a stone quarry and various businesses on the land without gaining consent of the co-purchasers. He further destroyed a dam wall separating Kalkfontein A from B and C to demonstrate the unity of his territory and thereby caused flooding during rainstorms. Besides misusing official money, he also sanctioned political protesters by flogging them in public as well as by cancelling their state pensions and welfare provisions that were channelled through his office.[9]

As political acts of disobedience proved ineffective, the co-purchasers in Kalkfontein stepped up their political protest during the late 1980s through petitioning for a government commission of enquiry into the misbehaviour of Chief Mahlangu. This political activism was effective, and the subsequently established Kruger Commission (1990) found numerous irregularities, expressing the opinion that 'the vast majority of the heirs of co-purchasers are in favour of the abolishment of the chieftainship and the disestablishment of the tribal authority' (Kruger Commission 1990: 45–46) and hence recommended both the dismissal of Chief Mahlangu and the general abolition of the local Ndzundza (Pungutsha) Tribal Authority. Yet the government only appointed another 'acting chief', while maintaining the tribal authority.[10]

The successor chief continued to allow outsiders to settle on Kalkfontein and, like Chief Mahlangu, engaged in dubious business

---

[9] Interview with Stephen Tongoane on 31 August 2010; cf. Claassens and Gilfillan 2008: 300.

[10] Interview with Stephen Tongoane on 31 August 2010 and Claassens and Gilfillan 2008: 300–01.

activities. Against this backdrop, representatives from both Kalkfontein communities jointly instituted legal proceedings in 1992 in the Pretoria Supreme Court (still operating under the old apartheid state) against the Minister of Regional and Land Affairs, the tribal authority, the 'acting chief' and the chief minister of the homeland KwaNdebele. The applicants thereby used the law to argue that their ownership rights as the heirs of the original purchasers were unlawfully undermined by the chief and tribal authority. This first legal strategy proved effective as the order of the Supreme Court in 1994 interdicted the 'acting chief' and the chief minister of KwaNdebele from permitting people to occupy the farm and from interfering with or dealing in the land in any way without the written consent of the heirs. Furthermore, as the Natives Land Act (1913) had meanwhile been repealed during the transition to democracy, the court ordered that the heirs were entitled to the transfer of the title deed, once formal conditions had been fulfilled.[11]

For that purpose the rightful owners of Kalkfontein A eventually used the Communal Property Associations Act (1996) in order to constitute the 'Katjebane Communal Property Association (CPA)', and elected Johannes Mahlangu as its chairperson. In contrast, the co-purchasers of Kalkfontein B and C opted for a trust arrangement, forming the 'Kalkfontein Community Trust' (of which Stephen Tongoane is currently Vice Chairperson). In 1997, after further pressure on the Minister of Land Affairs, land was finally transferred to the Katjebane CPA as compensation for those sections of their original farm that were lost to new residents. However, the official deed transfer of the remaining parts of their original section A had still not taken place when I was doing fieldwork.[12]

The situation for the Kalkfontein Community Trust has been somewhat similar in that these co-purchasers likewise failed in their continuous attempts to get Kalkfontein B and C registered in their names, as was their right according to the 1994 Supreme Court decision. Thus, in 2006 the Kalkfontein Community Trust chose to use a second legal strategy to secure their land rights, namely to launch proceedings in the Land Claims Court to have title transferred under the terms of the Restitution of Land Rights Act (1994). As happened before in the Supreme Court

---

[11] See *1994 02 24 Joseph Moema and Others v. Ndzundza (Pungutsha) Tribal Authority and Others (TPD 17808/92, unreported)*, section 8, as well as Claassens and Gilfillan 2008: 301–02.

[12] Interview with Johannes Mahlangu on 4 November 2010 and Claassens and Gilfillan 2008: 302.

under the old apartheid state, their new legal application was approved by the Land Claims Court, which in 2007 ordered that title to Kalkfontein B and C be transferred to the trust, as indeed eventually happened in 2008.[13]

As the 'acting chief' meanwhile passed away and a successor has not yet been appointed, the tribal authority is being run for the time being by its chairperson and continues to exercise political control and customary jurisdiction over the territory of Kalkfontein. Co-purchasers from both Kalkfontein communities have continued to question the legitimacy of this tribal form of governance both through letters of complaint to the local municipality (especially since welfare provisions continue to be channelled through the tribal authority, which has used these state funds as means of exerting political pressure) and by openly airing their discontent during a public meeting with representatives of the Mpumalanga House of Traditional Leaders. Yet none of these continuing forms of political protest has led to anything thus far.[14]

Within all these ongoing attempts to re-establish secure ownership rights, the emergence of debates on new legislation concerning traditional leadership and communal land rights has further complicated the picture. Media reports on controversies surrounding the corresponding bills led community representatives from Kalkfontein B and C to discuss the bills with their lawyers at the LRC. These co-purchasers were concerned that these future legislative acts could, yet again, jeopardise the security of their tenure. Thus, leaders from Kalkfontein along with representatives from other rural communities became politically engaged in opposing the Communal Land Rights Bill, sending a delegation to make written and oral submissions to the relevant parliamentary portfolio committee. During the limited involvement of the public in the legislative process – the constitutionality of which was challenged as well as part of the overall litigation[15] – the representative of the Kalkfontein Community Trust, Stephen Tongoane, 'stood up in Parliament to explain the history of the land and his community's reservations about the bill, and to ask the bill to be withdrawn and reconsidered after a more adequate consultation

---

[13] Interview with Stephen Tongoane on 31 August 2010 and Claassens and Gilfillan 2008: 302, 308.

[14] See founding affidavit by Stephen Tongoane, the representative of Kalkfontein B and C, in *Tongoane and Others v. The Minister of Agriculture and Land Affairs and Others* (TPD 11678/06), vol. I: 41–42 and Claassens and Gilfillan 2008: 304–06.

[15] See *2010 01 Stephen S Tongoane and 3 Others v. The National Minister for Agriculture and Land Affairs and 13 Others* (CCT 100/09), sections 167–255.

process with the rural people affected by its provisions' (Claassens and Gilfillan 2008: 304). However, despite strong opposition at the public hearings, the bill was approved with some amendments by parliament in 2004. Once again in the history of Kalkfontein, political activism had proven largely ineffectual.[16]

Hence, authorised by the community of co-purchasers in Kalkfontein B and C, and also in three other settings (namely Dixie, Mayaeyane and Makuleke), the Legal Resources Centre and the private law firm Webber Wentzel Bowens jointly embarked upon yet another legal journey to the promised land of tenure security by challenging the constitutionality of both the Communal Land Rights Act (2004) and the Traditional Leadership and Governance Framework Act (2003).[17] While the judgement of the North Gauteng High Court in Pretoria on 30 October 2009 dismissed the application, it basically followed the applicants' argument that the quasi-judicial rights of the minister to determine relevant 'communities', as well as the discretion of traditional councils without downward accountability mechanisms, put the tenure of communities such as the one in Kalkfontein at risk. The High Court therefore declared considerable sections of the Communal Land Rights Act to be unconstitutional and invalid, and immediately referred the case to the Constitutional Court.[18] In its subsequent judgement on 11 May 2010, the Constitutional Court found the Communal Land Rights Act unconstitutional in its entirety due to its improper procedural enactment, which had been one of the arguments put forward by the applicants.[19] The court also ordered that the procedural deficiency of the Act rendered it unnecessary to further consider whether its substantive provisions were consistent with the constitution or whether Parliament had sufficiently facilitated public involvement in the legislative process.[20] Thus the third legal strategy utilised by representatives of Kalkfontein B and C to prevent the local tribal authority to re-exercise control over their land, again, proved highly successful.

---

[16] Interview with Stephen Tongoane on 13 September 2010 and Claassens and Gilfillan 2008: 303–04.

[17] See *Tongoane and Others v. The Minister of Agriculture and Land Affairs and Others (TPD 11678/06)*.

[18] See *Tongoane and Others v. National Minister for Agriculture and Land Affairs and Others 2010 (8) BCLR 838 (GNP)*, sections 62–64 and 67.

[19] See *2010 01 Stephen S Tongoane and 3 Others v. The National Minister for Agriculture and Land Affairs and 13 Others (CCT 100/09)*, sections 90–166.

[20] See *Tongoane and Others v. National Minister for Agriculture and Land Affairs and Others 2010 (8) BCLR 741 (CC)*, sections 98–127 and 133.

THE JURIDIFICATION OF POLITICAL PROTEST
AND THE POLITICISATION OF LEGALISM:
SOME CONCLUDING REMARKS

Critical legal studies have propagated for decades as their mantra, echoing Marx, that all 'law is politics' (Tamanaha 2004: 74). In one sense, namely when referring to the domain of 'domination' through law, this statement is evidently a truism. It refers to little more than the fact discussed earlier that virtually every political authority at the very least rules *by* law, using legal rules as the medium through which to communicate and exercise political power and control. Yet in the second domain that is frequently mentioned as combining with domination to create the dual character of law (Roberts 1994: 962) – namely 'order' – the politics of law seems effaced: once established, a legal order can be seen as bracketing out the politics and historicity of its very constitution, as well as the obviously existing discretion within its judicial application, usually styling itself, at best, as apolitical and, at worst, as a doxic, 'natural' order of how things are done. It is especially this second sense of ostensibly depoliticising the use of law for truly political ends that Jean and John Comaroff seem to have in mind when talking about 'lawfare', namely the

> use of its own rules – of its duly enacted penal codes, its administrative law, its states of emergency, its charters and mandates and warrants, its norms of engagement – to impose a sense of order upon its subordinates by means of violence rendered legible, legal, and legitimate by its own sovereign word. And also to commit its own ever-so-civilized, patronizing, high-minded forms of kleptocracy.
>
> (Comaroff and Comaroff 2006: 30)

Seen in this light, both the globally increasing 'fetishisation of law' and the juridification of formerly political protest, in the course of which more and more issues are being addressed and negotiated in legal terms within and beyond courts, seem deeply worrying. The Comaroffs stand in a long tradition of critical engagement with processes of juridification,[21] which emphasises that this displacement of politics into the realm of the legal effectively leads to an ostensible depoliticisation of what, in fact, are ultimately political issues. This machination of 'the

---

[21] See, for instance, Kirchheimer 1928; Habermas 1987; Teubner 1987; Brown and Halley 2002; Mattei and Nader 2008. For an overview of different approaches to juridification, see Blichner and Molander 2008; see also Gerhard Anders's contribution to this volume.

anti-politics machine' (Ferguson 1994) of law comes with severe costs: not only does it lead to an increased rule by judges who are not themselves legitimated through a political process (Tamanaha 2004: 5); it also quite often entails an emasculation of the transformative potential of political agitation through the self-confinement to 'legal cases' that, in its appeal to laws, ostensibly instantiate rather than transform the existing order.

This line of critical reasoning seems to cultivate three basic expectations: first, that a legal framing transforms and profoundly modifies the nature of demands by formulating them in terms of the existing normative order; second, that the law thereby often reproduces the overarching *status quo*, while politics more obviously has the potential to profoundly change the order itself, as well as to substantially alter one's position within existing power asymmetries; and third, that the juridification of truly political issues creates the impression of handling them in a depoliticised fashion, which might hinder the more effective achievement of these goals through political struggle.

However, the case study presented here of the land struggle among the Kalkfontein communities, which has spanned several decades and taken place within fundamentally changing conditions shifting from apartheid's rule by law to the new substantive rule of 'good' law, seems to go against such expectations. While the various legal strategies utilised by members of these communities surely transformed their demands by prescribing the specific forms in which they could be expressed and processed, the same could be said of their earlier political engagements. Especially under conditions of apartheid, in which many of the often taken-for-granted forms of political action were simply illegal or violently oppressed, what could be meaningfully formulated and pursued through political protest turned out to be quite limited for the relatively powerless people in Kalkfontein. It was precisely this lack of political alternatives, combined with the apartheid state's own emphasis on legality, that made it generally promising for some of the anti-apartheid struggle to shift to the legal battlefield as a form of 'politics by other means' (Abel 1995: 12–14). What is more, for co-purchasers of Kalkfontein, legal strategies proved to be more effective than political actions for regaining at least some control over their land. Finally, far from reproducing the *status quo*, the various legal strategies utilised in Kalkfontein both profoundly altered the standing of the co-purchasers vis-à-vis the local tribal authority and substantially changed the overall order at various levels, most notably through the successful constitutional challenge of the Communal Land Rights Act in 2010. This case thus raises a challenging question: do we need to interpret law and politics differently?

In order to develop a better understanding of this empirical case, it might be helpful to assume that what appears from one point of view as the 'politics' of *setting collectively binding rules* might, from another point of view, be represented as the 'legalism' of *merely using such rules* – with specific advantages and disadvantages that come with representing one's activities in the terms of one or the other. In other words, whether one moves within fields ostensibly instituted as embodying either 'politics' or 'law', it seems often quite difficult (if not impossible) to say whether a certain action actually *is* political or legal. Instead, representing it either in 'political' terms that overstate the agency and power of the involved actors to define collectively binding rules largely at their discretion *or* in 'legal' terms that understate such agency and power (as well as the indeterminacy of law) at the expense of variously projected mechanisations of mere 'rule-application' seems to be more a matter of switching between two different and ultimately incommensurable codes than an issue of differential ontology.

In this sense, the legal code arguably defines and thereby transforms its objects in terms of an aspired adherence to an existing normative order of rules, while systematically evading questions of power. The political code equally defines and thereby specifically transforms the objects that can be processed in its name, yet does so in terms of power struggles over the very determination and implementation of such collectively binding rules. Over time, numerous interactions in the name of these codes can be seen as leading to path-dependent, historically contingent institutionalisations of 'politics' and 'law', each with their specifically enabling and constraining 'connectivity', as Niklas Luhmann calls it. What Luhmann observes for his 'social systems' also seems applicable to the political and legal codes:

> To be sure, interpenetrating systems converge in individual elements – that is, they use the same ones – *but they give each of them a different selectivity and connectivity, different pasts and futures.* Because temporalized elements (events) are involved, the convergence is possible only in the present. The elements signify different things in the participating systems, although they are identical as events: they select among different possibilities and lead to different consequences.
>
> (Luhmann 1995: 215 – emphasis in the original)

Each code has a different connectivity that evolves through the ongoing application of this code within its own path-dependently institutionalised and thus pre-structured setting. Switching from one code to another opens up a limited range of new potential consequences, while simultaneously precluding an equally limited set of others.[22] Against this backdrop, it becomes an empirical question whether a certain phenomenon is being processed by actors in terms of the political or legal (or any other) code; whether the matter of concern for certain actors empirically moves, for instance, from a political towards a legal framing (and hence becomes juridified) or moves in the opposite direction (and thus becomes politicised); and whether pursuing the matter in terms of one code or the other turns out to be more effective, depending on (among other factors) the currently existing connectivity for each code.

Using these terms to summarise the observations in this chapter, the former political protest against apartheid can be described as having been initially transformed in an ostensibly rule-setting act of political negotiations. These led to a profound juridification in the form of the South African constitution, as well as to a number of new land laws. The latter entailed, most importantly, the Restitution of Land Rights Act (1994), allowing for redressing past, 'racially' based dispossessions through restoration or compensation. Yet as has been shown, this political process was also profoundly shaped by both the transnational regime of the rule of law, which made its decidedly international presence felt during the negotiations, as well as by having to politically compromise between different positions, as represented by the various stakeholders in the transitional process. Given the establishment of a substantive rule of 'good' law under constitutional supremacy in post-transitional South Africa, the ostensibly political process of making new rules through legislation has now indeed become much more juridified, as the constitutional challenge to the Communal Land Rights Act has shown.

The co-purchasers in Kalkfontein lived through considerable historical changes, including the political shift towards homelands under apartheid and, ultimately, the juridification of former political protest during the transition to constitutional democracy, as described in this chapter. These changes proved to have far-reaching consequences with regard to newly emerging connectivities within both the political and legal fields. During apartheid, the political possibilities for the 'rightful owners' of Kalkfontein became greatly constrained. After having been

---

[22] Besides Luhmann (1995, 1997), other authors have similarly described such switches between different modes in terms of, for instance, 'frames' (Goffman 1974), 'contextualisations' (Gumperz 1982) or 'metacodes' (Rottenburg 2005).

forcibly removed from South Africa during the late 1970s through a process of moving homeland borders rather than people, their 'political rights' were profoundly reconstituted within the context of the tribalised homeland of KwaNdebele – an act that constituted their very problem rather than an arsenal for its political solution. When political acts of local disobedience proved to be pointless, a political petition to the South African government for a commission of enquiry seemed more successful. Yet the very conditions that helped to transform this political demand into a success, namely its political connectivity based on the non-enforceable character of such a commission's report, ultimately allowed the apartheid rule *by* law to continue its indirect rule *by* customary law in Kalkfontein. In the same vein, it is significant that all subsequent political engagements by the Kalkfontein community to secure their land rights against the local tribal authority failed, even under the seemingly changed political conditions of post-apartheid.

By contrast, all their legal actions – first with the Supreme Court still under apartheid, then under profoundly changed legal conditions in post-apartheid with the Land Claims Court and finally the Constitutional Court – were much more successful through timid and modest appeals to existing sets of overarching rules and by pleading that 'the law shall rule'. These merely legalistic uses of rules, declaring to be concerned with following, not changing rules, proved to be much more effective in actually setting new rules – most dramatically in the latest coup of forcing the South African government, through the Constitutional Court, to redraft central legislations for communal land rights – than any engagement with political rule-setting ever could have been.

In sum, a code-switching from engaging in the 'political' struggle of *setting the rules* towards a merely 'legalistic' *use of existing rules* has evidently been the much more effective strategy for co-purchasers in Kalkfontein to actually achieve their goals. As a matter of fact, the assertion that the heirs in Kalkfontein had to switch from a prior political code to a subsequently legal code is actually quite misleading empirically. To the contrary, it is rather their various political protests concerning the land that need to be seen as constituting occasional code-switches – that is, *politicisations* of an actually much more profoundly held *legalistic* attitude towards their 'rightful ownership' of the land. This locally prevailing 'legalism from below' (Eckert 2006), which consistently expressed itself in various legal strategies and also occasionally became politicised through switches to political action, became strongly apparent in various conversations during fieldwork. When asking different co-purchasers in

Kalkfontein to tell me more about 'their power struggle' with the chief, I was repeatedly corrected, somewhat indignantly, that their land struggle was actually not at all about 'politics' but solely about their 'rightful ownership' of the land, about 'defending what is rightfully ours'.[23] This insistence on a legalism of ownership and property, which had never corresponded to the reality of positive South African law but still expressed a profoundly held conviction about the rightfulness of an aspired-to property regime that had been legally impossible to instantiate at the time of buying the farms in the 1920s, was perhaps most strongly conveyed to me by Johannes Mahlangu, who fervently argued that 'it's *not* a matter of politics! My property is mine; I cannot involve politics in it! You play politics *on* the land, not *with* the land!'[24]

References

Abel, Richard L. 1995. *Politics by Other Means: Law in the Struggle against Apartheid, 1980–1994.* New York: Routledge.

Blichner, Lars C. and Molander, Anders 2008. 'Mapping juridification', *European Law Journal* 14 (1): 36–54.

Brown, Wendy and Halley, Janet E. 2002. *Left Legalism/Left Critique.* Durham, NC: Duke University Press.

Chaskalson, Matthew 1994. 'The property clause: section 28 of the constitution', *South African Journal on Human Rights* 10: 131–39.

    1995. 'Stumbling towards section 28: negotiations over the protection of property rights in the interim constitution', *South African Journal on Human Rights* 11: 222–40.

Claassens, Aninka and Cousins, Ben (eds.) 2008a. *Land, Power and Custom: Controversies Generated by South Africa's Communal Land Rights Act.* Cape Town/Athens, OH: Legal Resources Centre/Ohio University Press.

    2008b. 'Acknowledgements', in Aninka Claassens and Ben Cousins (eds.) *Land, Power and Custom: Controversies Generated by South Africa's Communal Land Rights Act.* Cape Town/Athens, OH: Legal Resources Centre/Ohio University Press, pp. x–xi.

Claassens, Aninka and Gilfillan, Durkje 2008. 'The Kalkfontein land purchases: eighty years on and still struggling for ownership', in Aninka Claassens and Ben Cousins (eds.) *Land, Power and Custom: Controversies Generated by South Africa's Communal Land Rights Act.* Cape Town/Athens, OH: Legal Resources Centre/Ohio University Press, pp. 295–314.

---

[23] Group interview with committee members of the 'Kalkfontein Community Trust' on 31 August 2010.

[24] Interview with Johannes Mahlangu on 4 November 2010.

Comaroff, John L. and Comaroff, Jean 2006. 'Law and disorder in the post-colony: an introduction', in Jean Comaroff and John L. Comaroff (eds.) *Law and Disorder in the Postcolony*. University of Chicago Press, pp. 1–56.

2009. 'Reflections on the anthropology of law, governance and sovereignty', in Franz von Benda-Beckmann, Keebet von Benda-Beckmann and Julia Eckert (eds.) *Rules of Law and Laws of Ruling: On the Governance of Law*. Aldershot/Burlington: Ashgate, pp. 31–59.

Commission on Restitution of Land Rights 2007. *Annual Report 2006/2007*. Pretoria: Department of Land Affairs.

Craig, Paul 1997. 'Formal and substantive conceptions of the rule of law: an analytical framework', *Public Law* 467: 467–87.

Crush, Jonathan and Jeeves, Alan 1993. 'Transitions in the South African countryside', *Canadian Journal of African Studies/Revue Canadienne des Études Africaines* 27 (3): 351–60.

Department of Rural Development and Land Reform 2011. *Strategic Plan 2011–2014*. Pretoria: Department of Rural Development and Land Reform.

Eckert, Julia 2006. 'From subjects to citizens: legalism from below and the homogenisation of the legal sphere', *Journal of Legal Pluralism* 53–54: 45–75.

Ferguson, James 1994. *The Anti-politics Machine: 'Development', Depoliticization, and Bureaucratic Power in Lesotho*. Minneapolis: University of Minnesota Press.

Goffman, Erving 1974. *Frame Analysis: An Essay on the Organization of Experience*. Cambridge: Harvard University Press.

Gumperz, John J. 1982. *Discourse Strategies*. Cambridge University Press.

Habermas, Jürgen 1987. *The Theory of Communicative Action*. vol. 2: *Lifeworld and System: A Critique of Functionalist Reason*. Boston, MA: Beacon Press.

Hellum, Anne and Derman, Bill 2004. 'Land reform and human rights in contemporary Zimbabwe: balancing individual and social justice through an integrated human rights framework', *World Development* 32 (10): 1785–1805.

2009. 'Government, business and chiefs: ambiguities of social justice through land restitution in South Africa', in Franz von Benda-Beckmann, Keebet von Benda-Beckmann and Julia Eckert (eds.) *Rules of Law and Laws of Ruling: On the Governance of Law*. Aldershot/Burlington: Ashgate, pp. 125–50.

James, Deborah 2006. '"The tragedy of the private": owners, communities and the state in South Africa's land reform programme', in Franz von Benda-Beckmann, Keebet von Benda-Beckmann and Melanie G. Wiber (eds.) *Changing Properties of Property*. New York: Berghahn Books, pp. 243–68.

2007. *Gaining Ground? 'Rights' and 'Property' in South African Land Reform*. Abingdon/New York: Routledge-Cavendish.

Kirchheimer, Otto 1928. 'Zur Staatslehre des Sozialismus und Bolschewismus', *Zeitschrift für Politik* 17: 592–611.

Klug, Heinz 1996. 'South African constitutional history', in Matthew Chaskalson (ed.) *Constitutional Law of South Africa*. Cape Town: Juta, 2.1–2.15.

2000. *Constituting Democracy: Law, Globalism, and South Africa's Political Reconstruction*. Cambridge University Press.

Kruger Commission 1990. Report of the commission of inquiry into alleged maladministration and irregularities by the ikosi and members of the Ndzundza (Pungutsha) tribal authority (appointed by the Chief Minister of KwaNdebele).

Love, Janet 2008. 'Foreword', in Aninka Claassens and Ben Cousins (eds.) *Land, Power and Custom: Controversies Generated by South Africa's Communal Land Rights Act*. Cape Town/Athens, OH: Legal Resources Centre/Ohio University Press, pp. xii–xv.

Luhmann, Niklas 1995. *Social Systems*. Stanford University Press.

1997. *Die Gesellschaft der Gesellschaft*. Frankfurt am Main: Suhrkamp.

Mattei, Ugo and Nader, Laura 2008. *Plunder: When the Rule of Law Is Illegal*. Malden, MA: Blackwell.

Ntsebeza, Lungisile 2005. *Democracy Compromised: Chiefs and the Politics of the Land in South Africa*. Leiden: Brill.

Palombella, Gianluigi 2009 'The rule of law and its core', in Gianluigi Palombella and Neil Walker (eds.) *Relocating the Rule of Law*. Oxford: Hart, pp. 17–42.

Platzky, Laurine and Walker, Cherryl 1985. *The Surplus People: Forced Removals in South Africa*. Johannesburg: Ravan Press.

Raz, Joseph 1979. 'The rule of law and its virtue', in Joseph Raz (ed.) *The Authority of Law: Essays on Law and Morality*. Oxford: Clarendon Press, pp. 210–32.

Reynolds, Noel B. 1989. 'Grounding the rule of law', *Ratio Juris* 2 (1): 1–16.

Roberts, Simon 1994. 'Law and dispute processes', in Tim Ingold (ed.) *Companion Encyclopedia of Anthropology: Humanity, Culture and Social Life*. London/New York: Routledge, pp. 962–82.

Rottenburg, Richard 2005. 'Code-switching, or why a metacode is good to have', in Barbara Czarniawska and Guje Sevon (eds.) *Global Ideas: How Ideas, Objects and Practices Travel in the Global Econcomy*. Malmö: Författarna och Liber AB, pp. 259–74.

Smith, Henk 2008. 'An overview of the Communal Land Rights Act 11 of 2004', in Aninka Claassens and Ben Cousins (eds.) *Land, Power and Custom: Controversies Generated by South Africa's Communal Land Rights Act*. Cape Town/Athens, OH: Legal Resources Centre/Ohio University Press, pp. 35–71.

Spitz, Richard and Chaskalson, Matthew 2000. *The Politics of Transition: A Hidden History of South Africa's Negotiated Settlement*. Johannesburg: Witwatersrand University Press.

Summers, Robert S. 1993. 'A formal theory of the rule of law', *Ratio Juris* 6 (2): 127–42.

Tamanaha, Brian Z. 2004. *On the Rule of Law: History, Politics, Theory*. Cambridge University Press.

  2009. 'A concise guide to the rule of law', in Gianluigi Palombella and Neil Walker (eds.) *Relocating the Rule of Law*. Oxford: Hart, pp. 3–15.

Teubner, Gunther (ed.) 1987. *Juridification of Social Spheres: A Comparative Analysis in the Areas of Labor, Corporate, Antitrust and Social Welfare Law*. Berlin/New York: De Gruyter.

Van Vuuren, Christo J. 1992. Die aard en betekenis van 'n eie etnisiteit onder die Suid-Ndebele. Universiteit van Pretoria.

Waldmeir, Patti 1997. *Anatomy of a Miracle: The End of Apartheid and the Birth of the New South Africa*. London: Viking.

Walker, Cherryl 2008. *Landmarked: Land Claims and Land Restitution in South Africa*. Johannesburg/Athens, OH: Jacana Media/Ohio University Press.

Zigomo, Muchena 2010. Minister says SA won't meet land-reform target. Mail & Guardian online, 26 February 2010. Website: www.mg.co.za/article/2010–02–26-minister-says-sa-wont-meet-landreform-target, last accessed 5 January 2010.

Case law

1994 02 24 Joseph Moema and Others v. Ndzundza (Pungutsha) Tribal Authority and Others (TPD 17808/92, unreported)

Tongoane and Others v. National Minister for Agriculture and Land Affairs and Others 2010 (8) BCLR 838 (GNP)

Tongoane and Others v. National Minister for Agriculture and Land Affairs and Others 2010 (8) BCLR 741 (CC)

Litigation documents

Tongoane and Others v. The Minister of Agriculture and Land Affairs and Others (TPD 11678/06)

2010 01 Stephen S Tongoane and 3 Others v. The National Minister for Agriculture and Land Affairs and 13 Others (CCT 100/09)

Legislation

Natives Land Act 27 of 1913

Native Administration Act 38 of 1927

Native Trust and Land Act 18 of 1936
Bantu Authorities Act 68 of 1951
National States Constitution Act 21 of 1971
(Interim) Constitution of the Republic of South Africa Act 200 of 1993
Restitution of Land Rights Act 22 of 1994
Communal Property Associations Act 28 of 1996
Constitution of the Republic of South Africa, Act 108 of 1996
Traditional Leadership and Governance Framework Act 41 of 2003
Communal Land Rights Act 11 of 2004

CHAPTER 6

RUMOURS OF RIGHTS

Julia Eckert

INTRODUCTION

This volume explores the dynamic by which law changes the perception of situations, problems and conflicts, as well as of the world and oneself within it for those who employ its norms and categories. We ask also how in turn law is transformed by being applied, interpreted and used by people to express their hopes and fears. In this article I attempt to look at these processes through the perspective of the particular properties of rumours. Rumours of rights travel across the globe, spreading legal norms in a particular manner. Attention to rumours of rights opens our view to processes of normative change, adoption and adaptation that are of a more general value for our understanding of law's transformations.

I start with the thesis that, along with commercial and governmental forms of legal export, rumours are one of the principal ways that law is spread. They are, of course, not an alternative to the former but their correlate, and they are thus part of processes of juridification. Upendra Baxi has provided us (in this volume and elsewhere) with the important

I want to thank Franz von Benda-Beckmann and Keebet von Benda-Beckmann for their intellectual and practical support that has made the research on which this article is based possible. I am indebted to the critical questions of the participants of the Law in Context – Berlin Research Network on Legal Culture(s) at the Institute for Advanced Study in Berlin, and the jour fixe of the SFB 700 at the Freie University Berlin, who helped me refine some of my arguments, although I am far from doing justice to their insights. Discussions with the members of the research group Law against the state – Özlem Biner, Brian Donahoe and Christian Strümpell – have given me much inspiration. I want to thank Gesine Koch for her constant support in all practical matters and her skilful finishing of the manuscript.

distinction between the politics *of* human rights and the politics *for* human rights, the former denoting policies to implement human rights, with all of its baggage of political interests and the geographies of global power, and the latter referring to movements for the alleviation of one's own suffering (Baxi 1998).[1] These movements are distinguished by the different impacts they have on the two decisive moments of the travels of law, namely the restructuration of economic or political power relations through legal interventions on the one hand, and processes of normative change on the other hand. Rumours are one way in which the two are connected: in rumours, that which is relevant to the hopes and fears of those engaged in politics *for* (human) rights is glimpsed, extracted, imagined or demanded from the politics *of* (human) rights.

In this article, I am concerned not with the politics *of* human rights, but the glimpses and imaginations of the politics *for* human rights in the rumours of law's possibilities and law's threats. These structure the adoption of new legal norms in a particular manner. Firstly, what is known about law is shaped by the fears and hopes of those who transmit the rumour and those who hear it. These processes of horizontal knowledge transfer thus select legal knowledge in relation to concrete situations, particular perceptions of problems and conflicts that differ from the often discussed top-down processes of legal dissemination. Secondly, because rumours entail uncertainty, they make routine reactions based on habitual normative orientations impossible. As such, they make more evident the potential of genuine action and the situational interpretative moments which are a general feature of normative orientations. Thirdly, rumours entail comparisons. Comparisons, by relying on categories of similarity and difference, have a universalising tendency, a propensity to construct matrices of comparability. The normative effect of the rumour lies thus both in its complex relation to pre-existing norms that influence but do not comprehensively determine the hearing of news, and the universalising tendencies of comparison inherent in it.

A RUMOUR OF A JUST COURT

Gopal Bhai is the president of a slum residents' association in a slum that is located on very precious land in a central suburb of Bombay.[2]

---

[1] Similarly, in legal fields other than human rights, we see various movements that might succinctly be distinguished as the politics of law (and rights) and the politics for law (and rights).

[2] Names of persons and places have been changed.

He was striving to have his slum included in the Slum Rehabilitation Scheme in order to safeguard the slum dwellers' residence 'rights' to this very land.[3] This scheme promised slum residents the construction of apartment blocks for their use on the land where they were living. In exchange, construction companies, or what in Bombay are called 'builders', were granted the right to develop the rest of the land commercially. The scheme had once been introduced by the Shiv Sena party, and is comparable to other schemes in other Indian cities that attempt to deal with 'the slum problem' (cf. Baviskar, this volume; Fernandes 2006: 137; Rao 2010). Gopal Bhai had at one point in the early 1990s joined the Shiv Sena party.[4] He had sought security for his colony and had delivered the votes of his area to Shiv Sena to guarantee safety, particularly of its Muslim residents, during the riots of 1993 in which the Shiv Sena had been centrally involved. Now he hoped the Shiv Sena would broker a deal with the builder. However, at some point, Gopal Bhai realised that he was being cheated by the builder, who was not planning to build apartments for the slum dwellers on the land where they had lived for so long and worked so hard to turn from a swamp into habitable land, but somewhere far away. This had regularly happened to other slum dwellers who had been relocated to far-away places, disrupting their economic networks, forcing them to travel for long hours between their new homes and their places of work and burdening them with the cost of travel (cf. Rao 2010). Gopal Bhai was desperate to save his slum from this fate – a fate that would probably have terminated his prospects as the president of the colony's residents' association as well. When he asked the Shiv Sena to employ its usual forms of pressure, this time against the fraudulent builder, he was forced to realise that the party was not really interested in helping him because it could buy more votes with the builder's money than would be lost by abandoning Gopal Bhai and his slum.

When Gopal Bhai realised this he said to me:

> Help me. You must know a lawyer. We need law. We want to use law. But we do not know enough. We need information. The powerful break the

---

[3] The Slum Rehabilitation Scheme made available public land on which slums had been established to commercial building companies. Investors were obliged to build housing (blocks of 225-square-foot flats) for the slum dwellers, and could develop the rest of the land commercially. Problems arose because the mixed-use characteristic of slums was not taken into account in the planning of the apartment blocks, so there was no space for workshops and other non-residential facilities.

[4] The Shiv Sena is a chauvinist regional party founded in the late 1960s that took on militant Hindu-nationalist positions in the 1980s (Eckert 2003).

law. We also have rights in law. Law makes us illegal, but the business that others make from us being illegal is even more illegal. We want to use the law against them. But we always lose out because we do not know the precise laws which give us the right, or tell us about whether the harassment is legal or illegal. We have made this land liveable. Without us, it would be a swamp. We have lived here for forty years. This is our land. The state (*sarkar*) has to give us our house.

So I brought a young lawyer to him who was active in housing and displacement issues. When he met Gopal Bhai the lawyer started telling him about the legal aid NGO he was working for, but after only a few sentences Gopal Bhai jumped up in his small house and screamed at the young lawyer and at me: 'I do not want any movement (*andolan*)! I have had enough of movements. I can't stand NGOs. I want law.'

The lawyer fled, and Gopal Bhai explained to me that movements were only for communism and that they only exploited the poor for their own political ends. He knew that there was a new court especially for poor people like him, and that this new court was using law for the poor, and the lawyers and judges there, unlike in all other courts he had encountered, did not ask for money. He had heard about this court from his neighbours. A story was making the rounds, namely that of a young Muslim man who had gone to this court because the police had falsely arrested him and beaten him up. This young Muslim had been awarded 15,000 rupees in damages – an unbelievable sum to Gopal Bhai, and an unbelievable event: that a young Muslim man living in the slums could be victorious over a policeman in court. Gopal Bhai said, 'He is also poor. He lives here too, but law was on his side.'

This story suggested to Gopal Bhai that law might be the way to go to get what he considered his and his fellow slum dwellers' rights: for all to live on the land that they had laboured to make liveable, a right he felt the residents had earned by virtue of the work they had put into turning this land from a swamp into land, by improving it over the years and 'making a living' in an extensive sense. His sense of entitlement and rights went beyond the labour that they had put into the area; it also came from the fact that they had been able to exist in an inhospitable city, depending only on themselves to survive, and from a sense that the poor contributed to the city in ways that were not acknowledged.

Law here appeared as a site of hope, of a just world in which the poor would not lose out – even though they might remain poor. It offered the possibility of affirming and realising existing values rather than overthrowing them, as Gopal Bhai assumed 'movements' – 'communism' and the like – wanted to do. His was not a fundamental critique of the political system he was living in; in fact, he objected to such critiques as he saw them as making for 'conflict'. In his experience, conflict brought only problems for people like him. They were the ones used by others to battle, as he knew from his years in the Shiv Sena, and they were the ones criminalised and punished afterwards for battling.

Law for him thus provided an alternative to collective action. It suggested peace rather than struggle, neutrality rather than opposition. It promised an avenue to something that to him was out there somewhere, namely (social) justice. Gopal Bhai and other slum dwellers have a clear idea of what they consider social justice, and also very concrete explanations of how social justice is subverted. Such explanations vary according to the specific case of injustice discussed and the specific social position of the teller. It might be the corruption of bureaucrats or the police; it might be the interests of the politically powerful; it might be a local rival and his connections; it might be 'the rich', or any group construed as 'the others' – whoever that might be in a particular instance. Rarely is it 'the system' as such, or the legal order of India that is held responsible for the plight of the poor and the injustice that they experience every day. In fact, a diffuse idea of law (and often of democracy) is highly valued, and it is the concrete persons charged with their implementation that are accused of preventing its realisation.

This idea of (social) justice residing in law (as well as the belief in democracy) needs to be explored, as it runs counter to the experiences that people like Gopal Bhai have every day. Gopal Bhai's faith in law arose despite his awareness of all the intricate ways in which law can be used in '(false) allegations'. In various local skirmishes he had been accused of all sorts of things – rape, murder, cheating, assault, fraud – and had used the weapon of (more or less false) allegations himself. He had been arrested on these allegations, beaten up by the police and set free after proffering a bribe. He had been involved in court cases that dragged on for years and were inconclusive in the end, but which had done harm simply by dragging on.

Moreover, Gopal Bhai was clearly aware of 'unjust laws', those that operated to the detriment of people like him, the laws 'that make us illegal'.[5] He distinguished between unjust laws and just laws, and between

---

[5] Poverty in the city is always accompanied by illegality. There are of course acknowledgements of legal status of the urban poor: ration cards and other forms of identity cards, voter registration lists, etc. Nonetheless, those living in the urban slums are all illegal in one or the other aspect of their circumstances. Their very residence in a certain place may technically be an

'the law' as a normative order of potential social justice and its subversion in the scheming and fighting in the slums. Nevertheless, the 'law' that he was referring to here was a site of hope, an idea of justice.

Gopal Bhai knew of this law-as-hope from a rumour. It was the story of the young Muslim man that he had heard, that 'someone' had told him.[6] That story gave him a new perspective on law and the courts, one that went against his previous experiences of battling local rivals by means of complaints and allegations at the police station. It was a perspective that resonated so much with his hopes, as well as with his beliefs as to how these hopes might be fulfilled, that it was able to overcome his experience of law to the contrary.

Gopal Bhai is not alone in this. Rumours are rife, so to speak, and law is much discussed in the slums (cf. Eckert 2006). Of course, law is mostly known by any slum dweller as an instrument of harassment by the police and the municipality. It is known to 'make us illegal' as Gopal Bhai says, and the magistrate courts are crowded with people, particularly those from the poorer sections of society, charged with various misdemeanours. Law appears as a weapon easily used by rivals and adversaries to pull one into the ambit of police attention. Rumours of law, therefore, are not always rumours of hope, but often of fear.

Despite these experiences, many turn to law to address their hopes and demands. Indians have a long history of addressing judicial institutions with their issues. For example, they liberally used the colonial courts from the moment they were set up (Galanter 1997: 19). Earlier discussions of the use of law in India have attributed this either to the litigiousness of Indians (e.g. Cohn 1959) or to the hegemonic sway of élite ideas (e.g. Chatterjee 2004).[7] However, since the advance of public interest litigation in the early 1980s propelled law to the forefront as an instrument of moral politics, filing a case is often also a matter of trying

---

'encroachment' on public land and an illegal use of space. The height of their house, its plumbing or the electrical connection may not meet specifications; the product of their labour or the conditions of its production, or any other vital issue connected to their livelihoods may contravene the law. If they beg, they violate the law against begging. There are no titles to land, building regulations and environmental rules are violated, special zones of living, working and engaging in trade may not be observed; in many cases they do not hold licences for their various trades, and many labour laws are violated in the workshops of the slums. Thus, for the urban poor, the most common experience of law is that of the many ways in which their forms of living and labouring are illegalised.

[6] Veena Das relates a similar currency of rumours in the slums of Noida, the role of the everyday occurrence of 'someone' having said something. See Das 2011: 330.

[7] Moog has refuted the alleged litigiousness of Indians (Moog 1993; cf. Wollschläger 1998).

to establish a specific morality of rights. Cases lodged in the various judicial institutions, whether it be the district courts, the high courts or the newly founded human rights commissions, express an understanding of citizens' rights and the expectations of a specific notion of governmental behaviour and governing norms – even if these are diverse and highly contested even among claimants (cf. Baviskar, this volume). This has been particularly true since the establishment of human rights commissions in India at the national level and in each state. From April 2007 to March 2008, the National Human Rights Commission received 98,332 complaints (NHRC 2008: 178). It had received similar numbers of complaints in preceding years. In the first months after the Human Rights Commission of Maharashtra was established in March 2001, it received 120 complaints a day (many of which concerned issues in which the commission was not competent).[8] Complainants addressed this new forum in the hope of being heard and of escaping the networks of patronage and the labyrinth of connections. Claims before the various institutions could thus be seen as an attempt to establish a specific reading of law.

RUMOURS AND HOPES

We need to pay attention to rumour as a mode of the spread of law. The spread of law and legal knowledge via rumours will open our view to interpretative processes which are shaped not only by existing legal concepts, but even more so by hopes and fears. They thus tell us something about normative change among those who put their hopes in law, as well as about the *jurisgenesis* (Cover 1992: 103) that begins in these movements.

Rumours are unauthenticated news whose truth is uncertain and whose source can (most often) not be determined.[9] The content of a rumour often changes in the course of its spread (Scott 1990: 145;

---

[8] Most complaints concerned harassment by the police. There were also many complaints about administrative failures, particularly in relation to pension rights. Many of these complaints were turned away because the commission was not competent in the matter in question. Discussions with claimants who had been turned away in 2001–2003 made it clear that their failure did not diminish their confidence in the law, but merely in the particular reading of their case by the specific judge involved.

[9] The functionalist strand of literature focusing on the social functions of rumour and gossip of affirming norms and thereby reinforcing community, in short, of social control, as discussed by Gluckman (1963), is not of concern here. Closer to the questions raised here are those authors who see rumours as a form of communication that has a particular relationship to authority, as suggested by Jean-Noel Kapferer (1990: 14).

Zitelmann 2000). One part of this transformation is the unsystematic selection of the content of the news, that is, the telling of the rumour according to the relevance structure of the teller and the 'hearing' of a rumour according to the relevance structure of the hearer. The other part is the creative interpretation of the news, the meaning making (and its normative dimension) that is particularly open in the case of rumours (Kirsch 2002: 70; Steward and Strathern 2004: 30). Rumours, more than other kinds of knowledge and because of their particular uncertainty, are strongly shaped by fears and hopes, and thus on the one hand by norms of what should or could be, and on the other hand by social constructions of danger and threat. Scott writes, 'as rumor travels it is altered in a fashion that brings it more closely into line with the hopes, fears and worldview of those who hear it and retell it' (Scott 1990: 145). Both fears and hopes relate to a situation and the ideas about the possibilities and threats inherent in it, as well as to existing norms of what ought to be.

Because uncertainty is part of the particular character of rumoured knowledge, it brings forth the open-endedness of situations in terms of the right course of action (*Handlungsoffenheit*). The pressures to 'decide' or choose among possible alternative ways of acting forces reflection on such alternative courses of actions. They throw open to questioning self-evident forms of reactions and often entail the re-evaluation of certain types of reactions in terms of norms, values and ends. Rumours cannot be responded to by routines; they demand the reflection of alternatives of acting.

At the same time rumours rely on *comparisons*: what happened there could happen here, because in some relevant manner the situations are the same. This points to a similarity between law and rumour: with law as well as with rumour people identify similarities and differences and isolate out certain factors in order to make a situation comparable. How the possibility of comparison is established in a situation and what is deemed comparable is telling. Gopal Bhai felt that it was the shared experience of living in a slum and of poverty that made the situation comparable: 'He also lives here, he is also poor'. Those were the factors that spoke against the system working for them and made the rumours of law's possibilities, evident in this case, so compelling.

Of course, not all rumours tell of possibilities. Many are about the futility of one's own efforts and the overpowering might of the opponent. My point here is that no matter whether rumours encourage or discourage, the comparisons between situations and between subject positions that they rely upon are a form of horizontal knowledge transfer in which norms are re-evaluated and opened up to include new possibilities in terms of acting. They also provide us with glimpses of what Nigel Rapport has called 'anyone', 'an actor with an identity over and above his or her membership in social groupings and cultural traditions' (Rapport 2010: 84), in that they highlight the moments of evaluation of one's own possibilities, of alternatives of action, of reflective interpretation.[10]

Rumours are most often discussed with regard to their role in heightening collective fears (e.g. Das 1990), in triggering frenzies (e.g. Zitelmann 1998) or in exacerbating social tensions (e.g. Elwert 1991; Subramaniam 1999; Spencer 2000). Their communicative and expressive character is analysed most often with regard to fear, uncertainty and insecurity (e.g. Das 1990; Scheper-Hughes 1992).[11] The other side of rumours, that of hope, is, however, rarely discussed, although here too rumours seem to play an interesting role. People act on rumours of possibilities, of opportunities; many a strategy, many a plan or endeavour is motivated by rumours of possibilities. Indeed, many processes that shape globalisation seem to rest on such rumoured notions: financial investments, economic strategies, migratory tactics about routes to safety and well-being (e.g. Harney 2006) and other such plans for the future. They are in part informed by seemingly sound assessments of market trends or shifting border policies, and they are motivated by speculation or risk calculation. To a large degree these are, however, based precisely on rumours of specific opportunities and their timing, unauthenticated news of possibilities.[12]

What can this attention to the rumours of rights tell us about the diffusion of law? Three aspects seem important to this case. The first one is the attention to processes of horizontal knowledge transfer that occur according to dynamics and selections that differ from the often discussed top-down processes of legal dissemination. The second one is

---

[10] I do not share Rapport's sweeping dismissal of the sociality of subjectivities and his (possibly strategically overstated) criticism of 'the Wittgensteinians'.

[11] Stuart Kirsch has examined the relation between the expression of collective fears in rumours and their appropriation and manipulation by the Indonesian state, which further escalated state terror (Kirsch 2002).

[12] There are, of course, other, more directed and regulated forms of the global transfer of (legal) knowledge, such as (legal) educational programmes, cooperations, the institutionalisation of standards and indicators, the formation of epistemic communities, travelling models and others. Rumour as a mode of the dissemination of knowledge particularly pertinent to processes of globalisation has not been examined much. Rights are yet one more of these rumoured potentials; in some ways, the global rights discourse could be called a rumour in itself.

the processual and situational nature of normative interpretations that is made apparent by observing rumours of rights. This follows the 'translation' of norms far beyond the professional translators that Levitt and Merry (2009) have described and thereby pays attention also to the interpretative processes that occur among those who are subjects of rumoured possibilities and who act on them. The third aspect is hence the normative effect of the rumour, its complex relation to pre-existing norms and the universalising tendencies of comparison inherent in the rumour. Attention to rumours of rights, to the stories about law that circulate, opens our analysis to include questions of how hopes and possibilities are perceived, how comparisons propel normative change and how particular interpretations affect legal norms when acted upon.

HORIZONTAL KNOWLEDGE TRANSFERS ABOUT LAW

In discussions about the spread of law or knowledge about legal norms, we most often examine the transmitters of law and legal knowledge: law firms (e.g. Garth and Dezalay 1996), NGOs (e.g. Keck and Sikkink 1998; Merry 2006; Levitt and Merry 2009), or international organisations (e.g. Li 2009) and such judicial institutions as the International Criminal Court (e.g. Anders, this volume; Clarke 2010). Analyses thus focus on the ways these organisations select, interpret and disseminate law; on their motives and aims; on the networks they operate within and the power relations that shape these networks; and their relation to specific target groups or audiences. These are fundamental questions for our understanding of the operation of law, or, to put it in Upendra Baxi's terms, of the politics *of* human rights. They are particularly pertinent considering the enormous economic and political interests that are involved. They do, however, provide little insight into other processes in which law, or ideas of law, travel. This forecloses a differentiated understanding of normative change that is at the centre of our understanding of the social significance of law. It possibly also forecloses insights into the dynamics between the politics of rights and the politics for rights, and the effects that they have on each other.

Attention to processes of horizontal knowledge transfer, especially in such vague forms as rumours, opens our view to what people hope and what they fear, what means they trust to approach their hopes, what ways of action they deem possible. This is because in the spread of rumours selection happens at every stage: what is transmitted and what is heard depends on what is deemed important either for hopes or for fears. Hence, such processes of horizontal knowledge transfers select according to different criteria than export-oriented law firms, governmental programmes or law-related NGOs with a particular mission and agenda. 'Selection', interpretation and hearing are structured by fears and hopes, and these are at most marginally shaped by the legal concepts that they might then adopt to name their intention. Thus, in paying attention to rumour as a form of horizontal transfer of knowledge about law and rights, we can gain insights into the ways that fears and hopes shape the interpretation, the reach and the adoption of particular understandings of rights and law.

It is precisely the shaping of hopes and needs into claims that is often critically examined when looking at processes of juridification. Legal anthropologists have often speculated on the degree to which so-called universal norms are inadequate to articulate the experiences and ideas of those whom they are meant to protect. They have shown how these experiences and ideas are transformed when reformulated according to legal categories (Felstiner et al. 1980/81); how the perception of a situation and of oneself is determined by the demands of legal reasoning (Merry 1990); and how an individualistic notion of the person underlies these norms and is incapable of representing alternative ideas of personhood (Collier et al. 1995; Strathern 2004). We have many examples of how legal concepts have transformed notions of 'community' (e.g. James 2006) and the perception of what it means to be indigenous (e.g. Donahoe et al. 2008), or to be a woman (e.g. Merry 2003) or a 'victim'. Juridification thus is not only a process of the colonisation of the lifeworld in the sense of Habermas; it creates a new world in its own image and according to (Western) law's assumptions about social organisation.

However important it is to scrutinise such transformative effects of law, it seems only of limited analytical value to stop at the deconstructions of normative imperialism. Such deconstructive perspectives seduce us to think in dichotomies about the travels of law: the dichotomy of modern or Western law and autochthonous legal orders; the dichotomy of hegemony and authenticity, of domination and resistance; that of individual rights and the sociality of being; or that between homogenisation and plurality; and, last but not least, that between law and politics (cf. Zenker in this volume). These dichotomies each detract from a processual approach to normative change and legal travels; they foreclose an analysis of the particular intertwining and merging of normative orders that Sally Merry (1988) and Franz von Benda-Beckmann (2002) have called for and that Fitzpatrick had earlier pointed to with his notion of 'combined law' (1983: 168).

Consider another case: Amita and Vikram got married in 2001. Both lived with their families in Dharavi. Amita was eighteen at the time and Vikram nineteen. Their parents had arranged the marriage, dowry had been paid in the form of pots and other kitchen utensils, and they conducted the wedding according to Hindu ritual. In March 2002 Vikram wanted to divorce. He said that Amita was unfit for marriage because of mental illness and that the marriage had never been consummated. Amita's mother, Tara, agreed to the divorce (Amita's father had long disappeared). Tara feared the worst: that her daughter might be physically harmed. She knew of so many cases in which girls had been severely ill-treated by their in-laws. The disagreement thus was not about whether or not to divorce, but about the rights over the dowry, especially Amita's *stridhan*.[13] Tara insisted on its return. Tara, always speaking for Amita, who never spoke herself because she was evidently in a state of severe depression, claimed that Amita's mental instability was due to the way Vikram had treated her during marriage, in particular his adultery. Vikram refused to return the dowry, claiming that he had been tricked into marrying a mentally ill woman. In this he felt affirmed by the counsel of the Jamaat, the caste council, but they were not willing to make a clear statement on the matter. To me they said that they could only help where the parties involved were willing to come to an amicable conclusion. They had counselled the two young people to mend their differences and stay together.

Vikram, however, turned to the local *Shakha Pramukh* of the Shiv Sena party, who threatened to drive Amita's family out of Dharavi.[14] Tara was very afraid of the *Shakha Pramukh*, so she went to a local (Muslim-led) NGO to find help. In response, the NGO mobilised its female clients to protest and threatened to file a case of 'dowry harassment' against

---

[13] *Stridhan* is the part of a woman's property which she can sell, give away, mortgage, lease or exchange. Besides the jewellery, clothes and bedding given at marriage, *stridhan* also includes the gifts to the woman before, during and after marriage. It includes property inherited by the woman from her family or husband's family; property received by her under a compromise or in lieu of maintenance; and property bought using proceeds from *stridhan*. Section 27 of the Hindu Marriage Act of 1955 stipulates that refusal to return *stridhan* upon divorce makes the husband liable to prosecution.

[14] *Shakha Pramukhs* are the heads of the local branches (*Shakha*) or party offices of the Shiv Sena (the RSS also uses the term). *Shakha Pramukhs* organise the activities and finances of the *Shakhas* with a relatively high degree of autonomy from the movement's leadership. Like the local big men of other political parties or gangs, they take on the role of adjudicator.

Vikram, a threat that would inevitably lead to police investigations. Although many 'dowry harassment' and 'dowry death' cases are not solved and might not even be taken seriously by the police, who often consider deaths related to dowry disputes to be matters of domestic accidents, a police investigation means being brought to the attention of the police and made vulnerable to police harassment, and is thus a serious threat.

However, a few weeks after the NGO had confronted the *Shakha Pramukh*, Amita's mother, in a meeting of the parties now involved in the case, declared that she now wanted not only the pots and pans, but also 135,000 rupees for 'maintenance'. When all others responded in surprise, she declared that she had heard that women were entitled by state law to maintenance after divorce.[15]

Another rumour was behind this sudden demand and her sudden increase in self-confidence, indeed one that was based on a misunderstanding. Tara told me that she had discussed the fate of her daughter with some of the women in her neighbourhood. At first she discussed it only grudgingly – she had wanted to keep the affair hushed up because she was afraid it would jeopardise the prospects of a second marriage for her daughter. But the case was making the rounds anyway, partly because Vikram's family were also going around telling their version of the story so as to establish it as fact. So one day, Tara said, someone had told her that the Indian Supreme Court – an entity well-known and equally mysterious in the slums – had awarded a Muslim woman a large settlement that was to be paid to her by her husband, who had divorced her. If a Muslim woman could get this, then surely it was also Amita's right. Everyone knew that Muslim women had at least as hard a lot as themselves.

I assumed then and still assume today (but cannot ascertain it) that this was the story of Shah Bano, the case that achieved notoriety because of the severe political upheavals that followed it. In the end, Rajiv Gandhi overturned the court's judgement granting alimony to Shah Bano when the Muslim Personal Law Board protested that the judgement was an infringement on minority rights and their legal autonomy. Shah Bano not only lost her alimony rights, but her case also came to symbolise the conservative politics of some representatives of Indian Muslims and

---

[15] I myself was so surprised by Tara's sudden confidence that I never asked how she came up with this precise sum, a sum that was well-nigh impossible for Vikram to pay as he earned only about 1,000 rupees per month.

their claims for minority rights, which in turn served to justify Hindu nationalists in their diatribes against Islam and the Muslims of India.

None of this Amita's mother knew. She did not know the name of the Muslim woman she had heard about and did not know who exactly had first mentioned her. None of her neighbours knew of Shah Bano, but all started talking about the right to maintenance and that this legendary site that was the Supreme Court had given a Muslim woman a lot of money and had taken this money from her estranged husband. Tara also wanted to write to this court (or rather, to have someone write a letter to the court for her) and tell the story of her daughter to whom such injustice had been done. The other 'rumour' – this one widespread and based in fact, but 'known' in the vague ways that rumours are – was that anyone can write to the Supreme Court and tell of their plight.

Tara never blamed her daughter for the failure of her marriage. She never told her to go back to her husband, and she once said that she was glad that her own husband had disappeared because he would not have taken Amita back. She feared for the safety of her daughter if she remained with her in-laws. In the course of talking with her neighbours about the fate of Amita, her position changed from one of trying to save her daughter from harm but being at the same time ashamed of the affair, to one where she assertively augmented her protective feelings with certain demands. She interpreted the legal rumour that she had heard through the filter of her understanding of Amita's situation: her husband had been a bad husband and had caused the current state of illness in Amita. He was responsible for the failure of the marriage and he was guilty of destroying her daughter's mental well-being. The money he was supposed to give was not only meant to ensure a livelihood for her daughter, but also as a punishment and an attribution of guilt.

Here again the rumour of a law, of a right, provided the frame in which certain interpretations of a situation could be named. Many factors shaped Tara's understanding. For one, it was her fear for her daughter, based on the stories (rumours, witnessing) of other daughters-in-law that had been harmed. These made her set aside all notions of propriety – of wifely duty or Hindu marriage law – that might have played a role.

This interpretation seemed to have emerged somewhat collectively, in the talk and gossip with her neighbours that Tara had initially been so worried about. The course of collective gossiping could have taken another turn: it could have resulted in the condemnation of Amita and her mental instability, or of Tara and her misguided marriage arrangement for her daughter. This version was probably circulating at the same time, at least among Vikram's supporters. The precise factors that led to the rumour of the right to maintenance overriding all other aspects of the story cannot be ascertained. Possibly Vikram's affair with another woman was detrimental to his credibility; maybe it was simply friendship and sympathy with Tara by some vocal local women who took the lead in defining the situation – I do not know. But this rumour grew into one which rather suddenly sidelined all other versions of this divorce and had Tara's female neighbours rally in solidarity. 'Maintenance' seemed to become the name for hopes and feelings that had found none before.

This often incidental, eclectic selection, specific to horizontal knowledge transfer and bound up with interests, aims and hopes different from those that motivate top-down processes of legal dissemination, needs to be examined with regard to the impact on other arenas of legal interpretation. It is the ground of the politics *for* human rights that Upendra Baxi (in this volume) mentions as an important source of the development of human rights. Of course, it is here not even quite politics: in particular, Gopal Bhai's aversion to social movements seems to confirm all fears that legal rights have an individualising tendency. However, his understanding of his rights was not individualistic; it related to collective experiences, collective labour and community. Even more evident was this social nature in Tara's and Amita's case: the rumour of legally prescribed maintenance turned into the defining narrative in the conflict involving Tara, Vikram's family and the *Shakha Pramukh* when her female neighbours adopted it with her, their talk reinforcing its urgency and primacy and elevating it above any other considerations pertinent to the case according to the different normative orders 'present' in the situation.

INTERPRETATION AND ITERATIONS

For such adoptions of new norms that are inspired by globally circulating legal concepts the term 'vernacularisation' has sometimes been used in legal anthropology (Merry 2006; Michelutti 2007; Levitt and Merry 2009). Vernacularisation means the adaptation of globally circulating norms, institutions or simply terms to locally valid normative languages and institutions. A 'universal' norm is translated into 'local culture', so to say. Theories of vernacularisation assume the meeting of two (or more) distinct normative systems. New and alien norms are adopted according to existing normative models into which people are socialised and within which they think and feel. Such adoptions and adaptations appear as a result of the fact that people live within one distinct system; theories of vernacularisation assume (often implicitly) that people are socialised into specific norms that not only shape but determine their perception of the world. Norms are shared by members of certain groups who are defined by such shared norms and are presumed to be normatively integrated and rather homogeneous. We can distinguish between those positions that consider all 'cultures' to be homogeneous in this sense, i.e. as relying on shared norms, and those who attest such high degrees of normative homogeneity particularly to non-Western, so-called traditional societies which are assumed to be less differentiated. These perspectives have to assume a degree of cultural determinism that binds 'members' of a norm group to their particular norms in a fundamental way of perceiving the world. In these perspectives, law, normativity and social action fall into one. They do not reflect the heterogeneity of norm orientations within those groups described as normative 'units', and they often do not assess the social processes by which certain norms gain dominance within particular social relations, or by which normative homogeneity or consensus is produced. The negotiations over norms that are inherent in all normative orders are obfuscated by the focus on the encounter between two apparently alien normative systems.

Of course, it would not be justified to employ instead a purely voluntaristic notion of normative orientation, or to speak of entirely situational and rational norm orientations (as might be suggested by some formulations of 'forum shopping'). There are limits to interpretation that lie in the norm itself, but also in pre-existing norms that shape people's interpretations of norms, or the 'doxa' in Bourdieu's sense (1977). A practice-oriented perspective points to the dynamic between normative or habitual orientation which shapes the understanding of a situation, and the open-endedness of action (Bourdieu 1977: 225) that is possible because of the singularity of each situation. This implies that every normative orientation is to some degree open to new interpretations, and that such interpretations are inherent in the application of a norm in a specific singular situation. Norms are transformed in iterations. Derrida's notion of iteration suggests that any use (in our case: of a norm) is also an interpretation and thus a transformation (Derrida 1991: 90). However, contrary to theories of vernacularisation and others that consider processes of normative hybridisation, this iterative transformation does not adapt a norm to an existing normative order. In other words, it is not a matter of mixing two distinct systems; rather it adapts a norm to a concrete situation, the interpretation of which

by the person who acts is of course also shaped by prevailing normative orientations. Any application of a norm to concrete circumstances
thus means interpretation. At the level of individual interactions we
thus come closer to the openness and indeterminacy in terms of action
that people face even within the limitations set by habitual normative
orientations – an openness or indeterminacy that is reinforced by the
uncertainty of rumour.

It is this interpretative act of Tara and Gopal Bhai that is of interest here because it points us to an alternative perception of normative
orientation and its transformations. These interpretations are transmitted in rumours of rights. They stand in an ambivalent relation to
other channels of the dissemination of legal knowledge, exaggerating
messages of hope, rejecting them as unbelievable, suspecting them of
unreliability – all depending on the circumstances of the hearer and
the issues at stake. In the case of Tara's norm adoption we see two processes of iteration: first, Tara introduces 'guilt' and responsibility into
the negotiation of the divorce of her daughter's Hindu marriage; then
she comes to apply a notion of 'women's rights' to the situation, thus
introducing an entirely novel category into the interpretation of the
social relations at issue in the case. In many ways the two norms that
she applies do not fit together: Tara was never opposed to dowry as such,
never considered its illegality in Indian law, and never saw women's
rights violated or denigrated thereby. For her it was the interpretation
of Hindu law that was faulty and that she wanted corrected by her
pointing to the husband's 'guilt' in making her daughter ill and unsuitable for marriage. Thus she did not break with the religious norms that
had guided her in arranging the marriage of her daughter, but wanted
them to be interpreted in a new way, a way that was to her the correct
way under the specific circumstances. This she battled for by drawing on norms provided by another normative system. The distinction
between the two, however, did not matter and was not even evident to
her. This points us to the possibilities that all legally plural situations
entail, namely that norms inform each other and are in the process
often synthesised, blurring seemingly fixed boundaries between different normative orders.

CONSTELLATIONS AND FIGURATIONS

Tara's adopting of the women's rights notion of maintenance could
be said to be a classic case of 'forum shopping', a case of her choosing

the legal forum and the normative order most suitable to her interests. However, in a perspective of 'forum shopping' we would not be able to see how these 'interests' emerged and thus her opting for one rather than another normative order could not be explained. After all, her 'interests' might have been to keep her daughter married – and avoid the burden of having to marry her off again or have an unmarried daughter. The notion of 'interests' is highly under-complex in this regard: the transition of Tara from her first role as a mother being relieved of her duty for her daughter upon marriage, to one worried for the safety of her daughter, to one adopting the category 'woman' as grounds for rights exemplifies the various possible 'interests' in conflict here, and the shift in roles that Tara underwent.

Moreover, observation of the 'act' of forum shopping needs to be complemented with the analysis of the possibilities of forum shopping, i.e. the unequal opportunities to choose the forum most beneficial to one's interests (once they have crystallised) and how such opportunities are structured. This points us to the constellations within which both 'interests' and roles, as well as opportunities for choice, are constituted. In Tara's case it was the empathy of her female neighbours, the precise reason of which cannot be known. It was also the fact that when faced with the wrath of the local women, the *Shakha Pramukh* lost interest in the case. For him, there was not much to gain from it, and more to lose, especially as he suddenly found himself in opposition to the women of his own party, members of the Mahila Aghadi, who (partly in competition with the Muslim-led NGO that had taken Tara's side) pleaded strongly for the maintenance payment. They presented this as the pro-woman position of Hinduism, although they had in many cases of marital conflicts counselled for adherence to traditional family roles. Their situational interpretation of what is Hindu tradition points us again to the frame that different normative orders provide for each other, either as a source of further reasoning and inspiration, or, as in this instance, as a bogey against which one can positively distinguish oneself. It also points us to the political constellations that were decisive in determining the conclusion of the case: the *Shakha Pramukh* withdrew because in his 'game', namely democratic competition, he had nothing to gain from siding with the wrong party. Norms did not play a part in his calculation.

Vikram, who suddenly stood alone with his version of the story, grudgingly agreed to return the *stridhan* and even to pay the maintenance sum of 135,000 rupees, a sum that he needed ten years to earn according to his own calculation.[16] The NGO refrained from accusing him of 'dowry harassment', and Tara did not have a letter written to the Supreme Court. We can only speculate on how these results feed into the rumour mill and breathe life into further iterations.

These are the multi-facetted relational processes at the core of normative change: the normative comparisons that are made, the linkages to normative publics that are sought – and which of these can successfully induce solidarity. Peter Fitzpatrick once pointed towards these relational processes with his attention to the historical struggles in which institutions were shaped by the interactions between various actors (Fitzpatrick 1983).[17] These processes can perhaps best be captured with Elias's concept of 'figuration' (1978), webs of (local and global) interdependencies. In the case discussed here, the relationship between Tara and Vikram was shaped by many strands of interdependence. It was, for example, shaped by the competition between the NGO and the *Shakha Pramukh*. That competition was in itself shaped by their differing dependence on the support of people, i.e. their different embeddedness in the realm of democratic politics. The particular ways in which Indian democracy works determined the behavioural logic of the *Shakha Pramukh*. It also propelled the discourse of women's rights to a certain prominence in a context in which chauvinist movements such as the Shiv Sena use the discourse of women's rights to distinguish themselves from their 'dangerous other', namely Muslims and Islam. Hence, the currency of women's rights was constituted by various movements within what could be called a global public in a historical moment in which Islam is perceived as most hostile to women's rights and the global security discourse legitimates itself also by claiming to protect women. (Of course, this line of justification in itself rests on the very currency of women's rights that had been struggled for by diverse women's movements across the globe.)

These figurations are all constituted by the often contradictory efforts to be heard, to distinguish oneself against another, to gain dominance and to forge alliances. They are also shaped by the means by which such dependencies and alliances are sustained through rules of majorities, brute force, money, a common enemy, law or a combination of the above.

---

[16] I have no information on whether Vikram even started to pay this sum. It seems very unlikely that, given his own meagre income, he would ever be able to comply with this demand.

[17] Fitzpatrick termed the outcome of such interactions 'combined law' (1983: 168), a term possibly slightly undermining his valuable insight that at issue were not simply combinations or hybrids, but institutions shaped in particular historical struggles.

FAILURE AND THE FUTURE

For Gopal Bhai, law had its limits; it did not prove as fertile with possibilities as it did for Tara. Gopal Bhai went to the Human Rights Commission of Maharashtra to present his case. The judge actually heard him, and in a somewhat strange twist of procedure told him at once that this was a case for Article 21 of the Indian Constitution, the right to life, but that Gopal Bhai's claim was no matter for the Human Rights Commission because no state agency was involved in either commission or omission. He sent Gopal Bhai away and recommended that he take his case to a *lok adalat* and come to an agreement with the builder there. Gopal Bhai knew about *lok adalats*, mediatory procedures that had been instituted in Maharshtra as part of the state's legal aid programme. Gopal Bhai was at once crushed and furious when he told me about his failure at the Human Rights Commission. He felt that *Lok Adalats* were only for compromises, but he did not want a compromise. He wanted to have what he considered the right of all slum dwellers: to stay on the land that they had turned into their home. 'A compromise gives me only half my right', he said.

National elections were approaching. Gopal Bhai went to the local Congress Party candidate. Gopal Bhai had always held the candidate in high regard as both a movie star and a person, and had once joined the Shiv Sena only for instrumental reasons. His heart, he had always said, was with the Congress Party. The Congress candidate arranged a contact to another builder, one close to his own party. After some negotiations, the Congress builder took over the contract with the residents of the slum. They in turn all voted for the Congress Party in the elections, and the Congress candidate won the election – for the first time after many years of Shiv Sena domination – and Gopal Bhai and his fellow residents now live in small apartments of 225 square feet next to a big shopping mall-cum-office-building complex.

For Gopal Bhai, patronage worked better than law. So was the rumour just a rumour? In many ways it was, but in others this rumour expressed and furthered a normative process: it gave a name to hopes; it made specific vague ideas of entitlements and the grounds on which they were based, namely having made a living in the city and contributing to it (cf. Das 2011; Holston 2011). In a way it turned hope into an expectation. Legal naming (Felstiner *et al.* 1980/1981) is not necessarily a misnomer, but is part of the iterative process of *juris genesis*. Thus, law is used not only for 'winning' but also for expressing certain values (Hirsch and

Lazarus-Black 1994: 16) and shaping them; legal norms are invoked in a normative manner. This is the case even where the chances of winning are slim, and where the reference to law has a predominantly symbolic nature, affirming certain values against prevailing practices that run counter to them. Changes might be small. They consist mainly in slow and sometimes contradictory changes of the norms of what is 'normal'. These norms influence how practices are evaluated and reacted to as acceptable or condemnable. These slow and small transformations in the ideas about the normal, that which is to be expected normatively as the right way of doing things, can in their cumulation add up to a more profound transformation of standards, of ideas of the good and proper order of things. The political directions that such transformations take are contingent.

References

Baxi, Upendra 1998. 'Voices of suffering and the future of human rights', *Transnational Law and Contemporary Problems* 8: 126–75.

Benda-Beckmann, Franz von 2002. 'Who's afraid of legal pluralism?', *Journal of Legal Pluralism* 47: 37–82.

Bourdieu, Pierre 1977. *Outline of a Theory of Practice*. Cambridge University Press.

Chatterjee, Partha 2004. *The Politics of the Governed: Reflections on Popular Politics in Most of the World*. New York: Columbia University Press.

Clarke, Kamari 2010. 'Rethinking Africa through its exclusions: the politics of naming criminal responsibility', *Anthropological Quarterly* 38 (3): 625–51.

Cohn, Bernard 1959. 'Some notes on law and change in India', *Economic Development and Cultural Change* 8: 79–93.

Collier, Jane, Maurer, Bill and Suarez-Navaz, Liliana 1995. 'Sanctioned identities: legal constructions of modern personhood', *Identities* 2 (1–2): 1–27.

Cover, Robert 1992. 'Nomos and narrative', in Martha Minow, Michael Ryan and Austin Sarat (eds.) *Narrative, Violence, and the Law: The Essays of Robert Cover*. Ann Arbor: University of Michigan Press, pp. 95–172.

Das, Veena 1990. 'Communities, riots, survivors: the South Asian experience', in Veena Das (ed.) *Mirrors of Violence: Communities, Riots and Survivors in South Asia*. Delhi: Oxford University Press, pp. 1–36.

2011. 'State, citizenship and the urban poor', *Citizenship Studies* 15 (3–4): 319–33.

Derrida, Jacques 1991. 'Signature, event, context', in Peggy Kamuff (ed.) *A Derrida Reader: Between the Blinds*. New York: Columbia University Press, pp. 80–111.

Donahoe, Brian, Habeck, Joachim Otto, Halemba, Agnieszka and Sántha, István 2008. 'Size and place in the construction of indigeneity in the Russian Federation', *Current Anthropology* 49(6): 993–1020.

Eckert, Julia 2003. *The Charisma of Direct Action. Power, Politics, and the Shiv Sena*. Oxford University Press.

2006. 'From subjects to citizens: legalisation from below and the homogenisation of the legal sphere', *Journal of Legal Pluralism* 53–54: 45–75.

Elias, Norbert 1978. *What is Sociology?* London: Hutchinson.

Elwert, Georg 1991. 'Fassaden, Gerüchte, Gewalt – über Nationalismus', *Merkur* 4: 318–32.

Felstiner, William, Abel, Richard L. and Sarat, Austin 1980/1981. 'The emergence and transformation of disputes: naming, blaming, claiming …', *Law & Society Review* 15: 631–54.

Fernandes, Leela 2006. *India's New Middle Class: Democratic Politics in an Era of Economic Reform*. Ann Arbour: University of Minnesota Press.

Fitzpatrick, Peter 1983. 'Law, plurality, and underdevelopment', in David Sugarman (ed.) *Legality, Ideology and the State*. London: Academic Press, pp. 159–82.

Galanter, Marc 1997. 'The displacement of traditional law in modern India', in Marc Galanter (ed.) *Law and Society in Modern India*. Delhi and New York: Oxford University Press, pp. 15–36.

Garth, Bryant and Dezalay, Yves 1996. *Dealing in Virtue: International Commercial Arbitration and the Construction of a Transnational Legal Order*. University of Chicago Press.

Gluckman, Max 1963. 'Gossip and scandal', *Current Anthropology* 4: 307–16.

Harney, Nicholas 2006. 'Rumour, migrants, and the informal economies of Naples, Italy', *International Journal of Sociology and Social Policy* 26 (9/10): 374–84.

Hirsch, Susan and Lazarus-Black, Mindie 1994. 'Performance and paradox: exploring law's role in hegemony and resistance', in Susan Hirsch and Mindie Lazarus-Black (eds.) *Law, Hegemony and Resistance*. New York: Routledge, pp. 1–31.

Holston, James 2011. 'Contesting privilege with right: the transformation of differentiated citizenship in Brazil', *Citizenship Studies* 15 (3–4): 335–52.

James, Deborah 2006. 'The tragedy of the private: owners, communities and the state in South Africa's land reform programme', in Franz von Benda-Beckmann, Keebet von Benda-Beckmann and Melanie G. Wiber (eds.) *Changing Properties of Property*. Oxford: Berghahn Books, pp. 243–68.

Kapferer, Jean-Noel 1990. *Rumours: Uses, Interpretations and Images*. Piscataway, NJ: Transaction Publishers.

Keck, Margaret and Sikkink, Kathryn 1998. *Activists beyond Borders: Advocacy Networks in International Politics*. Ithaca, NY: Cornell University Press.

Kirsch, Stuart 2002. 'Rumour and other narratives of political violence in West Papua', *Critique of Anthropology* 22 (1): 53–79.

Levitt, Peggy and Merry, Sally 2009. 'Vernacularization on the ground: local use of global women's rights in Peru, China, India and the United States', *Global Networks* 9 (4): 441–61.

Li, Tania 2009. 'The law of the project: government and "good governance" at the World Bank in Indonesia', in Franz von Benda-Beckmann, Keebet von Benda-Beckmann and Julia Eckert (eds.) *Rules of Law and Laws of Ruling*. Aldershot: Ashgate, pp. 237–56.

Merry, Sally 1988. 'Legal pluralism', *Law & Society Review* 22: 869–96.

1990. *Getting Justice and Getting Even: Legal Consciousness among Working-Class Americans*. University of Chicago Press.

2003. 'Rights talk and the experience of law: implementing women's human rights to protection from violence', *Human Rights Quarterly* 25 (2): 343–81.

2006. 'Transnational human rights and local activists: mapping the middle', *American Anthropologist* 108: 38–51.

Michelutti, Lucia 2007. *The Vernacularisation of Democracy: Politics, Caste and Religion in India*. London and New York: Routledge.

Moog, Robert 1993. 'Indian litigiousness and the litigation explosion: challenging the legend', *Asian Survey* 33 (12): 1136–50.

National Human Rights Commission (NHRC) 2008. Annual Report online available at: http://nhrc.nic.in/Documents/AR/AR08–05ENG.pdf, last accessed 28 June 2011.

Rao, Ursula 2010. 'Making the global city. Urban citizenship on the margins of Delhi', *Ethnos* 74(4): 402–24.

Rapport, Nigel 2010. 'Apprehending anyone: the non-indexical, post-cultural, and cosmopolitan human actor', *Journal of the Royal Anthropological Institute* 16: 84–101.

Scheper-Hughes, Nancy 1992. *Death without Weeping*. Berkeley: University of California Press.

Scott, James 1990. *Domination and the Arts of Resistance: Hidden Transcripts*. New Haven, CT: Yale University Press.

Spencer, Jonathan 2000. *On Not Becoming a Terrorist: Problems of Memory, Agency and Community in the Sri Lankan Conflict*. Berkeley: University of California Press.

Stewart, Pamela and Strathern, Andrew 2004. *Witchcraft, Sorcery, Rumor and Gossip*. Cambridge University Press.

Strathern, Marilyn 2004. 'Losing (out on) intellectual resources', in Alain Pottage and Martha Mundy (eds.) *Law Anthropology and the Constitution of the Social*. Cambridge University Press, pp. 201–33.

Subramaniam, Radhika 1999. 'Culture of suspicion: riots and rumour in Bombay, 1992–1993', *Transforming Anthropology* 8 (1 and 2): 97–110.

Wollschläger, Christian 1998. 'Exploring global landscapes of litigation rates', in Jürgen Brand (ed.) *Soziologie des Rechts*. Baden-Baden: Nomos, pp. 577–88.

Zitelmann, Thomas 1998. 'Bomben in Addis Abeba: Nachricht, Gerücht, Selbstinformation', in Jan Koehler and Sonja Heyer (eds.) *Anthropologie der Gewalt, Chancen und Grenzen der sozialwissenschaftlichen Forschung*. Berlin: Verlag für Wissenschaft und Forschung, pp. 203–16.

2000. Gerücht und paradoxe Kommunikation – systemtheoretische Implikationen der Gerüchteforschung. Manuscript on file with the author.

CHAPTER 7

PUBLIC INTEREST AND PRIVATE COMPROMISES: THE POLITICS OF ENVIRONMENTAL NEGOTIATION IN DELHI, INDIA

Amita Baviskar

INTRODUCTION

Public interest litigation (PIL) came into prominence in Indian jurisprudence in the 1970s as a means of addressing outstanding violations of fundamental rights guaranteed by the Indian Constitution. From being a tool for assisting vulnerable individuals and social groups in gaining access to justice, PIL has, since the late 1990s, been transformed into a far more complex device that shapes subjectivities as well as state practices across the spectrum of social activism. This essay argues that the changed meanings and effects engendered by PIL reflect larger shifts in Indian politics and society since the onset of economic liberalisation in the early 1990s. In particular, they signify that the formation of a judicial public sphere based on science and law, when embedded within the political economy of emerging urban land markets and labour deregulation and a discourse of 'world-class cities', is fraught with contradictions that undermine its original progressive intent.

This essay examines the use of public interest litigation by 'bourgeois environmentalists' in Delhi, who have deployed it to get the upper-level courts (Supreme Court and High Courts) to shut down factories and remove squatter settlements in the name of cleaning the city of pollution. These judicial orders, which have had severe and adverse impacts on workers' ability to find livelihoods and shelter in Delhi, have superseded the governmental realms of the executive and the legislature, and have short-circuited the processes of political negotiation that occur between workers, political representatives and government officials. How did the courts come to wield such overriding powers? This essay addresses this question by examining the shifts in the Indian polity in terms of the rise of an empowered urban elite that styles itself as the 'middle class' and that has come to monopolise the discursive construction of the 'public interest'. The ongoing collaboration between the upper courts and bourgeois environmentalists is also premised upon a shared understanding of what constitutes an 'environmental' issue and how it should be addressed.

I shall also show how such hegemonic agreements about 'environmental protection' and safeguarding the public interest are challenged on the ground – not so much through the actions of disenfranchised and dispossessed workers, but through the 'informal' arrangements made by state officials and politicians to maintain their sources of income and patronage. An analysis that situates law within a wider web of political practices shows how shifts in legal interpretations are shaped by the larger dynamics of social change.

PUBLIC INTEREST LITIGATION IN INDIA: A BRIEF OUTLINE

The first reported case of PIL in India occurred in 1979, when a case was filed in the Supreme Court by a lawyer on the basis of a news report published in the *Indian Express* highlighting the plight of thousands of prisoners in Bihar state who had spent several years in jail while awaiting trial.[1] Arguing that the right to speedy justice was a fundamental right, the judges ordered the release of more than 40,000 under-trial prisoners. This case illustrated many of the key features of the spate of PIL that was to follow. It created a new discourse of human rights by expanding the meaning of the fundamental right to equality, life and personal liberty.[2] In this process, the right to a speedy trial, free legal aid, dignity, means of livelihood, education, housing, medical care and a clean environment, as well as the right not to be subjected to torture, sexual harassment, solitary confinement, bondage and servitude, or exploitation, emerged as human rights. The initiative also democratised access to the courts by changing the rule of locus standi and allowing any public-spirited citizen or social action group to approach the court on behalf of an individual or group whose rights had been violated. It created a precedent for judicial monitoring of state institutions such as jails, mental asylums and the like, an

---

[1] *Hussainara Khatoon v. State of Bihar*, AIR 1979, SC 1360.
[2] www.ngosindia.com/resources/pil_sc.php, last accessed on 11 February 2011.

expansion of jurisdiction that was to later encompass almost all aspects of state administration. Finally, the court devised new mechanisms for investigation by drawing on the media, subject experts and government agencies, and making them report directly to it (Dembowski 2001).

In 1981, Justices V. R. Krishna Iyer and P. N. Bhagwati, who pioneered PIL in India, noted that when persons who 'by reasons of poverty, help-lessness or disability or socially or economically disadvantaged position [were] unable to approach the court for relief, any member of the pub-lic can maintain an application for an appropriate direction'.[3] Thus PIL focused attention on those whose social and economic position denied them access to justice and gave legal recognition to those 'public-spirited' citizens who claimed to represent the former. The initiative was premised upon the assumption that addressing the concerns of hitherto excluded sections of society was in the 'public interest'. Poverty and its attendant injustices were perceived as key concerns to be addressed by the courts.

Notably, public interest litigation started in the aftermath of the Emergency (1975–1977), a period when civil liberties were suspended, opponents of the ruling Congress party were imprisoned and tortured, press censorship prevailed, and many ordinary citizens were forced to undergo sterilisation and were evicted from their homes under 'wel-fare' programmes for family planning and slum clearance. During the Emergency, the higher judiciary was quiescent and did not object to the abuse of official power. It would seem that the subsequent 'activism' of the judiciary in the post-Emergency years, especially its vigorous pursuit of PIL, was intended to erase the stigma brought by its earlier passive acceptance of authoritarian state power.

In the late 1980s, the purview of PIL expanded from a primary focus on civil liberties to environmental issues. Perhaps the first case of this kind was filed in 1984 by a lawyer, M. C. Mehta, asking for the clos-ure of the Shriram Foods and Fertilisers factory in Delhi on the grounds of environmental hazard. Even as the petition was in court, there was an oleum gas leak from the plant which caused severe adverse reactions among hundreds of local people. Following close on the heels of the Bhopal gas disaster in December 1984, this alarming incident within the capital spurred environmental activist groups to implead themselves as concerned parties. Invoking Article 21 of the Constitution, which guar-anteed the right to life, environmentalists argued that the right to life included the right to a clean environment, an interpretation that was

---

[3] *S. P. Gupta v. Union of India*, 1981 (Supp) SCC 87, last accessed on 11 February 2011.

accepted by the Supreme Court. This period also witnessed a growing institutionalisation of environmental concerns: in 1985, the Ministry of Environment and Forests was formed and, in 1986, the Environment Protection Act was legislated. Other regulatory agencies and rules soon followed (Divan and Rosencranz 1991). Following the Bhopal tragedy, press coverage of environmental issues had also increased. Drawing upon newly available data from government monitoring agencies, environmental groups that had begun awareness campaigns in the early 1980s (CSE 1982) were able to harness heightened media attention to promote their concerns. Environmentalism in the 1980s thus brought together law, media and activist groups in a new alliance.

Notably, the big environmental issues of the 1980s – the Chipko movement against tree-felling in the Himalayan foothills and the Silent Valley campaign against the construction of a dam in a primary rainforest in Kerala in south India – did not approach the courts. Their key feature was the political mobilisation of local villagers and, in the Silent Valley case, students, to make demands on the government. In the process, they also cultivated support among members of the urban intelligentsia. In both cases, the central government responded directly to the movements: banning tree-felling on slopes greater than thirty degrees and cancelling the dam. Other campaigns against environmentally damaging practices and projects in the 1990s continued to engage in collective mobilisation and build support among metropolitan 'reference publics', but also began to file cases in court, making use of the legal opportunities now available. However, PIL remained a weapon of last resort, to be used only when the government had refused to accede to lawful demands made through the medium of non-violent public protest.

In the early 1990s, when India embarked upon a policy of economic liberalisation, environmental concerns were being routinely routed through the courts, often without any prior attempts at collective campaigning or approaching state regulatory agencies. As I discuss later in the essay, both economic liberalisation and increased recourse to the courts were premised on a common narrative of governmental incompetence and corruption. Instead of being the weapon of last resort for grassroots movements, PIL became the first and only strategy of elite urban-based NGOs. The prime beneficiaries of economic liberalisation have been urban elites, who have felt all the more empowered and entitled to demand a lifestyle that suits their growing aspirations. As the content of PIL shifted from the livelihood issues of pavement dwellers in the 1980s to the 'quality of life' concerns of affluent urban residents in the 2000s, so also did its target.

If the first wave of PIL was marked by the use of 'law against the state' to secure social justice, by the turn of the millennium it had become a different beast altogether: still against the state, but also against the poor, against factory workers, slum dwellers and forest users. It became apparent that 'public interest' now referred to different publics, and 'environmentalism' meant different issues to different people.

AIR POLLUTION AND EVERYDAY LIFE IN THE 1990S

'I was waiting this morning for the school bus to pick up my son, and I noticed that three of the four kids at the bus stop carried inhalers in their pockets. Man, that's scary!' said Anand Kapoor, an architect. Kapoor lives in Delhi's affluent Defence Colony neighbourhood, and has a ten-year-old who is asthmatic, a condition that seems to be more and more common among children in the city. Oft-quoted statistics in the media that 25 per cent of Delhi's children suffer from some chronic respiratory ailment provide a numeric gloss over the everyday experience of impairment, visits to the doctor and pharmacist, and the anxiety and expense suffered by parents.

Driving through Delhi's rush-hour traffic, pollution manifests itself in the smoke belched out by trucks and the acrid smell of unburnt hydrocarbons that cause burning, streaming eyes, coughing bouts and, later, blinding headaches. Many people on 'two-wheelers' (as scooters and motorcycles are called), who have no windows to roll up as they drive at the level of vehicular exhaust pipes, tie an ineffectual handkerchief across their noses and mouths. When asked whether it works, they shrug.

At some of the major traffic intersections in Delhi, the Central Pollution Control Board (CPCB) has installed giant digital displays of pollution levels as they are monitored. As people wait for the lights to change, they can check exactly what toxic cocktail they are imbibing, how much lead, carbon monoxide and suspended particulate matter. The metro news broadcast by the NDTV news channel regularly features a 'Pollution Watch' that follows the weather report. It records the levels of pollution recorded every day in the four major Indian metropolitan cities.

A child's body, a ride through the city, a set of statistics reported on television – these disparate sites are connected by a chain of signification that links somatic symptoms to proximate causes, suggesting diagnosis and remedy. The narrative that is created – the problem of air pollution in Delhi – conjures up a cause and a constituency, authorises action and enables exclusions, and obscures as much as it reveals. 'Air pollution' in the sense of an objectively verifiable series of chemical changes, may have existed in Delhi for some time, but it was only recognised as a *problem*, and especially one that demanded public action, at a particular historical and cultural conjuncture. The every-day experiences and media coverage described above are not 'natural' reflections of a pre-existing concern, but inform a collective cognitive process whereby a 'problem' came to be perceived. The narrative about 'the problem of air pollution' is produced by multiple historically and spatially located agents – different state agencies, particularly the judi-ciary, and an assertive middle class – to legitimise authoritarian inter-ventions in the lives of the city's working classes, who are employed in large and small industrial firms.

In response to litigation filed by an environmental activist-lawyer, the Supreme Court of India issued a series of directives in the latter half of the 1990s that resulted in the closure of thousands of industrial units in Delhi, India's capital. The petitions and the court's actions addressed the issue of air and water pollution, and were justified as being in the 'public interest'. The media and middle-class citizens, many with direct experi-ence of the increased incidence of respiratory diseases in the city, widely supported the environmentalist initiative. Affected factory owners' and workers' organisations did not succeed in getting the court to amend its decision. As a result, not only did many factory-owners suffer sig-nificant financial losses, thousands of poor workers lost their means of livelihood.

The pursuit of the 'public interest' in this era of liberalisation deprived a large section of Delhi's working class of their means of sub-sistence. Environmental benefits – clean air and water – were obtained at the cost of losing *working environments*, resources that sustained some of the most vulnerable citizens of Delhi. How did the middle class succeed in presenting health and hazard, beauty and order, as envir-onmental concerns that superseded the welfare of Delhi's working class? How did the environmental priorities of workers – jobs, food, shelter – come to be overlooked? Why were workers not represented in the decision-making process? Why was action routed through a *judicial* authority when the Indian government has an extensive administra-tive set-up for monitoring and regulating pollution? Was the closure of factories the most effective way of improving air quality? These issues indicate that environmental discourse under economic liberalisation came to be based on a separation of environmental concerns from social justice issues and the judicialisation of environmental action. This leads us to the central question: how did the courts facilitate the capture of 'public interest' by the private and particularistic concerns of urban elites?

The conjuncture of processes that enabled judicial action against air pollution can be related to capitalist restructuring of the real estate market under the regime of liberalisation and privatisation, which made the land on which factories were sited more valuable than ever before. Economic restructuring has also transformed Delhi's production economy from manufacturing to services and commerce. This process is eroding an industrial economy that, like construction, services and commerce in the city, relies heavily on 'informal' labour – ill-paid workers without any job security, who live in illegal shanty settlements in the city, are often migrants, and are denied recognition as legitimate urban citizens (Bhattacharya and Sanyal 2011). The invisibility of workers in the air pollution debate is also related to the dominance of corporate-owned media, which prefer to produce 'infotainment' – selling consumer products through the coverage of 'news' about health, beauty and lifestyles rather than discussing the realities of starving workers' families, hazardous industrial working conditions and dwindling public transportation. Connecting these processes, practices and positions enables an understanding of how a 'public interest' around the problem of air pollution was created.

The opening section, 'Jump-starting environmental justice', describes public initiatives to combat air and water pollution in Delhi.[4] The next section, 'Limits and contradictions of urban planning and judicial action', deals with debates around the city's Master Plan and the presence of polluting industries. It argues that the Master Plan and the court orders, while claiming to embody enlightened rational-legal 'public interest', were the products of asymmetrical political processes that marginalised working-class concerns. The following section, 'Pollution

---

[4] Due to lack of space, this essay does not discuss judicial efforts to control emissions from motorised transport. However, it should be noted that, even though 64 per cent of Delhi's air pollution in 1993–1994 came from motor vehicles and only 12 per cent from industrial sources, the courts focused on vehicular pollution only four years after it had targeted factories for closure. At the same time, the court's attention was only on cutting emissions from public transport vehicles and not privately owned vehicles. The resulting shrinkage of public transport adversely affected working-class commuters while affluent commuters went unscathed. See Kathuria 2002, 2005; Baviskar et al. 2006; Véron 2006.

and the constitution of a public', outlines the formation of the Indian state and middle class to show how pollution control has emerged from a historical trajectory of state management of landscapes and populations in order to improve them. It also explains why middle-class perceptions about clean air, represented by key actors like an environmentalist lawyer and judge, took the form of a transcendental discourse about the 'public interest'. The concluding section, 'Hidden violence, the workplace and workers', discusses laid-off workers' perspectives on the air pollution initiatives. Workers were constrained from expressing their own distinctive environmental concerns that prioritised stable and remunerative employment over work hazards and pollution. Excluded from deliberations about the 'public interest', workers became the silent victims of middle-class initiatives for clean air.

It must be recognised at the outset that there have been several environmental initiatives simultaneously under way in Delhi, of which the campaign against air pollution is only one. There is the removal of encroachments and squatter settlements from public lands, ordered by the courts in response to several public interest petitions filed by consumer rights organisations and affluent resident welfare organisations (Ghertner 2008; Menon-Sen and Bhan 2008; Baviskar 2009). Other contentious issues where environmental concerns have been raised include litigation about construction on the floodplain of the Yamuna river, the building of luxury hotels and shopping malls in green areas in south Delhi and the removal of cows and monkeys from urban environs (Baviskar 2010, 2011). Each of these initiatives brings together a range of social actors, working at and across multiple scales – courts, elected governmental officials (both state and central), different administrative departments, residential and business associations, transnational funding agencies, NGOs, media and even schools. Each of these initiatives merits examination on its own, as do the linkages between them. For the purposes of this essay, however, they form the larger context within which to understand the air pollution case.

JUMP-STARTING ENVIRONMENTAL JUSTICE

In 1985, environmental activist and lawyer Mahesh Chander Mehta filed a public interest petition asking the Supreme Court of India to order the closure of stone crushing units in Delhi 'which caused dust pollution, affecting half a million people. More than 2,000 tons of dust was being emitted into the air.'[5] Mehta contended that these industries violated the Air Pollution Act of 1981, as well as Delhi's Master Plan. In 1992, the court agreed – but this was not the end of Mehta's petitioning. He also asked the court to move 1,200 polluting industrial units away from Delhi, arguing that, since many of them were located in residential and commercial areas, they contravened the Master Plan's zoning provisions. As the following account shows, this category of 'non-conforming' factories (those that violated urban zoning regulations) was to become a major bone of contention in struggles against pollution in Delhi. In another petition, Mehta approached the court to act on the issue of the pollution of the Ganga and its tributaries, including the river Yamuna, which passes through Delhi.

The issue of air and water pollution in Delhi was therefore on the Supreme Court's agenda from the late 1980s, and periodic statements and directions were issued by the Bench. But little definitive action was taken until 1994, when the court took *suo motu* notice of a newspaper report about the pollution of the Yamuna.[6] The Central Pollution Control Board (under the central government's Ministry of Environment and Forests) and the Delhi government were made parties in the matter. In 1995, the court asked the Delhi Pollution Control Committee (DPCC), the state-level unit under the Delhi government, to categorise all industrial units in the city according to their pollution hazard, using the classificatory system employed in the Master Plan. It ordered the Municipal Corporation of Delhi, the agency responsible for licensing commercial activities in the city, not to renew the licenses of erring industries. In February 1996, the court ordered the Delhi state government to construct common effluent treatment plants (CETPs) to deal with the water pollution issue, and appointed the National Environmental Engineering Research Institute as a consultant to this process. It stipulated that industries that failed to install effluent treatment plants by 1 January 1997 would have to close. In April 1996, the court ordered the relocation of industries from residential areas.

These overlapping, even contradictory, orders that demanded prompt action from several state and private actors with different organisational capacities had little immediate effect beyond signalling the court's desire to address the pollution issue. Yet this spate of judicial orders precipitated several processes that unfolded over the subsequent decade. Although

---

[5] Interview with M. C. Mehta, *Frontline*, 22 December 2000, p. 17.
[6] 'And Quietly Flows the *Maily* Yamuna', *Hindustan Times*, 18 July 1994.

the various orders and their effects are inter-related, for purposes of clarity, they are presented here in three parts: (1) the 1996–1997 closure of hazardous, large and heavy industries; (2) the closure of industries that discharge effluents into the Yamuna in the year 2000; and (3) the closure and relocation of non-conforming industries, also in 2000. Aside from the judicial orders affecting industries, the Supreme Court in 1998 also initiated a major transformation of Delhi's transportation system, again in response to a public interest petition on air pollution. It is difficult to convey the complexity of these developments in the space of this brief account, and some generalisation and simplification cannot be avoided.

The first closures: hazardous and heavy industries

In July 1996, the Supreme Court targeted 168 factories classified as 'H' – noxious and hazardous. These factories, the court ruled, violated the 1990 Master Plan and had to be relocated or shut down within five months. If factory owners chose to relocate within the National Capital Region – adjoining districts of the states of Rajasthan, Haryana and Uttar Pradesh – they would have to pay each worker monthly wages during the period of the move, as well as one year's salary as a resettlement bonus. If owners opted to close their industrial units, workers would be entitled to six years' wages as a retrenchment allowance. Two months later, in September 1996, the court ordered the relocation or closure of another 513 non-conforming units by January 1997. In October 1996, it added another 46 hot mix plants, 21 arc/induction furnaces and 243 brick kilns to the list. All these firms were closed down by 1997.

The events around the closure of the initial 168 'H' category factories have been documented by the *Delhi Janwadi Adhikar Manch* (DJAM – Delhi Socialist Rights Forum). The Manch, a federation of trade unions and human rights organisations, was formed in December 1996 as a response to the Supreme Court's orders.[7] The Manch immediately started investigating the impact of the judicial orders on workers, organising meetings and public hearings, publishing reports (DJAM 1997a, 1997b), and attempting to represent workers' concerns before the court. Three trade unions affiliated with the Manch approached the Bench separately through their lawyers, asking to be heard in the air pollution case. The

[7] Many of the groups in the Manch were ideologically on the left of the Indian political spectrum. Notably, trade unions affiliated with the major political parties – Congress, BJP, CPI and CPI (M) – were not a part of the DJAM. Thus the Manch represented fairly small, radical groups with limited constituencies.

judges brushed them aside, merely remarking that the court would protect workers' interests and did not need the intercession of the unions.
This verbal assurance was not recorded as a part of court proceedings
and thus trade unions were later unable to appeal the judgment, as they
had not been recognised as affected parties.

Imminent factory closure had already spurred owners to take pre-
emptive action. The managers of many of the larger units saw the
court's order as an opportunity to profit from the sale of the land on
which their factories stood, and they were quite reconciled to the prospect of shutting down their industries and selling off capital assets.[8]
Anticipating closure, managers had begun retrenching workers well in
advance of the Supreme Court deadline (DJAM 1998). Managers also
used other devices to minimise their liability for workers' compensation.
Through various subterfuges, the owners of the remaining 167 factories
ensured that workers were laid off without compensation. Some factories declared that they were moving out of Delhi. This reduced their
liability to one year's wages. Yet, workers were not paid for the months
during which the factory was being shifted. In all cases, the number
of workers employed in the relocated unit was drastically reduced. In
effect, relocation meant that the majority of workers were laid off and
were not compensated.

Furthermore, factory management limited its liability to the narrow-
est possible definition of 'workmen', those who were on the rolls as permanent employees. This meant that large sections of workers employed
year after year as *badli* – casual workers or those hired through contractors – were denied compensation. According to the Manch's survey, up to
90 per cent of workers in some firms were not permanent, even after decades in service. Firms refused to accept that casual or contract labourers
were their employees, despite the fact that social security benefits were
deducted from their wages, indicating the firm's long-term, direct relationship with them. The majority of workers employed in these units
were thus laid off with no compensation.

---

[8] In many cases, the land had been given to them by the government at subsidised rates. With
economic liberalisation, the huge rise in the price of real estate in the heart of the city made
closing aging manufacturing units and converting the land to commercial use a very attractive
proposition. The Supreme Court had stipulated that a portion of vacated factory land would
have to be handed over to the government (30 per cent for industries below a certain size and 60
per cent for industries above), but several illegal land transfers happened anyway. A similar process happened in downtown Mumbai, when the closure of 'sick' textile mills opened up prime
real estate for commercial development, at great profit to mill owners (D'Monte 2001).

Permanent workers fared little better. According to the Manch, 'of those entitled to compensation ... our survey shows that compensation has not been paid to any worker although more than one year has passed since the order was issued' (DJAM 1997b).[9] When the Manch approached the Supreme Court and pointed out that the judge's orders were being violated, the court suggested that they should take complaints to the Labour Commissioner, an official whose previous inaction had already demonstrated his total apathy toward protecting workers' interests. Clearly, the attempt to clean Delhi's air and water had a severe adverse impact on workers' livelihoods, but the court dismissed it as a minor issue that pertained to a particular section of society, and deemed it not a justiciable public concern.

What was the scale of displacement? Notably, the only source of data on the number of workers rendered jobless by the Supreme Court is a survey conducted by the Manch (DJAM 1997b). No detailed figures are available with any government agency and, as the case of casual and contract labourers indicates, factory owners systematically under-report the number of people they employ.[10] The Manch estimated that 'in th[e] first phase, no less than 50,000 workers have lost their jobs and been dislocated with their families' (DJAM 1997b). To this estimate should be added the number of workers in ancillary industries supplying materials and services to the closed or relocated factories. Of Delhi's total population of 12 million at that time, the number directly affected by loss of employment (workers and their families) far exceeded 250,000, clearly a large section of the city comprised of its poorer population.

The closure of water-polluting industries
The second phase of factory closures occurred in 2000. As mentioned above, in February 1996 the court had stipulated that industries that failed to install effluent treatment plants by 1 January 1997 would have to close. Although the Delhi government drew up plans and cost-sharing mechanisms for joint public–private financed CETPs, a number of factory owners refused to participate, arguing that the scheme was too

[9] The Manch report goes on to note that Ayodhya Textile Mills, the only public-sector unit among the affected factories, was the only exception to this rule, giving six years' wages to its workforce.

[10] Under-reporting is a strategy to circumvent the provisions of the Labour Act and the Industrial Disputes Act, which mandate that firms employing more than ten workers provide them with certain entitlements. Under these laws, firms are required to contribute to workers' pensions and provident funds and other social security benefits, and must allow collective bargaining.

costly and that some of them were being unfairly targeted.[11] The Delhi government and industries could not come to any agreement, and over a three-and-a-half-year period no plants were built. In 1999, after setting further deadlines that the government failed to meet, the Supreme Court forbade the discharge of any untreated effluents from any factory in Delhi and Haryana into the Yamuna.

In late 1999 the Delhi Pollution Control Committee sent notices of closure to 1,142 industrial units. These firms were chosen through a survey conducted by 29 sub-divisional magistrates (administrators) of the Delhi government and engineers of the state pollution control committee, and on the basis of information provided by various industrial associations. To ensure effective closure, not only were the factories' gates locked, their supplies of water and electricity were also cut off. The closures did not go unopposed. On 12 February 2000, factory owners in the Seelampur area of the city mobilised physically to prevent the government's 'vigilance squads' from closing their units. Many other industrial units and associations also protested, arguing that they did not discharge effluents and met existing standards, or had already installed treatment plants. 372 of these units were allowed to re-open by January 2000. The process of closing and re-opening continued throughout the year: by July 2000, while 3,177 units had been issued closure notices, an unspecified number had been actually sealed and an unspecified number had been allowed to stay open or re-open (Adve 2000). Almost all the affected firms were small in scale, most reporting that they employed fewer than ten workers. The court issued no directions about workers' compensation and, since almost all the firms employed unorganised labourers, there is no documentation about the scale and impact of the closures.

The closure of non-conforming industries
The third, related, set of closures focused on 'non-conforming' industries (industries that violated the zoning provisions of the Master Plan). The Supreme Court had first ordered the relocation or closure of non-conforming industries from residential areas in April 1996, and set a deadline of 1 January 1997. In 1996, the DPCC contracted schoolteachers to conduct a survey of industrial units.[12] Of the 126,218 industrial units in the city, 97,411 (almost 80 per cent) were non-conforming.

---

[11] For an analysis of the complex technical and regulatory issues regarding effluent treatment plants, see Adve 2000.

[12] Schoolteachers in India are often conscripted to conduct enumeration exercises for the government, such as collecting census data.

Propelled by the court's initiative of setting deadlines and threatening punitive action against government officials, the Delhi administration was galvanised into action. In October 1996, the Delhi State Industrial Development Corporation (DSIDC) began to acquire land on the outskirts of the city in Bawana to relocate small-scale industries from residential areas. By July 2000, 52,000 applications for alternate plot allotments had been received – and not a single firm had been relocated, since Bawana only had enough land for 16,000 plots and the DSIDC officials could not decide which among the flood of applications should be selected.

The Supreme Court apparently decided that enough was enough. On 12 September 2000, the judges announced that 'all polluting industries of whatever category operating in residential areas must be asked to shut down'. Two months later, on 14 November, the court issued a show cause notice to the Chief Secretary, Delhi government, and the Commissioner of the Delhi Municipal Corporation, asking why they should not be punished for contempt of court for not implementing the court's orders. In panic, the Delhi government ordered the immediate closure of *all* non-conforming industrial units (and not just the polluting ones). This order, which affected more than 97,000 units, was unprecedented in scale. Over the next few days, as government officials, escorted by heavily armed policemen, went around sealing factory premises (locking their doors, disconnecting electricity and water), there were riots in Delhi. Factory owners and workers were out on the streets protesting. There was a city-wide *bandh* (shut-down) on 20 November.[13] Protestors set fire to government buses and stoned municipal officials. Police retaliated by firing on the protestors. Three workers were shot dead and hundreds were injured. Even the media, which had reported only desultorily on the progress of the litigation in the Supreme Court, took note of this outbreak of violence. Yet, restricted as they were to the industrial pockets of the city, even these dramatic events received only a few inches of column space for a few days. There were no in-depth accounts of how workers or small factory owners were affected, nothing that indicated that a huge section of the city's population stood to lose its livelihood.

On 28 November 2000, the Supreme Court chided the Delhi government for not distinguishing between polluting non-conforming and non-

---

[13] A *bandh* is a common form of collective protest, sometimes spontaneous but more often enforced by a political party or neighbourhood association. A *bandh* may also be a mark of respect (for the death of a public figure) or a precaution (in the case of anticipated violence such as riots).

polluting non-conforming firms. Soon after, undeterred by the protests, the judges criticised the government for its tardiness and set a deadline of 15 December 2000 for identifying all the non-conforming units, and a deadline of 7 January 2001 for shutting all polluting units among them.

On 15 December, the Delhi Pradesh Congress Committee, the state-level unit of the political party ruling Delhi, and the Delhi Manufacturers' Association staged a large demonstration near Parliament, trucking in thousands of workers. The target of their protests was the central government's Urban Development Ministry, which controlled the Delhi Development Authority, the body that prepared and implemented the city's Master Plan. The protestors blamed the Urban Development minister, Jagmohan, for arbitrarily trying to remove all industries from Delhi. It was not clear how the authority defined polluting industries, they said. Moreover, the livelihood of hundreds of thousands of workers and factory owners was more important than the Master Plan, and the protestors saw no reason why it could not be amended.[14] The protest thus blamed the onslaught on non-conforming units to the land-use classifications mandated in Delhi's Master Plan. This was also an attempt to deflect criticism from the Congress-led government of Delhi state and attribute the closure fiasco to the BJP-led central government. The Delhi government proclaimed a *nyaya yuddha* (battle for justice) against the central government and BJP members of Parliament elected from Delhi.

Between 2001 and 2003, many polluting industries shut down. The Supreme Court extended the deadline for closing all polluting non-conforming industries to 31 December 2002. The Delhi government submitted a revised list of thirty-three categories of polluting industries to the Supreme Court and announced that units under these categories would be closed down in phases.[15] The government also conceded that those industrial units that were non-conforming but did not pollute would be allowed to operate from their present premises for the time being. By November 2002, construction had started in the new Bawana Industrial Area, where 14,500 plots had been allotted by the DSIDC. An effluent treatment plant, housing for 3,000 workers' families, bicycle tracks and other facilities were also planned.[16] In February 2001, the

---

[14] *The Hindu*, Delhi edition, 16 December 2000.

[15] According to the Delhi government, the list of polluting industries was 'worked out by experts after a thorough study'. Of the 44 industries categorised in the earlier list, nine were deemed to be non-polluting, reducing the number to 35.

[16] By 2009 when I last checked, they had not been built. However, many of the squatters evicted from other parts of the city were resettled close by in Bawana, providing a ready supply of

Delhi government announced that it would approach the Ministry of Urban Development to 'regularise' (or re-designate as industrial) twenty-four areas classified as residential in the Master Plan.[17] It argued that more than 70 per cent of the land in these areas was occupied by industrial units, thus their de facto industrial status simply needed to be legitimised. Such a step would prevent the closure or displacement of 20,000 industrial units.[18] Almost two years later, on 12 December 2002, the Delhi Development Authority reversed its stand and accepted the Delhi government's proposal for in situ regularisation in twenty-four areas of the city. This move signalled the government's willingness to appease factory owners, an important political constituency, by finding a legal escape route that would protect their interests, a compromise that would pass muster under the court's scrutiny.

This change of heart in the Urban Development Ministry-controlled DDA was criticised in the English press. Voicing the opinion of its white-collar professional readership, *The Hindu* reminded its readers that the ministry had earlier rejected the proposed change of land use from residential to industrial, 'keeping in view the already deteriorating environmental conditions in Delhi and the ever-growing menace of illegal constructions and unauthorised encroachments'.[19] The newspaper darkly hinted that 'there are political and other interests involved in the exercise which on the face of it seeks to prevent the closure or displacement of nearly 20,000 industrial units but in reality overlooks not only the interests of residents of these colonies but all other citizens of Delhi as well'.[20]

workers. Also see Ramanathan (2004) for details regarding the shifting of chemical industries to Narela on the periphery of Delhi and the subsequent relocation of slum-dwellers into the area. Ramanathan argues that the courts have dealt with industrial hazard not by reducing the risk but by making vulnerable populations continue to bear an unequal burden of the risk.

[17] The Delhi government proposed another deft sleight of hand: changing the definition of a 'household unit' from a firm employing up to five workers and using up to 1 kilowatt of power, to a unit employing up to twenty workers and using up to 5 kilowatts of power. This move would literally domesticate the problem by reclassifying many current industrial units as 'household industries', giving them immunity from the Court's orders. But even this expansion, complained the Association of Small-Scale Industries, did not go far enough.

[18] *The Hindu*, Delhi edition, 13 February 2001.

[19] *The Hindu*, Delhi edition, 21 December 2002.

[20] It was rumoured that Jagmohan, the Urban Development minister, had been divested of his post because his intransigent attitude on factory closures was adversely affecting the popularity of BJP members of Parliament from Delhi. Small manufacturers and traders form a significant chunk of the BJP's electoral base in Delhi. Jagmohan was replaced by the more 'adjusting' Ananth Kumar, who was willing to accommodate the concerns of his party members from Delhi.

LIMITS AND CONTRADICTIONS OF URBAN
PLANNING AND JUDICIAL ACTION

The Supreme Court orders on the closure of factories contain many vexed assumptions and ambiguities. What is a *polluting industry*? The common-sense notion that a manufacturing unit must actually pollute – generate noxious or hazardous wastes (or noise) in excess of permissible levels – in order to be identified as a 'polluting industry' does not hold in this case. The 1990 Master Plan identifies twenty-seven polluting industries based on a list produced by the Central Pollution Control Board. The designation of a unit as polluting is not based on emissions but on what it produces and whether the manufacture of that product is classified as polluting or not. The classification of products in the 1990 Master Plan also has anomalies: 'While corrugated boxes are listed under category A, paper products are in category F and, in many cases, corrugated box manufacturers have been targeted for closure by the sealing squad under the argument that it is also a paper product' (Kathuria 2001: 194). Rather than investigate the specificities of each case and the particular practices adopted by individual units, the court uses only categorical designations devised by the CPCB as an approximation. Thus, even if the industrial unit controls its emissions to permissible levels, it may still be designated as a polluting industry. Yet all these issues became moot because the Delhi Pollution Control Committee (DPCC), the state-level counterpart of the CPCB, is woefully understaffed and would not be capable of checking emissions for every unit.

Workers' organisations and the Manch tried to downplay the importance of industries' contributions to air pollution, arguing that the vehicles of more affluent urban residents should be targeted before workers' livelihoods. But other analysts offered a different perspective, arguing that industrial emissions were also a serious hazard, especially for those who worked in them and that 'with the expansion of the urban sprawl in Delhi, many residential areas are now dangerously close to industrial areas housing hazardous units'.[21]

Yet relocation, which simply transfers the problem elsewhere, out of the Supreme Court's sight, was no answer. Closing down polluting industries to protect workers' health, without providing them with safe alternate livelihoods, merely exchanged one form of vulnerability for another. The Manch had initially adopted a 'jobs versus environment'

---

[21] R. Ramachandran, 'The Lethal Zones' in *Frontline*, 22 December 2000, p. 18.

stand on the issue of factory closure, dismissing pollution as the concern of privileged elites who did not care that workers were being deprived of their livelihoods. Confronted by the overwhelming concern about air pollution in the media and elsewhere, the Manch went on to acknowledge that pollution was not a trivial issue. It modified its stand to assert that the primary victims of polluted working conditions were labourers, and yet neither the court nor the government had addressed their plight. In the words of a commentator affiliated with the Manch: 'If the aim is to fight pollution and improve the health of the citizens then it should begin by addressing the issue in terms of the disproportionately high impact of pollution on the lives of the underprivileged sections of the population' (Navlakha 2000: 4471).

Another key concept on which the court's orders hinged was that of the *non-conforming industry*, an industrial unit that violates the land use provisions of Delhi's Master Plan of 1962, which designated functionally segregated zones for residential, commercial, institutional and industrial purposes. The Master Plan has emerged as a key point of reference for the debate on the closure of industries, and merits some explanation. Delhi's population almost doubled around 1947 when the partition of India brought more than 450,000 Hindu and Sikh refugees to the city. In order 'to check the haphazard and unplanned growth of Delhi', the Delhi Development Authority (DDA) was constituted in 1957 by an Act of Parliament. The DDA, a unit of the Urban Development Ministry of the central government, is the main body responsible for planning, acquiring and developing land in the city. The DDA prepared the first Master Plan in 1962 with expertise from the Ford Foundation. This Plan, intended for the period 1961–1981, divided the city into functionally segregated zones. In accordance with the Plan, and pursuing the goal of rapid industrialisation set out in the nation's second and third Five-Year Plans (1956–1961, 1961–1966), industrial estates were established on the outskirts of the city to support small-scale industries.

However, industrial development in the city failed to follow the Master Plan's design. Industrial growth outpaced the limited space provided in the industrial estates. Thousands of small industrial units sprouted up around the industrial estates and commercial centres to take advantage of the proximity of labour, materials and markets. With no more space available in the designated industrial estates, new firms were forced to occupy non-conforming sites. Despite being in violation of the Master Plan, most of these units were recognised by the government in that they were licensed, registered with the sales and excise departments, and received government subsidies and bank loans. Also, since the Plan had made virtually no provision for housing workers, squatter settlements had mushroomed all around the factories.

Such violations were not merely tolerated; they were actively encouraged by politicians and corrupt bureaucrats. Government practices regarding encroachments on public lands and non-conforming industrial units have been complex and contradictory; many different, often conflicting, pronouncements and acts have generated a fertile field for enterprising power-brokers. The possibility of eviction provides the context for negotiating bribes to look the other way. The simultaneous possibility of 'regularisation', or retrospective legalisation over time, spurs encroachers and non-conforming units to stay on and stake a claim. Thus the provisions of the Plan, as well as the multiple state practices around it, structure the fields of action of factory owners and workers. It should be noted that the most egregious violator of the Master Plan has been the Delhi Development Authority itself which, in the late 1970s, suddenly constructed several flyovers and sports complexes for the Asian Games 1982 in areas demarcated for other uses, and which has generally followed a policy of ad hoc accommodation of construction whenever it has been politically expedient.

After the lapse of the first Master Plan, the DDA prepared a 'Perspective Master Plan 2001' which was published in 1990 in the Gazette of India. After independent planners publicly criticised the document, the Delhi Urban Arts Commission, a body formed by an Act of Parliament in 1974, was entrusted with the task of reviewing it. The legal status of this Plan is ambiguous, yet it is frequently invoked in public interest litigation. This Plan (MPD 1990) designated twenty-eight industrial areas in Delhi and identified at least thirty-seven non-conforming areas where industries proliferated even though the area had been earmarked for some other use. The Plan also categorised various industries in terms of their pollution load, in order to select those industries that were suitable for an urban environment and identify those that should be shut down, relocated or prevented from being established in the first place.

At various points, the Supreme Court indicated that a non-conforming industry, even if it did not pollute, should either relocate or close down. Even in cases where a unit had been operating before the formulation of the Master Plan, it was retrospectively deemed to be in violation of it. The 1962 Master Plan (and its later versions MPD 1990 and MPD 2021), which the court treated as sacrosanct in this case, is a highly contested document, produced by planners without any process of representative consultation, and the courts have consistently condoned the Delhi government's systematic violation of its provisions over the years. Most non-conforming industries were able to establish themselves only by making regular payments to municipal authorities, an active collaboration between officials and factory owners. The Master Plan is based on projections about the rate of growth of Delhi's population and the city's anticipated and desired industrial and commercial profile – projections that were more than thirty years old at the time of the court's rulings and that had been proved wrong by several orders of magnitude.

The biggest ambiguity in the Supreme Court order was the fate of the several thousand workers who were laid off by one stroke of the judicial writ. Ostensibly, the court had been benevolent; it had stipulated norms for compensating permanent workers employed in the units being relocated or shut down. But the vast majority of workers who were affected by the court order were 'casual labourers' not officially registered as employees of particular firms. Under-reporting the number of workers employed is a common strategy and all the more so as industrial production is subcontracted to smaller firms in the 'informal' economy (NCEUS 2007). Much of this 'informal economy' – an umbrella category encompassing complex myriad arrangements of work, from family labour to seasonal employment – escapes the state's regulatory apparatus. Not being organised, not recognised as employees, hundreds of thousands of workers found no way of representing their point of view before the judge or the media, and lost their livelihoods.

The judicialisation of the problem of air pollution choked off a larger public debate about alternative policy options. As noted earlier, the overwhelming contribution to air pollution came from automobile emissions, yet the court focused on industrial pollution.[22] The Manch marshalled the evidence to make this case in a series of public hearings in the city, arguing that it was the vehicles of affluent citizens that should be the target of public action. Yet it was only in the late 1990s that automobile emissions became the subject of court action. Since the closure of factories would cause immense suffering to large numbers of industrial workers, was there a need to threaten non-conforming units that did not pollute but were only in violation of the Master Plan? And was closure the only way of dealing with polluting industries? A few chose to relocate outside

---

[22] Similarly, the bulk of water pollution is caused by untreated domestic sewage. Although the Court ordered the Delhi government to set up more sewage treatment plants, it has been far less energetic in pursuing this line of action.

Delhi, and presumably continue to pollute in other states. The option of helping firms adopt cleaner technologies or install pollution control equipment was not seriously examined. In one of its orders in 1996, the court had directed industrial units to set up common effluent treatment plants, but failed to pursue the matter, so even that possibility fell by the wayside. The failure to consider alternative strategies highlights the fact that the flurry of unilateral action by the court foreclosed a democratic process of representation, discussion and informed decision making. In the 'public interest' of preventing air pollution in Delhi, the rights of an entire class of poor workers to basic subsistence were brutally denied.

One reason for the court's swift and peremptory decisions has been the participation in the pollution cases of Justice Kuldip Singh, later famous as a 'green judge'. Kuldip Singh's reputation rested on his speedy dispatch of complex legal problems and his issue of strong diktats to recalcitrant bureaucrats. The failure to implement these diktats would lead to censure and the threat of senior officials being jailed for 'contempt of court'. Singh drew legitimacy from the radical tradition of public interest litigation of the 1970s such that, instead of being the last resort, the Supreme Court permitted itself to become the first body to which petitioners appeal, thereby short-circuiting the administrative process and even weakening it in the long term. Yet this new way of doing business was hailed by those who have access to the courts because it cut through red tape and obviated a painful, long drawn-out struggle for administrative responsiveness and accountability. As M. C. Mehta, the lawyer who initiated the pollution litigation, said:

> If there is a law, you respect it, you obey it, you enforce it ... You cannot set up hazardous and polluting industries in Delhi ... The law was there and all the industries, all the associations knew it very well ... Everybody knew. So if the law was there, then ... they [should] have voluntarily ... gone out of the city. Instead of doing that, they started lobbying with the government. All these politicians, they are vote-hungry people. They are all the time looking out for their seats and for their elections ... So they were doing that [and] all these industries were influencing them ... Nobody is complying with [the law] ... [There is] negligence on the part of the industries, on the part of the government of India, on the part of the state government and every possible machinery. So when they failed to protect the life and health of the people in this city then the court came into play.[23]

---

[23] Interview with Kavita Philip, 25 October 2002.

What this account leaves out is that environmentalists like Mehta made no attempt to directly influence or even address politicians, manufacturers or regulatory agencies, presuming that they were corrupt and compromised. Perceiving the political process as illegitimate justifies approaching the Supreme Court directly. The partnership of environmentalists M. C. Mehta and Kuldip Singh, advocate and judge, which resulted in directives that affected the lives and livelihoods of hundreds of thousands of workers and their families, people who had no representation in court, exemplifies the new efficient dispensation of justice in the 'public interest' that middle-class people acclaim.

As strong individuals who seem to galvanise a moribund system, M. C. Mehta and Kuldip Singh are vigilante icons who command the admiration and support of a broad public (excluding of course the workers and their supporters), and their actions are widely reported in the media.[24] Both have received several awards and frequently figure as invited speakers and celebrity guests at public ceremonies of the kind organised by the Rotary or Lions Clubs.[25] Together they attract the accolades of the upper classes, partly because they embody effective state action, and partly because they are seen to serve 'the public interest' by protecting the environment, with clean air and water appearing as universal goods that supersede questions of political economy. How did clean air become such a transcendental value, one that could trump issues of livelihood and social justice, and for whom?

POLLUTION AND THE CONSTITUTION OF A PUBLIC

For a subcontinent with a centuries-old obsession with matters of purity and pollution, a matrix that still organises much of social life, the problem of air pollution seems strangely inassimilable into older frames of understanding. While orientations to people, objects and spaces, especially in practices around food and sexuality, are shaped by concepts of caste and life-cycle event-related pollution, that set of concerns seems to be curiously at odds with a Western biomedical discourse around toxicity and risk. How do Hindu mourners in Delhi, who cremate their relatives on the bank of the river Yamuna, believe that they are cleansed of death's pollution by bathing in water made filthy by sewage and industrial sludge?

---

[24] On police vigilantism and public acclaim, see Eckert 2005.
[25] Mehta has won the prestigious Magsaysay prize, which honours outstanding social service in Asia.

One may trace beliefs about the relative harmlessness of water and air-borne wastes to Ayurvedic notions of the elements – air, water, fire, earth – as marked by constant traffic and flow of energy, such that their movement dilutes and diffuses the danger that these substances embody (Rosin 2000). In this view, sulphur dioxide from the Indraprastha thermal power plant, for example, is simply borne away by the wind, and cannot be a form of pollution that matters. The persistence of these beliefs acts as a powerful obstacle against mobilising public concern around the issue of pollution.

The transformation of public perceptions of environmental hazard was produced by a different discourse, one already made familiar by colonial and post-colonial health and hygiene projects.[26] Colonial ideas of 'improvement', of husbanding resources, controlling lands and peoples for the purpose of conservation, and better management for more efficient exploitation, were an intrinsic part of the colonial enterprise (Cowen and Shenton 1996; Mehta 1999). Empire was justified as an instrument of development, of 'fostering and leading new races of subjects and allies in the career of improvement' (Raffles, cited in Drayton 2000: 94). Promoting 'the internal Improvement … of a Powerful Empire' concerned 'the improvement of the people in regard to their health, industry, and morals', and not merely agriculture, mining and fisheries (Drayton 2000: 104). The pursuit of improved health and morals ranged over diverse terrain, such as school education, agricultural policy, public health and hygiene, population control, prison reform and personal law. The government as guardian drew upon expertise in new forms of knowledge (Cohn 1997), based on techniques of taxonomic classification and inscription that included maps, censuses and surveys of all kinds. Enumeration was essential to the act of producing order, rendering unruly reality legible (Scott 1998), and enabling bureaucratic action. It helped shape new collective identities, the modern politics of caste, religion, region and language, and modes of action. The same techniques of government were inherited by the post-colonial state and employed to pursue planned national development (Ludden 1992).

---

[26] Following Foucault's lead, there is a substantial body of work on the technologies of bio-power, on practices of rendering legible bodies and spaces, and ordering 'the conduct of conduct', which I will not review here. But some indicative references on public health are Anderson (1995), particularly his discussion on social improvement and smoke abatement in colonial Calcutta (1995: 328–35); Mitchell 2002; Greenough 2003; Tarlo 2003. On the creation of ordered urban spaces, see Holston 1989; Smith 1996; Caldeira 2000.

It would be misleading to point only to continuities between colonial and post-colonial governmentalities. The post-colonial discourse of sovereign nation-states, anchored though it was in the paradox of aspiring to independence by adopting a development path that required participation in the familiar inequities of global markets, an 'aid' regime, and Cold War militarism, created novel political opportunities (McMichael 1996; Khilnani 1997). The post-colonial era opened new institutional arenas for negotiating the conflicting imperatives of accumulation and legitimation – from electoral representation to socialist planning, liberal democracy created the possibility of new freedoms. Ideas of citizenship, forged in the freedom struggle's crucible, informed the sensibilities of assertive social groups who could make new demands upon the state. The Indian state created a large public sector that included research and educational institutions, capital-intensive infrastructure and heavy industries, as well as a large bureaucracy to control and regulate this sprawling edifice. The prominent position of the Indian middle class can be traced to the rise of nationalism in the colonial period (Chatterjee 1993), but its consolidation as a decisive hegemonic power occurred in the aftermath of independence (Deshpande 1997).

Though middle-class people saw themselves as upholders of the public interest, speaking for nature and the nation, their interests and ideologies were shaped by their subject positions. Their social location in the urban economy – in the professions and in commerce and finance – kept the middle classes detached from working-class lives and concerns. The absence of an organised working class in the city meant that opposing points of view could rarely make themselves heard in the public sphere. Instead, middle-class visions of the ideal city came to dominate and drive public action. Images of Singapore inform the model urban lifestyle that middle-class Delhites desire and to which they aspire.[27] The 'benevolent authoritarianism' of this city-state appeals to their sense of civic order and security, efficiency and prosperity. A city where spitting on the streets is punished by a hefty fine and where shopping and commercialised recreation are dedicated twenty-four hour activities is a utopia for those urban middle-class Indians who bemoan Delhi's chaos, dirt and lack of amenities.

The promise of development in post-colonial India, and the dream of model cities, was soon perceived by the middle class to have been

---

[27] Many upper-middle-class Indians have travelled to Singapore on vacation, and a growing number work there in the banking and IT sectors.

betrayed by a corrupt and inefficient bureaucracy. While it continued to have faith in the optic of enlightened public interest, to be determined by technocrats and judges, the middle class saw the process of governing as subverted by the 'politics' of vested interests. Thus governing should ideally be a rational, technically informed process that 'takes all factors into account' to generate enforceable decisions for compliant subjects. The state's failure to live up to this ideal led to disillusionment, which was only displaced by the emergence of activist-citizens like M. C. Mehta, and activist NGOs like CSE, who cut through red tape, disciplining not only erring bureaucrats but also working-class citizens. A middle-class citizen approvingly commented on the success of these initiatives in getting a moribund state to act:

> In terms of air [pollution] they've done a lot – moved to CNG, restricted entry time for trucks. Air quality has improved. [I know] through newspapers, TV. Now they have it on TV, everything about NO [nitrogen oxide], CO^2 [carbon dioxide] and dust ... It is only the judiciary and media which [are] keeping these things under control, otherwise the government machinery has failed. It is all because of the interfering politicians ... [who] do not support good officials. Two major factors that have led to failure are politicians and corruption. Media and judiciary are the only impartial ones. If they are not there, no one will know the truth.[28]

Yet this vaunted impartiality, their ostensible distance from 'politics', did not necessarily make the courts either just or enlightened. The courts' impatient dismissal of representations by workers, and their insistence on applying laws and rules that were palpably flawed, indicated an inherent bias in favour of bourgeois environmentalists – a class-based affinity made all the more attractive by the appreciative attention bestowed on it by the media.

HIDDEN VIOLENCE, THE WORKPLACE AND 'FREE' LABOUR

When middle-class citizens in Delhi praise the action against air pollution, the issue of displaced workers is rarely acknowledged. Middle-class privilege, as reflected in patterns of social and spatial segregation in the city, allows them to screen out facts that may disrupt the comfortable fictions of everyday life. One of these organising fictions is the idea of 'public

---

[28] B. M. Gupta, retired teacher and a member of the B Block, East of Kailash Residents' Welfare Association, in a discussion on public action around environmental issues in Delhi.

interest'. When confronted with the issue of workers' loss of livelihood, M. C. Mehta defends his campaign: 'Here twelve million people are suffering ... What is more important – people's life and health or jobs to a few people?' In this view, protecting the general population from respiratory diseases is a larger cause that overrides the specific suffering of a 'few people', even if they may be poorer and more vulnerable to malnutrition and ill health. Such a posing of the issue – benefit to many versus loss to some – conceals the class-specific effects of the air pollution initiative.

When critics point out the asymmetrical impact of the air pollution campaign, middle-class residents shelter behind self-serving reassurances: 'Oh, the government is bound to do something for workers.' Mehta asserts: 'The court has fully protected the interest of the workers ... Where is the injustice?' Mehta takes at face value the court's orders about compensation, without acknowledging that factory owners did not comply with them. When challenged about the efficacy of these orders, he shrugged off responsibility: 'It was the role of the politicians; it was the role of the trade unions ... When the court order was there they should have protected [workers'] rights through that order. If they don't do anything then [what] can you do?' This account blames politicians and trade unions for betraying workers, without admitting that the court gave them no room to represent workers' interests. That the court saw air pollution as a 'technical' problem devoid of social impacts is clear from the fact that, besides excluding trade unions as affected parties in its deliberations, its advisory committees contained only technical experts and environmentalists, and not representatives of factory owners or affected workers. The media, for its part, also made only token queries about the fate of workers and reported court proceedings without bothering to investigate their impact on the ground. Middle-class hegemony, operating through the court and the media, worked to conceal the violence perpetrated on workers.

That workers' concerns don't matter was clearly expressed by the then Labour Commissioner (LC) for Delhi, the senior-most official responsible for safeguarding the rights of workers in the city:

LC: The main issue of concern before the Delhi government is population – unchecked immigration in the city. This is the basic cause of all problems ... It also results in environmental problems. There have been two landmark judgements by the Supreme Court banning vehicles with non-clean fuel and the relocation of industries in non-conforming areas.

INTERVIEWER(I): Landmark judgement ... in what way?

LC: The Supreme Court acted on public interest litigation and acted to clean the air. Delhi is the fourth most polluted city in the world.

I: Has it improved?

LC: Oh yes. Recently kids were asked if they could see the sky and stars and they responded that they could see the stars now. It was bad [before], you could not see the sky, only black clouds.

I: But what about the workers?

LC: They were given compensation.

I: But what about the unorganised labour?

LC: Some must have gone back to their villages and others took up [other] jobs in the city. Water finds its own way. In practice no workers were laid off or dislocated. There are large-scale development activities ... Overall it seems everyone welcomes the efforts and is happy. Who would want to see dirt and no development?

In terms of changing air quality, the middle class regards the Supreme Court's action against air pollution in Delhi as a success. Pollution levels in Delhi were reduced temporarily until they were offset by the spurt in the number of private motor vehicles (Kathuria 2002, 2005). It was claimed that children can see stars in the sky. It is to be hoped that the incidence of asthma and other respiratory ailments will also decline, though there is no data to that effect. But what of the injuries suffered every day by the children of laid-off workers? They may have breathed cleaner air for a few months, but it didn't fill their bellies. They live in worse conditions; many have been pulled out of school because their parents cannot afford the expense. In the quest for cleaner air, why were these children not considered? The effects of the Supreme Court judgement on the vulnerable bodies of poor children, men and women remained invisible in the public eye.

CONCLUSION

The construction of the 'clean air' cause by a middle-class constituency with privileged access to the courts represented 'the environment' as a universal good, to be protected in the 'public interest', oblivious of the effects on workers. Workers, if they were considered at all, were dismissed as mobile migrants who could return to their distant villages or find other employment. Middle-class unconcern about the devastating effects of displacement for the poor was exemplified in the Labour Commissioner's remark, 'water finds its own way', naturalising their trauma as the simple ebb and flow of footloose and fancy-free nomads. Officially, the poor did not exist; they were absent from official records and, as long as they did not agitate, they were invisible.

Only to the extent that factory owners had some localised political weight that could result in the regularisation of their firms were workers able to hold on to their jobs. Disenfranchised by the legal interpretation of who constitutes the 'public', and excluded by the definition of an 'environmental' issue that failed to recognise their needs for food, shelter, safety and security, workers were doubly discriminated against. Ironically, this marginalisation and dispossession was effected by a legal innovation originally intended to protect their interests.

Despite the contradictions and contestations that marked different forms of state action around the issue of pollution in Delhi, at first glance it would seem that the alliance between judges, bourgeois environmentalists, media and the professional middle class had succeeded in what it sought. Certainly, the factories and workshops of industrial Delhi were banished to the periphery or confined to ghettos. Some of the larger factory sites were redeveloped as commercial real estate, while others remain in limbo, locked in litigation between multiple owners. However, the problem of air and water pollution continues unabated. With the steep annual increase in the number of private motor vehicles in the city, propelled by the shrinking availability of public transport as well as by liberalised access to consumer finance, air pollution is higher than ever. In the case of water pollution, despite additional steps such as the 2004 eviction of more than 200,000 poor squatters from the Yamuna embankment on the grounds that they were polluting the river, the river continues to be polluted because of the discharge of untreated domestic sewage from the city's 'developed' middle-class residential neighbourhoods. It would appear then that the public interest was not served. And yet, perhaps what the judicial activism against pollution did succeed in doing was creating a *spectacle* of law in action, a bravura performance of grand gestures that, regardless of its actual outcomes, conjured up a utopian vision of decisive action that legitimised the role of the judiciary as being 'above politics' and able to cut through it. Regardless of the private compromises that ultimately prevailed or the political negotiations that partially undid judicial orders, in the India of the liberalised era, the hegemony of a middle-class vision had been asserted through the exercise of law. In the era of economic liberalisation, public interest litigation around the environment became a creature of its times, transformed into the pursuit of elite private interests that excluded the poor.

References

Adve, Nagraj 2000. 'Industrial water pollution in Delhi: the Yamuna Maily case. An overview'. Delhi: Unpublished manuscript.

Anderson, M. R. 1995. 'The conquest of smoke: legislation and pollution in colonial Calcutta', in David Arnold and Ramachandra Guha (eds.) *Nature, Culture, Imperialism: Essays on the Environmental History of South Asia*. Delhi: Oxford University Press, pp. 293–335.

Baviskar, Amita 2009. 'Breaking homes, making cities: class and gender in the politics of urban displacement', in Lyla Mehta (ed.) *Displaced by Development: Confronting Marginalisation and Gender Injustice*. New Delhi: Sage Publications, pp. 59–81.

2010. 'Spectacular events, city spaces and citizenship: the Commonwealth games in Delhi', in Jonathan Shapiro Anjaria and Colin McFarlane (eds.) *Urban Navigations: Politics, Space and the City in South Asia*. New Delhi: Routledge, pp. 138–61.

2011. 'Cows, cars and cycle-rickshaws: bourgeois environmentalism and the battle for Delhi's streets', in Amita Baviskar and Raka Ray (eds.) *Elite and Everyman: The Cultural Politics of the Indian Middle Classes*. New Delhi: Routledge, pp. 391–418.

Baviskar, Amita, Sinha, Subir and Philip, Kavita 2006. 'Rethinking Indian environmentalism: industrial pollution in Delhi and fisheries in Kerala', in Joanne Bauer (ed.) *Forging Environmentalism: Justice, Livelihood and Contested Environments*. New York: M. E. Sharpe, pp. 189–256.

Bhattacharya, Rajesh and Sanyal, Kalyan 2011. 'Bypassing the squalor: new towns, immaterial labour and exclusion in post-colonial urbanisation', *Economic and Political Weekly* 46 (31): 41–48.

Caldeira, Teresa P. R. 2000. *City of Walls: Crime, Segregation and Citizenship in Sao Paulo*. Berkeley: University of California Press.

Chatterjee, Partha 1993. *The Nation and Its Fragments: Colonial and Postcolonial Histories*. Princeton University Press.

Cohn, Bernard 1997. *Colonialism and Its Forms of Knowledge*. Delhi: Oxford University Press.

Cowen, Michael P. and Shenton, Robert W. 1996. *Doctrines of Development*. London: Routledge.

CSE (Centre for Science and Environment) 1982. *The State of India's Environment: A Citizen's Report*. New Delhi: CSE.

Dembowski, Hans 2001. *Taking the State to Court: Public Interest Litigation and the Public Sphere in Metropolitan India*. New York: Oxford University Press.

Deshpande, Satish 1997. 'From development to adjustment: economic ideologies, the middle class and 50 years of independence', *Review of Development and Change* 2 (2): 294–318.

Divan, Shyam and Rosencranz, Armin 1991. *Environmental Law and Policy in India*. Delhi: Oxford University Press.

DJAM (Delhi Janwadi Adhikar Manch) 1997a. *The Order That Felled a City*. New Delhi: DJAM.

    1997b. *The Day After*. New Delhi: DJAM.

    1998. *Jansunvai* (Public Hearing). New Delhi: DJAM.

D'Monte, Darryl 2001. *Ripping the Fabric: The Decline of Mumbai and Its Mills*. New Delhi: Oxford University Press.

Drayton, Richard 2000. *Nature's Government: Science, Imperial Britain, and the 'Improvement' of the World*. New Haven, CT: Yale University Press.

Eckert, Julia 2005. *The 'Trimurti' of the State: State Violence and the Promises of Order and Destruction*. Working Paper No. 80. Halle/Saale: Max Planck Institute for Social Anthropology.

Ghertner, D. Asher 2008. 'Analysis of new legal discourse behind Delhi's slum demolitions', *Economic and Political Weekly* 43 (20): 57–66.

Greenough, Paul 2003. 'Pathogens, pugmarks, and political "emergency": the 1970s south Asian debate on nature', in Paul Greenough and Anna Lowenhaupt Tsing (eds.) *Nature in the Global South: Environmental Projects in South and Southeast Asia*. Durham, NC: Duke University Press, pp. 201–30.

Holston, James 1989. *The Modernist City: An Anthropological Critique of Brasilia*. University of Chicago Press.

Kathuria, Vinish 2001. 'Relocating polluting units: parochialism vs. the right to live?', *Economic and Political Weekly* 36 (3): 191–95.

    2002. 'Vehicular pollution control in Delhi', *Economic and Political Weekly* 37 (12): 1147–55.

    2005. 'Vehicular pollution control in Delhi', *Economic and Political Weekly* 40 (18): 1907–15.

Khilnani, Sunil 1997. *The Idea of India*. New Delhi: Penguin Books India.

Ludden, David 1992. 'India's development regime', in Nicholas B. Dirks (ed.) *Colonialism and Culture*. Ann Arbor: University of Michigan Press, pp. 247–83.

McMichael, Philip 1996. *Development and Social Change: A Global Perspective*. Thousand Oaks, CA: Pine Forge Press.

Mehta, Uday Singh 1999. *Liberalism and Empire: A Study in Nineteenth-Century British Liberal Thought*. University of Chicago Press.

Menon-Sen, Kalyani and Bhan, Gautam 2008. *Swept Off the Map: Surviving Eviction and Resettlement in Delhi*. New Delhi: Yoda Press and Jagori.

Mitchell, Timothy 2002. *Rule of Experts: Egypt, Techno-politics and Modernity*. Berkeley: University of California Press.

Navlakha, Gautam 2000. 'Urban pollution: driving workers to desperation', *Economic and Political Weekly* 35 (51): 4469–71.

NCEUS (National Commission for Enterprises in the Unorganised Sector) 2007. *Report on the Conditions of Work and Promotion of Livelihoods in the Unorganised Sector*. New Delhi: NCEUS.

Ramanathan, Usha 2004. 'Communities at risk: industrial risk in Indian law', *Economic and Political Weekly* 39 (41): 4521–27.

Rosin, Thomas R. 2000. 'Wind, traffic and dust: the recycling of wastes', *Contributions to Indian Sociology* 34 (3): 361–408.

Scott, James C. 1998. *Seeing Like a State*. New Haven, CT: Yale University Press.

Smith, Neil 1996. *The New Urban Frontier: Gentrification and the Revanchist City*. London: Routledge.

Tarlo, Emma 2003. *Unsettling Memories: Narratives of the Emergency in India*. Berkeley: University of California Press.

Véron, René 2006. 'Remaking urban environments: the political ecology of air pollution in Delhi', *Environment and Planning A* 38: 2093–109.

CHAPTER 8

LAW AGAINST DISPLACEMENT: THE JURIDIFICATION OF TRIBAL PROTEST IN ROURKELA, ORISSA

Christian Strümpell

INTRODUCTION

For years Orissa has been hitting the headlines in India and elsewhere for conflicts over land and mineral resources (cf. Mishra 2010; Sen 2010). These are fought out between various multinational and domestic companies, the state and the people living on the land that is to be opened up for mines and mills. The region's mineral riches have long been mined and processed into steel. In the late colonial period the industrialist Jamshedji Tata established the Tata Iron and Steel Company (TISCO) at Jamshedpur in what is now Orissa's neighbouring province of Jharkhand and was until 2000 part of Bihar. In the early post-colonial era the central government established the Rourkela Steel Plant (RSP) at Rourkela in Orissa's north-western Sundargarh district. The people who were displaced in both Jamshedpur and Rourkela were in their large majority 'tribals' or Adivasis, not caste Hindus. With regard to Jamshedpur, apart from their 'tribalness', not much is known about the people losing their homes, lands and forests

The field research for this article was conducted in Rourkela over twenty-six months between 2004 and 2009. I gratefully acknowledge the support of the *Deutsche Forschungsgemeinschaft* (German Research Council), the Free University, Berlin, and the Max Planck Institute for Social Anthropology, Halle, Germany. I am deeply indebted to Rajat Kumar Singh and Zoober Ahmed for their invaluable research assistance. I also remain grateful to Julia Eckert for her intellectual and practical support in carrying out this research. I want to thank Julia Eckert, Zerrin Özlem Biner and Brian Donahoe for their inspiring, critical and helpful comments on my research over the past several years, as well as on earlier drafts of this paper. Thanks are also due to Patrick Neveling and Christoph Bergmann for commenting on this paper, and to Brian Donahoe for his skilful editing.

to TISCO and Jamshedpur, their possible resistance or their whereabouts.[1] Concerning Rourkela, several government and academic reports from the 1950s describe in some detail the social, economic and political situation of the local society at the time of its displacement. However, their resistance against their displacement and their claims against the state for better rates of compensation or for better compensatory employment opportunities are only mentioned in passing.[2]

At the time I started conducting ethnographic research in Rourkela in 2004, the children and grandchildren of these displaced tribal villagers were once again raising these claims for rehabilitation and compensation. Unlike earlier, however, these claims are now often raised in a 'juridified' form, with reference to the law and in courts. In this paper I aim to trace the effects this process of juridification has on the claims the protestors forward and their relationship vis-à-vis the state providing the legal framework. A prominent scholarly strand considers this process to be evidence of the wider thesis that 'even at moments of rebellion, they [the subaltern classes] remain dominated by the ideas propagated by their oppressors' (Chatterjee 2005: 547). Following Eckert (2006; Chapter 6, this volume), I will argue against the inevitability in this proposition and interpret the process of juridification from below as an active assumption of citizenship and an active attempt by citizens to express and to act upon their specific interpretations of their citizenship rights in order to shape what they perceive to be the 'good order'.

Eckert (2006) focuses on the relationship between the state (police, etc.) and the citizen-ifying labouring poor in the megacity Mumbai. In this article I aim to show that her thesis also holds true for the struggle against the state that the 'tribal' or Adivasi citizenry in the provincial periphery of western Orissa engages in, despite the fact that India's tribal citizens are generally regarded as distanced and distancing themselves from the state (cf. Shah 2007). The displaced people in Rourkela actively use the law to resist modes of governance they face, and their recourse to law has to be regarded as an attempt to shape the 'good order'.

ROURKELA

When one arrives at the railway station, Rourkela appears not unlike other towns of a similar size in Orissa, and probably other union states

---

[1] Brief mention of them can be found in Orans 1958, Bahl 1994 and Simeon 1995.
[2] The reports that are available to me are Mishra 1958, Government of Orissa 1959, Sperling 1963.

in India. People describe the boroughs around the railway station, or Rourkela proper, as a densely populated, congested urban area with multi-storeyed buildings housing Rourkela's merchant families and their shops, offices and businesses, and slums of informal-sector labourers and small workshops that repair equipment for the local ancillary industries or for the steel plant itself. At the southern end of this bustling area the huge ovens and furnaces of the Rourkela Steel Plant (RSP) reach high into the sky. Its gates swallow and spit out thousands of steel workers at the change of shifts three times a day. Then they swarm out onto the broad, four-lane town highway, or 'ringroad', on motorbikes if they are regular, stably employed RSP workers, or on bicycles if they are contract workers employed via private labour contractors. In general the latter cycle to one of the many slums scattered all over the town or into the more or less urbanised settlements in its hinterland, while the former drive to their flats in the company township that the RSP maintains behind a chain of hills said to keep the steel plant's industrial smog away from it.

The contrast between Rourkela and the township is stark indeed. Well-maintained roads leading through the township are separated from whitewashed bungalows and one- to three-storeyed semi-detached homes near small parks and nurseries looked after by the RSP's horticulture department. RSP houses have front gardens and are all equipped with indoor plumbing and electricity at subsidised rates. The 24,000 company flats for workers and bungalows for officers, i.e. managers and engineers, share the same 'sectors', as the township neighbourhoods are called, each provided with well-equipped and staffed primary and secondary schools, community centres, playgrounds, markets and health centres. At the end of the poshest sector, where the bungalows of senior management are located, the company hospital offers its excellent medical services for a nominal fee to regular RSP employees, their spouses and their children up to the time they marry; for the rest of the population, however, the hospital charges market rates.

Two housing colonies established by the Orissa state housing board sheltering retired RSP employees (and some current ones as well) abut the steel township, as do two resettlement colonies established early on to rehabilitate the local peasantry displaced for the construction of the plant and township. Unlike the steel township, the housing colonies and resettlement colonies are looked after by the state government of Orissa, which is not able to compete with the high standards of civic infrastructure maintained by the RSP because the latter is an undertaking of the central government. Neglect by the state is more gravely experienced (and obviously more visible) in the resettlement colonies than in the colonies of the state housing boards. The latter provided different categories of houses in infrastructurally fully developed neighbourhoods to prospective leaseholders, whereas in the resettlement colonies the state government built only earthen roads and hand water pumps, and assigned levelled but otherwise undeveloped plots of 40 x 60 feet to each displaced household. Though they lack infrastructure and civic amenities, the residents hold legal title and are not encroachers on government land, as are the many slum-dwellers living in 'unauthorised' slums scattered between the different sectors or on the fringes of the steel township, many of which were established on the basis of an old village core pre-dating the Rourkela Steel Plant.

The spatial divides between Rourkela, the township, housing colonies, resettlement colonies and slums largely overlap with social ones. The spacious and orderly world of the steel township is reserved for RSP officers and RSP workers, the latter of which form a local 'aristocracy of labour' created by the post-colonial state's labour laws and policies.[3] 'Industrialise or perish' was the slogan of the early post-colonial era under Prime Minister Jawaharlal Nehru (Khilnani 2003 [1997]: ch. 2). Industrialisation would guarantee India economic autonomy and not mere political independence, and it would – no less important – provoke an inevitable and irrevocable modernisation of an Indian society riddled with regional imbalances, stark class inequalities and divisions of caste, ethnicity and religion. The key industries to start with were steel and energy. Because of their strategic significance and their symbolic importance as exemplary citizens of a nation-building project, the public-sector workforces were granted the right to a modicum of welfare and the right to collective organisation in trade unions (Breman 1999). They soon began to enjoy an almost inviolable job security, and wage levels and fringe benefits placing them firmly within the Indian middle class and leaving them without any common class interests with the great majority of the working class (Parry 1999, 2009, n.d.). In Rourkela workers with regular, and thus better, employment in one of the private companies live in Rourkela proper, in one of the housing colonies, or in one of the better-off slums, but they cannot be found among the residents of the resettlement colonies. In the latter and in the urban slums some people

---

[3] Other employees in government service such as teachers and policemen are also entitled to living quarters in the township, but usually they have their separate colonies maintained by their state government department.

also have regular RSP employment, but the majority ekes out a living with varying degrees of success as skilled and unskilled contract workers, craftsmen, self-employed drivers or petty contractors. Since India started liberalising its economy in the late 1980s, the 'displaced people's movement' has regained momentum precisely in these resettlement colonies and the urban slums that many pre-RSP villages have turned into.

THE BEGINNING

Rourkela was until the mid 1950s a settlement of some 2,000 people in the sparsely populated but mineral-rich hills of north-western Orissa.[4] To the West German and Indian experts surveying the region in search of a suitable site to build a steel plant it appeared relatively 'urban' in comparison to the 'tribal' hamlets and villages surrounding it. Rourkela had been part of the former princely state of Gangpur, one of the twenty-four 'jungle kingdoms' covering the forested hills of present-day western Orissa and ruled by *jungli* ('wild') despotic kings. These kingdoms were more or less voluntarily merged with the union state of Orissa, and thus with the Republic of India, in 1948. Since then Rourkela also hosted a few offices of the post-colonial state's administrative apparatus. As early as the turn of the twentieth century Rourkela had a train station on the Bengal–Nagpur railway, which connected the place to India's main industrial centres. This railway connection, the water supply from adjacent rivers, the proximity to rich iron ore and limestone deposits, and the fact that this was a 'backward' region in need of such a huge investment tipped the balance in its favour. On 15 February 1954 the government of India announced that the first public-sector steel plant of independent India would be established in Rourkela.

This decision was received enthusiastically in Bhubaneswar, capital of the state of Orissa, but the people in Rourkela and its thirty-one surrounding villages viewed the development with apprehension. Approximately 15,000 people or 3,000 households lived in these villages,[5] more than two-thirds of whom were Adivasis from the Munda, Oraon and Bhuiyan scheduled tribes, while the remaining one-third regarded themselves as Oriya, Bihari, Muslim or Marwari. After the state government issued the official notification of land acquisition on 22 February 1954, their

---

[4] The statistics referred to in this chapter have been taken from Mishra 1958.
[5] These numbers are only estimates since they are based on the 1951 census data, five years before the local population was displaced and resettled.

resentment turned into more open protest. They tried to obstruct preparatory work or refused to leave their fields and houses so that the state government, then ruling only by a marginal majority, felt forced to frequently renegotiate with the villagers over the terms of displacement and compensation. The small elite of former, and mostly Bhuiyan, village headmen (*ganju* and *gauntia*) and high-caste Oriya and Bihari professionals established various associations backed by Orissa's different major political parties. Their complaints were basically the same as the displaced villagers': that the money the state government offered as compensation was not enough and that monetary compensation alone was not sufficient. The villagers were for the most part categorised as 'backward' tribals and in need of special rehabilitation measures. After frequent visits of high-ranking ministers and administrators to Rourkela, the state government doubled the amount of compensation they granted to displaced people for the loss of fields, crops and houses.[6] In addition, it promised to provide each displaced household with a comparable area of land at alternative sites in reclamation camps some fifty to one hundred kilometres from Rourkela for those who wanted to continue working as farmers, and house plots in resettlement colonies adjacent to, but segregated from, the steel plant and township for those who opted for wage labour. They furthermore promised to provide employment to able-bodied displaced people on the construction site and, after the plant's inception, in their regular public-sector workforce. These negotiations were not always peaceful, and the state government regularly deployed armed police forces to intimidate and control villagers.

Apart from a handful of exceptions nobody challenged the process of land acquisition legally. Those who did belonged to the small local elite, but had to realise quickly that the land acquisition laws did not provide any room to challenge the state. Land in Rourkela was acquired under the provisions of the colonial Land Acquisition Act of 1894, which empowered the state to acquire against its market value any land in India for public purposes, in this case for a corporation owned or controlled by the state; and under the provisions of the Orissa Act XVIII of 1948,[7] which amended the 'public purpose' clause to include allied and ancillary industries regardless of whether they are in the private or public sector.

---

[6] Confusion continues to exist over the monetary compensation. While some officers and displaced people regard the payments from the government as compensation for lost land, others argue that the amount only compensated for the standing crops.

[7] The full form of that act is 'Orissa Development of Industries, Irrigation, Agriculture, Capital Construction and Re-settlement of Displaced Persons (Land Acquisition) Act, 1948'.

The eyewitnesses to the displacement process to whom I spoke all allege that many of the landlords and professionals siphoned off much of the compensation payments. The sums their fathers or grandfathers still got paid nevertheless seemed extravagant to them, and were often spent drinking and feasting, or were invested (and usually lost) in dubious business deals organised by migrant merchants with an eye for a quick profit. The eyewitnesses or their children also accuse the state government of never having properly demarcated the promised compensatory land. It sometimes also turned out to be barren or already under occupation. Everybody remembers the displacement as a moment of great grief and often also of humiliation and violence. If a patch of land acquired for RSP was required for further construction but was still occupied, the inhabitants were often barely left time to pack up their belongings and rudely pushed onto trucks to carry them to the resettlement colonies or reclamation camps. Many people told me that for many of their old relatives the situation then was so unbearable that they died. Those who left for the reclamation camps to continue their lives as farmers were mostly middle-aged couples with their small children. There were also many displaced villagers who preferred to work for wages on the various construction sites and build themselves huts in the resettlement colonies or – when possible – at their old village sites within and around Rourkela. After the steel plant's inception quite a lot of younger displaced villagers got recruited as unskilled labourers for the 'hot' shops of the RSP such as the coke ovens, blast furnaces and foundries. Protest against displacement and for different terms of rehabilitation abated for some years.

WORKING FOR THE RSP

By the late 1950s and throughout the following decades Rourkela's political arena was dominated by Oriya claims for public-sector employment. Orissa's fertile eastern coastal lowlands around the capital Bhubaneswar and the old temple town of Puri are regularly devastated by cyclones and floods. Many people from the coast soon started seeing the employment opportunities in the upcoming industrial hub of Rourkela as a way out of their economic insecurity. Some migrants who settled in Rourkela after their retirement – like so many did – told me a saying that was popular in coastal Orissa at the time: 'If it works out, it works out. If not, let's go to Rourkela' (*Hela to hela, no hela, chalo Rourkela!*). After arriving in Rourkela they had to compete against much more industrially skilled workers and engineers from Bengal, Punjab and the southern states. These 'foreigners' (*pardeshi*) allegedly distributed jobs, or at least the most lucrative ones, only among themselves and for no other reason than their shared ethnic identities. The hopes of Oriya migrants were thus soon shattered and it was easy for gangs of Oriya hooligans (*goondas*) engaged in protection rackets to stir them up against these 'foreigners'. The ethnic violence was rampant during this period and culminated in 1964 when a relatively small number of right-wing Hindu nationalists succeeded in instigating masses of people from all ethnic backgrounds to unleash a massacre against Muslims, claiming more than 2,000 lives (Ghosh 1981: 92–93; cf. Parry and Strümpell 2008).

The Orissa state government condemned the violence, but often proved incompetent to handle it. In fact it shared the general concern of Oriyas in Rourkela, i.e. that they would be outnumbered and subordinated to out-of-state-migrants. The state government made several pleas to the steel plant management to employ more people from Orissa. They argued that the disproportionate employment of out-of-state migrants ran counter to the very idea of public-sector undertakings being the leveller of regional disparities. The steel plant management – largely Bengali, Punjabi and Bihari – rebuffed these pleas with reference to the lack of industrial training of applicants from Orissa. The latter of course suspected this to be a mere act of ethnic discrimination against which their state government was unable to protect them. Asserting Oriya claims to the public-sector jobs generated in Rourkela thus turned into an important agenda for politicians from all major political parties active in Orissa.

The tide began to turn only in the late 1960s when the central government made it mandatory that, for jobs with a monthly wage below 500 rupees, public-sector undertakings recruit manual labourers from among a pool of candidates forwarded by the local employment exchange. This gave the local employment officer, a state government servant, considerable leverage over the recruitment process. This amendment occurred at the time the steel plant extended its production and again recruited steel workers by the thousands, and it was Oriya migrants from the state's coast who now got the jobs, not the Bengalis, Biharis and other 'foreigners'.

The hazardous jobs in the steel plant's 'hot shops', where coal is coked, iron melted and steel moulded, are still assigned to 'tribal' workers. In the eyes of non-tribal officers, unionists and co-workers, they are the ones who are backward and fierce enough to bear the heat and dust. Many displaced tribal villagers who had thus far been too young to work for the prestigious employer and who had undergone some technical training also applied for the new jobs in the steel plant's relatively cool and clean mills. But instead of getting those jobs themselves, they had to watch Oriyas – whom they consider to be as much 'foreigners' as the Oriyas regard Bengalis, Punjabis and others – getting all the jobs. This was done with the active support of the state administration, who insisted that they were protecting interests of the 'local people'.

Again a displaced people's association was formed to make their claims heard: that it was they who were locals, not the Oriya migrants from the far-away coast; that it was upon their former fields that steel and wealth were produced; and that it should therefore be they who receive secure and remunerative employment. They put forward their arguments in petitions to the state and central governments, though in vain. They allied with leaders of regional political parties demanding the establishment of a separate 'tribal' state, Jharkhand. They also allied with a new steel workers' union organised by 'tribal' workers to challenge the RSP's officially 'recognised union', which was the management's sole bargaining partner, staffed almost exclusively with Oriya and allegedly engaged in the marginalisation of non-Oriyas in Rourkela. The regional political parties and the new union received strong support from local displaced Adivasis, as well as from migrant Adivasis from other nearby places. They also received more or less tacit support from other groups of people who had experienced 'othering' and marginalisation at the hands of Oriya co-citizens. The displaced people's ire was directed against the state and in general against all Oriya colonisers from the coast. Protest marches, strikes and blockades were organised. Clashes with the police and security personnel were frequent. Given the town's earlier record of ethnic violence, the situation was taken seriously. On one of his visits to Rourkela in July 1973, T. N. Singh, the then steel minister of the central government, advised plant management and state government authorities to employ at least one person from each displaced household. A few hundred were employed immediately, and in the years to come others followed on account of what came to be known as the 'T. N. Singh formula'.

The movement died down after that because its leaders had been bought out, as most people cynically say, or because of its success, as some followers say. The steel plant's major union, allegedly backed by both management and state government, also managed to silence the 'tribal' union that had allied with the displaced people. However, fifteen years later, towards the end of the 1980s, a new trade union was again formed to challenge the officially recognised one, and a little later yet another wave of displaced people's movements appeared on the local scene. This time protests took on a more 'juridified' form.

THE JURIDIFICATION OF PROTEST

Contract workers against the state

The new trade union owed its emergence to a movement of RSP 'contract workers' demanding their regular employment. In the 1970s RSP management started to outsource work to private labour contractors. For tasks it declared not to be permanent and perennial to the production process, i.e. all maintenance work, management tendered contracts to private companies. These are known in general parlance as 'contractors' or *thikadar*, and the one submitting the cheapest bid would get the contract and then employ so-called contract workers to execute the tasks. Unlike regular and permanent workers, these contract workers did not enjoy the right to unionisation; they earned only up to 30 per cent of what a regular worker earned, did not enjoy fringe benefits and could be hired and fired at will. A large number of contract workers were and still are Adivasis, and their numbers grew quickly over the years. The managers, unionists and workers to whom I talked all estimated that by the mid 1980s around 10,000 contract labourers were working for the RSP under myriad contractors.

In the mid 1980s M. D. N. Panicker, an RSP clerk from Kerala who had already earlier engaged in RSP unions challenging the officially recognised 'Oriya union', started to organise the Rourkela Steel Plant Contract Labour Welfare Association for the regularisation of RSP contract workers. Earlier, some unions had tried to bargain with RSP management over the terms of employment of RSP contract workers. In the late 1970s the officially recognised union had reached an agreement with RSP management and its contractors that secured contract workers' continuous re-employment in case a contractor's contract terminated, but was taken up by a new one. The clerk interpreted this agreement to mean that the contract workers' jobs were in fact permanent and perennial to the production process, and in 1986 went to court to claim that the RSP was therefore bound to employ regular workers to perform them.

The struggle went on for almost a decade. Panicker survived a couple of attacks, averted numerous charges against him and rejected several offers to strike a deal with the RSP management or the contractors. On May Day 1987 nearly 3,000 contract workers were retrenched to prevent their regularisation. After only a couple of days the Supreme Court ordered their reinstatement and later directed the RSP management to ensure that no contract worker would be retrenched as long as the case was pending. The Supreme Court passed its verdict in May 1994, ordering the RSP to employ on a regular basis all contract labourers who had worked in one of 246 jobs identified as perennial and who had done so under one of its contractors for at least the last ten years. Starting from 1 January 1995, a total of 4,500 contract workers were regularised and entitled to the pay and perks of the privileged public-sector workers alongside whom they had worked for decades.

Panicker's growing popularity among contract workers also made him popular among the RSP's regular workers, who convinced him to form a trade union even before the Supreme Court passed its verdict. With their support he was able to establish his union as the strongest in terms of membership, which entitled it to the status of 'recognised union'. With the additional support from the regularised contract labourers his union has won all RSP trade union elections and thus retained its status as the recognised union ever since. The union celebrates the Supreme Court verdict every year on the night of 31 December, the night before the day the contract workers gained regular employment in 1995. In a speech he delivered on one such celebration in which I participated, and in several interviews I conducted with him over the years of my field research, the former clerk and now trade union leader expressed his strong faith in the law and his commitment to the struggle for the preservation of the 'rule of law'. He also obviously aims to express this faith in the union's emblem. It depicts a cogwheel inside which a line of Sanskrit is inscribed: *Satyameva jayate* ('Truth alone triumphs'; this is also India's national motto) and, looming large in the cogwheel's centre, the scales of Lady Justice.

The triumph in this case has of course been partial. All contract workers who could not prove their ten years of continuous service were immediately retrenched to prevent them from raising claims in the future. I met quite a number who said that they indeed had worked for RSP for ten years or more, but were unable to document it because their contractors had not maintained the insurance- and provident fund-cards that they are obliged to issue for their workers. They thus lost their source of income, however modest it had been. Also, the erstwhile agreement between the RSP management, the contractors and the once recognised union, which had been so crucial to the success of the case, was cancelled. Nevertheless, the 'juridified' approach to industrial relations that Panicker took appealed to Rourkela's working classes (and to some extent it still does). In the end, this approach did achieve the regularisation of contract labourers in numbers no political negotiation between unions and the RSP management, or indeed the management of any public-sector undertaking anywhere in the country, had ever done. Furthermore, it did so at a time when the RSP management was determined to actually reduce manpower levels significantly. The verdict was passed a couple of years after the government in Delhi officially declared a break with the Nehruvian legacy, with the intention of embarking on a 'new economic policy' and liberalising the economy. India's public-sector undertakings were privatised or, like its steel plants, restructured to compete in a global market. Profit generation now gained in prominence at the expense of employment provision. Subsequently, since the early 1990s the RSP has slimmed down its workforce from 37,000 to the current figure of 18,000, a figure that would still be lower if the RSP had not had to regularise a large chunk of its contract labour force.

The 'displaced people' against the state
The loss of labour

The reduction of manpower by 50 per cent over the last two decades was achieved not by retrenchments; as already mentioned, public-sector workers are well safeguarded against retrenchments and dismissals. The reduction of manpower was achieved by natural attrition. In the late 1980s workers of the first generation started retiring by the thousands and a new generation was recruited only in smaller numbers. Thus, few sons of retiring RSP workers were able to step into their fathers' footsteps. Children of RSP workers who grew up in the RSP township, with its above-average educational facilities, regard themselves as educated enough to compete for the narrowing number of privileged RSP jobs, or to earn a comparable income elsewhere. However, the situation of children of the local displaced people living in the resettlement colonies and urbanised 'villages' is very different. Few of them had acquired even the minimum educational qualifications necessary for applying for RSP jobs, which by that time had been raised to a passed matriculation exam upon completion of the tenth form.

The children and grandchildren of those displaced by the steel plant and town were thus excluded from the local labour aristocracy. They were left with little other option but to eke out a living as labourers in the local informal sector, as contract workers in the RSP or some other company, as self-employed drivers or by selling self-distilled illicit liquor, to name the most prominent examples. Or they would engage in associations and political parties striving to reclaim the place of the local displaced people in the public-sector steel workforce. In the late 1980s the Jharkhand Liberation Front (*Jharkhand Mukti Morcha* – JMM), a regional party struggling to establish a separate 'tribal' state, Jharkhand, encompassing among other areas the region around Rourkela, appeared on the local political scene. It has since then regularly won the support of the constituencies around Rourkela, notably in the resettlement colonies, at state legislative assembly elections.

Together with the JMM yet another displaced people's association was formed. Like its predecessor twenty years before, it staged demonstrations and strikes confronting plant management and – more vociferously – the state government. That the displaced people directed their anger especially at the latter was informed by their experience of the way the Orissa state government had exerted its authority to procure RSP jobs for Oriyas after 1968. When the Displaced People's Association and the JMM in 1994 organised a strike to prevent the construction of a mosque on land claimed by a local displaced Adivasi, the Hindu nationalist Bharatiya Janata Party muscled in to stir up anti-Muslim sentiments in Rourkela that just a year earlier had triggered ghastly communal violence in many towns of northern India. Though Rourkela remained peaceful then, its tainted record of inter-ethnic and communal relations (see above) made the central and state governments cautious. Several platoons of special police forces were sent in and violently crushed the strike.

Around the same time the RSP management, state government and the Displaced People's Association reached an agreement regulating the provision of compensatory RSP employment to all remaining 'uncovered' displaced households, i.e. households displaced forty years ago that still had not been compensated with jobs. The Displaced People's Association forwarded a list of approximately 1,000 uncovered households. The RSP management agreed to employ one person from each household, provided that he had matriculated, in batches of 100 per year, and the state government agreed to verify the identities of applicants. By 2008 only around 500 new workers had been taken on by the RSP. The leaders of the displaced people's association, as well as the displaced people in the resettlement colonies and urbanised 'villages', accused the RSP management and state government administration of unnecessarily delaying the process. They complained that steel plant and state officers simply lacked concern for tribal people. The former justified the slow progress by referring to a recent global steel crisis and the company's inability to recruit more staff, while the latter explained it away with reference to the complications of verifying the identity of claimants. The verification of identities is indeed a complex and painstaking administrative process, because it has to be established whether a claimant in fact is a descendant of one of the households displaced in the 1950s. These households had been registered – in the form of noting the names of their adult male members and the boundaries of their land in a book or *katha* – the last time being in a settlement in 1936. These records had often been so poorly maintained that it is difficult or even impossible to substantiate claims of descent. The displaced people are under the impression that a whole bundle of certified copies of documents are required, and gathering them of course costs time and money. Many people told me that they had spent sums of up to 3,000 rupees, or more than one month's wages for a contract labourer, to gather documents from various revenue departments. This is not to say that all these documents are in fact necessary or that it is indeed necessary to bribe administrators to get them. However, the widespread belief that this is the case prevents many people from poorer displaced households from even trying. In fact, almost all people who did pass in their applications for compensatory RSP employment at the local magistrate's office had close supportive relatives who had or still have such a job themselves.

Even if someone provides documents that pass the scrutiny of the state government officers, he or she can only expect an RSP job if no other descendant from that household has ever been employed in compensation for the household's displacement. As already mentioned, many displaced people in fact worked in the steel plant until their retirement in the 1980s. Nevertheless, they emphasise that the RSP in the beginning desperately needed workers and therefore recruited them on the open labour market, and not because of their displacement.

To check the households who over the decades had already been given compensatory employment, the RSP is supposed to forward to the local state government administration a list containing details of all workers for whom it has provided such employment so far. These lists, however, remain a major bone of contention. Only in 2006 did the RSP forward a list with 6,000 names on it, but it contained no further information. The Displaced People's Association alleged that most workers on this list were actually outsiders who had beguiled locals into giving their displacement certificates to them and were then working in the RSP under the names of the locals. Under the recently established Right to Information Act the Displaced People's Association then asked the RSP to forward a list with the home addresses of all the 6,000 displaced people it claims to have employed. The RSP complied, but the new list revealed that many individual workers mentioned on the earlier list had home addresses in other districts of Orissa, other states of India, or even in Nepal. Consequently, the Displaced People's Association challenged the tripartite agreement made in 1993 and demanded that a new list of 'uncovered' households be drawn up.

Since 2006 they have regularly organised sit-ins in front of the revenue office in Rourkela and occasionally staged demonstrations and strikes on the town's 'ringroad' to step up pressure on the steel plant and the state government. Now with a new agreement in the air many young people from the resettlement colonies and urbanised ex-villages are rushing to attend these gatherings in the hope that their dream of an RSP job might come true. The state government then urged the RSP to provide a new list containing the father's name plus the *katha* number, i.e. the number of their registered erstwhile plot of land. The RSP forwarded a new list in late 2007 that contained the required details of only 2,200 individuals, and some of them, it turned out, belonged to the same household. This list is now used by the local state government administration to verify the claims of the 8,000 or so displaced people who have submitted applications since 2006. In August 2009, state government administration and the steel plant management once again invited eighty-five individuals to undergo vocational training at the local industrial training institute before joining the RSP.

Both the RSP management and the state government emphasise that even if no household members have been provided with an RSP job the displaced people do not have any *rights* to public-sector employment. The RSP and the state government assert that it is solely because of their concern for the poor condition in which many displaced tribal families live now that they are even willing to consider going beyond the letter of the law and providing employment to all families who indeed have been left out so far. Throughout all the years since the displaced people lost their place in the steel plant, the Displaced People's Association or other informal groups seek to forward their claims not only through political patronage or by taking to the streets, but also through legal means, as the three main cases to which I will turn now illustrate.

Case one In 1991 a retiring RSP worker from the scheduled tribe Khumbhar, whose father had been displaced in the 1950s, approached Panicker for advice on how to claim employment for his sons and the sons of his neighbours in the resettlement colonies. Butu Khumbhar received financial support from a large number of displaced Adivasis living in and around Rourkela, and filed a case against the steel plant authorities for failing to provide public-sector employment (or, at a minimum, for failing to give preference when vacancies need to be filled) to all people displaced now and for the generations to come. He argued that compensatory employment in the public-sector undertaking constructed on their land had been provided only to a few of the displaced people, whereas all adults including future generations had been deprived of their means to earn a living. This was what the land that was taken away would have guaranteed, as it is an inheritable good. He argued that their displacement therefore violated article 21 of the fundamental rights in the Constitution of India, which guarantees all people the right to a livelihood.

The case was dismissed at the Orissa State High Court, and Butu Khumbhar then approached the Supreme Court. After a couple of years the Supreme Court declared in 1995 that the challenge he raised was void of any merit. The judges argued that the acts under whose provision land had been acquired provided only for monetary compensation and not for compensation with employment and that, to the contrary, guaranteed employment for all displaced adults for all time to come, or even their preferential treatment, would violate article 14 of the constitution guaranteeing the right to equality. They declared further that the 'T. N. Singh formula' that had been negotiated in 1973 only spoke about *one* regular RSP job per displaced household. The verdict that Butu Khumbhar showed me further emphasises what steel plant officers and state government administrators say today: that it was only because of the poverty of the persons who were displaced that the state took steps to ensure that each family was protected by giving employment to at least one member of the family.

Case two   In the late 1990s a local lawyer from a scheduled tribe whose forefathers had not been displaced advised a displaced people's association to file a case on other grounds. This time the displaced people claimed that the 'surplus land', i.e. the land that had initially been acquired for the construction of the steel plant and the township but that had not been utilised for that purpose, by law had to be returned to its original owners or their descendants. They further stated that, of the 20,000 acres the state government acquired by virtue of a notification in 1954 under the provision of the Land Acquisition Act of 1894 and the Orissa Act XVIII of 1948, the RSP had already returned 4,500 acres of surplus land to the state government. However, instead of returning this land to the local people, during the 1980s the state government assigned large parts of it to different state-run housing boards to establish colonies for retiring RSP workers, or to wealthy and influential private individuals. All of the latter, as well as all residents in the housing colonies, are migrants from Orissa's coast or elsewhere. After the country's turn to economic liberalisation, land became a very valuable asset, and the state government started selling further surplus land to private parties, just as the RSP started to advertise the possibility of purchasing company-owned living quarters. At the same time many slum-dwellers were facing the threat of eviction because their residences, which in fact are on land where their villages were prior to construction of the steel plant, are, technically speaking, illegal encroachments on either state government or steel company land.

Both parties sold land at the price of 4 million rupees per acre, a sum the displaced felt was exorbitant when compared to the compensation of 200–900 rupees per acre they had received fifty years ago. In the writ petition that members of the Displaced People's Association filed in the late 1990s,[8] they argued that under the provision of the Fifth Schedule of the constitution and under the Orissa Regulation (2) of 1956,[9] the transfer of land owned by a person from a scheduled tribe to any other person is forbidden and that the only exception to this regulation is the transfer of land for 'public purpose' as mentioned in the Land Acquisition Act and the Orissa Act XVIII. This clause is no longer valid if the land is not utilised for the public purpose it was acquired for, in which case it has to be returned to the original owners. The State High Court and, later on, the Supreme Court, however, held that the set-up of a steel plant-cum-township entails the establishment of other urban-industrial structures such as housing colonies, railway stations, industrial estates, markets and shopping malls. The courts dismissed the claim. In the end, only some residents from a few slums have been evicted, although the threat of eviction lingers on.

Case three The most recent legal claim was filed in 2005 by Tarkan Lakra, a former JMM politician who was also a member of the state's legislative assembly and a former RSP white-collar worker. Tarkan Lakra

---

[8] This writ petition was shown to me during my field research.
[9] The full term of the law is 'Orissa Scheduled Areas Transfer of Immovable Property (by Scheduled Tribes) Regulation, 1956'.

belonged to the scheduled tribe Oraon, and was born and raised in a village whose lands were partially expropriated in the 1950s. In the writ petition he forwarded to the court he challenged the legal validity of the whole land acquisition process. He argued that land acquisition in Rourkela had been pursued under the provision of the Orissa Act XVIII of 1948, but that this act had never been officially affirmed by the president of India as not violating the constitution that came into force in 1950. Without such an affirmation, he argued, the act is null and void. Therefore the land acquisition process lacked a legal basis and all of the land that was thereby acquired thus had to be returned to the descendants of its original owners. The Orissa State High Court declared the writ petition to be of no merit in 2008, and a little later the Supreme Court upheld that ruling.

How many of the people around Tarkan Lakra and the local displaced people's association ever really believed that case would have a chance at court is not clear, but I have never come across anybody who believed the case would succeed. However, all of them were convinced that the case would be turned down for political reasons, and not on legal grounds. As Tarkan Lakra and his neighbours in one of the resettlement colonies put it, the dismissal of their writ petition is what one has to expect when one is ruled by a regime of wild, violent domination, by a *jungli raj*. Their hope that law can get them 'justice' has been shattered for some time. When I talked again to Tarkan Lakra in 2011 he told me that he and some of his associates are now considering approaching the human rights commission in the state and at the centre, but this case is yet to be filed. Despite all odds the 'rumour of rights' Julia Eckert discusses in this volume thus also in Rourkela does not seem to lose its force.

LIGHT IN THE DARK ZONE

The trajectory of Rourkela's displaced people's struggles against dispossession and for rehabilitation delineated above suggests that this situation can properly be described as a process of 'juridification'. The displaced people frame their claims with reference to law and take recourse to courts now, but until twenty years ago they restricted themselves to seeking the patronage of political leaders (*netas*) and to strikes or individual acts of violence. Rourkela's politicians, lawyers, journalists, steel plant officers, administrators and activists, i.e. the local 'middle class' engaged in one way or another with the issue, consider this to be a recent phenomenon. Earlier, they told me, the displaced Adivasis had been much too timid to face the government and state officials. All middle-class informants relate this to the 'despotic' kings who had ruled the princely states without law, privileged their coterie, and fined and dispossessed their helpless subjects at will. These largely tribal subjects therefore always sought, with varying degrees of success, to keep the state at bay (cf. Shah 2007). After the 'merger' in 1948, the post-colonial state carried the 'rule of law' and democracy, progress and development, or 'light', into what people from Orissa's eastern coast consider the *andharua mulaka* – the 'dark zones' of the western hills (cf. Pati 2000).

However, according to Rourkela's middle class, the former tribal subjects still preferred to maintain their distance from the state and the Oriya representatives staffing its institutions. By doing so they themselves ruined the opportunities for development the state and the state-owned steel plant had offered them. That they now raise ill-advised claims on behalf of their displacement for which they had been compensated long ago and according to the letter of the law only shows how uneducated they still are.

The state laws' 'alienness' for the urban poor and the rural population is of course also an established scholarly notion. Thus, peasants instrumentally fabricated court cases to fight out disputes in nineteenth-century India because, Cohn argues, they did not share the social values inherent in British procedural law (Cohn 1987: 569). Their attitude to courts had not changed by the time of Cohn's field research in the 1950s and, following Upendra Baxi (1992), continues up to the present. As Julia Eckert (2006: 65) points out, the assumption of a fundamental clash of values also underlies studies holding that the use of state law by subalterns simply reveals the hegemonic sway the ruling classes enjoy.

Partha Chatterjee (2004) provides a prominent recent elaboration of this thesis. He claims that there exists in contemporary India a 'vast range of social practices that continue to be regulated by other beliefs and administered by other authorities than the ones provided by the state' (Chatterjee 2004: 50). Chatterjee also refers to them as the 'dark zones' which are nevertheless 'slowly, painfully and unsurely' being 'enlightened' by the governmental agencies of the modern state and thereby transformed into 'political society' (Chatterjee 2004). Political society emerges when a particular population group produced by governmental agencies as a target for particular welfare policies forms an association, imagines itself as a moral community, and, with the help of patronising mediators, raises claims to goods or services that are actually in violation of state law. Chatterjee states that these groups accept that their claims to, for example, settle on government land or to peddle goods without a license are illegal and contrary to good civic behaviour, but they demand to be treated as an exception and exempted from prosecution (Chatterjee 2004: 40; Chatterjee 2008: 61). The problem for the state is that it very often has to acknowledge these claims if it does not want to risk its legitimacy as a developmental state, but that at the same time it has to 'maintain the fiction that in the constitution of its sovereignty, all citizens belong to civil society and are, by virtue of that legally constructed fact, equal subjects of the law' (Chatterjee 2004: 74). The illegal claims therefore can only be negotiated on a political terrain where 'rules may be bent or stretched, and not on the terrain of established law or administrative procedure' (Chatterjee 2004: 60). This renders such negotiated paralegal arrangements uncertain and temporary, subject to the governmental agencies' calculations of political expediency.

Chatterjee illustrates his thesis with (among others) case studies of populations displaced by development projects in West Bengal, such as coalfields, ports and new towns. These case studies show that wherever the affected population groups were organised in associations to negotiate the terms of land acquisition and rehabilitation with representatives of both the government and oppositional parties, the agreements reached were indeed consensual and the outcome satisfactory because legal procedure was *not* followed (Chatterjee 2004: 69–73). He argues that '[i]t is over property then that we see, on the terrain of political society, a dynamic *within* the modern state of the transformation of precapitalist structures and of premodern cultures'. This, he claims, does not apply to India alone, but to 'most of the world' or to all places 'where just as the fictive ideal of civil society may wield a powerful influence on the forces of political change, so can the actual transactions over the everyday distribution of rights and entitlements lead over time to substantial redefinitions of property and law within the actually existing modern state'. Chatterjee concludes that 'the paralegal then, despite its ambiguous and supplementary status in relation to the legal, is not some pathological condition of retarded modernity, but rather part of the very process of the historical constitution of modernity in most of the world' (Chatterjee 2004: 75).

The relevance of Chatterjee's thesis for Rourkela seems obvious. The 'displaced people' are a population group construed as a target for specific policies by governmental agencies, and it gives itself the attributes of a moral community. The displaced people living in the slums into which their former villages have turned are illegally encroaching on government land and often engage in other illegal activities: they distil and sell illicit 'country liquor', help organise illegal cock fights and betting and pilfer electricity, to name but a few examples. They admit that a lot of their activities are illegal, and in order to negotiate them with government agencies they seek the patronage of ward counsellors, parliamentarians, unionists, police officers and other politically powerful people. Even with regard to issues like public-sector employment they seek patronage, and the political negotiations they engage in may lead to arrangements such as in 1973 or in the 1990s. Both these arrangements have been based on considerations of political expediency, and are regarded as exceptions from a rule, as the verdict in the second case quoted above explicitly mentions; they are, thus, paralegal. Rourkela's 'displaced people' hence display all characteristics of what Chatterjee calls 'political society'.

However, the claims forwarded by the displaced people introduced above reveal that Chatterjee's model is at odds with the 'politics of the governed' in Rourkela. Various plaintiffs on behalf of the displaced people as a whole accuse the state of having acquired their land without compensating them with the adequate means to earn a living, of having acquired land in excess of actual demand and of now selling it illegally to private 'outsiders' instead of returning it to its original owners, and, most recently, of doing all this without any constitutional basis at all. This contradicts Chatterjee's model, most obviously for two reasons. Firstly, in none of these cases do the 'displaced people' themselves make any claims to be treated as exceptions from an established rule, which in any case would be quite impossible because they frame their demands in legal terms and thus *per definitionem* in general principles (cf. Washbrook 1981; Fuller 1994). Secondly, the displaced people themselves in the first place consider the acts of the state and the public-sector undertaking to be illegal, and not their own. It is the state and its company that encroaches on their land without providing proper compensation and without a proper constitutional basis, they argue. That the high court judges reject their claims proves again that they are subjected to a state controlled by outsiders that rules them, the tribes, by wild, brute force. They are subjected to a *jungli raj*, as Tarkan Lakra says.

THE *JUNGLI RAJ*

The *jungli raj* is a prominent trope in discourses on Jharkhand, the 'tribal' state adjacent to Orissa and actually only a stone's throw (twenty kilometres) from Rourkela. In India's first steel town, Jamshedpur, less than a three-hour train journey north of Rourkela, the largely Bengali middle class refers to the *jungli raj* to explain the town's exceptionally high rate of violent crime (Sanchez 2010). This law and order problem is placed at the door of Jamshedpur's large population of Biharis and Adivasis, who allegedly have violence in their blood and thus maintain the town and its province as a 'pre-modern backwater' to the shining India of the metropoles. Sanchez (2010: 166f) argues that the *jungli raj* discourse portrays the region's problems as rooted in a local culture of violence and thus provincialises them. This discourse obscures the more general role violence plays in the actual operation of financial and industrial capitalism that towns such as Jamshedpur have been experiencing at an accelerating rate since India's economic liberalisation and since companies such as the local Tata Iron and Steel Company started the casualisation of large parts of their workforces.

In Rourkela the displaced Adivasis engage in the *jungli raj* discourse to emphasise that it is the post-colonial state, staffed with 'foreigners' from the coastal regions around the state's capital Bhubaneswar and in close cooperation with companies, that unleashes a wild regime upon them, void of legality, amassing incredible riches by violently dispossessing them and discriminating against them. The *jungli raj* discourse as Rourkela's displaced Adivasis use it thus represents a worm's eye view on the process of 'accumulation by dispossession' taking place in contemporary post-liberalisation Orissa. The expression 'accumulation by dispossession' was coined by David Harvey (2003) to formulate in general terms the notion that the current neo-liberal phase of capitalism repeats in an extended form what Marx once called 'original accumulation'. Dispossession or the enclosure of the commons nowadays also entails the privatisation of public-sector industries and government services, and often occurs along pre-existing social divides of class, gender and/ or ethnicity (Harvey 2003: 137–82). In Orissa it is predominantly 'tribal' lands that are acquired for mines and mills and it is – as the ethnography above has shown – predominantly Adivasi workers' children whose prospects for relatively remunerative and secure employment are shattered by the restructuring of existing industries. The 'tribal' and 'subaltern' reference to the *jungli raj* discourse in Rourkela reflects the provincial, geographically and socially uneven ways in which accumulation by dispossession unfolds in the Orissan context (cf. Strümpell n.d.).

This specific meaning the *jungli raj* has for Rourkela's displaced people, i.e. of a rule void of legality, depends of course on them taking recourse to the law and to courts in the first place. This juridification of protest, however, has so far not brought the outcomes the displaced Adivasis desire.

The reason why the displaced people referred to the law and approached courts at all at a given historical moment seems obvious. The extraordinary success of the contract labour case has – as Butu Khumbhar's story shows – apparently served as a shining example. That they continue addressing a variety of courts over a variety of claims seems to give support to Chatterjee's (2005) thesis on the inherently contradictory consciousness of subaltern classes. Revolting peasants, Chatterjee argues, often direct their anger at more or less minor officials, while 'the king or some higher authority [is] portrayed as the final court of justice' (Chatterjee 2005: 547f).

Julia Eckert (2006) argues on the basis of her ethnography of Mumbai slum-dwellers that Chatterjee's approach fails to make sense of the complexity of law's transformations in India, and possibly also other post-colonial settings. The 'idea of India' as it was born out of the independence movement propagated the idea of a state that is to fulfil its benevolent duties to its entire population (Chatterjee 1993: 200–19). After independence this idea was carried into all corners of the country, and it still continues to shape people's notion of what the state ought to be or what makes up the 'good order' it is supposed to guarantee. When people take recourse to state law to defend themselves against the state, this is not necessarily only about winning, Eckert argues (following Hirsch and Lazarus-Black). It is also about evoking certain values these very people understand to be part of the state idea, but which they often experience to be violated by governmental practices that representatives of the state themselves engage in (Eckert 2006: 65f). In that sense the recourse to law that the poor in Mumbai's slums and elsewhere take presents an active engagement with the rights, entitlements and duties citizens and the state have vis-à-vis each other. Eckert calls this process 'citizenship as resistance', and it implies that 'state legal norms become hegemonic by being used as a form of resistance against modes of governance that run counter to these norms' (Eckert 2006: 68). This does not, however, mean that these 'subaltern' citizens remain trapped in the ideological framework provided by their oppressors, as Chatterjee (2005: 547) puts it. The active engagement with the state's legal norms might also effect changes, however minor, in the understanding and the application of these very norms, just as attempts to transform the framework might unintentionally reproduce it (Eckert 2006: 70).

In Rourkela the active engagement of the displaced people with the state's legal norms has (so far) not effected any discernible change in the application of these norms. The trajectory of their protest nevertheless reveals that Eckert's thesis also holds true in the context of an industrial town in 'tribal' western Orissa. The RSP was established as the icon of the modern Indian state that acts as a benevolent employer, a 'mother and father' (*ma bap*) to its workers, providing employment and a decent living for all, not only profit for some (Parry 1999, 2009). It is exactly this idea that the displaced people continue to invoke in protest against the *jungli raj* way it is put into practice by the RSP management and by the Orissa state government.

CONCLUDING REMARKS

The assumption that the law of the modern state remains alien to large parts of India's people living in urban slums and rural villages is seriously wanting. Of course, the post-colonial state is, as Chatterjee argues, concerned about its legitimacy, and for that reason engages in political negotiations with various groups. These negotiations very often do not follow – and their outcomes often contradict – the rules established by law. These negotiations are 'politics' and their outcomes temporary, exceptional political arrangements. They thus constitute an aspect of a 'political society' that is fundamentally different from 'civil society'. Furthermore, the state and its governmental agencies actually actively produce the very population groups with whom it negotiates politically. They target certain populations for particular welfare policies, over which the populations and agencies then negotiate. In a certain way this is all true for the 'displaced people' in Rourkela, which makes them a prototypical people populating a 'political society' in Chatterjee's sense. However, in these negotiations the 'subaltern people' from Rourkela's slums and resettlement colonies do not simply beg to be treated as an exception for this or that particular moral – though not legal – reason. On the contrary, in their struggle against the state and the company they engage in reasoning that is not based on exceptions, but on general principles because it is legal reasoning. They refer to the law to protect themselves against what they perceive to be an arbitrary *jungli* rule constantly aimed at establishing a 'dark zone' of dispossession around them. In the various accounts Chatterjee provides to illustrate his thesis such voices are absent. This is so because the situation in West Bengal, where all his case studies come from, is very different from that in places like Rourkela (or Mumbai or probably most of the world). Chatterjee's references to the dark zone also suggest that his account theorises an elite perspective on the effects of the politics of dispossession pursued in contemporary India by what he calls civil society. In either case, and contrary to his claims, his arguments apparently remain poorly supported by ethnographic evidence. In Rourkela such an ethnographic approach reveals that the displaced tribal people actively appropriate the law to protest against the state's (and the RSP's) governmental practices and to struggle for a 'good order' that treats them as citizens, not subjects.

References

Bahl, Vinay 1994. *The Making of the Indian Working Class: A Case of the Tata Iron and Steel Company, 1880–1946*. New Delhi: Sage.

Baxi, Upendra 1992. 'People's law, development and culture', in Csaba Varga (ed.) *Comparative Legal Cultures*. Dartmouth: The International Library of Essays in Legal Theory Studies, pp. 465–82.

Breman, Jan 1999. 'The formal sector: an introductory review', in Jonathan Parry, Jan Breman and Karin Kapadia (eds.) *The Worlds of Indian Industrial Labour*. New Delhi: Sage Publications, pp. 1–40.

Chatterjee, Partha 1993. *The Nation and Its Fragments: Colonial and Postcolonial Histories*. Princeton University Press.

2004. *The Politics of the Governed: Reflections on Popular Politics in Most of the World*. Delhi: Permanent Black.

2005. 'Review of Emma Tarlo: unsettling memories: narratives of the emergency in Delhi', *American Anthropologist* 107: 547–48.

2008. 'Democracy and economic transformation in India', *Economic and Political Weekly* 43 (16): 53–62.

Cohn, Bernhard 1987. 'Some notes on law and change in North India', in Bernhard Cohn (ed.) *An Anthropologist among Historians*. Delhi: Oxford University Press, pp. 554–74.

Eckert, Julia 2006. 'From subjects to citizens: legalism from below and the homogenisation of the legal sphere', *Journal of Legal Pluralism* 53–54: 45–75.

Fuller, Chris 1994. 'Legal anthropology, legal pluralism and legal thought', *Anthropology Today* 10 (3): 9–12.

Ghosh, Srikanta 1981. *Violence in the Streets*. New Delhi: Light & Life Publishers.

Government of Orissa 1959. *Report on Rourkela*. Cuttack: Orissa Government Press.

Harvey, David 2003. *The New Imperialism*. Oxford University Press.

Khilnani, Sunil 2003 [1997]. *The Idea of India*. London: Penguin Books.

Mishra, S. 1958. *Rourkela: An Economic Survey*. Cuttack: Government of Orissa Press.

Mishra, Saroj 2010. 'As POSCO hits green roadblock, the mega project seems doomed', *Tehelka* 7 (43).

Orans, Martin 1958. 'A tribal people in an industrial setting', *The Journal of American Folklore* 71: 422–45.

Parry, Jonathan P. 1999. 'Lords of labour: working and shirking in Bhilai', in Jonathan Parry, Jan Breman and Karin Kapadia (eds.) *The Worlds of Indian Industrial Labour*. New Delhi: Sage Publications, pp. 107–40.

——— 2009. '"Sociological Marxism" in Central India: Polanyi, Gramsci, and the case of the unions', in Chris Hann and Keith Hart (eds.) *Market and Society: The Great Transformation Today*. Cambridge University Press, pp. 175–202.

——— n.d. The 'embourgeoisement' of a 'proletarian vanguard'. Unpublished manuscript.

Parry, Jonathan and Strümpell, Christian 2008. 'On the desecration of Nehru's "temples": Bhilai and Rourkela compared', *Economic and Political Weekly* 43 (19): 47–57.

Pati, Biswamoy 2000. 'Light in the "dark zones"? The congress, the states' people and the princes (Orissa, 1936–1939)', in Biswamoy Pati (ed.) *Issues in Modern Indian History: For Sumit Sarkar*. Mumbai: Popular Prakshan, pp. 198–230.

Sanchez, Andrew 2010. 'Capitalism, violence and the state: crime, corruption and entrepreneurship in an Indian company town', *Journal of Legal Anthropology* 1 (2): 165–88.

Sen, Suhit 2010. 'Vedanta hymn: the scion's political gambit', *Economic and Political Weekly* 44: 13–15.

Shah, Alpa 2007. 'Keeping the state away: democracy, politics and imaginations of the state in India's Jharkhand', *Journal of Royal Anthropological Society* 13 (1): 129–45.

Simeon, Dilip 1995. *The Politics of Labour under Late Colonialism: Workers, Unions and the State in Chota Nagpur, 1928–39*. New Delhi: Manohar.

Sperling, Bodo 1963. *Rourkela. Sozio-ökonomische Probleme eines Entwicklungsprojekts. (Rourkela: Socio-economic Problems around a Development Project)*. Bonn: Eichholz Verlag.

Strümpell, Christian n.d. 'Civilised workers and savage labour: Accumulation by dispossession and capitalism's own "Other" around an Orissan steel plant'. Under review.

Washbrook, David 1981. 'Law, state and agrarian society in colonial India', *Modern Asian Studies* 15 (3): 649–721.

CHAPTER 9

DOCUMENTING 'TRUTH' IN THE MARGINS OF THE TURKISH STATE

Zerrin Özlem Biner

The military conflict between the Turkish armed forces and the Kurdistan Workers' Party (PKK) militants has stretched over two decades. It has claimed more than 30,000 lives and resulted in thousands of casualties, the evacuation of villages, the displacement and disappearance of thousands of people and the formation of ethnic, social and political enclaves in contemporary Turkey. In 1999, the unilateral truce declared by the PKK helped to foster the transformation of state policy precisely at a time when the prospect of Turkey becoming a full member of the EU began to be discussed. In order to fulfil EU membership criteria, the Turkish parliament passed a series of legal and political reforms, including a number of constitutional amendments and changes to legal procedures. These reforms did not stop the military conflict. Rather they engendered a transition process fraught with contradictory, incoherent and progressive but paranoid practices of the state. In this process, there was neither an explicit acknowledgement of the state's violent practices under emergency law nor an official apology for the economic and moral injuries that resulted under the rule of emergency. The state eluded accountability for violations of citizenship rights by crafting

This chapter is based on my post-doctoral research conducted primarily in the towns and villages of south-eastern Turkey between July and October 2009. The names of informants and of towns and villages have been changed for reasons of confidentiality. The chapter significantly benefited from the insights of the organisers and participants of the workshops 'Possibilities of Reconciliation and Legalisation of Justice' (Halle/Saale, Germany, November 2008) and 'Law against the State' (Halle/Saale, Germany, April 2009). I am especially grateful to Julia Eckert, Brian Donahoe and Jane Tienne for their valuable comments on earlier drafts of the chapter.

legal devices designed to tackle claims of damages and losses under the scrutiny of supranational organisations such as the United Nations High Commissioner for Refugees (UNHCR) and the European Court of Human Rights (ECHR) during the EU-accession process.

This chapter is concerned with the forms and effects of such legal devices in contemporary Turkey. The particular focus is to analyse the discourses and practices of truth and justice produced through the implementation of the 'Law on Compensation for Losses Resulting from Terrorism and the Fight against Terrorism'. Enacted in 2004, the Compensation Law was designed to compensate citizens who had incurred material damages as a result of terrorism and the fight against terrorism from 1987 until 2004. The Compensation Law has been cited as the most concrete and effective step taken by the Turkish state to acknowledge responsibility for the losses and damages that resulted from the conflict. It is also regarded as a pragmatic attempt to put into practice the provisions of ratified international human rights treaties.[1]

The law was valid for all civilians, including village guards and members of the armed forces, who suffered losses that resulted from acts by both the PKK and the Turkish armed forces. The only non-eligible subjects were those who had been convicted under the Anti-Terror Law because, by legal implication, their alleged acts of terror were presumably the cause of the damages and losses at issue. In addition, damages that had previously been compensated for in kind or with monetary aid to returnees were deducted from the amount awarded, while damages already compensated for by decision of the European Court of Human Rights received no compensation under the new legislation (Ünalan et al. 2007).

This law stipulated that compensation was to be granted for losses resulting from physical damage to moveable and immoveable property, such as houses, animals and commercial property, as well as losses that resulted because a person was denied access to his property sometime during those years. Death and bodily harm were also included in the categories of compensation, though compensation for non-pecuniary damages suffered by people was not included. In cases of injury, disability and death, the law provided a fixed compensation amount determined according to the civil servant salary coefficients: 14,000 TRY for death; 2,000 TRY for injuries; 1,000–21,000 TRY for disabilities (Ünalan et al.

---

[1] For the first critical analysis of the new law, see Ayata and Yükseker 2005. For a detailed and comprehensive analysis of the implementation of the law, see Kurban et al. 2007.

2007: 93).[2] Applicants had the right to reject the amount awarded and to re-apply, first to the administrative courts and, if necessary, later to the supreme courts, to appeal the commission's decision. Litigation in the European Court of Human Rights was an option, but only after all the internal legal procedures had been exhausted.

The law entered into force in 2004 and was extended three times up until 2008, with several amendments. Human rights organisations and bar associations criticised the implementation of the law because of the absence of compensation for moral injuries, the inconsistent and arbitrary decision-making mechanisms of commissions and the standardisation and homogenisation of the categories of and compensation for injuries and damages incurred in the course of the conflict. Moreover, the decisions of the damage assessment commissions were imposed on the petitioners without allowing any space for discussion over the terms of the agreement. Any suggestions would be taken as a rejection of the offer and resulted in the prolongation of the decision-making process. The criticisms about the form and content of the law have been covered in the media, with the spotlight on individual protests and testimonies, as well as on official statistics that revealed a high percentage of rejections by the commissions. People often complained about the low amount of compensation and the rejection of files, and threatened to take their cases to the European Court of Human Rights. However, as will be discussed later in the chapter, in reality very few petitioners resorted to litigation to appeal the decisions of the commission. Despite their discontent, the applicants agreed to sign friendly statements with the state that renounced their right to litigation, which meant that they consented to the legal closure of their files in respect of the injuries they experienced under emergency rule between 1987 and 2004. The renouncement of the right to litigation applied not only to the national courts, but also international courts. In other words, the signature on friendly settlements (*sulhname*) was an official script that made material the reconciliation between the state and the injured citizens in the legal sphere and the recognition of injured citizens as legal subjects, and established a consensual limit to the acknowledgement of state accountability. In 2006 the government sent a report on the applications made under the Compensation Law from people who had previously filed petitions with the European Court of Human Rights. Evaluating the mechanisms and results of these assessments, the European Court of Human Rights ruled that the Compensation Law

---

[2] TRY is the Turkish Lira. One Euro is approximately equal to 2.53 TRY.

provided an effective domestic remedy and that applicants must exhaust this procedure before filing action in Strasbourg. On the basis of this evaluation, the court returned all pending applications (Kurban 2007). Following this decision, the issue of state accountability and the right to reparative justice have become an internal affair between the lawyers, the displaced villagers as the petitioners and the local bureaucrats of the damage assessment commissions.

It is possible to argue that the Compensation Law was turned into an effective tool to refashion the credibility of the Turkish state in the international arena. The accountable, care-taking and justice-delivering images of the state are constituted in particular against the scrutiny of the European Court of Human Rights and other supranational organisations. The state reconciled with the global norms of accountability and created inner mechanisms to cut off access to international institutions of justice. The consequences of the Compensation Law helped to justify the legitimacy of the state and foreclosed the possibility of making truth claims about state terror and of demanding retributive justice.[3] From the perspective of human rights lawyers, the law could have been used to document the atrocities of the state. Should the applicants have declined the friendly settlements, the files would have been taken to the administrative courts and the damage assessment commissions would have been stripped of their function. More significantly, the court system would have been incapable of dealing with the excessive number of cases, which would have justified recourse to the European Court of Human Rights. The aspirations of human rights activists did not come true. As mentioned above, the majority of the petitioners signed the friendly settlements and decided not to go to the administrative courts for a re-evaluation of the settlements. However, their acceptance of the terms and conditions of reconciliation, as implied by their signatures on their friendly settlements, does not mean that they have fully submitted to state rule. They resist going to the courts for reasons related to their distrust of the legal system and their fear of subjection to further interrogation by the state, as well as for financial reasons. They do not believe that the state courts could repair the injustices that have been caused by the acts of the terror. They do not perceive the Compensation Law as a path to reconciliation with the state or to the resolution of the Kurdish problem. Rather, they perceive it as yet one more charity package from the government that aims to establish its hegemony over the region.

[3] For similar criticisms of reconciliation projects, see Mamdani 1996; Wilson 2001, 2003.

While the applicants renounced their right to further litigation, they were able to use this process to collect evidence of the undocumented incidents of disappearances and murders, and they assess their situation in light of their aspirations and hopes for the future rather than the existing legal norms and opportunities. In other words, they anticipate an indeterminate moment in the future when they will be able to use the documents that they have collected to seek justice in the European Court of Human Rights. One might consider the formulation of their future aspirations as a sign of 'false consciousness' or of the 'fetishisation of law' (in this context, international law) (Comaroff and Comaroff 2006). Thinking through spaces of interpretations, I would like to argue that each applicant's engagement with the Compensation Law can be interpreted as an act of iteration. I use the concept of iteration with reference to Derrida (1992), who developed it against the idea that the contextual conditions of the enactment of a sign can be stabilised. Derrida argues that a sign enacted opens up the possibilities that it will move from one context to another, and it engenders new contexts in the process of re-enactment. As Eckert *et al.* argue in the introduction to this volume, these iterations are not independent of existing power relationships. They are structured within the given historical, political and economic contingencies. In what follows, I explore and reveal how the signs, norms and feelings that are engendered with the enactment of the Compensation Law destabilise the political discourses and practices of both the Turkish state and the human rights organisations as the hegemonic parties in the conflict.

PETITIONS AS OFFICIAL DOCUMENTS OF TRUTH

The enactment of the law was received with surprise, suspicion, uncertainty and cynicism, particularly by human rights lawyers. As a lawyer from a human rights organisation explained:

> We did not know what to expect of the law. We informed all of our members to come and give their testimonies. Villagers found it difficult to believe that the state would accept its responsibility and compensate for the damages incurred by the armed forces. They were suspicious of the purpose and the consequences of the law and they were uncertain about how to complain about the state to the state … We were not sure whether these petitions would ever be evaluated.

A young Kurdish man, Selman, whose family was evacuated from their village in 1993 following the murder of his father, explained their initial dilemma:

It was not an easy decision for us to apply for compensation under the law. There had been so many families whose members were taken to court under the Anti-Terror Law or whose children were in the mountains fighting for the PKK or whose relatives have been disappeared. For potentially suspect people like us, to use this law and submit petitions with claims, at the beginning it felt like we were informing on ourselves to the state. We were also worried that these applications could harm the struggle because, in most of the incident reports produced by the gendarme forces, the murders, evacuations and burning of the villages were indicated as acts of the PKK.

The procedure started with the submission of a petition to the damage assessment commissions, which were chaired by a deputy governor and composed of other local government officials (see below). There were several ways to file a petition. Petitioners could file individually at the governor's office; they could apply via a joint commission established by human rights organisations; and migrant associations or lawyers with power of attorney could file the petitions with the governor's office on behalf of their clients. Lawyers have been significant agents in this process, filing most of the petitions. They collected and submitted documents as proof of damage, and followed the progress of the case on their clients' behalf. They have become the 'translators' in mediating the process between the petitioners and the commissions. They standardised the petitions, which involved a formulation of the cause of damages and the construction of categories of material losses, and they followed the process of documenting and registering the damages and losses by the expert teams. It was often the lawyers who got involved with the commission members and who paid visits to the office to get updated information about the decisions of the commissions and the recent implementations. The lawyers also often signed the friendly settlements on behalf of the applicants. In exchange for these services, the clients paid 10–20 per cent of the compensation payment to the lawyers, which in turn made them big stakeholders in the new economy of transitional justice.

Returning our attention to the application procedure, applicants were required to submit their petitions along with any other documents, such as title deeds, incident reports, health reports, probate decisions and autopsy reports, that would prove their claims to injuries incurred and to ownership of the properties in question. Most significantly, they had to provide information that detailed how the event happened.

The petitions included the testimonies of the applicants explaining the cause of the claimed loss, with a list of the damaged or lost properties and/or people, and the requested amount of compensation for both material and immaterial injuries. According to the lawyers, the contents of the petitions changed over time due to the political intentions and local pragmatism of the applicants, and the circulation of various rumours. It was claimed that petitions blaming the Turkish military forces for the forced evacuation of villages were declined or delayed for an infinite period of time. The effect of this rumour (cf. Eckert, Chapter 6) was augmented by a parallel implementation of another procedure that took place during the course of the return to villages. The returnees, in exchange for official permission to return to their villages, were ordered to sign a statement which declared that the villagers had been evacuated by PKK militants. In the imaginary of the applicants, the ones who signed these declarations also received higher compensation. As one non-returnee applicant said: 'I did everything to stop my villagers from signing these declarations. They first agreed, but then they went ahead and signed anyway. Their applications were assessed faster and they received more money than we did.'

The circulation of such rumours also affected the attitude of the lawyers, who gradually began to draft standardised petitions devoid of the personal narratives about the experience of evacuation from the villages. The new version included a standard explanation formulated in the neutral terms of legal language, describing the cause as 'terrorism and/or terror events' and leaving out the identity of the perpetrator. A specific grammar was rendered for the production of the official scripts in such documents.[4] According to one lawyer, the standardised petitions reflected a common yet unstated logic of pragmatism shared by commission members (as the representatives of the state), the lawyers and the injured applicants. A lawyer who had experienced the forced migration himself put the underlying rationale as follows: 'Some of my clients were concerned about not stating the responsibility of the state in the petitions. They were concerned that such testimonies of denial could be used against them in the future. I convinced them that would not be the case. My struggle is to get as much money as possible for these people.' There were other cases where this pragmatic attitude engendered tension

---

[4] For critical analysis of mechanisms of transitional justice, in particular restorative justice, see Ross 2002 and Buur 2000. For a significant analysis on the use of legal language for the articulation of the experience of human suffering, see Hastrup 2003 and Das 2003.

between lawyers and their clients. Another lawyer who filed more than 1,000 petitions in the last four years expressed this tension:

> I draft petitions together with my clients. In all the petitions, I have high-lighted the fact that the people were evacuated and the villages were burned down by the soldiers. Unlike many other lawyers, I never con-sidered taking this statement out of the petition, despite the complaints of my clients who were badly treated by the gendarme forces for their testimonies in the petitions. Sometimes due to the fear of security forces or the anxiety about the acceptance of the petitions, two villagers give completely opposite accounts, one blaming the PKK and the other blam-ing the state for the same event.

DOCUMENTS AS PROOF OF TERROR

The decision about eligibility for compensation was made on the basis of the documentation. Applicants were required to provide documents as proof of the events that led to the claimed losses and damages, as well as proof of ownership of the mobile and immobile properties, such as houses, lands, trees and animals. They had to prove that the alleged losses and damages were incurred between 1987 and 2004; that they had been evicted from their villages or that their property had been burned or demolished; and that the injuries or deaths of relatives were incurred as a result of terrorism or the fight against terrorism. It meant searching for traces of loss and absence and looking for official evidence of that which remained unspoken, unnamed and unacknowledged. Perhaps not surprisingly, the majority of the applications were rejected due to insuffi-cient documentation.

According to the lawyers, the most difficult thing to obtain was the document that verified that the villagers had been evicted and/ or that their property had been burned. A list of the villages that were alleged to have been burned or evacuated was drawn up by the gen-darme forces and sent out to the local governors and their deputies who chaired the damage assessment commissions. The information on this document was considered to be legitimate proof of the claimed damages. However, the list was a ghost document, in particular for the lawyers, and no one except the commission members had access to it or to the information it contained about the officially acknowledged list of evacuated villages.

For villages not indicated on the list, the commission had to consult with the head of the village gendarme forces and ask them to check their records for the past and current state of the village, as well as the date and reasons for departure from the village of the indicated petitioners. In other words, gendarme records were a major source of information for evaluating the truth of the petition, particularly in cases where there was a lack of required documentation. This was significant because people who left their villages not as part of an *en masse* eviction but out of fear for their safety or under pressure from the PKK or village guards could be construed as having left their villages voluntarily, in which case their petitions would fall outside the scope of the law.

A lawyer representing clients who had moved to metropolitan areas protested against the rejection of their files because of the impossibility of providing proof of the atrocities that the state had committed under emergency law: 'During the investigation, the commission wanted us to provide the incident report that demonstrated the cause and the results of the event. The incident report is a document composed of the testimonies of the two parties. How could they expect us to provide a report for an event incurred by the gendarme forces?' Addressing the inconsistency of the commissions' decisions, an experienced lawyer spoke about the rejection of the petition of a client from a village that was not on the official (yet non-public) list of evacuated villages:

> My own village was burned down by the soldiers. Although it was not on the special list, they accepted the traces of fire as proof of evacuation. However, all other petitions from the villages that did not appear on the special list were rejected by the commission. Hundreds of times I asked the villagers whether they could provide me with a document indicating an incident of terror. They all remained silent. Months later, one of them remembered an incident that resulted in the killing of people from the village. I went to the prosecutor's office to find the report, which indeed verified the testimonies of the villagers. Yet by then it was too late to take the file to the administrative court.

The second major obstacle was obtaining documents for deaths and murders by unidentified perpetrators. According to statements from the lawyers, in the first years the majority of the files concerning deaths and murders were rejected due to insufficient proof. Only the files previously reported as murders by the PKK and which had previously been taken to the national security court were granted the right to compensation. Many of the anonymous murders without any incident report or autopsy report were rejected out of hand. The petitions of people who were convicted under the Anti-Terror Law and who applied for compensation for the death and injuries of their relatives were rejected by the commissions. As one of the lawyers working in the damage investigations commission revealed:

> The issue of anonymous murders and disappearances was really difficult to discuss. Most of the commission members were prejudiced against the victims, perceiving them as potential terrorists regardless of their age or other background information. If there was no document to prove the terror aspect of the event and if the petitioners had a previous conviction under the Anti-Terror Law, we would immediately reject the file.

DAMAGE ASSESSMENT COMMISSIONS

Damage assessment commissions were established in provinces to be the main implementers of the Compensation Law. They were chaired by the deputy manager and were composed of six members, five of whom were public officials from the provincial public departments of finance, agriculture, industry and public works, as well as a lawyer who was appointed by the bar association. The commissions were tasked with processing petitions, assessing damages, establishing compensation payments and preparing declarations of friendly settlement as well as protocols of non-agreement where applicants refused to sign declarations and decided instead to take the commission decision to the administrative court.

The commissions were in the middle of the nitty-gritty of everyday political struggles. Personal histories and local knowledge mingled with the results of the computer-analysed database that was designed to calculate the amount of compensation.

The commission members functioned like a court jury, with the authority to assess the acceptability of petitions and to determine the amount of compensation for each case. According to both lawyers and petitioners, there were significant inconsistencies between the decisions of different commissions. This was interpreted as being due to the political views of the deputy manager, who allegedly affected the decisions of other members. As one of the former lawyers of the commission said: 'Most of the commission members would act defensively in their evaluations of the petitions and submit to the decision of the deputy manager. There were no ethics in the decision makings of the commission members.' Accordingly, in their first decisions the commissions often rejected the assessment of petitions either on the grounds of lack of required documents or on the basis of reports from the gendarme forces, which often rejected the causal link between the evacuation of a petitioner's village and the state of terror in the villages. Where there was a discrepancy between the testimony of the petitioners and the information provided by the gendarme forces, the deputy manager tended to base the decision of the commission on the latter. As a lawyer who previously worked in the commissions aptly put it: 'What counted as evidence of truth was the documents, not the testimonies of the petitioners. There was no voice for the petitioners in these commissions; only the documents had weight.'

With the changing attitudes and decisions of the commissions, the only consensus between the members and among the commissions was on the criteria of non-eligibility of petitioners. Accordingly, as stated in the law, a person who was convicted under the Anti-Terror Law was not eligible to apply for compensation under the Compensation Law. The legal criteria about non-eligibility was further extrapolated by the commission members to include relatives of convicted individuals and of PKK militants. It was not uncommon for the commissions to reject petitions from the families of guerrilla fighters without providing any explanation, and the criminal records of husbands of female petitioners would be checked before the assessment of a petition in order to prevent 'abuses' of law.

Abuse was one of the key words in the vocabulary of the commission members when describing their mission. It follows that they were responsible for establishing justice for the injured citizens while, at the same time, distributing state resources in a just manner. What were the criteria of truth and justice for the commission members? One commission member told me:

> I have done everything to be just. Someone who left his village a hundred years ago applies for compensation under this law, or the village guard claims that his sister was shot dead by an anonymous person. I know that this murder was a crime of honour, but the village guard wants us to treat the case as an act of terrorism. I reject such petitions. Or a man has been convicted under the Anti-Terror Law and, hence, his wife files a petition. I immediately ask the secretary of the commission to check the criminal record of this woman's husband. If he was convicted, I refuse to assess the petition submitted by his wife. The Compensation Law clearly states the criteria of eligibility, of who is or isn't eligible to apply for compensation. In the future, inspectors will come to review our decisions and they will ask whether we have ever received petitions from terrorists or their families. These rejections are the proof of our law-abiding decisions.

Another commission member expressed this responsibility by describing the obligation to ask for documents in support of claims for damages and losses:

Our position is between the state and the citizens. I am a representative of the state but I am also aware of local facts. We – all the local commission members – know that there have been anonymous murders and disappearances in this region under emergency rule. Nevertheless, we need to have documents of proof.

PETITIONERS

The attitude of petitioners towards the implications of the law was perplexing. People who refused to apply or who had later decided to withdraw their applications associated the compensation with a 'blood payment', an association derived from their experience of blood feuds. In their imaginary, the state intended to pay this compensation to bring the conflict to an end, yet consenting to the state's terms implied accepting money in exchange for the blood of the people who lost their lives in this struggle.

On the other hand, the majority of people were inclined to sign friendly settlements with the state and renounce their right to litigation, despite the pervasive sense of dissatisfaction and injustice. Usually people resorted to litigation only when their cases had been rejected or the compensation offered by the commission was unacceptably low. According to the lawyers, this was related to the financial situation of the petitioners and to the high costs and long waiting period that litigation entailed. It was not exceptional for six to eight years to pass while petitioners exhausted the domestic legal regulations and applied to the European Court of Human Rights. One lawyer told me:

> Many times I suggested that my clients not sign the settlement declarations, but rather pursue their cases to litigation. Only a few agreed to do that. The majority of them signed the settlement declaration out of poverty or desperation, thinking that it would be the only payment they could ever possibly receive from the state. Some even thought that if they rejected the state's offer, they would be perceived as being subversive and that this, in turn, might irritate the state.

Another lawyer related the following incident: 'I have a female client, sixty years old, who witnessed the killing of twenty-five people in her village. She was tortured, imprisoned and finally released without any conviction. If she agreed to sign the friendly settlement with the state, why would others refuse to do so?'

The majority of petitioners perceived the payment not as compensation for the damages or losses suffered during the military conflict and the political violence, but rather as another form of economic aid from the government's charity policies, which were supported by the EU. This perception demonstrates the ambivalence in people's imagination of the Turkish state, which was simultaneously imbued with both violent and charitable practices. This was particularly true during the post-conflict transition process that was associated with the democratic and neo-liberal policies that were part and parcel of the EU-accession process. For human rights lawyers, this was a missed opportunity to document the truth and seek justice in the international arena. As one of the lawyers expressed it: 'The declarations of friendly settlements should never have been signed. We, Kurds, lost this legal battle. In the end, the only winner has been the Turkish state.' However I would like to argue that the reluctance to litigate did not merely produce desperation or absolute submission to the official line of reconciliation that foreclosed the possibilities of seeking justice. Altogether, despite its consequences, the process of applying for compensation enabled the subjects to confront past atrocities and to seek traces of their personal losses. At a broader level, it marked a new phase in their efforts to reveal and document the truth at both local and international levels, a new phase which would in the short run carry the potential to settle the accounts.

Petitioners' accounts were imbued with vivid images of the burning and evacuation of their villages, and they unequivocally held the state responsible for these atrocities. However, there was a clear gap between the narratives of their experiences of displacement and of their experience of applying for compensation under the Compensation Law. The notion of friendly settlement and the decision to renounce the right to litigation were totally absent from their narration of the Compensation Law. Rather, narratives about the law revolved around comparisons between the experiences of different petitioners regarding the amount of compensation and the waiting period for processing the application. The question was not about who signed the friendly settlement with the state but, rather, who did what to get the highest amount of compensation, which in turn created tensions among villagers, members of extended families and, in some cases, between clients and their lawyers. The Compensation Law became part of the war economy. At the same time its implementation perpetuated existing tensions based on different power relations.

Makbule is a fifty-year-old Kurdish woman who left her village with her extended family in 1993 and whose husband and brothers-in-law were killed by the gendarme forces. She described her ordeal to me in the following terms:

Before my brother-in-law [i.e. husband's brother] was killed, he told me that he would apply to Europe for money for our damaged property in the village, and asked me to give him the title deeds for the property, which I inherited from my husband. I agreed and did as he said. After he applied for compensation on behalf of the whole family, he was killed. I talked to the lawyers and learned that his application was accepted. Yet our family was allowed neither to return to the village nor to receive the money, and that is because, unlike others, we refused to sign the declaration statement that accuses the PKK of the evacuation. Even if we ever get it, I am not sure whether the wife of my brother-in-law will ever give me and my children our share.

Barut, a thirty-year-old Kurdish man, was also concerned with similar tensions between the villagers after their return to the village and their collective application for compensation under the law. His father was held responsible for the murder of seven village guards, and soon thereafter he was killed by another village guard from a different village though his body has never been found. This incident started a blood feud between two villages. Barut's village was evacuated, and two decades later they were allowed to return on the condition that the returnees make peace with the village guards. The villagers agreed on that. For Barut, this was unacceptable. In his view, all these villagers who used to be supporters of the Kurdish armed struggle are now submitting to military order as a survival strategy. Barut applied for compensation for the loss of his father as well as for other material damages, and he ultimately received some money in compensation for his losses. However, for him, what was important was to find his father's body, as well as the perpetrator of the murder. Despite the hostility of other villagers who saw him as a threat to their new order, Barut has been wandering in the open field searching for traces, following leads and contacting journalists to find and spread the truth. Finding his father's corpse was crucial not only to bring closure to his personal search, but also to seek justice in Europe, which in effect meant carrying the case to the European Court of Human Rights.

This process had similar effects on the future expectations and imagination of justice for Mehmet, another young Kurdish man who also lost his close relatives before and after the evacuation of their village in 1993. His two elder brothers joined the PKK, and his younger brother was in Europe as a political refugee. He applied for compensation under the law on behalf of the whole family, and he managed to receive money for his father's death and the material damages to their property in the village, which was completely burned down after being evacuated and was even erased from the map. As he says: 'The village is not shown on the map of Turkey any longer'. Mehmet did not find the amount of compensation sufficient and wanted to resort to litigation and ultimately to take the case to the European Court of Human Rights. However, he was stopped by his lawyer. As Mehmet explains:

> Most of our property in the village was registered as state property. Actually, the majority of the land in the evacuated villages was confiscated by the state. At the time I applied for compensation, I did not have title deeds for our property, so I was concerned that we might already have lost what we had. As a matter of fact, I was more concerned with the possibility of causing the loss of another person in the family. Someone like me with a murdered father, disappeared uncles and guerrilla brothers cannot avoid thinking of the next tragedy. What awaits us next? What does the state think of us now?

Despite his submission to the law and acute sense of injustice, Mehmet was optimistic about the long-term consequences of the law:

> Only with the Compensation Law, for the first time, have we had the chance to document what we were forced to witness here. The people who applied for compensation through this law attempted to document their losses. Now at least we have the evidence documenting the truth of the evacuated villages and the disappeared people. Each of these documents of friendly settlement is also a document of official acknowledgement of what has happened here.

This was the beginning of a new phase for Mehmet. This process would have long-term effects and change the conditions for seeking justice. His hopes, like those of all the other protagonists of this ethnography, lay in a timeless and difficult project of attaining the power to change the conditions of communicating truth and of gaining legitimacy for the Kurdish struggle in the transnational sphere. He expressed his hopes passionately:

> Since I applied under this law, I have been collecting many documents, including ones about my daily life, such as bus tickets, telephone bills, membership cards, maps and photos of daily encounters. I will keep them because in two decades' time I believe we will have the opportunity to reveal to Europe what really happened here.

BY WAY OF A CONCLUSION

Despite its consequences, the Compensation Law should be interpreted neither as a success of the state nor as a failure of the citizens or human rights organisations. The application procedure composed of drafting petitions with narratives of displacement and claims of injuries and damages, collecting and submitting documentation, and encounters with damage assessment commission members, initiated a new process which allowed the reiterations and transformations of hegemonic norms and discourses. The state, on the one hand, used the law to re-establish its hegemony at the local, national and international levels. The human rights organisations pursued standardisation of the narratives of loss and suffering, on the basis of which they constructed a legal persona for the displaced victims of terror and war. The subjects of this ethnography have been subjected to and used by the hegemonic discourses of both parties for contradictory purposes. Yet in the process they have managed to open up spaces for new discourses and practices that have allowed them not only to return to their evacuated villages, but also to follow the illegible traces of the undocumented incidents of murder and disappearance. In this political contingency, the practices of submission to the law and hence the renunciation of their right to further litigation do not diminish the hopes and expectations of the subject-citizens to seek justice. Yet their expectation does not lie with their future confrontation with the state. In their legal and political imaginary, the state is neither the subject of reconciliation nor the provider of justice. Their imaginary for justice lies first in the expectation of finding traces of the bodies of their disappeared relatives or the perpetrators of such anonymous killings, and then in the possibility of carrying the case to 'Europe', as the abstract representative of justice, at some time in the 'future', as an unspecified and hoped-for moment in time.

References

Ayata, Bilgin and Yükseker, Deniz 2005. 'A belated awakening: national and international responses to the international displacement of kurds in Turkey', *New Perspectives on Turkey* 32 (2005): 5–42.

Buur, Lars 2000. 'The South African Truth and Reconciliation Commission: a technique of nation state formation', in Thomas B. Hansen and Finn Stepputat (eds.) *States of Imagination: Ethnographic Explorations of the Postcolonial State*. Durham, NC: Duke University Press, pp. 149–81.

Comaroff, Jean and Comaroff, John L. 2006. 'Law and disorder in the postcolony: an introduction', in Jean Comaroff and John L. Comaroff (eds.) *Law and Disorder in the Postcolony*. University of Chicago Press, pp. 1–56.

Das, Veena 2003. 'Trauma and testimony: implications for political community', *Anthropological Theory* September (3) 3: 293–307.

Derrida, Jacques 1992. 'Force of law: the mystical foundation of authority. Deconstruction and the possibility of justice', in Drucilla Cornell, Michel Rosenfeld and David G. Carlson (eds.) *Deconstruction and the Possibility of Justice.* New York: Routledge, pp. 3–67.

Hastrup, Kirsten 2003. 'Violence, suffering and human rights', *Anthropological Reflections* 3 (3): 309–23.

Kurban, Dilek 2007. 'Internal displacement: developments in international law and practices in other countries', in Dilek Kurban, Deniz Yükseker, Ayşe B. Celik, Turgay Ünalan, A. Tamer Aker (eds.) *Coming to Terms with Forced Migration: Post-Displacement Restitution of Citizenship Rights in Turkey.* Istanbul: TESEV, pp. 60–70.

Kurban, Dilek, Yükseker, D., Celik, A. B., Ünalan, T., and Aker, T. A. (eds.) 2007. *Coming to Terms with Forced Migration: Post-Displacement Restitution of Citizenship Rights in Turkey.* Istanbul: TESEV.

Mamdani, Mahmood 1996. 'Reconciliation without justice', *South African Review of Books* 46: 3–5.

Ross, Fiona 2002. *Bearing Witness: Women and the South African Truth and Reconciliation Commission.* London: Pluto Press.

Ünalan, Tugay, Celik, Betül and Kurban, Dilek 2007. 'Internal displacement in Turkey: the issue, policies and implementation', in Dilek Kurban, Deniz Yükseker, Ayşe B. Celik, Turgay Ünalan, A. Tamer Aker (eds.) *Coming to Terms with Forced Migration: Post-Displacement Restitution of Citizenship Rights in Turkey.* Istanbul: TESEV, pp. 77–108.

Wilson, Richard A. 2001. *The Politics of Reconciliation in South Africa: Legitimizing the Post-Apartheid State.* Cambridge University Press.

2003. 'Anthropological studies of national reconciliation processes', *Anthropological Theory* 3 (3): 367–87.

CHAPTER 10

THE ONES WHO WALK AWAY: LAW, SACRIFICE AND CONSCIENTIOUS OBJECTION IN TURKEY

Erdem Evren

INTRODUCTION

On 24 January 2006 the European Court of Human Rights (ECHR) settled the case of Turkish conscientious objector Osman Murat Ülke, ruling that the Turkish state had violated Article 3 of the European Convention on Human Rights. The case addressed a series of prosecutions and criminal convictions Ülke had endured in the aftermath of his public refusal to do his mandatory military service in 1995. From 1996 to 1999 Ülke was prosecuted several times and imprisoned for a total of two years for refusing to wear a military uniform and for not complying with the orders of military officials. Each time he was released from prison he was sent right back to his military unit, where he faced the same charges of insubordination and would again be transferred back to prison. In the decision unanimously taken by all seven judges of the court, the fact that the punishment received by Ülke did not exempt him from the obligation to perform military service was construed as making Ülke potentially liable to prosecution for the rest of his life. Moreover, because the recurring nature of the charges and sentences had resulted in Ülke's being

This article benefited significantly from the comments of the organisers and contributors of the workshop 'Law against the State', held on 14–16 April 2010. I am especially grateful to Amita Baviskar, Özlem Biner, Tobias Kelly and Christian Strümpell for their valuable comments. To Christian Strümpell I also owe a sincere apology for being frivolously resistant to some of the points that he brought to my attention at the time I presented this paper. These suggestions later proved to be crucial to my discussion here. I also want to thank Alice von Bieberstein, Enis Oktay, Nadine Püschel and Umut Yıldırım for helping me improve several aspects of this article. Their guidance and friendship were exceptional.

deprived of such basic citizenship rights as the freedom to go abroad and the right to marriage and to legal custody of his son, the court took the view that the criminal convictions amounted 'almost to "civil death"' and caused him fear, anguish and vulnerability. Accordingly, the Turkish state was sentenced to pay a total of 11,000 Euros for its degrading treatment of Ülke.[1]

Almost all the conscientious objectors prosecuted and convicted by the Turkish state since Ülke's application to the court in 1998 have turned to this international body of jurisdiction with the claims that the acts carried out by the state violate a number of articles of the Convention. And yet, strongly identifying with the principles of anarchism and anti-authoritarianism and refusing to partake in any aspect of hierarchical institutions in principle, Turkey's conscientious objectors often reflect on the ambivalence of carrying their activism into the legal system. Some of them speak of the ECHR as a technically circumscribed legal institution that is not immune to international power relations, and discuss their appeal to the court with a pinch of cynicism. Others, drawing attention to the fact that the court in Ülke's case carefully refrained from passing official judgement on the legal status of conscientious objection in Turkey,[2] regard their own efforts to be not only in conflict with their political views, but fundamentally futile. In fact, submitting an application to the ECHR is generally regarded by these objectors as a disturbing, if not compromising, process from which they 'do not expect much' in the end.

Based on my ethnographic research in Istanbul, Ankara and Izmir, this chapter seeks to understand why recourse to law constitutes a vital dimension of conscientious objectors' political dissension despite being

[1] For the court decision in French, see www.echr.coe.int; for the press release in English, see www.cmiskp.echr.coe.int/tkp197/view.asp?item=1&portal=hbkm&action=html&highlight=%FClke%20%7C%20turkey&sessionid=48108470&skin=hudoc-en, last accessed 27 July 2011. For a useful article that discusses the legal meaning and implications of the decision, see Gürcan 2006.

[2] 'The Court points out that, in its *Thlimmenos v. Greece* judgement ([GC], no. 34369/97, § 43, ECHR 2000-IV), it did not find it necessary to examine whether the applicant's initial conviction and the authorities' subsequent refusal to appoint him amounted to interference with his rights under Article 9 § 1. In particular, the Court acknowledged that it did not have to address, in that case, the question whether, notwithstanding the wording of Article 4 § 3 (b), the imposition of such sanctions on conscientious objectors to compulsory military service might in itself infringe the right to freedom of thought, conscience and religion guaranteed by Article 9 § 1. The same applies in the present case. As the case raises serious questions under Article 3 of the Convention, the Court does not find it necessary to pursue its examination of the applicability of Article 9.'

considered contradictory and ineffective. Here, I focus on how these conscientious objectors get precariously caught in the midst of their intersubjective relations with the state and their fellow activists in their refusal to serve in the army. Consequently, I consider the jurisdiction of dissension in the light of two things: first, the radical exclusion sustained by the state through the termination of the objectors' civil rights; and second, the sacrificial role that conscientious objectors fulfil with regard to the rest of the movement. In doing so, I try to show how legality, extra-legality and political activism get entangled in a number of different ways.

Recent scholarship on the claims brought to courts against the state by various political actors has rightly emphasised the affective investments of people – their hopes, fears, anger, visions of empowerment or disempowerment, etc. – in translating political struggles into legal demands. These studies have invariably revealed law to be a contested and ambiguous site in so far as the experience-near local knowledge and ideals of justice and rights of people converge and collide with the realities of juridical processes amid the mobilisation of legal orders.[3] Notwithstanding these aspects, in this chapter I contend that the use and effects of juridification and the subjectivities that they elicit are implicated in a different kind of ambivalence that law hinges on which is often neglected in this literature but recognised by theorists such as Giorgio Agamben (1998): the indistinction between legality and extra-legality; the co-habitation of rule with its exception. In other words, by following Agamben's work, I would like to suggest that as much as the juridification of protest entails the uncertainties of law, a more profound uncertainty with regard to what falls inside and outside of law's boundaries can trigger the use of law as protest.

The punishment regime that the ECHR observed to be in effect in the case of Osman Murat Ülke lays bare at least two related processes whereby the purview of law is implicitly conflated with its exterior. In the first instance, the state turned Ülke into a channel of crime and a constant target of punishment by attaching the same criminal offence to him several times. Consequently, the fact that this crime can in no possible way be absolved other than by serving in the army carries the further implication that he is stripped of all his civil liberties and

---

[3] Several contributors to this volume draw attention to the affects generated by the juridification of activism. For a relatively early article that makes similar points but nevertheless stresses the enabling role that the use of law against the state plays, see Merry 1995.

protections, and effectively rendered a non-citizen. This is, however, not a mere consequence of a legislative loophole or a single instance of misconduct. Since Ülke's application to the ECHR, at least five other activists have been subjected to the same repetitive exercise of prosecution and conviction and forced to live in similar abject conditions in terms of their civil rights. As late as 2010, one conscientious objector was arrested and sentenced to seven months in a military prison for the second time. The Turkish state clearly perseveres in disregarding the unequivocal verdict of the ECHR by refusing to amend its punishment regime targeting conscientious objectors. It thereby perpetuates a modality of rule that ceases to be rooted in the rule of law, or at least one that invalidates the clear-cut divisions between legality and illegality. I therefore ask: how does a legal order continue to exist side by side with its suspension and, more importantly, what implications does that have for the legal and political subjectivities of those people who fall under its sway?

Agamben (1998) designates the miserable socio-legal existence that leaks out of the perimeters of lawfulness as 'bare life'. The 'bareness' of life essentially concerns the ramifications that being positioned 'before the law', that is, prior to legal institutions, has on the political and biological lives of subjects. One important idea that stems from his discussion is that law renders certain bodies socially and physically 'killable' by expelling them from the scope of its institutions (Das and Poole 2004). Here, although Agamben refers mainly to the Jews who perished in concentration camps as the most salient example of bare life in modern times and goes on to scrutinise how the state of exception and martial law laid the ground for their persecution, his larger analysis rests on a figure that he pulls out of archaic Roman law called *homo sacer*: a criminal who can be murdered by any citizen with impunity but cannot be sacrificed. Agamben construes *sacer* in some senses as the emblem of a new subjectivity that is constituted at the intersections of the juridical and biopolitical models of power in liberal democracies. In so far as the state preserves the form that it takes under these regimes in governing communal life, he concludes, subjects of certain racial, ethnic or sexual groups will continue to be reduced to objects of violence in a manner that exceeds the realms of law and sacrifice, and the bare life that they embody, with all the paradoxes it poses, remains to underlie modern politics.

My ethnographic material on Turkey sheds light on how the prosecuted conscientious objector inhabits an abject zone of life that is reminiscent of the bareness within which *homo sacer* is materialised.

This is officially referred to as 'civil death'. But contrary to Agamben's interpretation of *sacer* as an entirely passive victim of violence, I claim that these activists challenge the state from their place of banishment as the sacrificial mode that their activism intentionally or unintentionally acquires gives life to the broader movement. The resentments and disappointments caused by them being the only ones absorbing the suffering inflicted by the state, however, eventually compel these objectors to face yet another exclusion – this time a voluntary one that usually involves a retreat from anti-militarist activism and coincides with the reluctant utilisation of international human rights law against the Turkish state. In what follows, then, I recount the different ways in which bare life, ultimately thought to be void of law and sacrifice by its theorist, calls back the juridical and the sacrificial. The intricate relationship between the two, I propose, is what essentially affects the transformation of the subjectivities that unfold in activism and state violence.

'IT IS KILLING ME'

Military service has been compulsory for all able-bodied male subjects of Turkey since 1927, in other words, almost from the very beginnings of the republic in 1923. Unlike in western European countries, there has been no legal arrangement that provides an alternative such as civil service. The duration of the service is usually around six months for university graduates (with medical doctors and engineers being an exception), and fifteen months for the rest of the recruits. The daily routines of life in the military barracks range from receiving basic training in warfare to learning the ceremonial aspects of soldiering, and from attending educational seminars to serving in the various units of the division or the brigade. Long-term conscripts are particularly singled out for verbal and physical abuse and punishment during these activities. Even though cases of physical and/or mental injury, suicide or fatality are not uncommon, very few of them are investigated or made public.

In addition to the legal liability that it occasions, military service turns out to be a fairly potent institution that has an influence on a number of aspects of civilian life. Although no legal necessity is specified in the laws, the discharge papers issued upon completion of the service usually serve as a prerequisite for formal employment. In particular, men desiring to pursue careers in civil service are expected to have fulfilled their obligation so that their employment will not be interrupted by conscription.

Furthermore, military service is also commonly perceived as a rite of passage where boys are turned into men. In many cases, males from rural areas are allowed by their families to get married only after they have completed their service. The discipline and orderliness of life in the barracks are believed to instil maturity and a sense of accountability that are deemed integral to proper forms of adult masculinity. Hence, as military service is understood as a necessary step before forming conjugal relations, initiation into its rituals is normalised and naturalised by the majority of the population.[4]

In 1990, Vedat Zencir and Tayfun Gönül, known as anarchists active in the Aegean city of Izmir, sent their conscientious objection statement to be published by the weekly political magazine *Sokak* ('Street'). Seen against the backdrop of military service's power as a naturalised and culturalised institution, this first public declaration of conscientious objection created unexpected reverberations around Turkey. Having gradually grown disillusioned with the socialist organisations that they had been affiliated with in the 1980s, Zencir and Gönül eventually disowned Marxism and Leninism and came to view violence and hierarchy as the essence of any form of oppression. Soon after the national daily *Güneş* ('Sun') covered their story and reprinted their objection declaration, they were prosecuted and charged with the criminal offense of 'alienating the people from the institution of military service'. Zencir was acquitted of all charges and Gönül's conviction and sentence of three months in prison was reduced to a fine. This result emboldened a small group of activists closely following the case to convene in Izmir and establish the first War Resisters' Association (Savaş Karşıtları Derneği) in 1992.[5]

Zencir and Gönül's act of refusal to serve in the Turkish military on the grounds of objecting to becoming part of 'any structure or institution that is organised around killing human beings' (cited in Altınay 2004: 88–89) coincided with a political mood that was becoming prevalent after the military coup in 1980. Armed Marxist–Leninist groups capable of mobilising hundreds and thousands of people prior to the military intervention were practically wiped out within days as the majority of their militants were murdered, imprisoned or went to live as asylum seekers in European countries. According to Coşkun Üsterci,

---

[4] A new body of ethnographic literature sensitive to the gendering dimension of the military and of military service has developed in the last decade or so (see, e.g., Gill 1997; Ben-Ari 1998; Goddard 2000; Sinclair-Webb 2000 and Altınay 2004).
[5] For this early history of the conscientious objectors' movement, I am drawing on Altınay's (2004) important work on military service in Turkey.

a veteran of the anti-militarist movement and formerly a militant of one those revolutionary groups, it was the question, 'Why did we get defeated despite having so many organisations?' that triggered socialist activists' disillusionment with Marxism and Leninism. One view that powerfully foreshadowed a new way of doing politics diagnosed violence and hierarchy as the impediments to the formation of an organic relationship with the people. The revolutionary armed groups that were active until the military coup, according to Üsterci, simulated the state in that they garnered support by virtue of holding the gun in their hands. Ordinary people took their side not simply because they identified with their ideological stance, but also because these revolutionaries were able to dominate their towns and villages. Socialists were building castles of revolution in the air (and on the ground), while the escalation of violent conflict with the state was exacerbating the demise of a democratic public sphere. In the face of these political hierarchies and organisational authorities nourished by violence, Üsterci and others roughly defined their purpose as devising a non-violent form of activism to disrupt the chain of command inherent in both the state and the revolutionary groups fighting against it.

It is not a coincidence, then, that early conscientious objectors prosecuted by the state initially received support mostly from some of the former socialist cadres and a younger generation of activists who were concurrently questioning violence, hierarchy and authority. Several of them were already calling themselves anarchists at that time. Osman Murat Ülke was one of those activists who took an active role in promoting the idea of conscientious objection through international conferences, discussion groups and objection declarations. His recurrent prosecutions and convictions between 1996 and 1999 prompted a general interest in anti-militarism and conscientious objection which was translated into more or less short-lived campaigns and small-scale groups in other parts of the country. However, two decades after Zencir, Gönül and Ülke almost single-handedly introduced conscientious objection into the vocabulary of political activism in Turkey, the number of objectors barely reaches 100. Among other things, due to the movement's persistent mistrust of collaborating with socialist and human rights organisations, these early efforts always failed to bring about the desired snowball effect.

The incongruous relationship between the anarchists and the activists of other political affiliations within the general anti-militarist movement is in many ways an offspring of the lingering tension over the new form and diction that radical politics was to adopt in the 1980s and 1990s. Some of those groups and individuals that abandoned the idea of using violence as a legitimate form of protest against state oppression while retaining their Marxist or socialist claims began to look for ways of organising and mobilising beyond the classic Leninist party model. Human rights groups, non-governmental organisations and various short-term political campaigns seeking to reach the widest possible spectrum of leftist groups and figures have gradually prevailed over the more traditional instruments of political activism. Simultaneously, a fierce theoretical discussion on the role and potential of civil society for counter-hegemonic struggles was filling the pages of virtually every single leftist publication at the time. Demands for the recognition of civil liberties and human rights that had been crushed by the military intervention were appended to and in some cases superseded the rhetoric of class struggle. Often led by a core group of activists, the new modus operandi that these political struggles sought to achieve was to secure the endorsement of well-known intellectuals and other public figures who could lend legitimacy and visibility to these causes.[6] Anti-militarist activism and/ or opposition to mandatory military service was merely one of the many agendas that these leftist activists were pursuing within the broader task of contributing to the democratisation of the country.

Despite their recent arrival on and negligible presence in the political scene, anarchists too were engaging with and responding to the transformation of political activism through readings, publications and regular meetings in the 1990s. From the classic anarchist texts, they had acquired the conviction that any resistance against the state, that is, the ultimate form of organised domination and authority, must espouse non-vertical structures of assembling. From the then recently translated historical studies on and first-person accounts of the Kronstadt uprising and the Spanish Civil War, they had imbibed a strong prejudice against the idea of ever working together with socialists who do not discard the pillars of Marxism and Leninism. Certainly, the majority was advocating a certain version of social anarchism or anarchist communism sensitive to social and economic inequalities. Nevertheless, due to the absence of any ties with workers and trade unions, their activism was largely

---

[6] The most prominent example of this was the freedom of speech campaigns of the early 1990s. Known also under the name 'Freedom of Thought' (Düşünceye Özgürlük), in these campaigns several human rights activists came together with well-known intellectuals to republish articles that had been censored by the authorities.

confined within the boundaries of university student circles, and eventually took a decisive post-left turn that entirely rejects the conventional structures of leftist politics built around rank and file organising. The struggle against mandatory military service was crucial here in terms of bringing together the anarchist movement's most fundamental issues, such as the critique of violence, authority and hierarchy. Consequently, it became arguably the most effective means for the dissemination of anarchist ideas in the following two decades.[7]

One anecdote told to me by an informant suggests that the conflicts between anarchists and other activists opposing the mandatory military service go back to as early as the beginning of the 1990s. Inspired by their counterparts in Izmir, a group of activists came together in Istanbul in 1993 to establish the second War Resisters' Association. In contrast to the Izmir organisation, however, the anti-militarists in Istanbul were predominantly comprised of socialist individuals from various groups, and advocated a campaign-based struggle that aspired to gain strength through the support of writers and journalists. My informant, who as an anarchist perceived this form of mobilisation, as well as the internal structure of the association, to be authoritarian from the very beginning, remembers a meeting that he attended to articulate his objections. As he entered the smoke-filled room where the discussion was to take place, he saw a rather comfortable armchair apparently left empty for the president of the association, who was expected to arrive soon. Irritated by this, he deliberately went and sat in that chair under the gaze of the other members as a political gesture aimed at subverting this symbolic hierarchy. The soaring tension quickly turned into a quarrel, and the strife between the two camps, which is still apparent today, suddenly boiled over. While the anarchists were accused of being 'deranged utopians' (*ütopik meczuplar*) who lack the vision to grasp how politics function, let alone to successfully oppose the state and the military in Turkey, the leftists were attacked on the grounds that they acted like 'bureaucrats' who reproduce the conventions of their political organisations prior to the military intervention. Although never openly disowned by the anarchists, it

---

[7] A latent source of inspiration that later gave shape to anti-militarist protests was the notion of 'street politics' as it was appropriated by groups such as *Reclaim the Streets* in the UK and the US in the 1990s. Starting with theatre, this performative aspect later took a completely parodic turn, where certain rituals and symbols of the military service and militarism in Turkey were made fun of. The 'Militurizm' gatherings in 2004 and the 'Militurne' organisation in 2008 are two important examples of this.

was the leftists who strategically embraced the use of law and a political discourse based on rights and justice.

If it is partly its activists' reluctance to cooperate with groups and organisations that are not governed according to anarchist principles that at some level hindered the expansion of the movement, the other reason is the state's aggravating reactions against the conscientious objectors. Unlike the earlier activists, the objectors imprisoned and convicted by the state in the last decade not only suffered from the repetitive exercise of jurisdiction, but they also were subjected to assaults and mistreatment in military prisons. In almost all cases, these acts were perpetrated by fellow inmates under the silent approval of the military officers. As a result, several individuals who sympathised with the idea of conscientious objection either moved away from the movement or withdrew their own objection.

Yet, the most immediate implication of conscientious objection concerns the legal situation known as civil death (*civiliter mortuus*). Civil death refers to the total deprivation of a person's civil rights due to a conviction for a crime usually committed against the state. Originally a legal institution in medieval Europe, where a former convict who had lost his civil rights could actually be killed or injured by any person with impunity, in contemporary legal theory it is recalled in the discussions about some of the juridical restrictions of the rights of ex-felons who have completed their sentences.

In the case of Turkey, conscientious objectors who are detained and prosecuted by the state are often released after serving a part of the sentence on the condition that they go back to their unit to complete their military service. Due to the non-recognition of conscientious objection by the Turkish jurisdiction, the objector's refusal to comply with this order automatically qualifies him as a deserter. A warrant is subsequently issued for the arrest of the activist, which once again poses the threat of detention, prosecution and mistreatment. In the midst of this vicious cycle, the objector loses by implication all his civil rights, including the right to travel, to work, to marry, to health care, etc.; in short, all of the rights and privileges that ensure his participation in civil society and his protection against unlawful conduct on the part of others.

During my fieldwork in Istanbul, a conscientious objector, Mehmet Tarhan, who had earlier agreed to talk to me, did not show up in the small activist café where we had decided to meet. Tarhan is a well-known activist who was detained in Izmir in April 2005 and spent a total of eleven months in a military prison, where he was severely beaten up by other prison inmates. Released in June 2006, the cases brought against him on the charge of 'insistent insubordination before the unit with the intent of evading military service entirely' are still pending due to a number of disagreements between the local Sivas Military Court and the 3rd division of the Military Court of Cassation. Wondering why he missed our appointment, I called him on his mobile phone only to be informed by a metallic voice that the person that I called could not be reached at that moment.

When I met Tarhan a week later in the activist organisation that he works for, he told me what had happened to him that day:

> [On the day that I was going to meet you], I was assaulted and mugged in my own flat. The guy put a knife to my friend's neck and took our mobile phones. I can identify him, I know the places where he hangs out; actually I can find him. But there is no way I could go to a police station and file a complaint. Because by going to the police, I would be saying, 'OK, there's the guy [who mugged us] and, by the way, you can arrest me'. I'm feeling pretty bad [since the incident]. It is not so much the assault and the mugging but this state of helplessness. It is killing me. Knowing that I can do nothing about this is horrible.

This contemporary mode of absolute disenfranchisement, which is nevertheless partly imbued with its antiquarian and medieval manifestations as Tarhan's story illustrates, rests on the idea of exception as it is explicated by Giorgio Agamben (1998). According to Agamben, the fact that the sovereign is by definition invested with the power to annul the validity of the juridical order creates a dual paradox according to which not only the sovereign but also the subjects who become targets of this exception to the rule can be said to exist both inside and outside the law. The exclusion by law of certain groups from the scope of legal institutions is undertaken with the intention of including them within the mechanisms and processes acting upon their biological qualities and capacities. In some cases, this takes an extreme form whereby the positioning of certain bodies prior to the law enables the sovereign (read: the modern state) to mark them as 'killable'. Civil death falls within this most radical kind of exception as it implies the possibility of an actual death with impunity. While the prosecuted activist loses his civil protections through the suspension of the legal order, he is simultaneously contained in a new category of people who may not be entitled to the same biological rights as other citizens. Note, however, Tarhan's claim that 'it is not so much the assault and the mugging but this state of helplessness' that is killing him. In addition to the social, legal and physical variants of the deprivation that constitute bare life, he seems to suggest there is also an affective component to this exclusion. This, it seems, can at times be the hardest and, as we shall see, can contribute to the resentment that surfaces between the prosecuted conscientious objectors and the rest of the movement.

'THERE IS NO POLITICS WITHOUT SACRIFICE'

Even though Mehmet Tarhan's description of his socio-legal condition implies a sense of political inertia against those practices that render him both socially and physically killable, other prosecuted objectors resort to tactics that denote more agency in a way that has important implications for the rest of the movement. Another objector's story is illuminating here.

On 7 December 2006 Çorlu Military Court took the decision to detain and imprison conscientious objector Halil Savda on the grounds that he presented a flight risk. Savda had already been prosecuted and sentenced to three months and fifteen days' imprisonment on the charge of 'insistent insubordination before the unit' by the same court in December 2004. After spending one month in Çorlu Military Prison, he had been released provided that he go back to his unit in Çorlu, Tekirdağ within forty-eight hours. Instead, he went to Istanbul in February 2005 and played an active role in establishing the Conscientious Objectors' Platform (*Vicdani Ret Platformu*) over the course of the next one and a half years. During this time, his lawyers filed an appeal against his 2004 conviction.

In June 2006 the 3rd Chamber of the Military Court of Cassation examined the case and ruled that the Çorlu Military Court's initial verdict should be annulled due to the procedural incompetence of the investigation, namely, the lack of a psychiatric examination. However, it also rendered the judgement that the defendant's refusal to wear his military uniform and attend musters, as well as his declaration of objection, would require his prosecution on the charge of 'insistent subordination before the unit with the intent of evading military service entirely', rather than mere 'insistent subordination before the unit'. As defined under Article 88 of the Military Penal Code, the former offence would entail a more severe punishment for Savda – from six months to five years' imprisonment, compared to a maximum sentence of one year stipulated under

Article 87 for the latter. Thus, the case was referred back to the Çorlu Military Court for retrial.

On 7 December 2006 Halil Savda showed up at the courthouse for the first hearing of the retrial prosecuting him under Article 88 of the Military Penal Code, despite the fact that he had been cautioned by his lawyers that, because he had been living as a fugitive since February 2005, participating in the trial would lead to his immediate detention and imprisonment. He was indeed detained, and this led to his second imprisonment under Article 88. This was followed by further prosecutions, convictions, assaults and attempts to subject him to a psychiatric inspection over the next couple of years. In the meantime, the anti-militarist/conscientious objectors' movement was leading a turbulent political life, first witnessing the launch of the 'Campaign for Solidarity with Halil Savda' by his fellow activists, then a gradual dissolution of the Conscientious Objectors' Platform that Savda had played a crucial role in establishing prior to his second imprisonment.

Savda justified his decision to attend the trial despite being fully aware of its punitive consequences, saying it was a response against the condition of civil death that arises from the state's policy to turn a blind eye to conscientious objectors. He went on to suggest that his act was not only meant to protest against the radical exclusion suffered by objectors in Turkey, but also to contribute to efforts to render conscientious objection visible and powerful. When objectors passively bear this social banishment, according to Savda, they in fact help to perpetuate the state's dismissal of the public discussion of conscientious objection. Therefore, at the time he opted for his quasi-voluntary imprisonment, he discerned it as the only viable means to further his political cause.

Savda was not the first activist to resort to this tactic. Osman Murat Ülke also took the same approach following those few instances in which he was not sent back to his military unit after being released from the military prison. Ülke's participation in his trials in the face of a warrant issued for his immediate detention stemmed from a conviction that was widely shared during this early phase of the anti-militarist/conscientious objector's movement. Generating more public awareness of their challenge against mandatory military service and disseminating the idea of conscientious objection were the first and foremost priorities of the activists. Accordingly, Ülke was also of the opinion that a premeditated imprisonment would better serve these purposes than a fragile liberty.

Whether it took place as a consequence of a semi-deliberate decision or of an undesired course of events, the imprisonment of Ülke, Savda, Tarhan and others indeed enhanced the recognition of anti-militarist ideas in Turkey. Every time a conscientious objector was detained or put in a military prison, their fellow activists quickly mobilised through press releases and demonstrations that were covered by national newspapers on a more or less regular basis. Left-leaning journalists and writers who sympathised with anti-militarism expressed support for these objectors at the risk of opening themselves up to the notorious charge of 'alienating the people from the institution of military service'. Moreover, campaigns launched in the names of imprisoned objectors rendered the movement relatively more open to cooperating with political groups and individuals outside the anarchist/anti-authoritarian circles. In short, those phases in which the conscientious objectors' movement gained momentum over the past twenty years have almost always coincided with an objector being in prison.[8]

The fact that the potential and influence of the conscientious objectors' movement largely depends on the extent to which its activists suffer at the hands of the state entails a form of political activism that I will call the 'sacrificial mode of dissension'.[9] The general demands of the movement are articulated through the individual suffering of the objector, with the intention of attracting the attention of the general public. Ironically, despite their strong disapproval of the leftists who perceived this form of publicity essential for the success of the anti-militarist causes, the suffering that the anarchists depended on in one way or another served similar purposes. In the cases of Halil Savda and Osman Murat Ülke, the sacrificial function materialises as the objector utilises law as a means of magnifying his victimisation by turning himself in to the authorities. Two different episodes of assault targeting Mehmet Tarhan, on the other hand, indicate that exposure to violence tolerated or permitted by the state bestows victimhood on the activist in that his suffering reveals the blatantly extra-juridical mechanisms. Either way, the sacrificial role that

---

[8] Here, I have to make it clear that the growing publicity that the movement received had a very limited positive effect on the actual number of people who declared their conscientious objection. The suffering and violence experienced by the prosecuted conscientious objectors did indeed render the movement more visible. However, as I mentioned earlier, for the same reason several people who would otherwise consider becoming objectors changed their minds.

[9] A number of other analysts have discussed the relation between political activism and sacrifice (e.g. Feldman 1991; Arextaga 1997; Bargut 2010).

the prosecuted conscientious objector performs is acknowledged and reflected upon by the activists themselves. As Halil Savda put it:

> Unfortunately, there is a general political culture in Turkey that affects the anti-militarists as well. Struggles gain ground with grievances. When we activists are not thrown into prison, a powerful anti-militarist/conscientious objectors' movement does not make progress. The discussions concerning conscientious objection gradually fade away. Maybe I attended my court hearing as a result of this culture, of this political sentiment. But I am not the one to judge what the consequences were [for the movement outside].

Mehmet Tarhan, on the other hand, takes a more critical stance in his observations:

> [If the problems that I encounter are resolved one day], then it would set me at ease for committing myself to my political activities. It would terminate the state of living like a fugitive. But it would also strike a heavy blow to the movement. Unfortunately politics goes hand in hand with necrophilia in this country. There is no politics without sacrifice. This is not only the left's problem, it is also our problem. If your grievances are prevented, so to speak, then obviously you no longer assume the position of a victim. Therefore, whereas you have several people working in the campaigns [in support of the objector in prison], there is no one around once you get out of prison. And the problems are not over or anything. People concretely want to see that there is a victim; I mean, there has to be blood.

I would like to take a step further here and argue that the presence of an imprisoned objector not only serves to empower the movement, but also protects other conscientious objectors against prosecution, conviction and possible state violence. However much I find this claim empirically difficult to substantiate, the chronology of anti-militarist movement in Turkey suggests that there have never been two conscientious objectors in prison at the same time. What is even more intriguing is that some anecdotes shared with me during my fieldwork reveal a certain degree of reluctance on behalf of the state to proceed against the activists under certain conditions. A few activists who declared their conscientious objection years ago and have been maintaining a low public profile since then mentioned that they were taken into custody a couple of times during police controls and taken to a police station nearby. Expecting to be sent to their military units under a gendarmerie escort, these objectors were curiously released without any charges after spending a couple of hours in detention. Given that these events took place at the time there was another conscientious objector serving his prison sentence in a military prison, it seems that the state deliberately avoided the increasing publicity that a wholesale assault against the movement might give rise to.

If such is the case, then René Girard's (1977) celebrated argument that 'the sacrificial process prevents the spread of violence' can be invoked here to explore this second association that the sacrificial mode of dissension infers.[10] Girard argues that the practice of sacrifice involves a deliberate act of alleviating the tensions, feuds and rivalries taking place within the community by concentrating the violence upon a chosen victim. This sacrificial substitution that occurs at the expense of a victim averts the danger of escalation and restores harmony within the community. The sacrifice, in short, protects the community from its inner violence.

Clearly the violence in question in the case of the conscientious objectors in Turkey is unilaterally directed against the activists by the state. Nevertheless, only a few of them – seven out of seventy objectors in the past twenty years, to be precise – have fully endured the legal, extralegal and physical variants of this violence. This, in turn, has prevented the suffering of their fellow activists. The sacrificial role that the prosecuted conscientious objector performs between the state and the rest of the activists, therefore, not only lends vitality to the movement, but at the same time constitutes a protection for it.

Girard makes a clear distinction between tribal and modern societies, claiming that the sacrificial process exists only in the former. All sacrificial victims share the common characteristic of lacking a link with the rest of the community, which in turn eliminates the risk of vengeance in the aftermath of their death. If sacrifice in tribal societies represents an act of violence without the danger of vengeance, this function is replaced by the judicial system in modern communities. 'The system', Girard argues, 'effectively limits [the act of violence] to a single act of reprisal, enacted by a sovereign authority specialising in this particular function' (1977: 15). In other words, law breaks the 'chain reaction' that vengeance triggers.

---

[10] Girard notes that the process of sacrifice is always partly unknown to its participants: '[T]he sacrificial process requires a certain degree of misunderstanding. The celebrants do not and must not comprehend the true role of the sacrificial act' (1977: 7).

In this chapter I have argued, following Agamben, that law, rather than pertaining to two different modalities of violence prevention, is in fact founded on violence, or more precisely, is contingent upon the violence that its suspension induces. But unlike him, I have tried to demonstrate that law also mediates intricately with sacrifice, and that this convoluted mediation is where the political dissension of conscientious objectors comes into being. On the one hand, the sacrificial act seeks to defy, even to momentarily interrupt the violence that the (extra)-juridical system elevates into vengeance. On the other hand, the prevention of this vengeance, as well as the struggle against it, is maintained only when certain victims fall under the influence of its intensity.

'WHAT HAPPENS IF THAT CHILD RUNS AWAY FROM THERE ONE DAY?'

Can we say that the prosecuted objectors' recourse to the European Court of Human Rights carries the intention of bringing an end to the 'state vengeance' fostered by the local juridical system in the form of civil death? Does it also attest to a way out from the sacrificial role that the conscientious objector is compelled to play between the state and his fellow activists? Can we envision a radical non-violent political movement that can protect itself from state violence and grow stronger not at the expense of some of its activists' suffering?

This last question has been occasionally posed within the movement especially during the phases when the activists began to show signs of fatigue and despair. An anti-militarist activist and conscientious objector, Yavuz Fani, who has closely witnessed the evolution of the movement since its inception, tried to explain the ebb and flow of energy within the movement. 'The struggle came to a halt at some point, particularly in Izmir,' Fani said. 'The organisation in Izmir during that time began to invest all its energy exclusively in the case of Osman Murat Ülke.' Fani referred to Ursula K. Le Guin's short story 'The ones who walk away' to make his friends understand what might happen if they put too much hope in one person. Le Guin's tale (2000) depicts a utopian city called Omelas, where the entire welfare and happiness of its citizens depend on the condition that a single child is locked up in a dark cellar. She writes:

> They all know it is there, all the people of Omelas. Some of them have come to see it, others are content merely to know it is there. They all

know that it has to be there. Some of them understand why, and some do not, but they all understand that their happiness, the beauty of their city, the tenderness of their friendships, the health of their children, the wisdom of their scholars, the skill of their makers, even the abundance of their harvest and the kindly weathers of their skies, depend wholly on this child's abominable misery.

Once the young inhabitants of the city reach the age of puberty, they are taken into the basement room to learn the miserable truth about their city for the first time. Initially shocked and disgusted by the suffering of the unfortunate child, most of them gradually accept the situation and go back to their normal lives. A few, however, cannot come to terms with it and silently walk away from the city.

Fani continued:

> I mean, it is not our welfare, happiness and peace that are in question here, but I was still using Le Guin's story to tell my friends about the troubles of building an entire political struggle upon the confinement of an activist, on the imprisonment of Ossi [Osman Murat Ülke]. And I was asking: what happens if that child runs away from there one day? How would the movement exist without him?

The image of the child locked in the dark basement in Le Guin's story sadly captures a number of themes that I have pursued in this chapter – the bareness of life, the state of exception, violence and sacrifice – in an attempt to make sense of what it means to be a prosecuted conscientious objector in Turkey. Yet, as Yavuz Fani rightly predicted years ago, due to the failure of the movement to bring about a political struggle that does not stand upon the suffering caused by the state, in this story the one who walks away turned out to be the 'miserable child' in question. Osman Murat Ülke and some other objectors severed their ties with the movement and are currently leading quiet lives away from activism. Mehmet Tarhan likewise distanced himself from the movement. Even though he mentioned to me that his retreat has more to do with his desire to focus on LGBT (lesbian, gay, bisexual, and transgender) activism than any kind of break with the anti-militarist struggle, his candid remarks about the sacrificial role of the prosecuted conscientious objectors suggest that his resentments might have played a role in this decision. As for Halil Savda, after he was released from prison for the last time, he became instrumental in establishing a separate organisation called the Conscientious Objection Platform for Peace (Barış için Vicdani Ret Platformu). As it is comprised of human rights groups and other leftist activists, the majority of anarchist/anti-authoritarian activists refrain from taking part in this platform.

Although Osman Murat Ülke is still obliged to do his military service and will potentially face an arrest for the rest of his life, the decision of the ECHR provides protection that makes it virtually impossible for the Turkish state to resume the cycle of detention, prosecution and imprisonment. Even if the struggle to force the Turkish state through international law to legally recognise conscientious objection is lost, some consequences of civil death previously affecting him seem to have been averted, at least for the time being. Because the applications lodged at the court by other objectors have still not been settled, it is difficult to say for sure if this will be the case for these activists. In the last couple of years, in reaction to the ECHR's decision regarding Ülke's case, the state adopted a new strategy by declaring a number of prosecuted conscientious objectors, including Halil Savda, medically unfit for serving in the army on the grounds of 'anti-social personality disorder'. As far as the general conscientious objectors' movement is concerned, its future remains unclear despite the gradual spread of resistance against mandatory military service in other social and political circles, most notably the recent emergence of objectors who refuse to serve on the grounds of their Kurdish identity or Islamic convictions.

CONCLUSION

I began this chapter by pointing out that the ambiguities and paradoxes inherent in the utilisation of law against the state can be affected by a deeper ambivalence concerning the question of what qualifies as legal or illegal in the first place. Following Agamben's insights about the state of exception and the bare life that it engenders, I suggested that the condition of civil death that the prosecuted conscientious objectors in Turkey become subject to can be construed as an example of law culminating in something unlawful. Accordingly, I tried to understand the reluctant use of international human rights law in the light of the radical exclusion that the Turkish state engages in by suspending the validity of law.

My analysis of the relation between political dissension and juridification, however, offers a more fragmented and varied picture than the duality suggested by 'law against the state', drawing attention to the dynamics within the group where some activists take on the role of sacrificial figure for the rest of the group. Here, rather than considering law merely as a weapon that is used by political activists, I also construed it as the material that their legal and political subjectivities are woven of. In this chapter, three 'layers' have been given special attention: first, the way in which the exception to the rule facilitates the legal condition known as civil death; second, the prosecuted conscientious objectors' attempts to reveal the 'illegality of law' by turning themselves in to the authorities; and third, the resort to international law in order to seek protection when the struggle based on this tactic of sacrifice fails.

References

Agamben, Giorgio 1998. *Homo Sacer: Sovereign Power and Bare Life*, trans. Daniel Heller-Roazen. Stanford University Press.

Altınay, Ayse G. 2004. *The Myth of the Military Nation: Militarism, Gender, and Education in Turkey*. New York: Palgrave Macmillan.

Arextaga, Begona 1997. *Shattering Silence: Women, Nationalism and Political Subjectivity in Northern Ireland*. Princeton University Press.

Bargut, B. 2010. 'Spectacles of death: dignity, dissent and sacrifice in Turkey's prisons', in Laleh Khalili and Jillian Schwedler (eds.) *Policing and Prisons in the Middle East: Formations of Coercion*. New York: Columbia University Press, pp. 241–61.

Ben-Ari, Eyal 1998. *Mastering Soldiers: Conflicts, Emotions and the Enemy in an Israeli Military Unit*. Oxford: Berghahn Books.

Das, Veena and Poole, Deborah 2004. 'State and its margins: comparative ethnographies', in Veena Das and Deborah Poole (eds.) *Anthropology in the Margins of the State*. Santa Fe, NM and Oxford: School of American Research Press and James Curry Ltd., pp. 3–33.

Feldman, Allen 1991. *Formations of Violence: The Narrative of the Body and Political Terror in Northern Ireland*. University of Chicago Press.

Gill, Lesley 1997. 'Creating citizens, making men: the military and masculinity in Bolivia', *Cultural Anthropology* 4 (12): 527–50.

Girard, René 1977. *Violence and the Sacred*. Baltimore: Johns Hopkins University Press.

Goddard, Victoria 2000. 'The virile nation: gender and ethnicity in the re-construction of Argentinian pasts', *Goldsmiths Anthropology Research Papers* 4.

Gürcan, Ertuğrul C. 2006. 'İnsan Haklarında Bir Sırat Köprüsü: Avrupa İnsan Hakları Mahkemesi'nin Vicdani Ret Kararı', *Mülkiyeliler Birliği Dergisi* 251–59: pp. 30–33.

Le Guin, Ursula K. 2000. 'The ones who walk away from Omelas', in Ursula K. Le Guin *The Wind's Twelve Quarters*. London: Victor Gollancz, pp. 275–84.

Merry, Sally E. 1995. 'Resistance and the cultural power of law', *Law & Society Review* 29 (1): 11–26.

Sinclair-Webb, Emma 2000. 'Our bulent is now a commando: military service and manhood in Turkey', in Mai Ghossoub and Emma Sinclair-Webb (eds.) *Imagined Masculinities: Male Identity and Culture in the Modern Middle East*. London: Saqi Books, pp. 65–92.

Ülke v. Turkey 2006. http://cmiskp.echr.coe.int/tkp197/view.aspitem=1&portal=hbkm&action=html&highlight=%FClke%20%7C%20turkey&sessionid=48108470&skin=hudoc-en. Last accessed 27 July 2011.

EPILOGUE: CHANGING PARADIGMS OF HUMAN RIGHTS

Upendra Baxi

PREFATORY REMARKS

The text in your hands offers a series of fragments of thought concerning some ways of understanding the changing paradigms of human rights, which I call respectively the 'modern', 'contemporary', 'trade-related and market-friendly' and 'post-human'. Any such understanding remains complicated by the term 'human rights' and the notion of 'paradigm'. It is not my intention here to reiterate the analysis of changing paradigms of human rights offered in my recent work (see Baxi 2007, 2008). Rather, I offer a few remarks by way of retrospect as well as sites of some fresh provocation, in full awareness that what gets said here may not respond to the richness of ethnographic insights that this volume presents overall, by way of a critical anthropology of law in general and in particular of human rights.[1]

Perhaps, my interest in the paradigm talk may well have been formed by my early schooling in the famous contestation between Max Gluckman and Paul Bohannan, although neither explicitly invoked the notion of a paradigm! At stake remained then the concerns about singularity and comparison: Bohannan (1957) thought that responsible and responsive practices of anthropology of law ought to articulate the singularity of 'folk-concepts'; Gluckman (1955) leaned towards rendering 'folk' concepts into comparable conceptions (such as 'law', 'property' and 'sovereignty') (see

---

[1] Compatible, though in many ways different from the project as proposed by Mark Goodale, among significant others (see Goodale 2006: 485–511). Perhaps the difference lies in 'juridification' presented both as a promise and peril.

also Comaroff and Roberts 1981; Conley and O'Barr 1990; French 1996). I do not know how either protagonist may have addressed the 'folk/comparative' concerns in relation to human rights; however in this volume the tension between singularity and comparability (universality) becomes even more palpably escalated by a third element that I call 'solidarity' (to adapt a category of Kant in the *Third Critique* (2000), the practices of 'subjective universality' – grasped here at least as a collective growth in moral sentiment resisting barbarism of power in all its forms).

Thus stand offered richly in the various contributions some fresh starts in understanding of the idea of human rights via various prisms: 'juridification' both as a hegemonic and counter-hegemonic frame; the community of rights (human rights as relational notions and practices towards freedom and autonomy); struggles over 'voicing' and 'silencing' of the 'human' element in the appropriation of human rights (as we now know these); the practices of public as insurgent reason (the 'fury') in reclaiming rights; and the prism of transgressive translation. What remains for me then is a supplementary task of directing marginal attention to notions of paradigm and paradigm shifts as, perhaps, not too impertinent an offering to the richness of diverse concerns about singularity and solidarity.

In my writing about and on human rights, I had not quite thought it necessary seriously to challenge the meaning of 'paradigm', and instead used the notion rather loosely as signifying a model or map. On second serious thoughts an anxious engagement with the notion of 'paradigm', which is heavily contested in social and scientific theory and philosophy, seems necessary. The scientific meanings and uses of the notion demand a more rigorous analysis. It will simply not do to adopt the voguish usage of the notion by the mass media, which constantly refers us to 'paradigm shifts' as routinely occurring, or the usage in human rights and social movement contexts (in which 'paradigm warriors' seek to 'subvert' or 'smash' the 'dominant paradigm'). If the media almost equate 'paradigm' with style or fashion, activists signal by 'paradigm' a set of ideological beliefs and some other folk uses of the notion as an equivalent of a rough tourist guide that offers the pleasures and perils of quick visitation to alien sights and experiences.

However, in specialist discourse, from its origins in grammar and rhetoric the notion of a paradigm has moved, ever since Thomas Kuhn (1962), to signify a scientific community's ways of 'knowing'.[2] Indeed,

---

[2] Kuhn (1962: 15) maintains that: 'In the absence of a paradigm or some candidate for paradigm, all the facts that could possibly pertain to the development of a given science are likely

such a community is constituted by a common consensus among its practitioners as to what constitutes a scientific method yielding verifiable true knowledge. The history of sciences is a history, however, of 'paradigm shifts' which occur when metaparadigms change – a new paradigm takes place of the old (Copernicus, Darwin and Einstein, for example). Thomas Kuhn's pioneering work narrating paradigm shift has opened up narratives of the paradigmatic groups, leading to further explorations in the way of sociology of knowledge, now rechristened as 'social epistemology' (Fuller 2000; Nickels 2003).

Further extension of Kuhn's work has led to various contentions which suggest a multitude of meanings.[3] One may mean by 'paradigm' many things – 'metaparadigms' ('unquestioned' metaphysical 'presuppositions'); the 'shared commitments of any disciplinary community'; or 'exemplar' (whose function it is to permit a way of seeing one's subject matter on a *concrete* level, thereby allowing *puzzle-solving* to take place) (Eckberg and Hill, Jr. 1979: 928).

Kuhn rather explicitly cautioned us all against an open space for appropriation of his thought to social science and theory when he said, '[i]f … some social scientists take from me the view that they can improve the status of their field by first legislating agreement on fundamentals and then turning to puzzle-solving, they are badly missing my point' (quoted in Eckberg and Hill, Jr. 1979: 928). Why this caution? Is it because social sciences and humanities remain incapable of establishing – 'legislating' – a general conception of the fundamentals of method? Or is it so because the subject matters they deal with remain inherently intractable – such as ideas of truth, beauty, goodness and justice? What explanatory powers may the notions of paradigm and paradigm shift carry when annexed to social theory and humanities? Or, indeed, may these notions be made more diffuse in the process, so much so as to even imperil the paradigm-talk in science?

Of course, Kuhn's caution has been widely, and perhaps wisely, disregarded by social theorists. Thus, Michel Foucault distinguished the

---

to seem equally relevant.' In contrast, 'normal science' signifies 'research firmly based upon one or more past scientific achievements, achievements that some particular scientific community acknowledges for a time as supplying the foundation for its further practice' (1962: 10). Science here signifies natural sciences: 'no natural history can be interpreted in the absence of at least some implicit body of intertwined theoretical and methodological belief that permits selection, evaluation, and criticism' (1962: 16–17).

[3] See, for example, Phillips 1974; and in a different context, Hafner 1998. See further Babich 2003; Musgrave 1970.

notion of *episteme* from that of a paradigm, and Giorgio Agamben (2009: 32), in his quest for 'completing Foucault', insists that what we need is a 'paradigmatic ontology' – going beyond 'the cognitive relations between the subject and the object' to the question of 'being'. At this level, much more work needs to be done than what I offer today concerning the competing paradigms of human rights. I doubt, though, that those concerned with social theory or anthropology of human rights may ever go so far as to absorb Agamben's call for 'philosophical archaeology', which reminds us of the need to think beyond 'paradigmatic' thought-ways so far as to invent a 'method' that enables us to understand afresh a 'world supported by a thick plot of resemblances and sympathies, analogies and correspondences'. Yet, may I say, even if densely, that any attempt to decipher the future of human rights calls precisely for this order of archaeological vigilance?

For me, this call at least signifies the need for giving dignity of discourse to the other of the 'paradigm' – the '*sub-*'paradigmatic (folk-)ways of knowing the world and acting with and upon it. 'Commonsense' stands thus represented as opposed to scientific ways of knowing. And we now hear about a 'new' commonsense as questioning these hegemonic ways, putting 'science' in question (see Santos 1995); when that 'sub-paradigmatic' may become 'non-paradigmatic' altogether remains an open question. Further, not being paradigmatic at all may signify being pre-paradigmatic ('pre-modern') or para-/trans-paradigmatic ('postmodern').

The introduction of the other of paradigmatic raises a threshold anxiety about talking of human rights paradigm or paradigm shifts. Put another way, the caution of Kuhn, if no longer pertinent to social theory, may still haunt folks (including myself) who may still speak about human rights paradigms.

ON BEING AND REMAINING HUMAN

What constitutes the idea of 'human' remains variously constructed and contested in spiritual, religious, 'secular-ethical', 'scientific' and 'politico-juridical' traditions of discourse. A certain kind of 'ontology' has always been at work in the work or labour of 'defining' that which we call 'human'. In each tradition, the distinctively 'human' provides different imageries. And there is no way in which I may in this conversation elaborate these, save risking the following summary remarks:

(a) In so far as the spiritual idea of human is regarded seriously, the 'spiritual' emerges as not always coinciding with the 'religious';[4] in this way we arrive at the idea of human as a trans-religious being (notably manifest in indigenous peoples' traditions but not only on that site).

(b) With all the variations in the origins and development of religious traditions, the idea of human as divine subject remains paramount; to be sure, different pious hermeneutical traditions present this in the languages of theological voluntarism (obedience to God's will) or theological rationalism (God's reason, requiring a pious human interpretation of His word); and the difference crucially matters as so many histories of theistic 'natural rights' fully yield to view.

(c) The secular/secularizing idea of human remains anchored in *the freedom of conscience as making us all equally human*. It is this freedom/faculty that makes possible the emergence of the notion of an equal right to freedom to choose, establish and practise 'religion', or to remain agnostic or atheist.

(d) In its different itineraries, the 'secular-ethical' idea elevates the human as an autonomous moral person endowed with the capability of free will and reason (human as a moral agent). An otherwise born human may thus be regarded as less than human, or sub-human or an inferior human.

(e) The 'scientific' idea de-hyphens the 'secular-ethical'; 'human' is grasped here as an evolutionary entity and as an experimental subject, not always guided by the telos of the moral or ethical.

(f) The politico-juridical idea offers human as an ideological construction, a form in which different ways of understanding and constituting 'human' form the specificity of the articulatory practices of domination and resistance.

Given even this bare listing, any human rights paradigm talk remains aggravated. What consensus by way of 'normal science' may we arrive at amidst this welter of conceptions? In what ways, for example, does the spiritual idea of being and remaining 'human' speak to having 'human rights'? May it not be the case that in this conception the idea of being human remains entirely sensible outside the talk of having human rights? Further, how may we relate the religious conceptions of the idea of having

---

[4] For example, see the distinction between 'spiritual' and 'religious' as outlined in the talk by the Archbishop of Canterbury, Rowan Williams (2008). Dr Williams contests the idea of 'spiritual' as a form of 'post-religious consciousness'.

human rights, given the insistence that the human is a divine creation, subject to God's Word and World? How may, or even how should, peoples of faith receive the 'truths' of contemporary secular enunciations of human rights, and some secular theologies thus framed? How may we tell stories about the convergence between theistic *iusnaturalist* traditions and the contemporary 'secular-ethical' and the 'politico-juridical' notions of what it may mean to say human and 'having' human rights?

At least since the Universal Declaration of Human Rights (UDHR) secular-ethical and juridico-political discourses demand infinite inclusion; via the birth-metaphor all humans thus remain proclaimed entitled to dignity. But this inclusivity also remains rife with the propensity towards strategic exclusion of who may count as human beings or persons. The 'imperialism of the same' (to adapt a phrase from Emmanuel Levinas 1969: 87) in the acts of enunciation of the 'human' then invites us all rigorously to rethink the very politico-juridical contrast between 'inclusion' and 'exclusion'. Even as 'we' include, 'we' also exclude – *sans papiers* or the undocumented alien migrants, for example, or 'terrorists'.

More is at stake as well. Already the work of the distinction between human and non-human is challenged by a critique of anthropocentrism in the construction of the idea of 'human'. Giorgio Agamben (2004) calls our deliberative attention to the operations of what he names the 'anthropological machine'. Animal rights theory and the animal rights movement fully suggest that defining human in terms of moral agency, rather than the capacity to suffer pain, distorts our understanding of what, after all, we may wish to mean by 'human'. Indeed, Peter Singer (1979) has singularly drawn our attention to the comparison of women to beasts of burden, thus not eligible to count as 'human'.[5] Our unexamined speciesist ways of thinking have often led to practices that exile from the realms of rights a large number of human beings – including slaves, indigenous peoples, women, people living with disability, people of different sexual orientation, children, the 'insane', and I may further

---

[5] Singer writes: 'When Mary Wollstonecraft, a forerunner of later feminists, published her *Vindication of the Rights of Women* in 1792, her ideas were widely regarded as absurd, and they were satirized in an anonymous publication entitled *A Vindication of the Rights of Brutes*. The author of this satire (actually Thomas Taylor, a distinguished Cambridge philosopher) tried to refute Wollstonecraft's reasoning by showing that it could be carried one stage further. If sound when applied to women, why should the arguments not be applied to dogs, cats and horses? They seemed to hold equally well for these "brutes"; yet to hold that brutes had rights was manifestly absurd; therefore the reasoning by which this conclusion had been reached must be unsound, and if unsound when applied to brutes, it must also be unsound when applied to women, since the very same arguments had been used in each case.'

add the masses of subjects of European colonisation, the imperialist Cold War and now the wars on 'terror'.[6]

This reduction of human beings to 'beasts of burden' or 'brutes' – to the status of things – is, you may contend, no longer normatively the case, given the situation of the UDHR and its subsequent normative progeny. Yet it may not be gainsaid that normative inclusion often signifies various orders of existential exclusion.[7] On a different register, non-humans – whether animals or objects in nature such as oceans and rivers, mountains, trees and forests and variegated forms of biodiversity – stand conceived as resources or commodities placed at the service of the human species. One may wish to say that this imagery is now being transformed by a growing recognition and even concern for the human rights of non-human animal persons or objects in nature. Even so, these performances – whether the preservation of rainforests, endangered species, biodiversity, and now the politics and emergent 'law' of climate change – raise the concern about the extent to which the idea of human rights may be extended to 'nature' as such.

To complicate matters, allow me to refer to the not so indeterminate futures of cloning humans as future figurations of a free techno-science market economy. The birth metaphor of the UDHR does not quite extend to human-like entities thus produced, in the not-so-distant future, as 'commodities' just like the cloned sheep and other transgenic animals. 'Commodities' represented as insentient objects remain inherently ineligible for any ethical or moral solicitude; these entities stand devoid of the capacity for self-determination (lacking faculties of reason and will), and they may not be ever said to be subjects of pain and suffering. No doubt the future human clones, even when conceived as genetic warehouses for the amelioration of the 'naturally' born, will remain capable of pain and suffering; yet the dominant techno-scientific capital argument remains just this: such clones are commodities produced by the market and as such their actual or potential suffering matters but little. One may extend this analogy as well to forms of artificial intelligence and related life-forms (see Baxi 2007: chapter 6).

Understandably, the idea of human as a techno-scientific experimental human subject may constitute for many of us a nightmare of human

---

[6] For further elaboration of these points, see the themes and literature in Baxi forthcoming.

[7] The practices of contemporary economic globalisation remain intelligible only because of the recurrence of this tendency. The logics of neo-liberalism promoting flexible labour markets, and thus pursuing global competitive advantage, means all over again that sentient human beings are reduced to the status of the order of things.

rights (as we know them). Yet it remains the case that evolutionary life sciences and neurobiological thought-ways and research agendas continue to insist that understanding humans as a species (whether via the human genome project or its further applications) is not a denial of other related ideas of human, but rather a way of deepening that understanding. The short point rather here is that the old paradigm of construction of the human is now signified by the construction of the post-human – one in new techno-scientific dressings that promises the emancipation of the 'human'. This is scarcely an occasion to map or unravel forms of continuities/discontinuities thus marked. Put simply, the progress narratives reincarnate themselves, though this time around perhaps less driven or riven by 'ideological' disputations.

HAVING RIGHTS

The second term – rights – in the phrase 'human rights' (hereafter: HR) has been as controversial as the first. For most philosophers or theorists the idea of human rights as a set of moral rights remains at stake; this entails construction of an idea of self in society, usually presented as a rational self that seeks autonomy to choose, pursue and fulfil designs of the good life, freely chosen. Understandably, we find a kind of moral economy at work in identifying the basic rights, as any reader of the listing of basic rights in the corpus of John Rawls (1993; 1999) and Jürgen Habermas (1995) well knows.

The 'thin' conceptions of basic rights – equality, liberty and dignity which lay, as it were, the 'groundwork of metaphysics of morals' of HR – contrast with the 'thick' ones enacted by a massive proliferation of international, supranational, regional and constitutional human rights enunciations. Typically, almost paradigmatically, for lawpersons what matters is the idea of rights as juridical rights (see Sen 2004: 315–36; see also the critique in Baxi 2007: 30–75). Juridification of human rights raises a number of different kinds of questions concerning their 'nature,' 'number' and limits.[8]

---

[8] By 'nature' I mean here primarily distinctions made between 'enforceable' and not directly 'justiciable' rights. By 'number', I refer to the distinction between 'enumerated' and 'unenumerated' rights, the latter often articulated by practices of judicial activism. By 'limits' I indicate here the scope of rights thus enshrined, given that no constitutional guarantee of human rights may confer 'absolute' protection. The 'negotiation' process is indeed complex; it refers to at least three distinct though related aspects: 1) judicially upheld definitions of grounds of restriction or regulation of the scope of rights; 2) legislatively and executively unmolested judicial interpretation of the meaning, content and scope of rights; and 3) the ways in which the defined bearers

Few discussions about HR achieve clarity of what is to be meant by this term. I suggest in *Future* (Baxi 2008: chapter 1) that the expression HR constitutes a false totality. Whether conceived in ethical or juridical terms, HR comprises a whole variety of normative texts concerned with *values, principles, norms, standards, rules* and *practices/conduct*. And these distinctions matter.

Understanding human rights *values* remains a complex and even contradictory affair. The study of values (axiology) is a difficult yet necessary enterprise. Difficult because one needs to understand the idea of values not as rationalisation of strategic interests – what 'we' desire – but as an ethical platform of what 'we' ought to desire. In this sense, 'having rights' does not just mean having interests (claims/desires/wants), but a reflexive capability of *taking interest in our interests* (see Habermas 1995). If so, 'having human rights' is an affair not just of claiming rights for oneself but for others as well. It is in this sense that Alan Gewirth (1997) speaks to us about a 'community of rights' going beyond the conventional distinctions between civil and political rights on the one hand, and social, cultural and economic rights on the other. The notion of a community of rights acquires an even deeper meaning with its recognition of human rights as human needs (cf. Nussbaum 2000, 2006).

'Having rights' entails a grasp of mutuality and interdependence as both necessary and desirable. Necessary, because values in the latter sense remain inherently pluralistic; put another way, different cultural/ civilisational traditions define the notion of the good life differently. The question then is not so much about the voguish debate concerning the 'universality' and 'relativism' of human rights that remains both vexatious and unproductive, but rather one that concerns an understanding of the translation of particular values into universal ones. Eva Kalny (2009), among significant others, puts this well when she suggests that ethnography of human rights yields the conclusion that what stands represented by way of universality of contemporary human rights values remains a manifestation of a specific configuration of the European experience. All this accords rather well, if I may say so in an abrupt way, with my own insistence that we distinguish between claims of *universality* of human rights values and their *globalisation* (see Baxi 2008: chapter 5). Further, this cannot be a merely juridical task; it entails the

of human rights choose or choose not to exercise their rights, this in turn presupposing that they have the information concerning the rights they have and the capability to deploy them in various acts of living.

labours of philosophical anthropology or what Agamben (2009) more fecundly calls 'philosophical archaeology'.

Rendering HR values into juridical ones is a task of translation (as more than literary translation). Put concretely, in internationally arrived at human rights, value enunciations often get impoverished; further, they even get 'lost' in translation in national legislations and related policy statements. It is clear thus that the HR values otherwise so manifestly embodied in the Genocide Convention, the Torture Convention, the concept of 'crimes against humanity' (elements of which are defined in the Statute of the International Criminal Court) and the CEDAW find different incarnations in national law regimes.[9] In a way, then, one is talking about the 'juridification' of human rights (Baxi 2008: chapter 7). If so, even human rights theorists and practitioners need to learn about, if not immerse themselves in, the theory of translation. It remains particularly important to stress the distinction between 'dominant' and 'transgressive' practices of translation (Baxi 2009), and recent work on 'juridification' (including this volume) does hold some exciting potential.[10]

Of course, 'the task of translation' (to adapt a scintillating phrase from Walter Benjamin (1968)) in an age of production of the values of human rights takes us further afield and at least (for the present purposes) in four directions: concretisation, authorship, languages and politics. A brief remark concerning each is necessary.

'Concretisation', at least as speaking to the politico-juridical acts of translation, is no simple affair. Because 'values' remain poor guides to practical action, any understanding of the translation practices needs further to grapple with the tasks of translation of these into human rights *principles, standards, norms, rules* and *institutional practices*. At the risk of appearing dogmatic, the differentiation in these normative forms remains insufficiently grasped in contemporary human rights discourse. If the first three categories seem closer to the tasks of translating values, the last two may not be regarded as insignificant.

The concern about acts of authorship of HR values, whether on a secular-ethical or politico-juridical register, is indeed crucial to their translation. Contrary to common theoretical propaganda, the authorship of HR is not at all *unique* to the Euro-American tradition. Every culture and civilisational tradition develops its own conceptions of

---

[9] See, as to this, a precious study by Beth A. Simmons (2009).

[10] See Blichner and Molander 2008. The five types of juridification they offer (see the introduction to this volume) may well help us further grasp translation and transgression.

rights as social relations. This entails a different type of genealogical understanding of human rights values than available in the present state of knowledge. It remains my firm conviction that suffering peoples and communities in resistance are the historically first authors/inventors of human rights values, standards and norms, even when the further translation of all these into rules always remains a politico-juridical endeavour.[11] Accordingly, I have canvassed the need to develop differential understandings of the contrast between the politico-juridical and a struggle-based narrative of human rights languages and development.

Translation from secular-ethical to politico-juridical values further entails understanding of different languages of human rights. In *Future* (Baxi 2008: chapter 1), I have thus suggested the following incommensurable 'languages': HR as languages of governance; as shared sovereignties (to take some enormously different realms – the European Community and war on 'terror' for example); as moral/ethical languages; as 'doctrinal'/'juridical' languages; and as languages of resistance and even of insurrection.

All this has further led me to develop a distinction between the politics *of* and *for* HR. Shortly put, if the former inexhaustibly directs energies towards the maintenance and replenishment of the ends of power and domination, the latter presents itself as practices and forms of transformative politics for dignity and justice for all humans everywhere. The universality of the politics *of* HR has been much more explored than that of its other – the politics *for* HR.

Talking about HR in the languages of 'paradigm' and of 'paradigm shifts' thus presents difficult questions concerning the very existence of a disciplinary tradition ('normal science' as Kuhn (1962) calls this.) Because there exists no such 'normal science' concerning HR, we lack a lens through which we may study HR paradigm shifts. Yet it is clearly the

---

[11] See Baxi 2008: chapters 1 and 2. At a discussion event with fellows at the Kate Hamburger Kolleg Institute for Law as Culture, Bonn (22 June 2011), Professor Werner Gephart raised a concern about 'competing frames of suffering'. This calls for an understanding always (and I have always recognised this) of the heterogeneity of *sources*, *experiences* and *voices* of human and social suffering. I have argued that their coming together in certain historic conjunctures articulates new forms of human rights, repudiating certain formations of radical evil (in the sense that early Hannah Arendt (1968) gave to it as states of affairs that we may never ever fully understand or forgive). 'Competing frames of suffering' pluralises the notion of radical evils rather than resourcing Arendt's normalisation of it in terms of their 'banality'. That description in Arendt must of course be read alongside her remarkably insightful enunciation of the 'right to have rights'. Even when the contributions to this volume do not explicitly engage these aspects, I read these as deepening our understanding of the 'competing frames of suffering'.

case that shifts, often seismic, in the attribution of meanings of the idea of being and remaining human and having rights do transform our ways of understanding of the growth and change in collective human moral sentiment. Communities of sentiment often undergo transformations as vast as those of 'normal' science; or to put it differently, the sub-paradigmatic may also offer histories of crises and change. *Faute de mieux*, I seek to redefine the frontiers thus presented on different registers contrasting the 'modern' and 'contemporary' HR paradigm shifts, now in turn confronted by a paradigm of trade-related, market-friendly HR paradigm.

THE 'MODERN' HUMAN RIGHTS PARADIGM

The modern human rights paradigm (MHRP) begins its itineraries by the reduction of human into things – objects of a brutish will to power – slavery and colonisation offering some enormous examples. This corresponds with the idea of progress which, as fostered by the philosophies of European enlightenment from Immanuel Kant (who after all justified placing the subjugated colonial peoples under the 'moral tutelage' of European peoples) to Karl Marx (who regarded colonisation as breaking the fetters of feudalism and as marking the advent of a dialectically emancipatory regime of global capital), was the principle that justified practices of violent social exclusion of the colonised subject-peoples.

HR values thus emerged as installing 'justified' forms of *conquest globalisation*. This is a complicated story, but in the main, once the idea of human was equated with having the twin faculties of reason and will, those said to be devoid of these were either not human (therefore reduced to the status of things or animals) or inferior humans (beings subjected to the 'benevolent' despotism of the 'white man's burden' thought-ways) – and had to be brought to a certain standard of 'civilisation'. In sum, conquest of the non-European others constituted a civilising mission, accompanied always with the three other 'Cs' – commerce, Christianity and civilisation. These four 'Cs' define the basic structure and the essential features of MHRP. Epistemic racism marched ahead with the powers of conquest and domination. To encompass a long archive briefly here, all this meant that, in the main, 'human rights' were a 'whites-only "affair"'.[12]

---

[12] I derive this phrase from Robert Young (2001). See also Galeano 1997; Prahsad 2007; and Baxi 2008: chapter 2, for related literature and a further development of this thematic.

One must, however, distinguish between the dominant MHRP and its myriad subaltern traditions. The latter was archetypically represented by Francisco de Vitoria, who notably evoked the Christian doctrines of natural law and natural rights as a principal weapon of criticism (though far from being possessed with a modicum of historic impact; see Simpson 2004; Anghie 2005; and Baxi 2006a). The juridico-political categories of imposed human subjectivities that thus constructed the idea of 'human' may not be fully grasped outside categories of resistance.

Further, we thus arrive at an understanding of the rise of legal positivism that begins altogether to discredit the origin of the idea of human and having human rights in any theologically grounded, or secular, *iusnaturalist* tradition. This idea was now to be severely constructed in terms of the power and prowess of the Westphalian understanding of the notion of the state and its law. Understandably, then, the narrative of MHRP gives birth to the idea of liberal human rights as rights of property holders against power of the state. The owners of the colonial means and ends of production elevate the idea of being human as myriad exuberant forms of a hyper-colonising European 'possessive individualism' – the rights of selfhood that elevate the 'sacred' rights of contract and property as the foundation of human freedom and moral agency. A wave, or even a tsunami, of the contemporary narratives the 'dark side of the Enlightenment' leaves intact overall, at least from my narrative standpoint, the structures of MHRP thought-ways.

THE CONTEMPORARY HUMAN RIGHTS PARADIGM

In contrast, the contemporary human rights paradigm (CHRP, dating from the adoption of the UDHR) accentuates the growing inclusion of all humans – that is those born as humans (indeed the UDHR specifically invokes and even rests upon a birth metaphor as the basis of all human rights). If the MHRP remained celebratory of such exclusion, the CHRP seeks its near-total (that is normative) reversal; one way thus to understand what constitutes 'human' is to equate the idea of being 'human' with the imagery of 'having human rights'.[13]

---

[13] Regardless, and at a most general level, it is of course important to avoid an entirely *rights-based understanding* of the idea of being and remaining 'human'. I may somewhat dramatise this by saying that, while having rights may be a *necessary* condition for being and remaining human, it is not a *sufficient* condition; put differently, the idea of being 'human' still remains ethically intelligible in a world without rights. *Not having 'rights' does not make one not/non-human, except that those who have all the rights so think. Indeed, the rightless peoples throughout history articulate*

The CHRP order of inclusiveness is made complex by juridical classification of some human rights as enforceable and as civil and political, and others as social, economic and cultural. The complexity aggravates by the constant tendency to convert human *needs* into human *rights*, generating an 'overproduction' of HR norms, principles, standards, rules and institutional practices via several mechanisms. Human rights theorists and philosophers who develop the idea of HR as moral rights critique, and even condemn, this proliferation, whereas the practices of the assemblages of human rights and social movement activists suggest that what we have today are not too *many* but too *few* normative and institutional developments. I shall not pursue this storyline here (see further Baxi 2008: chapters 4, 5 and 7).

A remarkable aspect comprises the growing participation of the residual 'old' and the 'new' social movements. People's movements against despotic rule everywhere have contributed to a renascent HR culture – from the Czech to the Arab Spring. However, this contemporary referent remains under-inclusive of similar 'springs' in other arenas of the global South, including the various coloured revolutions in post-socialist societies. Leaving this aside, what matters is the emergence of a New Sovereign – a formation in which the *constituent* power of peoples enacting forms and grammars of insurgent reason lead to an overthrowing of *constituted* powers. In a different register, social and human rights movements have made pioneering contributions in their role in the making of international human rights norms, standards, principles, rules and institutional conduct. Further, in many parts of the world today, the movement of peoples and processes have led to the renovation of adjudicatory power and process, especially via the initiative for judicial activism (see Simmons 2009: note 25). All this has contributed to a slow but steady growth of moral sentiment, redefining variously yet with enormous influence the idea of legitimacy of sovereign power and function.

However, and increasingly, theoretic/philosophical anxieties also register a high growth curve! I have in mind the provocations offered by leading progressive Eurocentric thinkers that I fondly name the 'club' of 'A to Z' (from Agamben to Žižek). We all have much to learn from

alternate visions of what it may mean to say 'human' and 'having rights'. Should you be puzzled by this observation, do please have a look at the other of the Universal Declaration of Human Rights (UDHR), especially the Zapatista charters of human rights. These articulate a notion of being 'human' as one with 'nature'. And these too, in turn, molest profoundly our received understandings of human rights as heavily secularised and un-'natural' conceptions of whatever it may mean to say 'human' and 'having' human rights.

this critique of the CHRP, poignantly accurate in terms of an exposé of the latent and manifest 'imperialism' of human rights talk and action by the hegemonic nations, or the vanguards of the new 'Empire' (see for example Douzinas 2007; Bowring 2008). However, it would constitute an egregious error to take this seriously as an entire gesture of 'dismissal' or 'termination' of the idea of being human and having human rights.

To concretise somewhat, I read the A-to-Z thinkers as providing a precious critique of what I call the politics *of* human rights (the appropriation of the ethical languages of human rights for domination). Suchlike concerns direct our attention, often militantly, towards stances of theoretical anti-humanism (ever since Heidegger) and no doubt remind us of the barbarity of power which consists in the construction of political Darwinism, a form of sovereign bio-politics in which some peoples are represented as more authentically 'human' than others.

TRADE-RELATED, MARKET-FRIENDLY HUMAN RIGHTS PARADIGM

This paradigm (hereafter, TRMFP) suggests the salience of the reconstruction of the idea of a collective legal personality as a bearer of human rights. Multinational and national corporations, as well as the diffuse communities of direct foreign investors, have always claimed a wide range of legal rights; what now happens is that they begin to claim the same order of human rights as made available to individual human beings under the UDHR. We ought to pause here to note that the liberal, contemporary HR paradigm, which has such plentiful difficulties in speaking to the collective or group rights (of 'minorities'), hesitates but little in its fullest recognition of the human rights of these communities. In this sense, we arrive at a conception of 'corporate legal humanity' (to evoke the phrase-regime of Anna Grear (2010)).

I will not detail in this conversation the salient aspects of the TRMFP already enunciated in *Future* (Baxi 2008: chapters 8 and 9). Yet I ought to draw your attention to an imaginary Declaration of the Human Rights of Global Capital (2008: 259–64); and in addition and very briefly draw attention to some salient features.

In the first place, corporate legal humanity claims a primacy for human rights of the 'communities' of multinational/global corporations and diffuse personifications of direct foreign investors, while also denying as fully as possible the individual and collective human rights of the workers. Conceptually, then, the owners of the means of production are presented as the 'essence' of this new form of 'humanity' that denies the 'humanity' of the owners of nothing more than labour-power. In a sense this constitutes a form of human rights regression – a recrudescence of aspects of the MHRP!

Second, these 'communities' now claim a superior order of human rights than rendered available to human beings under the auspices of the CHRP. To mention a few examples:

- The human right to freedom of speech and expression extended to collective rights of global capital now translates as the right of 'commercial' free speech and expression, even going so far as to inhibit (and in some contexts to prohibit) any free exercise of human rights of individuals and social action groups.
- The robust human rights of corporate freedom of speech and expression as including (especially as judicially-blessed in the United States, but also elsewhere) the right to fund electoral campaigns so as to exclude political representation and participation by subaltern groups and voices.
- The human rights of global capital to a borderless world for the flows of global capital, but also its right to a bordered world and often cruelly as concerns migrants named as undocumented aliens.
- Its human rights as associational rights that may trump the human rights of human beings (see Schneiderman 2008).
- The human right of immunity and impunity of corporate legal humanity (agents, managers and related normative cohorts of 'toxic capitalism') even in the face of planned failures of catastrophic 'corporate governance' exemplified now by the more than a quarter-century old and un-redressed sufferings of the Bhopal-violated humanity (see Baxi 2010).

The TRMFP distinguishes itself by claims of politics *of* human rights that consist in the languages of *impunity* as well as of *immunity*. This stands demonstrated by the fact that, even as corporate legal humanity claims the same order of human rights, the state-like, yet state-transcendent, global corporations and the communities of foreign direct investors decline the courtesy of being held accountable in terms of human rights responsibility. The phenomenon of the UN global compact – rightly described as 'Global Compact, Little Impact' – actually authorises these entities to self-select HR norms, standards, rules and institutional practices that they may sometimes respect. The recent story of cruel normative abortion of the UN Draft Norms on the Responsibilities of Transnational

Corporations and Other Business Enterprises with Regard to Human Rights further reinforces the point.[14]

I need go no further to suggest the vitality of the TRMFP, which entrenches a post-Enlightenment progress narrative entailing, as Anna Grear (2010) reminds us fully, a new form of 'colonisation' of human rights. Perhaps an equally apt description may echo Kwame Nkrumah's withering description of 'neo-colonialism' as '*power without responsibility and exploitation without redress*' (1965).

A CONCLUDING REMARK

Put another way, and entirely evading the question of how such a narrative scramble may authorise even a word in conclusion, all I may say is that the TRMFP needs to be understood as a register of human rights *regression*, rather than constituting any *progress* narrative. This act of reading remains even more imperative, given the normative triumph that converts juridical enunciations of human rights obligations and responsibilities into mere declarations of acts of global social policy such as the Millennial Development Goals and the development of the right to development (see Baxi 2006b).

These now fully dominant practices of translation of human rights languages into statements of mere global social policy – these vastly enfeebled languages of corporate social responsibility, ethical investment, bioethics modes of 'good' corporate governance – ought to be fully confronted by the never-ending stories of reproduction of the 'third worlds' of suffering humanity, now also including the global-finance-crisis re-constituted 'first world'. If this task is to be ever fully attempted (let alone completed), we need to think and act *sub*-or even *non-paradigmatically*.

How this may ever be done remains a critical question. Already, people's struggles (constituting a new sovereign) as well as some social movements have begun to convert the moment of crises of global governance into opportunities for global social action. I have here in view many a success story, exploiting the inner contradictions of a neo-liberal regime (see for example Hardt and Negri 2009). How may we then decipher these developments, bereft of the imagery of a secular messianic

---

[14] See Baxi 2008: chapter 9, though I here refer to more recent labours of John Ruggie, UN Secretary General Special Representative, who even denies the dignity of a 'third-class funeral' for these 'norms', advocating instead unmitigated voluntarism – a TRMFP right of global capital to pick and choose standards of human rights that may or may not govern MNC conduct.

time, articulated differently in terms of a 'coming community' (Agamben 1993) or 'democracy to come' (Derrida 1994: 105–73)? In sum, then, theory and praxes for human rights in the contemporary 'post-neo-liberal conjuncture' need to confront its *disinvention* of human rights by feats of their *re-invention*. I read the volume in your hands as richly contributing to this *programmschrift*.

References

Agamben, Giorgio 1993. *Coming Community*, trans. Michael Hardt. Minneapolis: University of Minnesota Press.

2004. *The Open: Man and Animal*, trans. Kevin Attell. Stanford University Press.

2009. *The Signature of All Things: On Method*, trans. Luca D'lasanto and Kevin Attell. New York: Zone Books.

Anghie, Anthony 2005. *Imperialism, Sovereignty, and the Making of International Law*. Cambridge University Press.

Arendt, Hannah (ed.) 1968. *Illuminations*, trans. Harry Zohn. New York: Shocken.

Babich, Babette E. 2003. 'Kuhn's paradigm as a parable for the Cold War: incommensurability and its discontents from Fuller's tale of Harvard to Fleck's Unsung Lvov', *Social Epistemology* 17 (2–3): 99–109.

Baxi, Upendra 2006a. 'New approaches to the history of international law', *Leiden Journal of International Law* 19: 555–66.

2006b. 'A report for all seasons? Small notes on reading *in larger freedom*', in C. Raj Kumar; and D. K. Srivastava (eds.) *Human Rights and Development: Law, Policy and Governance*. Hong Kong: Lexis/Nexis, pp. 495–514.

2007. *Human Rights in a Posthuman World: Critical Essays*. Delhi: Oxford University Press.

2008. *The Future of Human Rights*. Delhi: Oxford University Press.

2009. 'Translating terror: siting truth, justice, and rights amidst the two "terror" wars', in Esperanza Bielsa and Christopher W. Hughes (eds.) *Globalization, Political Violence, and Translation*. New York: Palgrave-Macmillan, pp. 45–71.

2010. 'Writing about impunity and environment: the "silver jubilee" of the Bhopal catastrophe', *Journal of Human Rights and the Environment* 1 (1): 23–44.

(forthcoming). Animal rights as companion human rights The 19th I. P. Desai Memorial Lecture, Centre for Social Studies, Veer Narmad University, Surat, 2009.

Benjamin, Walter 1968. 'The task of the translator in an age of mechanical production', in Hannah Arendt (ed.) *Illuminations*. New York: Shocken, pp. 69–83.

Blichner, Lars C. and Molander, Anders 2008. 'Mapping juridification', *European Law Journal* 14 (1): 36–54.

Bohannan, Paul 1957. *Justice and Judgement among the Tiv.* London: Oxford University Press.

Bowring, Bill 2008. *The Degradation of the International Legal Order? The Rehabilitation of Law and the Possibility of Politics.* London: Routledge-Cavendish.

Comaroff, John L. and Roberts, Simon 1981. *Rules and Processes: The Cultural Logic of Dispute in an African Context.* University of Chicago Press.

Conley. John M. and O'Barr, William M. 1990. *Rules versus Relationships: The Ethnography of Legal Discourse.* University of Chicago Press.

Derrida, Jacques 1994. *Spectres of Marx*, trans. Peggy Kamuf. London: Routledge.

Douzinas, Costas 2007. *Human Rights and Empire: The Political Philosophy of Cosmopolitanism.* London: Routledge-Cavendish.

Eckberg, Douglas Lee and Hill, Jr., Lester 1979. 'The paradigm concept and sociology: a critical review', *American Sociological Review* 44: 925–37.

French, Rebecca R. 1996. 'Of narrative in law and anthropology', *Law & Society Review* 30 (2): 417–36.

Fuller, Steve 2000. *Thomas Kuhn: A Political History of Our Time.* University of Chicago Press.

Galeano, Eduardo 1997. *Open Veins of Latin America.* New York: Monthly Review Press.

Gewirth, Alan 1997. *The Community of Rights.* University of Chicago Press.

Gluckman, Max 1955. *The Judicial Process among the Barotse of Northern Rhodesia.* University of Manchester Press.

Goodale, Mark 2006. 'Toward a critical anthropology of human rights: commentary', *Current Anthropology* 47: 485–511.

Grear, Anna 2010. *Redirecting Human Rights: Facing the Challenges of Corporate Legal Humanity.* London: Palgrave Macmillan.

Habermas, Jürgen 1995. *Between Facts and Norms: Contributions towards a Theory of Discourse Ethic*, trans. W. Rehg. Cambridge, MA: MIT Press.

Hafner, Peter 1998. 'Theories and paradigms in sociology', *Philosophy and Sociology* 1 (5): 455–64.

Hardt, Michael and Negri, Antonio 2009. *Commonwealth.* Cambridge, MA: Belknap Press.

Kalny, Eva 2009. 'Against superciliousness: revisiting the debate 60 years after the adoption of the universal declaration of human rights', *Critique of Anthropology* 29 (4): 371–95.

Kant, Immanuel 2000. *Critique of the Power of Judgment*, trans. Paul Guyer and Eric Matthews. New York: Cambridge University Press.

Kuhn, Thomas 1962. *The Structure of Scientific Revolutions.* University of Chicago Press.

Levinas, Emmanuel 1969. *Totality and Infinity: An Essay on Exteriority*, trans. Alphonso Lingis. Pittsburgh: Duquesne University Press.

Musgrave, Margaret 1970. 'The nature of a paradigm', in Imre Lakatos and Alan Musgrave (eds.) *Criticism and the Growth of Knowledge*. Cambridge University Press, pp. 59–90.

Nickels, Thomas (ed.) 2003. *Thomas Kuhn*. Cambridge University Press.

Nkrumah, Kwame 1965. *Neo-colonialism: The Last Stage of Imperialism*. London: Thomas Nelson and Sons Ltd.

Nussbaum, Martha 2000. *Women and Human Development: The Capabilities Approach*. Cambridge University Press.

2006. *The Frontiers of Justice: Disability, Nationality, Species Membership*. Cambridge, MA: Belknap Press.

Phillips, Derek L. 1974. 'Epistemology and the sociology of knowledge: the contributions of Mannheim, Mills, and Merton', *Theory and Society* 1: 59–88.

Prahsad, Vijay 2007. *The Darker Nations: A Biography of the Short-lived Third World*. New Delhi: Leftword Books.

Rawls, John 1993. *Political Liberalism*. New York: Columbia University Press.

1999. *The Law of Peoples*. Cambridge, MA, London: Harvard University Press.

Santos, Bonaventura de Sousa 1995. *Towards a New Commonsense: Law, Science, and Politics in the Paradigmatic Transition*. London: Routledge.

Schneiderman, David 2008. *Constitutionalizing Economic Globalization: Investment Rules and Democracy's Promise*. Cambridge University Press.

Sen, Amartya 2004. 'Elements of a theory of human rights', *Philosophy and Public Affairs* 32: 315–36.

Simmons, Beth A. 2009. *Mobilization for Human Rights: International Law in Domestic Politics*. Cambridge University Press.

Simpson, Gerry 2004. *Great Powers and Outlaw States: Unequal Sovereigns in the International Legal Order*. Cambridge University Press.

Singer, Peter 1979. 'Killing humans and killing animals', *Inquiry* 22: 145–56.

Williams, Rowan 2008. The spiritual and the religious: is the territory changing? Lecture given on 17 April 2008.

Young, Robert 2001. *Postcolonialism: An Introduction*. Oxford: Blackwell.

INDEX

Made in the USA
San Bernardino, CA
18 February 2016